GAMING
THE MARKET

Wiley Trading Advantage

Trading without Fear/Richard W. Arms, Jr.
Neural Network: Time Series Forecasting of Financial Markets/E. Michael Azoff
Option Market Making/Alan J. Baird
Money Management Strategies for Futures Traders/Nauzer J. Balsara
Genetic Algorithms and Investment Strategies/Richard Bauer
Managed Futures: An Investor's Guide/Beverly Chandler
Beyond Technical Analysis/Tushar Chande
The New Technical Trader/Tushar Chande and Stanley S. Kroll
Trading on the Edge/Guido J. Deboeck
The New Science of Technical Analysis/Tomas R. DeMark
Point and Figure Charting/Thomas J. Dorsey
Trading for a Living/Dr. Alexander Elder
Study Guide for Trading for a Living/Dr. Alexander Elder
The Day Trader's Manual/William F. Eng
Analyzing and Forecasting Futures Prices/Anthony F. Herbst
Technical Analysis of the Options Markets/Richard Hexton
New Commodity Trading Systems & Methods/Perry Kaufman
Understanding Options/Robert Kolb
The Intuitive Trader/Robert Koppel
McMillan on Options/Lawrence G. McMillan
Trading on Expectations/Brendan Moynihan
Intermarket Technical Analysis/John J. Murphy
Forecasting Financial and Economic Cycles/Michael P. Niemira
Beyond Candlesticks/Steve Nison
Forecasting Financial Markets/Tony Plummer
Inside the Financial Futures Markets, 3rd Edition/Mark J. Powers and
    Mark G. Castelino
Neural Networks in the Capital Markets/Paul Refenes
Option Strategies, 2nd Edition/Courtney Smith
Trader Vic II: Analytic Principles of Professional Speculation/Victor Sperandeo
Campaign Trading/John Sweeney
The Trader's Tax Survival Guide/Ted Tesser
Tiger on Spreads/Phillip E. Tiger
The Mathematics of Money Management/Ralph Vince
Portfolio Management Formulas/Ralph Vince
The New Money Management: A Framework for Asset Allocation/Ralph Vince
Trading Applications of Japanese Candlestick Charting/Gary Wagner and
    Brad Matheny
Selling Short/Joseph A. Walker
Trading Chaos: Applying Expert Techniques to Maximize Your Profits/Bill Williams

GAMING THE MARKET

Applying Game Theory to Create Winning Trading Strategies

Ronald B. Shelton

JOHN WILEY & SONS, INC.

New York • Chichester • Weinheim • Brisbane • Singapore • Toronto

This text is printed on acid-free paper.

This publication is designed to provide accurate and authoritative
information in regard to the subject matter covered. It is sold
with the understanding that the publisher is not engaged in
rendering legal, accounting, or other professional services. If
legal advice or other expert assistance is required, the services
of a competent professional person should be sought.

ISBN 0-471-16813-0

10 9 8 7 6 5 4 3 2

Foreword

I t's not often that a refreshingly new idea appears in the field of trading strategies or risk management, but Ron Shelton has taken pieces from game theory and betting strategies and transformed them into a new, visual way to make trading decisions. His own use of the term "gaming" probably best describes the purpose of his approach. In a very practical way, Ron Shelton shows the chances of a successful trade, which is based on your own trading strategy, its profit objective and your own choice of accepting either a small or big risk, and, instead of a single answer, you get a picture of the extent of its potential success or failure. He has been able to put a value on trading situations which can increase your ability to manage risk as well as clarify expectations—both essential ingredients for success.

Surviving and profiting from trading is dependent upon the accumulation of knowledge, the selection of the most robust methods, an understanding of risk, the acceptance of change, and the flexibility to move forward. Those are big hurdles to overcome. Fortunately, those who have prospered over the years of hectic markets have either been very lucky, or, more likely, have already moved down this path, sometimes unaware of their own subtle development. They have evolved and, subsequently, their way of dealing with markets has become more sophisticated. However, these advances need not be complex or illogical.

Although the modern stock and financial markets have been active for well over a century, they have been permanently altered throughout the years by the forward motion of technology. For the past twenty years, the ability to access data and display charts on a screen has caused a revolution in price analysis and trading methods. Equipment that allows real-time calculation of relationships between world stock markets, or the creation of strips to substitute for single-maturity interest rates has expanded our thinking well beyond Charles Dow's breakthrough when he applied charting to his hand-calculated index of thirty stocks. Without communication and computers, these applications could not exist. To make life even more competitive, programmable platforms, which have enormously reduced the development time for trading strategies, also are being widely used.

Market analysis, as we know it, surfaced at about the same time that the International Monetary Market introduced currency futures trading in 1972. Although the dominant form of high-powered evaluation was a hand-plotted point-and-figure chart, it was soon replaced by what then seemed the highly sophisticated simple moving average. This was a technical leap forward because it was no longer Keltner's 10-day moving average. Moving averages of all lengths, weightings, and combinations, and followed shortly by exponential smoothing, dominated the technicians' toolbox for the next ten years. The simplicity and success of those methods, in markets that had never been subject to such analysis, made more complex methods unnecessary.

During the next ten years competition expanded, due to a steadily declining U.S. dollar, gold reaching $800 per ounce, and double-digit inflation. More market participation was met with better technology for accessing and manipulating data and increased the expectations of both the investor and the analyst. By displaying historic prices easily on a quote machine or a computer screen, we fell into the trap of hindsight. Using much more versatile electronics, we could now see too easily what we *should* have done yesterday. Unfortunately, the tendency was to be too critical of our own performance and compare our modest net returns (sometimes losses) with the maximum profit we could have captured had we known more. When used in this way, the tools themselves can become our worst enemy and our biggest problem—we come to expect too much.

At the same time we were struggling to control the power given to us by the computer, we could integrate massive amounts of data and solve practical problems that were previously unthinkable. In the 1980s bank profits soared from fixed income arbitrage programs made possible by large-scale automated access to data on interest rate instruments of different maturities, and the ability to instantly calculate those that yielded the best returns and others that had fallen out of line. While the idea was simple in concept, it was the technology that had been missing.

Most of all, larger, faster computers became affordable by those studying the markets, and made access to information and the ability to manipulate prices commonplace. The issue was one of understanding what to do with all of it, and how to compete successfully now that basic techniques, such as trend following, have been so heavily used that profits from these methods are more erratic and too often unrewarding. In essence, many market trends have been overtraded and market noise has replaced those trends that were once profitable price moves.

To overcome this problem, other more advanced techniques have been developed, represented in may ways by the neural network. This development process has taken advantage of computer power and provided a level of sophistication far beyond the simple optimized backtesting that has been the most common analytic tool since computers became popular. Using a genetic algorithm, neural networks can combine any number of technical, fundamental, and statistical data in a non-linear, even discrete manner, to find solutions to problems that were not possible only a few years ago. When a neural network has a verifiable physical solution, such as a complex orbit, the method is invaluable; but when there is no solution for a specific trading technique, a neural network process is likely to find one anyway. This method is so powerful that it can piece together information that is entirely coincidental into what appears to be a perfect solution. It is typical of the problems currently facing everyone trying to develop a trading program. In short, common sense is still the best way to separate a valid solution from an absurd one.

In the final analysis, it is neither the computer power nor the new methods that succeed; it is the person that keeps a level-headed approach. Each idea that is studied to improve trading and profits must make sense before the computer begins its job of coordinating and calculating all the facts. It is never the computer solution that is a success, it is your solution. The computer is simply a tool to validate your idea.

Ron Shelton has worked from a sound idea to a computer solution. He has first solved the problem of risk and probability, then validated it using the computer. The result is simple, creative, and enlightening. Most importantly, it is realistic. By solving a problem without optimization, the results are clearly achievable. The solutions may not always be perfect, and each market does not always return large profits with only insignificant losses—that combination can only be achieved through hindsight.

I have found this new approach particularly interesting because it has been given visual representation. You can actually see the areas of risk and opportunity for a trading system and use that visual presentation to improve your trading. Mr. Shelton has taken a simple, sound idea; converted it into a clear trading tool; described how to use it; and moved us a step forward.

PERRY KAUFMAN

Wells River, Vermont

Preface

The goal of this book is to examine the behavior of financial markets from a completely new and different perspective. The book uses game theory to develop a model of financial market behavior. Game theory is a mathematical discipline used in a wide variety of economic applications. For any given situation, the outcomes (payoffs) and courses of action (strategies) are diagrammed algebraically. A few calculations then show which strategies yield positive payoffs. Can a set of strategies be found for the financial markets that yield positive payoffs?

The basic idea is that when you take a position in a market, you are really playing a game against the market. Profitability doesn't lie in your actions alone, it lies in the interaction between your position and the market's price fluctuations. If you go long, you are essentially betting that the price will go up. Whether or not you make a profit will be determined by the market. If the price goes up you will make money, but if it falls you will lose money.

To have a game, each player must have a desired outcome or goal. The goal of the individual is obvious. It is to make money. But what is the goal of the market? Simply put, the market wants you to lose money. This may be a provocative thought, but it is quite reasonable in the context of game theory.

Game theory answers the essential questions that investors face on every trade: How much risk do you take? A little or a lot? What is the likelihood of the profit objective being reached? Is the expected value of this trade positive or negative?

The book begins with an introduction to game theory to familiarize readers with its techniques and conventions. From there it progresses to the financial market game. A model of the interaction between market behavior and the individual is developed, which shows whether or not any particular trade will be profitable.

The book's underpinning is a research paper I wrote in college. I studied economics in school, and concentrated on game theory my senior year. I wanted to apply game theory to the futures market and see if a viable trading strategy could be developed. For more than ten years, I have continued to refine the model and statistically test it. I also trade futures and options in my spare time for my own account. The result of the academic research and real life experience is this book.

The book is intended for traders, investors, stockbrokers, and others who take a serious interest in the market. Although it is fairly technical in some respects, anyone who reads it can benefit from it. Even though some of the equations in the model are challenging, being strong in math isn't a prerequisite to understanding the book and putting the ideas to work in your own portfolio. The completed model is easy to follow, and the formulas can be programmed into a spreadsheet program quite easily. Additionally, the model incorporates a graph of the result so that the likelihood of loss or profitability can be seen at a glance.

Writing this book has been not only challenging and rewarding, but a lot of fun. I especially want to thank my agent and editors for all of their hard work in making this book happen.

Acknowledgments

I want to thank all the people who helped make this book possible. They include friends, relatives, and colleagues. They are Nanette Bellefleur, William Weber, Perry Kaufman, Wendy Becker, Pam Van Giessen, Kim Nir, Tom Robinson, Cathy Shelton, and John Ryff. And, of course, my parents.

Contents

Foreword   *v*

Preface   *ix*

Acknowledgments   *xi*

CHAPTER 1:   WHAT IS GAME THEORY?   1

    Basic Game Theory Terms and Ideas   4
    The Decision-Making Problem   6
    What Is a Game?   8
    A Simple Game   12
    The Prisoner's Dilemma   17
    Iterated Games   19
    Zero Sum Game   24
    Games against Nature   25
    Pros and Cons of Game Theory   28

**CHAPTER 2:   BASIC IDEAS ABOUT
FINANCIAL MARKETS**   30

**CHAPTER 3:   THE INTERACTION BETWEEN
PRICE FLUCTUATIONS AND RISK
ACCEPTANCE LEVELS**   39

    Realistic Scenarios   41
    Financial Markets as a Parlor Game   50

**CHAPTER 4:   CONSTRUCTING A GAME
THEORETIC MODEL**   **55**

   Market-Strategy Notation   57
   Speculator Strategy Notation   58
   Payoff Notation   58
   Mathematical Representation of the Game Table   59
   When to Accept Less Risk   62
   When to Accept More Risk   66
   Separation of Less Risk and More Risk   71
   The Completed Model   74

CHAPTER 5:   UNDERSTANDING THE MODEL   **76**

   Determining the Probability of Adversity   79
   An Estimation of the Probabilities of Adversity   87

CHAPTER 6:   TREASURY BOND FUTURES   **100**

   Intraday T-Bond Price Movements   106
   A Practical Application   114
   How Changes in the Risk/Reward Variables Change the Regions 123
   A More Sophisticated Approach: Take the Trend into Account 127
   Developing a Trading System   134
   Another Test   139

**APPENDIX A: MATHEMATICAL REPRESENTATION
OF THE MODEL**   **161**

**APPENDIX B: FREQUENCY DISTRIBUTION FOR
EXPIRING MONTH T-BOND FUTURES PRICES**   **165**

**APPENDIX C: RELATIVE FREQUENCY
DISTRIBUTION FOR EXPIRING MONTH T-BOND
FUTURES PRICES**   **168**

**APPENDIX D: QUICK BASIC PROGRAM FOR
RELATIVE FREQUENCIES**   **171**

**APPENDIX E: RELATIVE FREQUENCIES BY
OSCILLATOR CONDITIONS**   **175**

Index   *205*

1

What Is Game Theory?

Most of what has been written about financial markets treats the subject as a science. Asset allocation models are developed, yield curve formulae are analyzed, various indicators are scrutinized, etc., all with the hope of being able to determine the best investment strategy to employ. Much of the analysis consists of statistically analyzing past market behavior in an attempt to predict future market behavior. The very nature of statistical analysis is suggestive of "scientific" credibility; that is, a method that uses rigorous analytic techniques will generate scientifically valid results.

What is the track record of all this analysis? Most equity mutual funds don't have rates of return greater than those of the broad market indices. Many mutual funds actually have rates of return less than market averages. The fund that is "hot" this year is invariably "cold" next year (and vice versa). The same is true for individual stock pickers: the *wunderkind* who has the Midas touch this year almost never replicates his performance. There are certainly exceptions to this, but in general the track record of the professionals is not very good.

The Wall Street Journal has a running "contest" that illustrates this point. First they have several investment professionals pick a few stocks. Then the editors tape stock listings to a wall and throw darts at them to pick a random series of stocks. After a time the returns earned by the professionals are compared with the returns earned by the darts. The darts win as often as the pros.

From this perspective it looks like financial markets can be viewed as a game. This book isn't about how to throw darts, but the subject of gaming the markets isn't one that has been explored in very much detail. Are financial markets really just a game? What is a game? How is a game analyzed and quantified? If the markets are a game, then is it possible to find a winning strategy? What are the rules of the game? Who are the players in the game? These questions and more are explored in this book, and some of the answers are surprising.

The first few paragraphs may have seemed to make light of rigorous quantitative analysis, but rest assured that game theory is highly quantitative and rigorous. A game theoretic approach to financial markets is no less "scientific" than any other; it is merely unconventional. If playing the financial markets can be seen as a form of a game, then why not use the science of games to analyze them? Don't conclude that game theory must be a "lightweight" science because most people play games for recreation: On the contrary many games are played with deadly earnestness.

Game theory is a branch of mathematics that studies games. It is unfamiliar to most people, but with a "primer" most readers won't find the concepts difficult to grasp. This chapter will lay a foundation to that effect. Many examples will be used to illustrate various concepts of game theory. These examples don't directly relate to the financial markets, but they will explicate important concepts that need to be understood to comprehend the later chapters which deal directly with financial markets. Readers who are familiar with game theory may elect to skip this chapter but should probably read it anyway as a quick refresher. The ideas and concepts that need to be grasped are not excessively complicated, but a basic understanding of game theory is essential. After building a solid foundation, readers will be able to follow the construction of a game theoretic model demonstrating that optimal solutions *do exist* for the game of playing the financial markets.

Exactly what is game theory anyway? Game theory is the study of conflict of interest between individuals, organizations, or entities. These conflicts are referred to as games. Each individual (i.e., player) has more than one course of action (i.e., strategy) available, and the outcome (i.e., payoff) of the game depends on the interaction of the strategies pursued by all of the different players. No single player can determine the outcome of a game through his actions alone. The outcome is the result of the actions of all the players in a particular game. To have a conflict of interest, different players must prefer different outcomes. If different players desire the exact same result, there isn't any conflict of interest. Game theory is very specific as to what constitutes a different outcome. If I want to win and you want to win, we don't desire the same outcome (i.e., to win). I want to be the winner, and you also want to be the winner. These are very different outcomes.

John von Neumann is generally credited as being the father of game theory. The Hungarian-born von Neumann was a mathematician and physicist. In 1930 he was offered a professorship at Princeton University, which he accepted. Many people have never heard of von Neumann, but he had one of the most illustrious scientific careers of the twentieth century.

Von Neumann was part of the team of scientists that developed the atomic bomb under the aegis of the Manhattan Project for the U.S. government during World War II. After the war von Neumann turned his attention to the nascent field of computers. He had become aware of the world's first computer, the ENIAC, that was developed for the U.S. army during the war. Von Neumann decided to build a better computer, and he did so at Princeton University. Later as an advisor to IBM, von Neumann's ideas about computers defined computers as we know them today: the use of digital technology, the binary numbering system, sequential processing, and the use of stored programs, just to name a few. Von Neumann is widely recognized as the father of digital computers, and the vast majority of computers in the world today are known as "von Neumann" style computers. This includes all PCs. It is no mean feat to be considered the "father" of two of the most important intellectual advances of the twentieth century!

Von Neumann's mental abilities and contributions to advancing the frontier of knowledge were as great as those of Edison, Einstein, and Tesla. (Readers who are unfamiliar with von Neumann and his work may wish to read a biography of this towering figure.) Von Neumann loved to play games of all types, especially poker. Although his analytic mind easily grasped the mathematical probabilities associated with poker, the bluffing and gamesmanship intrigued him. When playing a poker hand, one may have calculated the odds and bet accordingly, but a skilled bluffer can walk away with the pot with nothing in his hand. Von Neumann wondered if there was a mathematical analysis that might determine when to bluff, for what size bet, and so on. He had written a few mathematical papers that analyzed "games," and he decided to make a rigorous examination of games. Von Neumann teamed up with Princeton economist Oskar Morgenstern to study the mathematical aspects of gaming, and in 1944 they jointly published a book titled *Theory of Games and Economic Behavior.*

The *Theory of Games and Economic Behavior* is a tour de force; it is one of the most influential books written in modern times. Even though it isn't a very well-known book, it has nevertheless influenced high-level policy in many areas. The most widely known policy areas affected by game theory are military strategy and nuclear war strategy.

The *Theory of Games and Economic Behavior* is very difficult to read. Written by two mathematicians, virtually every page of the book is filled with complex formulas and notations. A lay person will find it mostly incomprehensible; many professional mathematicians struggle with it as well.

BASIC GAME THEORY TERMS AND IDEAS

Many of the conceptual ideas of game theory can be illustrated using "parlor games" such as card games, dice, board games, chess, and checkers, but the theory itself is a methodology used to analyze the actions of each player in a mathematical fashion. The title of von Neumann and Morgenstern's book deliberately included the phrase "Economic Behavior" as much of the theory has to do with analyzing production and consumption decisions as "choices" in a game. The theory is not limited to parlor games and economic decision making: The focus is on the analysis of situations where people have strong preferences for one result over another and are only able to exert partial control over the result. The parlor and economic games are used to illustrate the underlying concepts.

To have a "game," each player must have several possible strategies, each of which leads to a different payoff. Payoffs may be negative (i.e., undesirable to the player), or they may be positive (i.e., desirable to the player). Most games involve the potential for both negative and positive payoffs, although some games involve a set of payoffs that are either all positive or all negative.

Each player typically ranks the possible payoffs in order of preference. This can be a very tricky business. In general in a game of checkers each player tries to win. We could easily assign a payoff of "1" to a winning game and a payoff of "−1" to a losing game. This seems to be a rational ranking of the two possible outcomes to a game of checkers. But what about the case where an adult is playing against a child and wants to lose on purpose? How should the payoffs be ranked? A player must be able to identify clearly and accurately the different payoffs and rank them in order of preference. Failure to have a clear grasp of the payoffs will generally cause players to pursue muddled strategies.

The payoffs for games are expressed in terms of *utility*. Modern utility theory holds that utilities are ordinal: If a person prefers outcome "A" to outcome "B," the outcome "A" is said to have more utility for that person than outcome "B." The outcomes can be ranked numerically. Outcome "A" may be assigned a numerical value of "10" and outcome "B" assigned a numerical value of "5." This doesn't necessarily imply that outcome "A" holds twice as much utility as outcome "B," but it does imply that the player prefers outcome "A" to outcome "B."

Because games have more than one player, we have to assign utilities to the various possible outcomes for both players. The utility that player "X" receives for a win may be "10" and the utility that player "Y" receives for a win may also be "10," but we cannot say both players have the same preference for a win because their utilities are equal. Each player's utilities are ordinal only with respect to themselves. A simple example will illustrate this point.

Suppose two people are in a contest in which the prize is a surfboard valued at $99.95. One contestant is a nineteen-year-old man who lives in southern California and loves to surf. The other contestant is a farmer from Kansas. Although both players may prefer to win the contest rather than lose, it is probably safe to say that winning means more to the surfer (and hence has more utility) than winning means to the farmer. Even if both contestants are surfers, the utility isn't necessarily equal: One surfer may be broke and in need of a new surfboard, and the other surfer may be well-to-do and already own several surfboards, all of which are of better quality and worth more than the prize.

The amount of utility that any person receives for any given outcome is a highly personal thing. Consider again the case where an adult and a child are playing checkers, and the adult is trying to lose. The outcome where the child wins (i.e., the adult loses) may have the highest utility for the adult. Similarly in a game of poker, each player generally tries to win as much money as possible. It seems reasonable to conclude that the utility each player receives is directly related to the amount of money he or she has won. But what of the player who loves to bluff more than he or she cares about winning? The player who wins $1 from a successful bluff may get more utility than the utility another player gets from holding a winning hand that nets $10.

It is clear from the above examples that utilities are ordinal. They can be ranked for each player, but the rankings are not directly transferable to each different player. The utility a player receives for each of the game's outcomes is known as the player's *utility function*.

Game theory assumes that each player is trying to maximize his utility. Furthermore each player is assumed to know his or her own utility function, as well as those of other players.

A player that attempts to maximize utility is known as a "rational" player. The strategy that will yield the highest expected utility is known as the "optimal" strategy. Game theory restricts itself to games played by rational players. For a rational player to choose the optimal strategy, he must know the other player's utility functions (as well as his own), or he may pursue a strategy the other players will thwart. If a strategy is thwarted, it cannot be an optimal strategy.

Although this looks good on paper, the real world is much messier. How often in competitive situations (i.e., games) does an individual know all of his possible strategies and the utilities associated with them and also all of the possible strategies and utilities of the other players? Probably not very often.

THE DECISION-MAKING PROBLEM

People make decisions every day. Decisions need to be made because people find themselves in situations where they have more than one course of action available, and each different action will lead to a different outcome. People try to make decisions that will result in the most favorable outcome.

Some decisions are easy to make. Both the courses of action and the possible outcomes are easily identified. The question of which restaurant to go to for lunch can be decided by determining how much time you have for lunch, the amount of money you have to spend, and your personal preference for various types of food. If you only have 45 minutes for lunch and only want to spend $5, you may elect to go to a fast-food restaurant. If you are entertaining an important client, you may have an expense account and not be worried about time, so you may elect to go to a fancy restaurant.

Other decisions become more complicated. How much money should you save each month for your child's college education? A decision can be reached after examining tuition costs, room and board costs, the rate of inflation you expect will prevail until the child reaches college age, the rate of return you expect to make on your investments during the same time frame, and so forth. You can construct an equation using the above information and solve it for the required monthly savings.

Still other decisions require you to take a course of action without knowing all the variables that can impact on the outcome. If you have $10,000 to invest, do you put it all in one stock? Split it up among several? Buy a mutual fund instead? Keep it in a shoe box under your bed? You may use a lot of complicated analytical techniques to try to determine how to make the highest return on your money, but the actual return you realize will have a lot to do with factors outside your control. If you put it all in the stock of Company "X," it may turn out that their management is incompetent and the company goes into Chapter 11 bankruptcy. If you put the $10,000 into a bond fund, the government may incur huge deficits that raise the inflation rate, making your bond fund investment lose money.

In general decisions are made under four possible conditions. These are (1) decision making under certainty, (2) decision making under risk, (3) decision making under uncertainty, and (4) decision making under a combination of risk and uncertainty.

Decision making under certainty occurs when each choice is known to result (without fail) in a known outcome. For example a plant manager may have "X" number of orders for a product but limited production capacity. Furthermore he must retool his machines between each order's production run, because the orders are for somewhat dissimilar products. In what order should the different production runs be scheduled so as to produce all the orders in the shortest time? The plant manager may use the technique of linear programming to solve this problem.

Decision making under risk occurs when each decision results in a specific outcome that occurs with some known probability. Gambling falls into this category. If someone is playing blackjack and has "14" showing, should the player hold or accept an additional card? The decision is made by counting how many cards are face-up, which cards they are, estimating the probability of getting a "7" or less, and deciding accordingly.

Decision making under uncertainty occurs when each decision results in a specific outcome that occurs with an unknown probability. If you are driving home during rush hour and want to minimize the time spent commuting, should you take your "usual" route or try an alternate route? Either decision results in a specific outcome (arriving home), but on any given day which route is fastest may be unknown to you.

Decision making under a combination of risk and uncertainty generally occurs when there is a conflict of interest between decision makers. Both parties are at risk and are uncertain what the other will do. During the Cold War, both the United States and the former Soviet Union possessed enormous nuclear arsenals and were highly antagonistic toward each other. Should one power or the other launch a first strike? Only launch in retaliation? What if the enemy's first strike destroys the other's capacity to strike back? Should they strike first to keep from being struck? Game theory is the study of "conflicting interest" problems.

WHAT IS A GAME?

Games can be characterized as having one or more *moves*. Each player has the choice of what move to make when it is his turn. Legal moves and choices are determined by the rules of the game. All the choices made by an individual player from the beginning of the game to the end of the game are called a *play*.

Take tic-tac-toe for example. Player "1" may place an "X" in the lower right-hand box for his first move and player "2" may place an "O" in the center box for her move. Play continues until the game is over. If we were to write down all of one of the player's moves in sequence, the resulting list is considered a *play*. A play contains all the moves from the beginning to the end of the game. This is also synonymous with a *strategy*.

Let's look at an even simpler game. A player is required to roll a fair die and then flip a fair coin. The player wins if the die shows an even number and the coin lands heads up. The player loses if the die shows an odd number or the coin lands tails up. The possible outcomes can be drawn as shown in Figure 1.1.

The drawing in Figure 1.1 is known as a connected graph. Such a graph consists of nodes and branches. Each branch is a move in the game. Each node is a "decision point." In game theory a connected graph of the game is known as a *game tree*.

The first node (at the left of the drawing) represents the player's choice of whether or not to play the game. Branching out from this node are six branches, each corresponding to the roll of a fair die. After

FIGURE 1.1   The game tree for "roll a die and flip a coin." Each node on
the tree represents a decision point. Each play is shown by a complete
branch of the tree, from the starting point on the left to the final result
on the right. A losing play is depicted with a broken line.

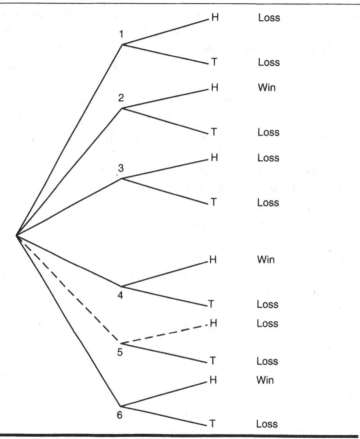

the die has been cast, the player must flip a fair coin. The "decision"
point when the coin is flipped is indicated by the six nodes at the ends
of the die-rolling branches. The result of the coin toss (heads or tails) is
shown by the next set of six pairs of branches extending from the nodes
at the ends of each of the die-rolling branches.

It is easy to see which plays of this game result in wins, as well as
which plays result in losses. Obviously casting a die and flipping a coin
aren't "strategies" in the sense that the player has any control over the

outcome, but they are "strategies" in the sense that the player knows what the result will be in the event they occur.

The column to the right of the tree lists the outcome of each particular play, that is, either a win or a loss. There are 12 possible outcomes, of which three are winners. Tracing through each branch of the tree from start to finish contains all the moves in a play. A losing play (depicted with a broken line) is shown in Figure 1.1.

Note that a player knows where he is on the game tree at any given time during the game. If a player rolls an odd number on the die, he might as well quit playing the game because it isn't possible to win.

Let's draw the game tree for tic-tac-toe (Figure 1.2). Only the first two moves are shown. There isn't enough space to show them all.

The left-most branch of the tree consists of player 1's possible choices. Because player 1 has an open board, he may place an "X" in any of the nine squares. Therefore there are nine branches on the game tree corresponding to player 1's initial choice of moves.

The node terminating player 1's first move represents the beginning of player 2's first move. There are eight branches stemming from each of the nodes. Because player 1 has filled in one box with an "X," there are only eight remaining boxes where player 2 can place an "O." Following from this, player 1 will only have a choice of seven squares from which to choose his second move, and player 2 will only have a choice of six squares for her second move, and so on. This pattern repeats until all of the squares are filled.

The resulting game tree will be a diagram of all the possible plays that can take place during a game of tic-tac-toe. Note that a player knows where he is on the game tree on any given move, just as he knew where he was on the game tree when playing "roll-a-die and flip-a-coin." In general games in which the players know where they are on the game tree are known as games with *perfect information*.

The game tree for tic-tac-toe is fairly large, but it can be graphed with a little patience. It isn't necessary to do so, because anyone who has played tic-tac-toe knows that it always results in a tie. The rules are simple and the "game space" is limited to nine squares, so the players always know where they are on the game tree. This being the case, the result is always a tie. Either player can always make moves in such a manner as to keep the other player from being able to win. This is why adults don't play tic-tac-toe and children do: Adults have played tic-tac-toe enough to know where they are on the game tree and to realize the game is pointless. Children haven't played the game enough and

FIGURE 1.2   The game tree for "tic-tac-toe." The entire game tree isn't shown because there isn't enough room.

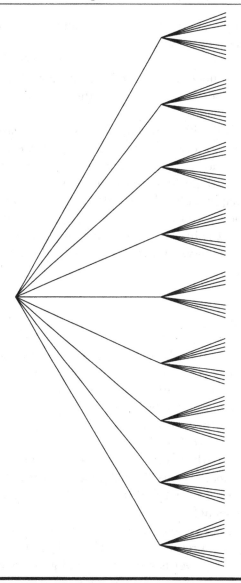

are still looking for a "strategy" that they can play from start to finish which will enable them to beat their opponents. Such a strategy does not exist.

The game of tic-tac-toe is finite: It cannot consist of more than nine moves. It may consist of less than nine moves if one player allows the other to get three squares in a row, but it can never have more than nine moves. Von Neumann and Morgenstern showed that for any two-player game with perfect information, there are a finite number of moves that can be made.

There are games with these characteristics that cannot have their game trees drawn. For example the game tree for chess is so large that it can't be drawn. However, chess does have a game tree. It is also a two-person game with perfect information, so it is finite. Theoretically it is possible to map out *all* the possibilities for the game of chess from start to finish. Such a job would probably be one of the most monumental undertakings in the history of mankind, and it is extremely doubtful that it could be done, even using the largest and most powerful computers in existence.

A SIMPLE GAME

It is often more useful to diagram a game in a table or matrix rather than in a game tree. This is especially true for two-person games. A *game table* is constructed with the possible outcomes on the inside and the possible strategies on the outside.

To demonstrate this concept, let's look at a game called "Leftover Pie." A mother with two children has a large slab of leftover pie in the refrigerator. Both children want a piece, so it must be divided as evenly as possible. If the mother cuts the slab in half, invariably one child will insist that the other child got the "bigger" half and that the pie division isn't "fair." What should the mother do?

Every parent knows the answer to this question! One need not be a game theory expert to resolve this conflict. Merely have one child cut the slab in half (this player is the cutter), and give the other child the first choice of slices (this player is the chooser). Neither child can now claim the process is unfair. If the cutter makes one slice much bigger than the other, the chooser has first dibs and will take the big slice. Equity is ensured.

Let's draw out the game of "Leftover Pie" in matrix format. The matrix can be drawn showing the payoffs accruing to either each individual player or to both players simultaneously, but for simplicity's sake let's look at the game from the point of view of the cutter. This means that the payoffs shown are the cutter's (see Figure 1.3).

Each player's strategies are represented by either the rows or the columns. In our example the cutter has the rows and the chooser the columns. In Leftover Pie each player only has two strategies available. The payoffs resulting from the interaction between the two players are shown inside the matrix.

If the cutter makes the division as evenly as possible (i.e., plays the "fair" strategy), the payoff to the cutter will be one half of a slice. If the cutter makes one piece disproportionately large (i.e., plays the "unfair" strategy), he will get either the small piece or the large piece.

The actual outcome of the game doesn't depend on the strategy chosen by either individual player, it depends on the strategy chosen by both players. Neither player can determine the outcome through his actions alone. It is only the combined actions of both players that determine the actual payoffs.

Note that the earlier discussion of utility has a bearing on the outcome of this game. This game has assumed that both players want to maximize the size of their slice of pie. In game theory terms, each player is attempting to maximize their utility, and we are defining utility as being positively correlated with the size of the piece of pie. If one of the players doesn't like pie, then our assumption about the "utility of pie" doesn't hold. Then again, if one player doesn't like pie, they

---

FIGURE 1.3 The game table for "Leftover Pie," with the payoffs shown from the cutter's point of view. The cutter's only two strategies are to "cut fairly" or to "cut unfairly."

		CHOOSER	
		Choose Big Slice	Choose Small Slice
CUTTER	Cut Fairly	1/2 slice	1/2 slice
	Cut Unfairly	less than 1/2 slice	greater than 1/2 slice

wouldn't play the game in the first place: The "pie averse" child would just tell the other child to have the entire leftover pie.

However, assuming the children are "rational players" and that "utility" is positively correlated with the quantity of pie received, it's obvious that player 1 (the cutter) won't be able to do any better than get a half slice. If the cutter unfairly divides the pie, the chooser will take the bigger half. The optimal strategy for the cutter is to try to divide the pie as evenly as possible.

The cutter decides in which row the outcome will rest by playing either a "fair" strategy or an "unfair" strategy. In general the row player will seek to maximize the minimum amount available to him in any row and then choose that row. This is known as the *maximin.* In our example the top row has a minimum amount of pie equal to "one half." The bottom row has a minimum amount equal to "less than one half." Because the row player (the cutter) wants the largest minimum available, he compares the minimum payoffs and chooses his strategy.

If the cutter pursues the "fair" strategy (i.e., top row), he has a minimum payoff of "one half" of the pie. If he pursues the "unfair" strategy, he has a minimum payoff of "less than one half." Because "one half" is greater than "less than one half," the cutter's maximin is obtained by pursuing the "fair" strategy.

The row player's tactic is to find the minimum payoffs for each row and select the strategy that has the higher minimum. The row containing the maximin strategy varies with the particulars of the game.

Similarly the chooser (i.e., column player) seeks to maximize his payoff by selecting the strategy that will leave the other player with the *smallest* payoff; that is, he minimizes the column maximum (this is the *minimax*). This is because the payoffs are expressed in terms of the row player.

If the chooser selects "choose big" as his strategy, the maximum amount in the left column is "one half"; if he selects "choose small" as his strategy, the maximum amount in the right column is "more than one half." By employing the minimax, he should select "choose big" because by doing so the most the cutter will receive is one half. The column player's strategy is to find the maximums in each column and select the strategy that yields the smaller maximum.

Does the above hold true if we look at the game from the chooser's point of view? Figure 1.4 shows the game of "Leftover Pie" from the chooser's perspective; that is, the payoffs shown are the payoffs accruing to the chooser.

FIGURE 1.4 "Leftover Pie" as shown from the chooser's perspective. The chooser has the option of choosing either the big slice or the small slice.

		CHOOSER	
		Choose Big Slice	Choose Small Slice
CUTTER	Cut Fairly	1/2 slice	1/2 slice
	Cut Unfairly	greater than 1/2 slice	less than 1/2 slice

The chooser will seek to maximize the minimum payoff available, and the cutter will try to leave the chooser with the smaller payoff. The chooser has a minimum payoff of "one half" if he plays the "choose big" strategy, and a minimum payoff of "less than one half" if he plays the "choose small" strategy. The maximum of these two minimums is attained by playing the "choose big" strategy.

The cutter will select the strategy that minimizes the maximum available to the chooser. By playing "fair" the maximum the chooser gets is "one half," and by playing "unfair" the maximum the chooser gets is "more than one half." Of these two strategies, the minimum maximum is left to the chooser by playing the "fair" strategy. The outcome of the game is the same if looked at from either the chooser's or cutter's point of view.

In general, if the payoffs are expressed in terms of player 1, then player 1 will use the minimax strategy, and player 2 will use the maximin strategy.

Game tables are often drawn showing the payoffs to both players. The usual mathematical convention of *(row, column)* is used to illustrate the payoffs. For each cell the row player gets the *row* payoff (or left-hand entry), and the column player gets the *column* payoff (or right-hand entry). Figure 1.5 shows the "combined" payoff matrix for Leftover Pie.

When the maximin is equal to the minimax, the outcome is known as the *saddle point*. This is the payoff generated by rational play. The "solution" to the game is the payoff achieved when both players employ their optimal strategy. The game is said to be in "equilibrium" when a solution exists. As will be demonstrated later, not all games have saddle points.

FIGURE 1.5 The game table for "Leftover Pie" shown in conventional form of *(row, column)*. The payoffs to both players are shown. The row player gets the *row* payoffs, and the column player gets the *column* payoffs.

		CHOOSER	
		Choose Big Slice	Choose Small Slice
CUTTER	Cut Fairly	(1/2, 1/2)	(1/2, 1/2)
	Cut Unfairly	(< 1/2, > 1/2)	(> 1/2, < 1/2)

By rationally selecting their strategies based on the concepts of minimax and maximin, each player is able to guarantee himself a certain minimum payoff. In other words each player is able to find a strategy that ensures a certain payoff. Player 1 might do better than receive his minimum payoff if player 2 doesn't also play his optimal strategy, but player 1 can *guarantee* himself a minimum payoff no matter what. The complement holds true for player 2: He can *guarantee* himself a minimum payoff by playing his optimal strategy as well. A player's minimum payoff is known as his security level.

In Leftover Pie both players receive a positive payoff; that is, they both receive some part of the pie. Not all games have minimum payoffs that are positive. In many games a player faces a situation where he is guaranteed a loss. By employing the minimax, he can limit the amount of loss he will receive. Having a losing payoff is undesirable, but being able to ensure that the size of a loss won't exceed a certain amount is a form of a "win" in itself.

This is an important point: Game theory suggests there are strategies that guarantee a player some minimum payoff.

Herein lies the attraction game theory holds for someone interested in financial markets. If the "game" you play when you buy or sell stocks (or other financial instruments) can be clearly identified, then it should be possible to find an optimal strategy that will *guarantee* a certain minimum payoff, that is, find a strategy that has a security level. This is an extremely important point. Game theory seeks to identify the payoffs associated with each strategy, and the optimal strategy will *guarantee* the security level payoff. If the guaranteed payoff in the financial market game is *positive*, then an individual is *guaranteed a profit*.

THE PRISONER'S DILEMMA

The Prisoner's Dilemma is the most well-known "game" that has been analyzed by game theory. The term "prisoner's dilemma" was first coined in 1950 by Albert Tucker of Princeton University. The structure of the game is quite simple. The police have apprehended two criminals. They have evidence that the pair committed a serious crime, but the evidence isn't strong enough to convict them. The state must get one of them to turn "state's evidence" and rat on the other to get a conviction. Additionally, the police have enough evidence to convict them both on a lesser charge. The prosecutor orders them held in separate cells so they can't communicate with each other. The prosecutor then meets with each in turn and offers the following deal:

1. If one prisoner turns state's evidence and testifies against the other suspect on the serious charge, the state will drop all charges against the testifier. The state will then send the other prisoner to prison for 25 years.
2. If both prisoners take the deal and confess, the state will send both of them to prison for 10 years.
3. If neither prisoner confesses, the state will convict both on the lesser charge and send them to prison for three years each.

What should the prisoners do? We can diagram their options using a payoff table (Figure 1.6).

Because both prisoners have been given the same deal, the payoffs are the same to both. The payoffs are shown in the usual (*row, column*)

FIGURE 1.6   The classic case of the Prisoners' Dilemma. Payoffs are shown for both prisoners and are expressed as years in prison.

		PRISONER "A"	
		Keep Silent	Confess
PRISONER "B"	Keep Silent	(3 Years, 3 Years)	(25 Years, No Time)
	Confess	(No Time, 25 Years)	(10 Years, 10 Years)

notation. If prisoner B confesses, he will either get no time in prison or serve 10 years, depending on what prisoner A does. If prisoner B keeps silent, he will either get 3 years or 25 years, once again depending on what Prisoner A does. Prisoner A is faced with the same dilemma.

Assuming each prisoner wants to spend as little time in prison as possible, what choices will be made? If a prisoner keeps silent, he is guaranteed a prison term. If he confesses, he may not serve any time at all. The optimal strategy is for each prisoner to confess. In game theory terms, each prisoner will choose the strategy that maximizes the minimum payoff.

If this isn't clear, let's look at the problem expressed in terms of utility, where utility is negatively correlated with time spent in prison. If a prisoner spends three years in prison, it is really three years that have been taken away from him. We can assign this outcome a value of -3 (utility of negative 3). The same reasoning applies to the other payoffs. If the payoff table is constructed with negative numbers to represent jail time (i.e., actual utility), it is easy to see that the two strategies yield minimums of -10 and -25 respectively, and that -10 is obviously the maximum of the two (Figure 1.7).

The "equilibrium" outcome of both prisoners confessing seems counterintuitive to many people. Because both prisoners are in the same boat, why should one rat on the other? They are both equally at risk. It seems to make sense for both of them to keep their mouths shut.

Various researchers have questioned the "optimal" outcome of both prisoners confessing. Empirical studies have been conducted to see if people really behave this way. Obviously a researcher can't threaten

---

FIGURE 1.7   The Prisoners' Dilemma shown with the payoffs expressed in terms of utility (the presumption is that years in prison is negatively correlated with utility!).

		PRISONER "A"	
		Keep Silent	Confess
PRISONER "B"	Keep Silent	$(-3, -3)$	$(-25, 0)$
	Confess	$(0, -25)$	$(-10, -10)$

test subjects with long prison terms as part of an experiment, so they typically set up a game that pays off in pennies.

Two subjects are put in different rooms. Neither subject knows who is in the other room. Both are given a payoff table showing the possible strategies as well as the payoffs. They are given a few minutes to decide which strategy they are going to play, and after making their decision, they inform the researcher. The researcher pays them according to the outcome and keeps a log of the result. An example of a payoff table used in this type of experiment is shown in Figure 1.8.

The game is a prisoner's dilemma, but the names of the strategies have been simplified. The nomenclature of calling the strategy in which a player tries to maximize his own payoff has come to be known as the "defect" strategy, whereas the strategy that affords an equitable payoff to both sides is called the "cooperate" strategy. Most of the studies suggest that people will play "defect" most of the time.

Other researchers have wondered whether the choice of strategies changes if the subjects are allowed to repeat the game many times. Games that are repeated over and over are called *iterated games*.

ITERATED GAMES

The most famous study of iterated games was conducted by Robert Axelrod of the University of Michigan. He created a tournament to test various prisoner's dilemma strategies.

What makes an iterated prisoner's dilemma different from a one-shot prisoner's dilemma is that players have to take into account how

---

FIGURE 1.8 A game table for a typical "Cooperate/Defect" game that pays off in pennies. Researchers often use games like this to measure behavior empirically.

		CONTESTANT #1	
		Cooperate	Defect
CONTESTANT #2	Cooperate	(5, 5)	(0, 10)
	Defect	(10, 0)	(2, 2)

their behavior in any one round will affect the other player's behavior in subsequent rounds. In a one-shot prisoner's dilemma, only the present has any value. This being the case, it makes the most sense for a player to defect. If an iterated game is being played, future gains and losses have to be taken into account as well.

Axelrod set up a tournament where each player submitted a strategy in the form of a computer program. The tournament matched each program against every other program submitted, as well as against itself. This ensured that every strategy had a chance to test itself against all other strategies. Each game was played for 200 iterations. Provisions were made so that each player was provided feedback on what their opponent did during each iteration. The payoffs were in points according to the diagram in Figure 1.9.

The most points that a player can win during any round is 1,000. If a strategy got the maximum of 5 points per iteration for each of the 200 iterations, the strategy could win 1,000 points. Similarly the least amount that can be won is zero. This would be the payoff if a strategy never won a single iteration. Axelrod totaled the number of points won by each strategy for each round of the game. After all strategies had played against all others, the winner was the strategy with the highest number of points.

Axelrod received fourteen entries to the tournament. Some of the entries were pretty complex computer programs; others were quite simple. Some strategies were extremely predatory; that is, they tried to

FIGURE 1.9 The game table for Axelrod's tournament. The payoffs are in points (which were an arbitrary measurement). Contestants were invited to submit computer programs that tried to win the highest number of points over the course of many iterations. TIT FOR TAT proved to be the winner.

		PLAYER #1	
		Cooperate	Defect
PLAYER #2	Cooperate	(3, 3)	(0, 5)
	Defect	(5, 0)	(1, 1)

take advantage of their opponent whenever possible. Other strategies recognized that the total points likely to be won were highest if the strategies cooperated and tried to get a high payoff for both players.

He also included three strategies of his own that weren't submitted by any of the contestants. These are pretty simplistic strategies that didn't stand much of a chance of winning, but Axelrod wanted to be able to see how well they did.

The first of Axelrod's strategies played "cooperate" for each iteration. This strategy is called ALL C. This strategy will do well when it plays against ALL C or a strategy that tries to cooperate, but it will be decimated by a predatory strategy.

The second strategy was the inverse of ALL C. This strategy decided that it would never cooperate, it would "defect" all of the time. It was called ALL D. This is the safest strategy, as it can never be taken advantage of. It also corresponds to the "classic" prisoner's dilemma solution of defecting. It is a highly predatory strategy in that in never attempts to cooperate.

The last strategy was called RANDOM. This program randomly played either cooperate or defect during each iteration.

If ALL D were playing ALL C, it's obvious that ALL D would win each and every round. ALL D would score 1,000 points, and ALL C would score zero. If ALL D were paired against itself, it would only score 200 points per game. If ALL C were paired against itself, it would score 600 points per game.

The winning strategy was called TIT FOR TAT, and it was submitted by Anatol Rapoport. TIT FOR TAT was the simplest strategy entered in the tournament. TIT FOR TAT cooperated on the first iteration, and then played the opponent's strategy on each successive iteration. For example, if the opponent played "defect" on the first iteration, TIT FOR TAT would defect on the second iteration. TIT FOR TAT "echoes" its opponent's strategy for each successive iteration.

What makes TIT FOR TAT such a successful strategy? If TIT FOR TAT were playing a cooperative strategy such as ALL C, then both strategies would win 3 points per iteration, for a total of 600 points per game. When paired against a predatory strategy such as ALL D, TIT FOR TAT would lose the first round but would defect in every successive iteration, thereby keeping it from being taken advantage of. TIT FOR TAT would score 199 points, and ALL D would score 204 points. The cooperative strategies would score well when playing against each other but get really hammered when playing against a defect strategy.

The defect strategies would do poorly against each other but score well against cooperative strategies. TIT FOR TAT did extremely well when playing against cooperative strategies and would come out nearly tied with the defect strategies.

Because the tournament was based on the *total* points for all games played, TIT FOR TAT would rack up a lot of points when it was playing against cooperative strategies but only score slightly worse than the defect strategies when playing against them. The total points scored by TIT FOR TAT were the highest of the tournament. TIT FOR TAT's average score was 504.50 points per game. TIT FOR TAT can't actually "beat" any other strategy in terms of scoring more points in any individual game, but it outscored every other strategy in total points for the whole tournament.

Axelrod decided to hold another tournament. He provided entrants with the results of the first tournament. The challenge for the contestants was to enter a strategy that could beat TIT FOR TAT. Sixty-two entries were received for second tournament. TIT FOR TAT was the winner again.

Axelrod was curious if this tournament could be modified to reflect Darwin's theory of natural selection. A biologist may have a test tube of a certain type of bacteria. If a researcher then introduces a different variety of bacteria into the test tube, after a time one of the two bacteria may prove to be superior and have dominated the other. This can be ascertained by looking at the proportion of the two types in the test tube. If the test tube were filled with 50% each of bacteria A and bacteria B, then after a day the researcher might find that 90% of the bacteria were type A and only 10% type B. He could then infer that type A dominates type B.

Axelrod substituted computer "colonies" of strategies in place of bacteria in test tubes. He would let the strategies play many rounds, each consisting of many iterations. Then he had the strategies "reproduce" offspring. Reproduction was based on the total points each strategy scored. The points a particular strategy scored determined the number of "offspring" it had. The more points, the greater the number of offspring. The game would then continue based on the new mix of strategies, including their offspring. Thus each new generation would include greater numbers of the more successful strategies and lesser numbers of unsuccessful strategies.

Initially weak strategies such as RANDOM and ALL C died out very quickly. The highly exploitive strategies were successful in reproducing large numbers of offspring, as was TIT FOR TAT. Eventually the exploitive strategies began to run out of "food" (i.e., weak strategies), and they began to "starve." The number of the predators began to drop off with each successive generation. After many generations TIT FOR TAT was the most predominant strategy in the computer "test tube." This strongly suggested that TIT FOR TAT is the optimal way to play an iterated prisoner's dilemma.

Axelrod wanted to see just how powerful a strategy TIT FOR TAT really is, so he concocted another experiment. Starting out with a colony of many exploitive strategies (say, 100 ALL D strategies), a few (say, five) TIT FOR TATs are introduced into their environment. The ALL Ds take advantage of TIT FOR TAT (i.e., score 204 points versus TIT FOR TAT's 199 points), but they do poorly against each other. Eventually, TIT FOR TATs will have played against each and every ALL D and a few of the other TIT FOR TATs. An ALL D strategy can expect to win one point per iteration. That is, they score one point when playing against either another ALL D or TIT FOR TAT. However, TIT FOR TAT will score one point per iteration when playing against an ALL D, but it will score three points per iteration when it plays against another TIT FOR TAT. Thus TIT FOR TAT's "average" score per iteration is slightly higher than one. After allowing the computer to play the game for many generations, the TIT FOR TATs eventually came to supplant the ALL Ds. A small colony of TIT FOR TATs was able to enter a large and hostile population of ALL Ds and defeat them!

In a one-time prisoner's dilemma, each player has to choose either one strategy or the other. Each strategy is known as a *pure strategy.* If someone is playing an iterated game, they can play a different strategy during each round. A player might decide to "defect" 60% of the time and "cooperate" 40% of the time. This is known as playing *mixed strategies.* It is still possible to play a mixed strategy in a one-time prisoner's dilemma by deciding that you will "defect" with a probability of 60% and "cooperate" with a probability of 40%. This might be accomplished by writing "defect" on six slips of paper and "cooperate" on four slips of paper, putting them in a hat, and then playing whatever strategy you draw from the hat.

The financial market game is definitely an iterated game. You can lose money on a stock today, but you can still go back to the market and make a different play tomorrow. You can iterate the game until you have either made so much money you don't know what to do with it, or you have gone bankrupt.

This game is also played with mixed strategies. Investors may develop numerous strategies and play them with varying probability in different markets, over different time frames, under different market conditions, and so on. There are probably an infinite number of strategies that can be played, and they can be played in any combination.

ZERO SUM GAME

Zero-sum game is the one term from game theory that has entered the English language as an everyday expression. Most games that people play for recreation are zero-sum games. In chess each piece captured is a loss for the other player. Winnings in poker represent someone else's losses. When a baseball team is victorious, an increase is made to that team's "games won" statistic, and the losing team adds to its "games lost" statistic.

A zero sum game is defined as a game where the payoff to player 1 is the *exact* opposite of the payoff to player 2. The phrase "zero-sum game" is often tossed about quite loosely by people who don't understand it. Many people think that if two people are in a situation where one person may profit at the other's expense, then they are playing a zero-sum game. This is not necessarily true—perhaps there was a better strategy the loser failed to see. Because one player gains and the other loses doesn't necessarily imply that the situation is zero-sum. To have a "true" zero-sum game, there must be exactly opposite payoffs to each player. Zero-sum games are also known as *strictly competitive* games, and these two terms are often used interchangeably. None of the games diagrammed in matrix format so far have been zero-sum games.

It is often said that many financial markets are zero-sum games, especially the futures market. This is because what one person wins, another person has lost. This may be true if your opponent were another person, but your opponent is not another person. Your opponent is the market.

The futures market is a zero-sum game in the sense that all the winners' profits come at the expense of the losers. How would this be diagrammed in a game table? If we assign the entire class of "buyers" the row positions and the entire class of "sellers" the column positions, we could probably construct a game table, but how useful is this approach? In reality both buyers and sellers play the game against the market. If you are a short seller, you make money if the market drops and lose money if the market rises. Similarly someone who takes a long position makes money if the market rises, and loses if the market drops. There is a seller for each buyer, so one of them will make money at the other's expense.

Assume someone shorts a futures contract. That means they've sold a contract. There has to be a buyer. If the price drops and the seller makes money, can we assume that the specific buyer who was on the other side of the trade has lost money? No.

Perhaps the buyer was closing out a short of his own. Perhaps the short seller is a floor trader who doesn't expect to hold the position longer than a few hours and only plans on making a few ticks. The buyer may be an institution that is initiating a hedge position they expect to hold for several months, so a few tick drop in the next few hours doesn't affect their decision making. Although it is true that the net winnings of the entire futures market are zero (i.e., the positions of the entire classes of buyers and sellers net out to zero), it doesn't hold that for any *individual* player the game is zero sum.

The key idea is that after a position is taken, profitability depends on what the *market* does, not what the party on the other side of the trade does. From this perspective each trader is competing against the market and not against the other traders.

GAMES AGAINST NATURE

If taking a position in a financial market means you are playing a game against the market, then the market must represent nature. This is central thesis of this book: Buying and selling in financial markets is analogous to playing a game against nature. Most of the rest of the book is devoted to explicating this game. Before we delve into the intricacies of the financial market game, let's look at games against nature in more detail

Games can be played by entities other than people. Obviously two corporations can play games with each other during the normal course of business. A person may play a game against a business. These two examples still involve the human element; that is, corporations don't "think" in the conventional sense, the people that work for them think and make the decisions. There is a subclass of games where one of both players is not a "thinking" entity. These games are known as games against nature.

In game theory nature is broadly defined as natural phenomena or the "state of nature" that might exist. An individual must choose between several options (Option 1, Option 2, Option 3, etc.), and the outcome of the situation will depend on the "state of nature" that prevails after the individual chooses his option. Typically the individual knows what the possible states of nature are but has no idea with what probability the various states of nature will occur.

Games against nature are unique in the sense that the payoffs are somewhat artificial. In Leftover Pie each child attempts to maximize their slice of pie. If you are playing a game against nature, what payoff is nature trying to win? Game theorists assign nature the inverse of the human player's payoffs; that is, if the human player were to lose "2" by employing a particular strategy, then nature wins "2." This is a mathematical convention that allows us to have two players with conflicting interests.

What sort of game might a person play against nature? Let's say someone has recently purchased a vacation house on Long Island. Furthermore the house isn't on Long Island proper; it is on one of the barrier islands on the south side of the island. Our intrepid homeowner has priced property insurance and decided that it is too expensive. He has foregone the protection provided by insurance in the hope that a hurricane won't destroy the property. Whether or not the person takes a loss isn't determined solely by the decision not to buy insurance, it will also be determined by whether or not Mother Nature has a hurricane strike Long Island.

The above situation can be diagrammed as demonstrated in Figure 1.10. Payoffs are to the homeowner. Clearly this person is playing a game against nature (. . . and it's not nice to fool Mother Nature!).

Games against nature can be more complex than the above example. Assume you are a geologist for an oil company. You have drilling rights for two parcels of land. Your budget will only allow you to drill at one of the sites. Whether or not you strike oil depends on the "state of nature" that exists at the site you choose to drill. This can be diagrammed as shown in Figure 1.11. Although this example oversimplifies the oil exploration business, it does illustrate the concept of a game against nature. The game is diagrammed with pure strategies. In reality nature "plays" this game with mixed strategies.

Let's expand the game a little to show the concept of nature playing mixed strategies. Assume the geologist has determined that there is a probability distribution that accurately reflects the likelihood of

FIGURE 1.10 Playing a game against nature. Do you buy insurance if you live on the beach or not? Whether or not your property is destroyed depends not only your decision but on Mother Nature.

		NATURE	
		No Hurricane	Hurricane
HOMEOWNER	Buy Insurance	Property intact, but out the price of insurance	Property is rebuilt, paid for by insurance
	Don't Buy Insurance	Property intact, insurance premiums are in the bank	Property is destroyed, homeowner pays cost

striking oil at each of the sites. If the probability of striking oil at site A is 35% and the probability of striking oil at site B is 65%, then isn't nature playing mixed strategies of "oil at site A" 35% of the time, and "oil at site B" 65% of the time?

This game can be further expanded to make it more realistic. Nature may vary the probability of striking oil at each site by depth, and the geologist may have constraints on how deep of a well can be sunk due to budgetary considerations. For example if the probability of striking oil varies by depth, there may be (at site A) probabilities of 10% at the 500-foot depth, 15% at the 600-foot depth, 25% at the 750-foot depth, 18% at the 1,000-foot depth, and so on. A similar but not identical probability distribution will also exist for site B.

FIGURE 1.11 The "Oil Prospecting" game. Probably not a good real world example but illustrates the many different ways to define "the state of nature."

		NATURE	
		Oil at Site A	Oil at Site B
GEOLOGIST	Drill at Site A	Strike Oil	Dry Well
	Drill at Site B	Dry Well	Strike Oil

The game may be expanded for the geologist as well. His budgetary constraints may limit him to drilling to a total depth of 700 feet. He may do this by drilling 700 feet in one bore at either site, 350 feet at both sites, or 500 feet at site A and 200 feet at site B, and so on.

It would be very difficult to diagram the expanded game, but it is possible. It is unlikely that oil companies use game theory alone in deciding where to drill for oil.

Playing the financial markets is analogous to playing a game against nature. If someone buys a mutual fund that tracks the S&P 500, whether that investment makes money or not is determined by the market, that is, nature. Markets make their moves just as hurricanes make their moves. After you have decided to play, the state of nature that exists (i.e., market conditions) determines the profitability of the investment. You make your move, then the market makes its move. You can't persuade the market not to crash anymore than you can persuade a hurricane not to hit Long Island.

However, if the strategies employed by the individual and the market can be clearly identified, then a game table can be constructed. Mathematical analysis of the game table will reveal which strategies are profitable (and unprofitable), given various states of nature that may prevail.

PROS AND CONS OF GAME THEORY

Game theory can be used to analyze complex problems in a systematic manner. It focuses on studying the outcomes that result from employing different strategies. It is particularly well suited to the study of problems where the various participants have conflicting interests. Rigorously applying game theory techniques can reveal solutions that guarantee a participant a certain minimum payoff.

The biggest problem in using game theory as an analytic tool is that the "answers" you get are based entirely on the assumptions used to create the model. The strategies and their respective outcomes must accurately represent reality, or else the solutions are invalid. If the identification of the strategies and the payoffs is inaccurate, you may get a "solution" to a game that in fact is incorrect (or does not exist). A mathematically precise answer can be deduced from a game table: Whether or not the answer has any validity depends on the assumptions used in its construction.

This can be seen from some of the examples discussed in this chapter. Is it logical that both prisoners will rat each other out? If this premise is wrong, then the game theoretic answer is meaningless. Is it logical that the two children will split a piece of leftover pie fairly? Would you really drill for oil using the oil prospector game as a guide?

Financial markets are complex entities. Anyone can create a game table that suggests an optimal strategy, but it is the *assumptions used to construct the game* that determine its validity.

The topic of game theory is rich, complex, and diverse. I have only scratched the surface in this chapter. Many of the topics discussed deserve an entire book, not merely a few paragraphs or a few pages. However, the focus of this book is to create a game theoretic model of the financial markets and not serve as a game theory textbook. This chapter has been written with enough detail so that the rest of the book can be followed. The basic concepts of game theory have been sufficiently examined so that the reader can follow the discussion of how game theory can be used to describe how financial markets behave and the construction of a model that quantifies that behavior.

2

Basic Ideas About Financial Markets

F or a game theoretic model to have any relevance to the real world, the premises on which it is built must accurately depict reality. In the previous chapter, some of the games made good representations of reality, and others did not. "Leftover Pie" is a pretty good example of a game that closely approximates a real-life situation. The oil prospecting example is much too simplified to be of any use in the real world. If a game theory model of a particular phenomenon is not well grounded in the actual parameters of the situation, then the model is useful for ivory tower discussions but not much else.

A game theoretic model of financial markets has to be built on a set of premises and assumptions about how the markets actually behave. If it isn't, it will be useless as a method of analyzing particular investment decisions with respect to their potential profitability. Accordingly the premises and assumptions used to develop the model need to be explained, and they must withstand scrutiny.

Fundamentally the first question that needs to be asked is: Why do people invest? Primarily to make money. There are people who buy and sell stocks for the thrill of it, but most people invest with the idea that they will be able to make a profit. This holds true for individual investors as well as institutional investors, pension fund managers, and so forth. There may be instances where investors want to make "paper" losses as part of complicated tax avoidance schemes, but these instances are anomalies.

What methods do people use to make money; that is, what are their investment strategies? Some people are highly risk averse. These people may buy government bonds and hold them to maturity, thus avoiding any price risk. They are content to make the stated coupon rate on the bonds. Others may have a slightly greater appetite for risk and may choose to put their money in "blue chip" stocks that have a long history of regular dividend payments. These people are happy to make the dividend, and any increase in wealth due to the appreciation of the stock's price is considered as gravy. Many people also purchase stocks that have a fair dividend return with some potential for price appreciation. These investors are trading some risk for the added benefit of potential price increases.

There is also a large middle ground of investors that use mutual funds for their investments. They don't feel that they either have the time or the expertise to pick stocks, so they are content to buy into a fund and make the average rate of return. Even within the universe of mutual funds the pattern described in the paragraph above is evident. There are income funds (i.e., "safe" dividend funds), growth funds (i.e., price appreciation funds), bond funds (i.e., coupon interest funds), and so forth.

At the other end of the spectrum, there are people who are extreme risk takers, such as floor traders in the futures markets. These traders may not hold a position longer than several hours and may "scalp" the difference in small price changes as profit. There are institutional money managers who spend hours each day doing research on stocks in an attempt to find attractive buys. Some of these buys may be quite risky, but the managers have done their homework and feel confident about their prospects for success.

Even though it seems as if there are huge differences between different types of investors, there are some consistent patterns in their behavior. Broadly speaking there are two classes of participants in financial markets: *Investors* and *speculators*. Most people will tell you that they are investors, not speculators. The word "speculator" has a somewhat pejorative connotation in our society, and besides "speculating" sounds riskier than "investing."

What is the difference between investing and speculating? I heard a definition a long time ago that I think perfectly describes the difference. Investors look to the market to make a predictable rate of return; speculators look to the market to make money from price changes.

People who purchase (and hold) bonds are investors, as are people who buy stocks primarily for the dividends. The universe of investors is not limited to individuals; many professional money managers are

investors. The mutual funds that are classified as income funds generally pursue rates of return, not price changes. The managers of these
funds will often utilize a variety of hedging techniques by trying to ensure that negative price changes will have as little effect on their portfolio as possible. These techniques typically negate the effects of
positive price changes as well. Insurance companies' portfolios are
heavily weighted to the investment end of the spectrum, as well as
many employer sponsored 401-(K) retirement plans.

Speculators, on the other hand, want to make money from price
changes. Obvious examples of speculators are floor traders (locals) at
the various futures exchanges and foreign currency arbitrageurs. However, if we define speculation as the desire to make money from price
changes, the universe expands considerably. Many people who swear
they are investors are, in actuality, speculators. If someone buys into a
stock index mutual fund that tracks the Standard & Poors 500, they are
really hoping that the stock market will go up. They are speculating. If
your brother in-law tells you that XYZ Corporation is a "good buy" and
you act on the advice, you are speculating.

There is a television commercial for one of the national daily investment newspapers in which an interviewer elicits comments from
several supposedly "average" investors, who all extol the virtues of the
newspaper. One woman says that she uses the paper to "monitor her investments, keep track of her investments and look for new growth opportunities." Anyone who is looking for "new growth opportunities" is a
speculator, not an investor.

Investing and speculating are really just the two ends of a continuum. There are probably very few "pure investments," just as there are
very few "pure speculations." Most opportunities have a mix of both of
these characteristics but lie closer to either one end or the other of the
continuum. If you think about all the "deals" offered by the financial
community, you will conclude that there is a lot more speculation going
on than is apparent at first. Everyone who reads this book has some
"investments" that are really speculations.

Many people have lost a great deal of money in the market by not
knowing when they are investing and when they are speculating.
Whenever you evaluate a potential "investment," ask yourself: Am I
buying this for a rate of return, or am I buying this for price appreciation? Speculation is inherently more risky than investing, and requires
a different frame of mind to do successfully. Being honest with yourself
vill save you quite a few dollars in the long run.

The biggest mistake most people make when speculating (aside from not knowing when they are speculating!) is not quantifying the downside. *Know how much you are prepared to lose.* If the market turns against you and your losses reach the level you were willing to risk up front, then get out. This is the main philosophical difference between amateurs and professionals: the professionals nearly always know exactly how much they are willing to lose. If they have made a bad decision, they cut their losses at their predetermined level and get out. Amateurs typically think "well, I've lost "x"$ already . . . things can't possibly keep going this bad . . . the stock will turn around if I just hold it a little while longer." They end up losing their shirts. Meanwhile the professional has moved on to a different opportunity.

This book is primarily about speculating. Because virtually everyone speculates to some degree, most people will find it useful.

Assume you have made the decision to buy a particular stock or other financial instrument. You are hoping for an upward price change. You have correctly decided that this is speculating, not investing. What situation do you face?

First risk is unavoidable. Naturally you want to minimize the amount of risk you take, but you have to accept some risk when you purchase the security. How much risk do you accept? Painting with a broad brush, you can either accept "relatively more" risk or "relatively less" risk. How much is "more" and how much is "less"? No one knows for sure, but it varies with each person, as well as on the merits of the particular opportunity.

The Hunt brothers attempted to corner the silver market in the early 1980s. They lost billions. They had to accept risk in their attempt to corner the market. One can safely presume they accepted "more" risk rather than "less" risk. A friend of mine purchased stock in a fast-growing restaurant concern. He only spent $1,000 on the opportunity, so he probably accepted "less" risk. The point is that on any speculative decision you make, you can either accept relatively "more risk" or relatively "less risk." Money is generally the only determinant of the level of risk acceptance.

It is also to note that it isn't the absolute magnitude of money that determines the amount of risk, rather it is the relative amount of money given the individual's financial picture. If the Hunt brothers risked $1,000,000 on a particular deal, they may be accepting less risk (for them). Perhaps my friend who bought into the restaurant stock had $10,000 that he could afford to lose on the deal, so his risk of

$1,000 was less risk. If my friend only had $1,250 to his name when he bought the stock, risking $1,000 should probably be considered more risk.

Putting all of the above together, let's say you realize (obviously) that the point of making a trade is to make money. You have a particular instrument in mind. You have correctly determined that the opportunity is speculative and that you are speculating. You have analyzed your own particular financial situation along with the merits of the opportunity. You have quantified what you consider "more" risk and what you consider "less" risk for this particular deal. Biting the bullet, you call your broker and buy. What happens now?

Whether or not you make any money doesn't depend on anything you do at this point. Your fate is in the hands of the market. The market will either move against you to the point of your risk acceptance level and you will lose money, or the market will move favorably with respect to your position and you will make money. Clearly you are playing a game against nature, and nature is the market.

After you make the trade, the price will fluctuate from the entry price. The price will keep fluctuating each day until either your profit objective is reached or your risk acceptance level is reached. This is the only absolute certainty about any financial market: The prices will fluctuate.

Most market researchers try statistically to model price fluctuations or price movements. These analyses take many forms. Many market research firms give predictions such as: At what level will the Dow Jones Industrial Average be six months from now? Will gold rise or fall in value, and by how much? Will interest rates go up or down? Will the bottom fall out of the pork-belly futures market? Everyone is trying to predict the direction and magnitude of future price fluctuations. There is no sure-fire way to predict the future. There are models that have performed well over time, but they are far from infallible. There is no "Holy Grail" in terms of absolute certainty. The financial markets present even the most sophisticated player with a degree of uncertainty or randomness.

Fundamental factors generally determine the overall direction any particular market will take. For example during times of rising interest rates, bond prices will fall. Precisely how fast bond prices will fall, how far they will fall, and so on, is uncertain. There are so many external factors (economic factors, political factors, the mood of the players in the market, fear, greed, etc.) that determine the exact movement of prices that it is impossible to make accurate predictions.

Even if a particular financial instrument is trending strongly in one direction or another, there will be plenty of fluctuation within the overall trend. For example if there are strong corporate earnings and a broadly expanding economy, then stock prices generally rise. However, there will still be plenty of days that the market closes down. Look at the bull market of the 1980s. Stock prices generally rose between 1982 and 1987, but studying a chart of the data reveals that prices rose unevenly. The overall direction of the market was up, but there was plenty of up and down variation during the bull run.

Some events are completely unpredictable. The Crash of '87 is a perfect example. The "panic mood" of a crashing market will defeat the plans of even the best group of analysts.

Take a look at the price charts of a variety of markets. The time frames and price levels will all be dissimilar, yet the charts will also be very similar in appearance. Studying a wide variety of price charts leads one to conclude that the above discussion holds true for any market and any time frame. Prices will fluctuate. Sometimes they will exhibit a clearly identifiable trend, other times they will not. Even within trends, prices don't move in a smooth line, they exhibit varying degrees of up and down movement or randomness. This is often referred to as "noise" by analysts.

Quantifying the downside in terms of relatively more risk and relatively less risk can be easily drawn on a chart (Figure 2.1).

This particular chart is of the Hang Seng (Hong Kong) stock index. The chart displays 16 months of data. In this example the purchase price is represented by point "A"; "less risk" has been chosen as an index level of 6,600, and "more risk" is an index level of 6,300. The amounts of "less risk" and "more risk" have been arbitrarily selected: They can be any amounts at all. These values are used to illustrate the concept.

It isn't necessary to always show the historical values of the instrument on the chart. The same risk acceptance levels for the Hang Seng example can be shown as in Figure 2.2.

It is often convenient to show the price history when drawing the risk acceptance levels and profit objective on the chart, but it really isn't necessary. Once you have taken a position in a market, the past becomes an irrelevancy. The only thing that matters is what the price will do from that point onward.

This convention will be used in illustrating price charts. Price will be on the vertical axis, and time will be on the horizontal axis. Generally, the buy price is about mid-way up the vertical axis and the "less risk" and "more risk" lines are drawn from there.

FIGURE 2.1 This is an historical price chart showing eighteen months of the Hang Seng Index. The speculator buys at the current price of 6,750. He or she also decides that "less risk" is a 150-point loss (an index level of 6,600), and that "more risk" is a 450-point loss (an index level of 6,300).

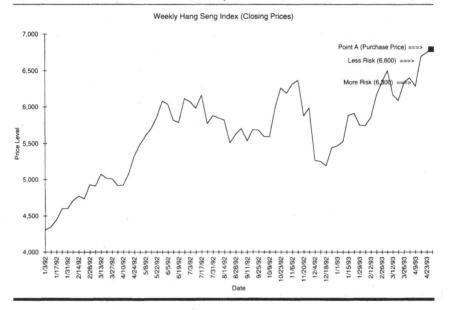

FIGURE 2.2 After the trade has been made, the past becomes irrelevant. The only thing that matters is what will happen in the future. This chart shows the situation faced by the speculator on a going forward basis.

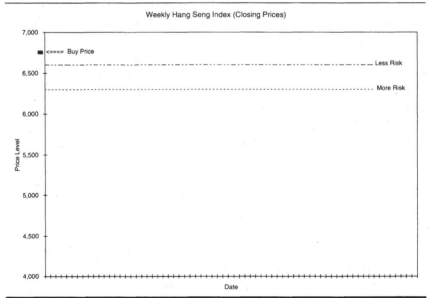

In addition to quantifying the downside, you should also quantify your profit objective. Failure to quantify a profit objective (and take your profits when your objective is reached) often leads to situations where a once-profitable trade deteriorates into a losing trade. This can be easily illustrated (Figure 2.3). In this chart we see that the price began to move favorably after the buy was made. Unfortunately the instrument began to fall in value after awhile. A once-profitable trade is now losing money. The speculator is now faced with closing out the trade at a loss. Human nature often leads to the type of reasoning as described above (things can't keep going badly . . . the stock will turn around if I just hold it a while longer). This type of logic generally results in a poorly performing portfolio.

If our speculator had also quantified a profit objective, his chart would have looked like Figure 2.4.

The result would have been a profitable trade. This should make it abundantly clear that both the upside and the downside need to be determined in order to have much prospect for success.

FIGURE 2.3 **An example of a price chart where the risk acceptance levels have been drawn, but a profit objective hasn't. A once profitable trade has turned into a money loser.**

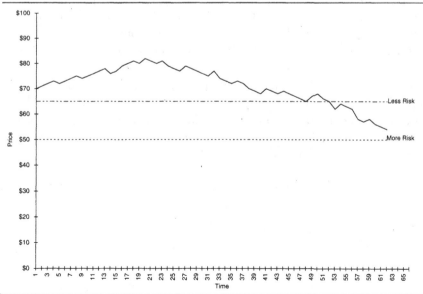

FIGURE 2.4 The same price chart as shown in Figure 2.3, but the profit objective has been added. Presumably the speculator would have closed out the trade at a profit when the objective was first reached.

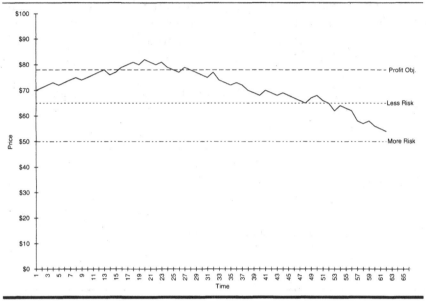

In summary we can say that there are two types of participants in the financial markets—investors and speculators. Investors are interested in making a predictable rate of return from their investments through interest payments, dividends, and so on. Speculators, on the other hand, are interested in trying to profit from changes in the price of the instrument. To be a participant in the market, risk must be accepted. Either relatively more risk can be accepted, or relatively less risk can be accepted. Speculators should also have a clear profit objective in mind and not merely "hope" that price changes will be favorable and that they can conclude the transaction at a profit.

3

The Interaction Between Price Fluctuations and Risk Acceptance Levels

O nce the decision has been made to take a position in the market by buying or selling a particular security, the interaction between the security's price fluctuation and the speculator's risk acceptance level and profit objective will determine whether or not a profit will be made. This is consistent with a requirement of game theory, namely, that the outcome is determined by the choices made by both players, not just one player.

Speculators take positions in markets, and market prices fluctuate. The speculators' strategies involve determining how much risk to accept. The market will then fluctuate prices. Sometimes the fluctuation will result in the speculator making a profit, and sometimes the fluctuation will cause the speculator to lose money. The amount of money lost will either be "relatively little" or "relatively more," depending on the amount of risk the speculator assumes. Clearly it is the interaction between the speculator's actions and the market's action that determine if a trade is profitable. Are there patterns which can be identified that describe this interaction?

To answer this question, let's look at some charts showing risk acceptance levels and a profit objective, and see the result of different price fluctuations. Broadly speaking there are really just a few possible outcomes. At a fundamental level, either a trade will make money or it will not.

The concepts of "less risk," "more risk," and "profit objective" need further clarification at this point. It is assumed that an individual is willing to hold a security until the price reaches one of these targets. These targets must be *effective* targets, that is, targets that represent an individual's actual risk and reward appetites.

If the risk acceptance levels and profit objective are set idiotically, then it is possible that neither are reached. For example assume someone buys Microsoft stock at $85 per share. They decide that "less risk" is a price of $10 per share, and "more risk" is a price of $5 per share. They've also decided their profit objective is a price of $1,000 per share. This results in a price chart (Figure 3.1).

If someone really makes these risk and profit determinations, then they may end up holding their shares a very long time. Perhaps their great-grandchildren will still be holding the shares in the year 2100 and waiting for their profits.

FIGURE 3.1 This example shows unrealistic risk and reward levels for Microsoft. Care must be taken in determining the profit objective and risk amounts. If they are set so far from the current market price as to be unreachable, then using any type of analysis will be fruitless.

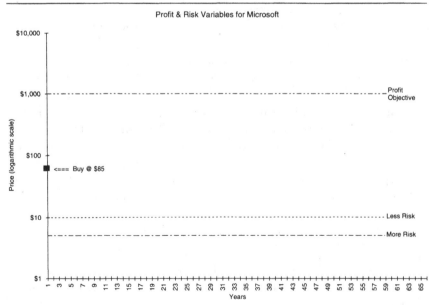

If the speculator in this case decides (after holding the stock for a few years) that he will really sell at a profit if the share price hits $125, then the original determination of a profit objective of $1,000 per share was incorrect. Similarly if the risk acceptance levels were reevaluated and set at a price of $75 for less risk and $65 for more risk, then the original amounts didn't reflect the individual's actual risk appetite. The point is this: Make sure your risk acceptance levels and profit objectives have some basis in reality. The instrument you have in mind should stand a reasonable chance of hitting one of the three targets.

REALISTIC SCENARIOS

There are several possible outcomes that can result if the profit objective and risk acceptance levels are set realistically. The trade will either make money or lose money. The loss will either be large or small,

FIGURE 3.2   An example of entirely favorable price movement. The price doesn't fluctuate adversely enough to reach either risk acceptance level. Price movement like this can be termed *zero adversity.*

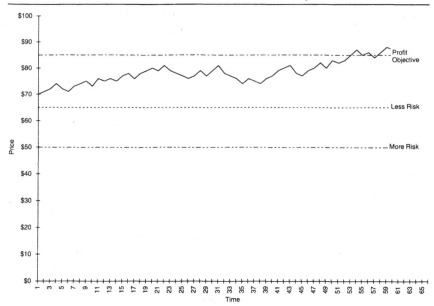

depending on the risk acceptance level. Each scenario will be examined in turn.

Let's start with the cases where the speculator has correctly predicted the direction of the market; that is, there is no price fluctuation against his position severe enough to cause the trade to hit *either* risk acceptance level. In other words let's look at a very profitable trade. Figure 3.2 shows the market rising after a buy. In this case it really doesn't matter whether more or less risk is accepted; the market movement is completely favorable. Clearly if the market movement is completely favorable it doesn't matter how much risk is accepted. The profit made by accepting more risk is the same as the profit made by accepting less risk. This pattern of price movement can be termed *zero adversity.*

Figure 3.2 only illustrates one possible scenario in which prices don't move against the speculator's position. There are many other charts that can be drawn that have the same outcome. Some other examples showing zero adversity are illustrated in Figures 3.3A and 3.3B.

FIGURE 3.3A   Another example of zero adversity. The market looks like it is in a trading range. The profit objective is set near the anticipated top of the range, and the "less risk" amount is set somewhat below the range.

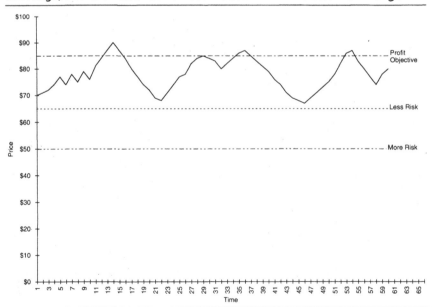

FIGURE 3.3B It seems as if the profit objective is set too high, but holding the trade eventually yields a winner. The price never went against the position enough to cause a loss.

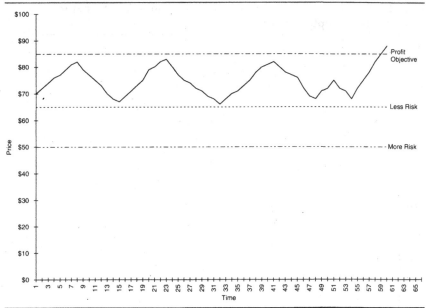

Next let's look at a situation where the market has moved *somewhat* against the speculator's position (Figure 3.4). Market movement that goes somewhat against the speculator's position are price changes that will cause the speculator to lose money if less risk were accepted but would have resulted in a profit if more risk were accepted. This example shows that accepting less risk results in a loss, whereas accepting more risk results in a profit.

This pattern of price movement can be termed *moderate adversity*. It is characterized by price movements that will only cause a loss if less risk is accepted. Greater risk acceptance still yields a profit. Once again Figure 3.4 is just representative of the concept of moderate price adversity. The same idea can be illustrated with many different price charts (Figures 3.5A and 3.5B).

Any pattern of price movement that will cause a loss if less risk is accepted, yet still yield a profit if more risk is accepted, falls into the category of moderate adversity. Figures 3.5A and 3.5B are examples of

FIGURE 3.4   The situation of moderate adversity. The price went far enough against the position to cause a loss if "less risk" were accepted but not far enough to cause a loss if "more risk" were accepted. This illustrates the trade off between less risk and more risk: Sometimes you are better off accepting more risk.

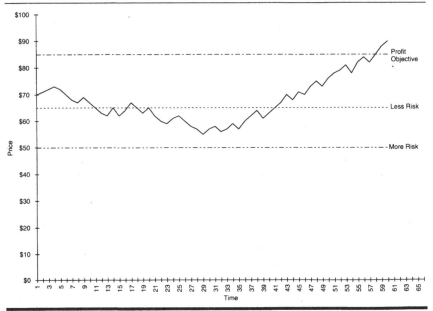

moderate adversity. There are any number of patterns of price movement that fit the definition of moderate adversity.

Lastly look at what happens when the market moves completely against both risk acceptance positions. In this case the less risk acceptance position results in a small loss, and the large risk acceptance position results in a large loss (Figure 3.6).

The profit objective was never reached. Accepting less risk results in a small loss, and accepting more risk results in a large loss. This pattern of price movement is termed *major adversity*.

As in the previous examples, many different price movement patterns yield the same result. A couple of these are shown in Figures 3.7A and 3.7B.

FIGURE 3.5A Another example of moderate adversity. If less risk were accepted, the position got closed for a loss quite early. The market eventually recovered and those who accepted more risk were rewarded.

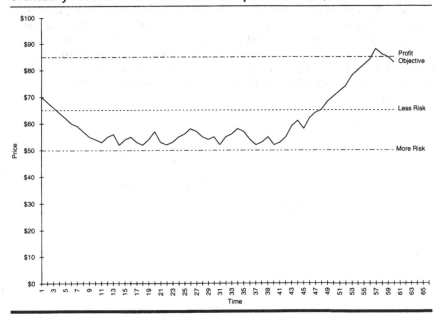

FIGURE 3.5B A seesaw market in a general up-trend. Once again accepting less risk results in a loser, but accepting more risk results in a winner.

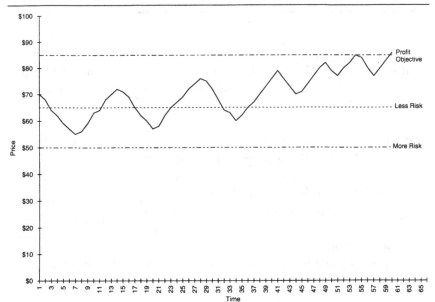

FIGURE 3.6 This is major adversity. The price went against the position enough so that either strategy loses money. If less risk were accepted, the loss would be of much less magnitude than if more risk were accepted. This is the trade off between risk acceptance levels: It is better to have accepted more risk if the market under conditions of moderate adversity. Accepting more risk under conditions of major adversity yields much greater losses.

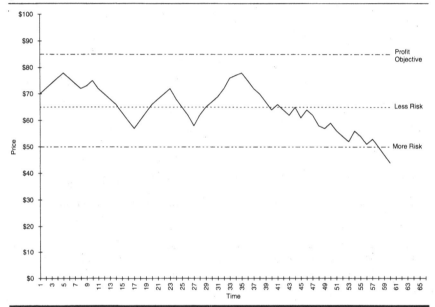

It is possible to classify *all* market price movements into the categories of no adversity, minor adversity, and major adversity. These classifications are:

1. The speculator accepts less risk, and then prices move favorably. The result is a profit to the speculator.
2. The speculator accepts more risk, and then prices move favorably. The result is a profit to the speculator.
3. The speculator accepts less risk, and the prices move moderately against the speculator. The result is a small loss to the speculator.
4. The speculator accepts more risk, and prices move moderately against the position. The result is a profit to the speculator.

FIGURE 3.7A   Another price chart showing major adversity. Ouch!

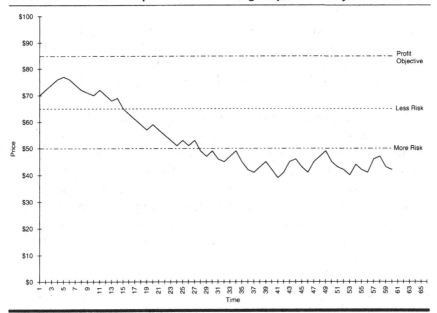

FIGURE 3.7B   Major adversity again. Note that the more risk level was set very close to where the market bottomed. A little lower and this would have been a moderate adversity scenario.

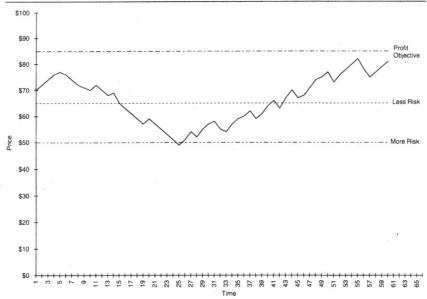

5. The speculator accepts less risk, and then prices move severely against the position. The result is a small loss to the speculator.
6. The speculator accepts more risk, and then prices move severely against the position. The result is a large loss to the speculator.

If you quantify your risk acceptance levels and profit objective, then the pattern of price fluctuation that subsequently occurs will result in one of the six outcomes discussed above. There is *no* price line that can be drawn that will not yield one of the above six results. If you are not convinced of this, draw some charts with risk acceptance levels and a profit objective, and see if you can draw a line that doesn't result in one of the above outcomes. The lines you draw will, of course, vary from the examples shown here, but the outcomes will fall into one of the six categories.

Some readers may think that a price line that never fluctuates enough to reach either the risk acceptance level or the profit objective is an outcome that hasn't been taken into account. An example of price line with this characteristic is shown in Figure 3.8.

FIGURE 3.8   The price refuses to hit any of the criteria. This is similar to the Microsoft example, although the levels aren't set absurdly. Eventually the price will fluctuate enough either to yield a profit or cause a loss.

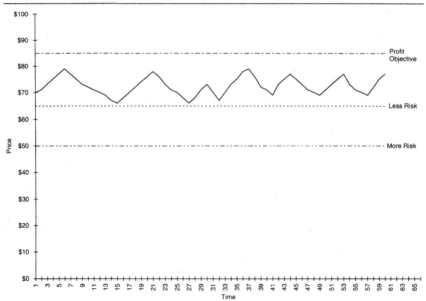

Unfortunately this price line violates the premise of the argument. We have defined the risk acceptance levels and profit objective as amounts that the individual has determined to be satisfactory, and the individual is *willing to hold* the instrument until one or the other is reached. Eventually the market price will fluctuate enough to reach either the risk acceptance level or profit objective.

Observe that even though there are six categories, there are only three possible outcomes that can result from any one trade. This is because the speculator must decide if he is going to accept More Risk or Less Risk on any particular trade, and there are three outcomes associated with either of these choices. In other words the speculator decides how much risk to accept. There are two options: either take more risk or take less risk. The market then decides how to fluctuate prices. The market may either fluctuate them so as to cause the speculator zero adversity, minor adversity, or major adversity. After the speculator makes his choice, then one of three possible *states of nature* will prevail.

The above discussion also holds true for short sales. A short sale is where the individual sells a particular instrument first, then buys it back at a later date. Typically the instrument to be shorted is "borrowed" from the brokerage firm. The broker will require a high margin against the short. In some markets, such as the futures markets, the margin required to short is identical to the margin required for a buy, so there is no additional cost to be a short seller. For clarification of this point, the next diagram shows the profit objective and risk acceptance levels for a short sale. Note that this is merely the inverse of the diagrams we've looked at so far: A short seller makes a profit when the value of an instrument declines and loses money when the price rises. Figure 3.9 shows a profitable short sale. The speculator hoped that prices would decline, and they did. The trade was concluded at a profit. The risk acceptance levels are naturally set at prices *higher* than the price that initiated the trade.

Clearly there really is no difference in the concepts of risk acceptance levels and profit objectives between being either long or short the market. Because of the added cost of margin requirements associated with being a short seller, profit objectives generally have to be higher to be able to recoup margin costs. The same logic applies to commissions and other transaction costs. The profit objective must be set high enough to recoup these costs.

On any given trade, the speculator decides how much risk to accept (either more or less) and a profit objective, and the market "decides"

FIGURE 3.9   A short sale with zero adversity. The concepts of profit, moderate adversity, and major adversity apply to short selling. Be aware that because of extra costs, such as margin, the profit will need to be set proportionally higher than on a long position.

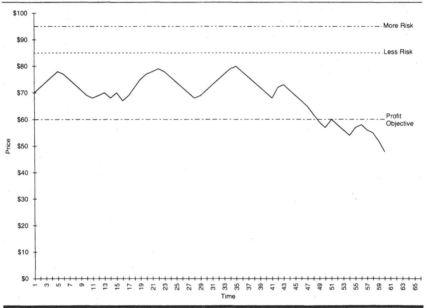

whether there will be favorable price changes, moderately adverse price changes, or severely adverse price changes. From this perspective playing the financial markets is beginning to look less like a sophisticated mathematical undertaking and more like a simple parlor game.

FINANCIAL MARKETS AS A PARLOR GAME

Let's create a game that mimics the financial markets. The game isn't very complicated and can easily be played with a group of friends. The game plays best if there are at least six players but will work with less. One person plays the role of the "Market." The other players are the "Speculators."

The "Market" player draws an X-Y graph with price on the vertical axis and time on the horizontal axis. Make sure to put a scale of prices on the vertical axis. The remaining players (i.e., the "Speculators") should write down their risk acceptance levels and profit objective.

The "Speculators" should write down both of their risk acceptance levels, but only choose one of them to play. The players should agree on how many "rounds" will be played. Start with a new X-Y chart for each round. Also agree upon the amount of money each speculator starts with. This is similar to *Monopoly*, where each player starts with the same amount of cash. Make sure that the price scale on the vertical axis of the X-Y chart is consistent with the amount of money each "Speculator" has.

For example you may decide that each "Speculator" will start with $1,000. A reasonable price scale would be $0 at the bottom and $100 at the top. A game length of ten rounds is sufficient. Each "Speculator" can change their strategy for each round, that is, play "less risk" during Round 1 and "more risk" during Round 2. "Speculators" can also change the magnitude of "less risk" and "more risk" for each round. For example "Speculator A" may have "less risk" of $10 and "more risk" of $20 during Round 1 and may decide to play "more risk." However, each player can change these parameters for the next round. "Speculator A" may decide that "less risk" is $15 and "more risk" is $25 for the second round and may play either choice during the round.

The rule is the "Speculator" writes down his or her choices for "less risk," "more risk," and "profit objective." Then one of the risk levels must be chosen. These choices cannot be changed during the course of a round, only between rounds.

Next have the "Market" player draw a price line, varying it any way he wants. The resulting chart will end up looking similar to all of the ones shown so far in this book, or like the price charts seen in newspapers and magazines.

Each "Speculator" compares his or her actual choices for risk and profit with the "state of nature" that the "Market" player created. Each "Speculator" must keep track of his or her wins and losses. The winner is the "Speculator" that amasses the most money during the course of the game.

To make sure that the game mimics real life as much as possible, allow short sales. This will prevent the "Market" player from merely drawing a downward sloping line and making all of the rest of the players losers.

If you play this game many times in a row (i.e., iterate the game), the resulting price charts will end up looking very randomized. Some will have a lot of wide fluctuations, some will trend strongly either up or down with little fluctuation, some will move "sideways," and so on.

All in all the charts will look like the charts you see in *The Wall Street Journal*. For each individual "speculator," each of the price charts will fall into one of the six categories previously discussed.

During one "round" or play of the game, Speculator 1 might see that his result is a small loss, Speculator 2 might record a profit, and Speculator 3 might have a large loss. The results depend on the risk acceptance level and profit objective that each speculator decided on, whether each is long or short, and the actual market conditions that prevailed relative to each individual's position.

The "Market" player doesn't get to win anything in this game. This parlor game merely demonstrates how price changes affect speculators.

It is likely that you and your friends will get bored playing this game very quickly. It will seem hard for any of the speculators to beat the market (i.e., record a profit) with any regularity.

However, this game closely mimics the reality of playing the financial markets. Billions of dollars are traded every day in the real-life version of this game. Can we use game theory to find a way to come up with a set of strategies that will enable us to beat the market?

Game theory requires at least two players in a game and that their identities are known. Who are the players in this game? There are two players: the speculator and the market. Although game theory typically analyzes games between two people, we have seen that there is a sub-class of games called *games against nature* in which one of the players is an abstract entity. In this case the abstract entity is not "Mother Nature" but the market. From this perspective the financial market game is analogous to a game against nature.

There are some differences between "nature" and a financial market. First the market doesn't come up with prices in a vacuum: Prices are really the net result of the buying and selling decisions of all the individual speculators and investors in the market. It is also generally presumed that an individual has no influence at all on nature, yet in the financial markets a participant may have an effect on the price movements due to his own actions. If the market is small and thinly traded, a large order will tend to move the prices either up or down. If a person making the order is generally known to other participants to be shrewd or represent "smart money," then his actions may gather "coattails" in the sense that others may follow his lead.

This can cause prices to move in an "unrandom" manner. These caveats are of more concern in small markets or in markets for individual stocks. In large, deep markets such as T-Bonds, the S&P 500,

Eurodollars, and so forth, the effect that any individual has is negligible. In contrast a small, thin market may not always "give" prices to the participants, instead the participants may directly affect the prices that are observed.

The market also plays the game against all of the participants simultaneously. Millions of shares are traded each day on the New York Stock Exchange. All these shares have buyers and sellers. Which buyers and sellers will make money and which buyers and sellers will lose money is something that is *individually* determined for each participant. Whether or not I make money is completely unrelated to whether you make money. We each play against the market separately.

Because game theory analyzes games where there is a conflict of interest between the players, we need to look at the goals of the players in the financial market game and see if they are in conflict. What are the goals of the two players? The goal of the speculator is to make a profit, but what is the "goal" of the market? Simply put the market's goal is to try and make the speculator lose money.

We should assume that the market "tries" to make the speculator lose money by attempting to fluctuate prices in such a manner so as to make it impossible to find a good combination of risk acceptance levels and profit objectives. Having the market's goal the direct opposite of your own creates a conflict of interest. Also because we are exploring a theory that will enable an individual to find a way to beat the market, assuming that the market is also trying to "beat" you is also the most conservative approach. Ascribing a motive to an abstract entity like "the market" allows us to analyze the market's strategies as if the market is a thinking being or a "live" player in the game.

To have a game theoretic construction, we have to be able to draw a game table outlining the strategies of each player, as well as the payoffs. This should be done from the perspective of the individual speculator, because the point of the analysis is to find a set of strategies that will enable an individual to beat the market. What are the possible strategies an individual speculator can play? This has already been answered. The speculator can either accept relatively "more risk" or relatively "less risk."

What about the market? The market's strategies are price movements *relative to the speculator's position.*

A few examples should clarify this concept. Referring to Figures 3.2, 3.3A, and 3.3B, we saw that if the market price moved in a favorable direction, the speculator makes money. This pattern of price

FIGURE 3.10   The game table for the financial market game. The payoffs shown are to the speculator. The table incorporates both the speculator's strategies and the market's strategies.

		SPECULATOR	
		More Risk	Less Risk
MARKET	Zero Adversity	Profit	Profit
	Minor Adversity	Profit	Small Loss
	Major Adversity	Large Loss	Small Loss

movement (i.e., market strategy) can be called *zero adversity*. Similarly in Figures 3.4, 3.5A, and 3.5B, we saw that if the market moves somewhat against the speculator, a position of "more risk" acceptance results in a profit, whereas a position of "less risk" acceptance results in a loss. This market strategy is termed *minor adversity*. Lastly if the price movement is altogether unfavorable to the speculator, accepting either "less risk" or "more risk" results in the speculator losing money (as in Figures 3.6, 3.7A, and 3.7B). This market strategy is termed *major adversity*.

There are two possible strategies the speculator can play, and three possible strategies the market can play. Note that $3 \times 2 = 6$, and six is the number of possible outcomes that can result from the interaction between price movements and risk acceptance levels, as we saw earlier.

Given the above the game table for a financial market can be illustrated as Figure 3.10.

4

Constructing a Game Theoretic Model

N
ow that we know what the game table looks like for the game of speculating in the financial markets, what good is it? As the speculator you may decide that you should maximize the minimum (i.e., employ the maximin). Looking at the game table suggests that you should play the strategy of Less Risk, because this column has a minimum of a small loss, which is larger than the minimum in the More Risk column, which is a large loss.

Similarly the market will "look" at the payoff table and "decide" to play a strategy that leaves you with the smallest maximum (i.e., employ the minimax). This strategy is Major Adversity. This row's maximum is a small loss, which is the smallest maximum available.

Hence the most likely outcome is that you will lose money. The "solution" offered by game theory is that the speculator will play the Less Risk strategy, and the market will play the Major Adversity strategy, resulting in the speculator losing money. This game is unattractive. Why on earth would anyone want to play this game? No one would. However, in the real world a lot of people do play the markets. Some of them make money, at least some of the time. Why is this so if game theory suggests that it isn't possible to win this game?

The solution of Less Risk and Major Adversity is a solution based on the concept of pure strategies. The solution requires that the speculator always play the strategy of Less Risk, and the market always play the strategy of Major Adversity. Because this renders the game entirely pointless from the speculator's point of view, how does the market "entice" people to play this game?

In the last chapter, we created a board game that is a facsimile of the real world. If you played this game with a few friends, you saw that the market player had to draw a very random set of price lines. This is because the market player didn't know what each speculator's risk acceptance levels were nor what their profit objectives were. In the real world, the market doesn't know if you are willing to risk $1 or $10 on any particular trade, nor does the market know if you are satisfied with $1 in profit or $10 in profit. The market also doesn't know if you are a short seller or if you have gone long on any trade. Furthermore the market has to play the game against all of the other players simultaneously. It has to make its decision on which strategy to play under conditions of both risk and uncertainty.

Given the myriad of players and their strategies, the market will try to fluctuate prices in such a manner so that as many people as possible lose money. From the point of view of any individual speculator, these fluctuations will make it look as if the market is varying its strategy each different time the game is played. Recall from Chapter 1 that playing each different strategy with various probabilities is called playing mixed strategies. The reason that people play the financial market game is because the market doesn't play a pure strategy, the market plays mixed strategies.

The speculators also play mixed strategies. They vary their risk and reward amounts each time they play the game. They have to, because they don't know how advantageous it is to play either strategy with any regularity, due to the market's continually changing mixed strategies.

How often should an individual play either strategy? Is there a way to find a solution showing the mix of strategies that will enable a speculator to ensure a positive payoff?

We need to be able to calculate the payoffs to the speculator for any set of strategies the speculator plays against any set of mixed strategies that the market may play to determine the merits of playing any one strategy at any particular point in time. This has to be done in the general case, because to have a cogent theory, the solutions must hold true for each and every individual speculator, no matter what strategy they play.

The remainder of this chapter will develop an algebraic explication of the payoffs and strategies associated with both players (the market and speculator) utilizing mixed strategies. A series of equations will be developed from the game table that accurately model the behavior of financial markets. A chart will be constructed along with the equations to aid in visualizing the model. The model not only shows when it is profitable to accept either "less risk" or "more risk" but also when it is unprofitable to do so.

Most of the mathematics will be relatively uncomplicated. This chapter will concentrate on the "why," not on the "how." For readers who are interested in studying how these equations are derived, please see Appendix A. This appendix contains a detailed discussion of the mathematics used to derive the model's equations.

MARKET-STRATEGY NOTATION

The market will play one of three strategies. These strategies are to fluctuate prices in a way that causes major adversity to the speculator, fluctuate prices in a manner that causes minor adversity to the speculator, or fluctuate prices in a manner favorable to the speculator. These events will occur with an unknown probability. These events must be represented symbolically in order to analyze them.

Let:

$$p_1 = \text{the probability the market plays "Minor Adversity"}$$

$$p_2 = \text{the probability the market plays "Major Adversity"}$$

$$1 - p_1 - p_2 = \text{the probability the market plays "Zero Adversity"}$$

It is safe to say that the market will fluctuate against the speculator's position with Minor Adversity part of the time. Of course it is unknown how often this will happen, but it will happen. Let's define the market playing the strategy of Minor Adversity as p_1.

Similar reasoning applies to the instances when the market fluctuates against the speculator's position with Major Adversity. It's unknown how often the market will move against a position in a severe manner, but it inevitably will at one time or another. This market strategy (Major Adversity) is defined as being notated by p_2.

The above notations are in terms of the probability that either event will occur. Because the market is playing mixed strategies, the sum of the probabilities of playing all of the strategies must equal 1. Therefore if the market plays Minor Adversity with a probability of p_1 and Major Adversity with a probability of p_2, then it follows that Zero Adversity occurs with a probability of $1 - p_1 - p_2$.

The cases we are most concerned with are the two cases where the market's strategy results in a potential loss to the speculator. The model should be developed in such a fashion that these are the two conditions for which optimal solutions are found. Additionally it is much more likely that a speculator experiences market conditions that aren't favorable, so it seems logical to try to solve for the adverse situations rather than for the more unlikely situation of zero adversity.

SPECULATOR STRATEGY NOTATION

A speculator may play two different strategies: More Risk or Less Risk. The speculator may play the More Risk strategy with some probability and the Less Risk strategy with some probability. The speculator is playing mixed strategies, just as the market is. At this point we don't know how advantageous it is to play either strategy with a certain probability, so let's define the probabilities of playing the two strategies as follows:

Let:

q_1 = the probability the speculator plays "More Risk"

$1 - q_1$ = the probability the speculator plays "Less Risk"

Once again the sum of the probabilities of playing both strategies must equal one, because it isn't possible to play both of the strategies more than 100% of the time.

PAYOFF NOTATION

Next we need to make a mathematical representation of the payoffs. Recall that there are three different payoffs: a speculator may make a profit, he or she may lose money equal to the Less Risk amount, or he or she may lose money equal to the More Risk amount.

Let:

w = profit to the speculator (this is a "win")

$-x$ = loss equal to the "Less Risk" amount (this is a "small loss")

$-y$ = loss equal to the "More Risk" amount (this is a "large loss")

Where:

$$w > x > y$$

At this point we don't need to know the specific dollar amounts associated with a profit, a small loss, or a large loss. All we need to know is the relative magnitude of these variables. Obviously, a profit is greater than a small loss, and a small loss is greater than a large loss.

MATHEMATICAL REPRESENTATION OF THE GAME TABLE

Putting the above ideas into the game table shown in Figure 3.10, it is clear that a mathematical representation of the game table takes the form shown in Figure 4.1. For clarity I have redrawn Figure 3.10 above the algebraic version to allow the reader to easily compare the "English" version of the game table with the mathematical version of the game table.

The market's strategies, the speculator's strategies, and the payoffs are multiplied together to derive the equations that describe financial market behavior. The techniques used are matrix multiplication and

FIGURE 4.1 The top game table shows the strategies and payoffs in plain English. The bottom game table has the algebraic equivalents.

		SPECULATOR	
		More Risk	Less Risk
MARKET	Zero Adversity	Profit	Profit
	Minor Adversity	Profit	Small Loss
	Major Adversity	Large Loss	Small Loss

		SPECULATOR	
		q	$1-q_1$
	$1-p_1-p_2$	w	w
MARKET	p_1	w	$-x$
	p_2	$-y$	$-x$

some simple algebra and factoring (see Appendix A for a detailed exposition). The result of the math is two equations that coincide with the speculator's two pure strategies; that is, either accept less risk or accept more risk. These equations are written in terms of the market's strategies and payoffs. These equations are:

More Risk Strategy $\Rightarrow (w + x) \, p_1 - (y - x) \, p_2$ [TERM 1]

Less Risk Strategy $\Rightarrow w - (w + x) \, p_1 - (w + x) \, p_2$ [TERM 2]

These equations can be further analyzed to determine under what market conditions a trade will be profitable or unprofitable. For example the equation corresponding to "More Risk Strategy" can be used to find out when a speculator should accept more risk (and hence also determine *when not* to accept more risk). The "Less Risk Strategy" equation can answer the same questions for the appropriateness of employing a strategy of less risk at any point in time. Additionally comparisons can be made between the relative attractiveness of using either strategy by comparing the two equations with each other. The two equations have been named "TERM 1" and "TERM 2" for clarity.

To determine when it is advantageous to play one strategy or the other, we need to start by isolating the pure strategies in terms of their profitability. Each of the speculator's strategies must be compared with each of the market's strategies, and the results must be quantified.

A diagram will be constructed that goes along with the algebraic exposition. The diagram will make the model much easier to interpret. This will be especially important to the reader who isn't strong in mathematics. Most of the math is about as difficult as high school algebra, so most readers will be able to follow the mathematical argument as well as the diagram.

It's been established that there are three things that can happen after you take a position in the market: either you make a profit equal to your objective, or you take a loss equal to your Less Risk amount, or you take a loss equal to your More Risk amount. In other words two of the three things that can happen to you are bad.

To speculate successfully it's necessary to quantify the downside. After all this is where the risk lies. To facilitate this let's draw our diagram so that it is in terms of the speculator losing money.

Each of the three things that can happen (win, lose a little, lose a lot) happen with some unknown probability. These events are mutually exclusive. This means that only one of them can happen on any one trade. If you get stopped out of the market for a small loss, you obviously haven't either made a profit or suffered a large loss. The highest probability that any event can occur is 100%. Given this it is possible (although unlikely) that the market will stop you out for a small loss 100% of the time. It is also possible that you will be stopped out for a large loss 100% of the time. It is also possible (although extremely unlikely!) that you will never get stopped out and make a profit 100% of the time. Because we want to develop our model in terms of getting stopped out for either a large loss or a small loss, the diagram will reflect these two possibilities.

Let's put the market's strategy of Major Adversity on the vertical axis, and the market's strategy of Minor Adversity on the horizontal axis. The highest value either axis can have is 100%, because neither condition can prevail more than 100% of the time. This implies that all combinations of Major Adversity and Minor Adversity can *never* sum to more than 100%. This being the case, a diagonal line drawn between the 100% mark on both axes will contain *all* possible combinations of the market's strategies of Major Adversity and Minor Adversity. Drawing this results in a "probability triangle" (Figure 4.2). The probability

---

FIGURE 4.2   The probability triangle showing the likelihood of loss. All combinations of market strategies can be described by points within the triangle.

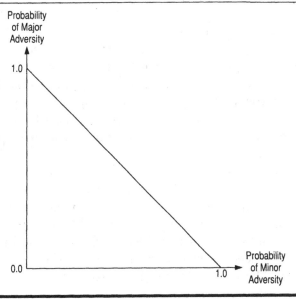

triangle will be divided into several regions. These regions will show when it is advantageous to accept less risk, when it is advantageous to accept more risk, and when it is advantageous not to play the game at all.

We need to quantify the desirability of the speculator playing any one of his available strategies to begin to flesh out the model.

Generally speaking a speculator has only two strategies: either accept Less Risk or More Risk. Because game theory affords us an analytic method to determine when a player is guaranteed a certain payoff, we can solve for when it is optimal to accept either More Risk or Less Risk. Recall that payoffs are not necessarily positive. This implies that in solving for when a positive payoff is guaranteed, we are also solving for when a negative payoff is guaranteed. Indeed it is highly likely that a speculator will lose money under a variety of market conditions.

In analyzing a speculator's strategies, we have concentrated on those which involve taking a position in the market. However in reality if we know *when* to take a position in the market (i.e., play the game), we also know *when not* to take a position in the market (i.e., don't play the game). The development of this model will show when it is advantageous to take a position, along with when it is disadvantageous to do so. Conditions where it is disadvantageous to take a position will correspond to the "Don't Play" region of the probability triangle.

WHEN TO ACCEPT LESS RISK

The "Less Risk Strategy" equation represents the pure strategy of playing the game with a small stop. The equation is written with several variables. These are the amount that can be won (w), the amount that can be lost due to a small stop (x), and the probability that the market will either give you minor adversity (p_1) or major adversity (p_2).

The speculator determines the values of w and x by his individual risk-to-reward appetite. The market determines with what probability p_1 and p_2 will occur.

If this equation is greater than zero, the speculator will make a profit. If it is less than zero, the speculator will lose money. Because the speculator is only in control of the variables x and w, we need to express the equation as a strict inequality, and solve in terms of p_1 and p_2. In other words let's find out for which market conditions it is *always advantageous* to accept less risk by finding out when the "Less Risk Strategy" (i.e., TERM 2) is greater than zero.

Let:

Less Risk Strategy > ZERO

$$w - (w + x) p_1 - (w + x) p_2 > 0$$

Solved:

$$\frac{w}{w + x} > p_1 + p_2 \qquad\qquad \text{[Equation A]}$$

or (in English . . .)

$$\frac{Profit}{Profit\ plus\ Less\ Risk} > \begin{array}{l} Probability\ of\ Minor\ Adversity\ plus \\ Probability\ of\ Major\ Adversity \end{array}$$

Let's call the result of this operation "Equation A" instead of "Less Risk Strategy Equation Greater Than Zero" for brevity.

What does this mean in English? First $w/(w + x)$ is the ratio of profit to profit plus the less risk amount. This ratio has to be *greater* than the sum of the probabilities of Major Adversity and Minor Adversity occurring in order to be successful playing the strategy of Less Risk.

What are the implications of Equation A? First of all note that if the probability that Minor Adversity occurs is zero (i.e., p_1 is equal to zero), then the probability of experiencing Major Adversity (i.e., p_2) has to be *less* than $w/(w + x)$ to have a winning trade. The opposite holds true as well: If the probability of Major Adversity is zero (i.e., p_2 is equal to zero), then the probability of experiencing Minor Adversity (i.e., p_1) has to be *less* than $w/(w + x)$ to have a winning trade. Additionally all summations of both Minor Adversity and Major Adversity (i.e., p_1 and p_2) have to be *less* than $w/(w + x)$ to make a profit.

Incorporating Equation A into the probability triangle is shown in Figure 4.3.

The area beneath the line is shaded to show the region of profitability. The unshaded area corresponds to the area of loss; that is, market conditions that will cause the trader to take a loss. Observe that because Equation A was developed as a strict inequality, the line dividing the two regions is not included in the shaded area. Points on the line are included in the area of loss.

The shaded region is labeled Less Risk. This region shows the combinations of market strategies where it is profitable to make a trade that accepts less risk. The unshaded area is labeled Don't Play. This region

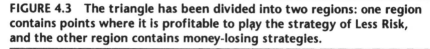

FIGURE 4.3 The triangle has been divided into two regions: one region contains points where it is profitable to play the strategy of Less Risk, and the other region contains money-losing strategies.

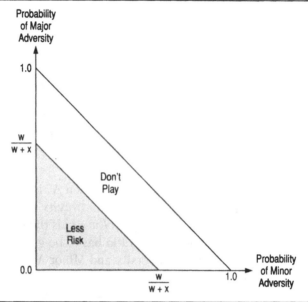

shows the combination of market strategies that will cause a speculator to lose money if he accepts less risk.

Let's take a closer look at where the intercepts lie on the two axes of Major Adversity and Minor Adversity. If the probability that there will be no Major Adversity is zero (i.e., p_2 is equal to zero), then it is clear that Equation A will yield an intercept on the Minor Adversity axis of $w/(w + x)$. The converse is also true for the Major Adversity axis: If there is no Minor Adversity (i.e., p_1 is equal to zero), then the intercept on the Major Adversity axis is $w/(w + x)$.

Also observe that the line delineating the demarcation between the Less Risk region and the Don't Play region must be of lesser magnitude than the "unity" line that defines the entire probability triangle. The intercepts have been shown to be $w/(w + x)$ for each axis. Because by definition the denominator of this equation is greater than the numerator, the intercepts will always evaluate to less than one.

To ensure that the implication of the analysis is clear, I have re-drawn Figure 4.3 and added several points shown as "A," "B," and "C" (Figure 4.4).

Points "A" and "C" lie within the Less Risk region. Point "B" lies within the Don't Play region. Dotted lines have also been added to each point showing their coordinates with respect to Major Adversity (p_2) and Minor Adversity (p_1).

The axes are defined in terms of the probability that the market will produce conditions of either Major Adversity or Minor Adversity with respect to the speculator's position. Take point "A" for example. The implication of the model is that if the coordinates of point "A" (in terms of p_1 and p_2) are less than $w/(w + x)$, then the trade will be a successful one.

This is true in a probabilistic sense. Any one individual trade may be a loser, but if the trade is made repeatedly, the winners will out-weigh the losers by a large enough margin to yield profitable results

FIGURE 4.4 **The coordinates of a point are used to determine it's profitability. Points "A" and "C" have coordinates less than w/(w + x) and will yield a profit. Point "B" is in the unprofitable region.**

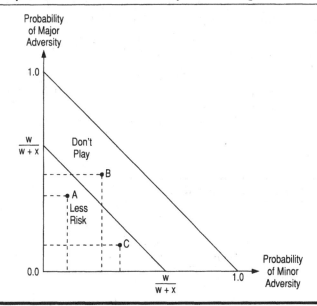

overall. The model doesn't suggest that each and every trade that falls within the parameters of $w/(w + x)$ will necessarily be profitable, only that over time the dollars won will be greater than the dollars lost. Recall the discussion of iterated games from Chapter 1. Because we have postulated that speculating in financial markets is an iterated game, we are really looking for solutions in an iterative (or probabilistic) sense.

The line dividing the Don't Play region from the Less Risk region is determined by parameters set by the speculator. This line will vary from individual to individual, based on each individual's risk to reward appetite. The value yielded by $w/(w + x)$ is not a constant that holds true for all players in all markets. It is a value that is different for each and every person. Because we are developing a model in the general case, it must hold true for each and every person, no matter what their individual circumstances are.

WHEN TO ACCEPT MORE RISK

Determining when it is advantageous to accept more risk isn't as straightforward as determining when to accept less risk. This is because it is only advantageous to accept more risk when the market is playing Minor Adversity. Under this market condition, a strategy of Less Risk will cause a small loss, but a strategy of More Risk results in a profit. To clarify this point, let's take another look at the game table (Figure 4.5).

When is it more advantageous to play More Risk than it is to play Less Risk? Under market conditions of Zero Adversity, both strategies yield a profit. The speculator is indifferent between the strategies. Under market conditions of Minor Adversity, a strategy of More Risk generates a profit, and the strategy of Less Risk causes a loss. Clearly

FIGURE 4.5   The algebraic game table.

		SPECULATOR	
		q	$1-q_1$
	$1-p_1-p_2$	w	w
MARKET	p_1	w	$-x$
	p_2	$-y$	$-x$

under market conditions of Minor Adversity, it is advantageous to utilize the More Risk strategy. Finally if market conditions correspond to Major Adversity, both of the speculator's strategies are unprofitable, but the Less Risk strategy causes a smaller loss than does the More Risk strategy, so it less advantageous to play More Risk.

We know that if TERM 2 evaluates to a positive number, then we are guaranteed a positive payoff when Less Risk is played. To find out when the strategy of More Risk yields a positive number when the strategy of Less Risk doesn't, we have to analyze TERM 1 while TERM 2 is *negative.*

To make a profit playing Less Risk, the positive payoff associated with TERM 1 must be greater than the loss associated with TERM 2. In other words the magnitude of TERM 1 has to be greater than the magnitude of TERM 2 for the sum of the two terms to be a positive number. These magnitudes can be found by comparing TERM 1 with the absolute value of TERM 2.

Assume:

$TERM\ 2 < 0$

(This ensures we are only looking at conditions where Less Risk produces a loss and More Risk doesn't.)

Then if TERM 1 is greater than the absolute value of TERM 2, accept more risk:

$TERM\ 1 > |\ TERM\ 2\ |$ *(i.e., play More Risk strategy)*

But if TERM 1 is less than the absolute value of TERM 2, don't play the game:

$TERM\ 1 < |\ TERM\ 2\ |$ *(i.e., don't play the game)*

Algebraically we can find the dividing line between when it is attractive to accept more risk versus when it is attractive not to make a trade by comparing TERM 1 to the negative of TERM 2 as follows:

Let:

TERM 1 = The negative of TERM 2

$$(w + x)\, p_1 - (y - x)\, p_2 = -w + (w + x)\, p_1 + (w + x)\, p_2$$

Solved:

$$p_2 = \frac{w}{w + y}$$

or

Probability of Major Adversity $> \dfrac{Profit}{Profit\ Plus\ More\ Risk}$

Let's call this "Equation B" for brevity.

Observe that Equation B is in terms of Major Adversity (p_2) only. Recall from our definition of the game that if the market plays Minor Adversity and the speculator plays the pure strategy of More Risk, the outcome results in a profit. Minor Adversity only results in a loss if the speculator plays a Less Risk strategy. Because we are looking for a solution where we can still make money under conditions of Major Adversity, the solution should only be in terms of that variable.

Equation B implies that if the probability of Major Adversity (p_2) is greater than $w/(w + y)$ then the trade will lose money, and that if the probability of Major Adversity (p_2) is less than $w/(w + y)$ then the trade will make money. In game theory terms, if the probability of Major Adversity is greater than $w/(w + y)$, then Don't Play, and if the probability of Major Adversity is less than $w/(w + y)$ then play the pure strategy of More Risk.

Let's diagram this result on a probability triangle (Figure 4.6).

As in the prior analysis, I have shaded the region where it is advantageous to play the pure strategy of More Risk, and left unshaded the region where it is disadvantageous to play More Risk. Once again points on the line are included in the Don't Play region.

The same reasoning used to understand the implications of playing the pure strategy of Less Risk holds true for the strategy of More Risk. Points within the shaded area represent profitable trades, and points within the unshaded area represent losses.

The following diagram adds points "A," "B," and "C" to the More Risk chart. The interpretation is the same as before: If the actual probabilities of Major Adversity and Minor Adversity are equal to or less than the coordinates of a point, then trade is a winner. Point "A" is a profitable trade, whereas points "B" and "C" are unprofitable trades (Figure 4.7).

Once again the solution must be interpreted in a probabilistic sense. All three points (A, B, and C) will have both winning trades and losing trades. However, the sum of all the winners and losers will have a net

FIGURE 4.6   The case of whether to accept more risk. The triangle has
again been divided into two regions. In this case the dividing line is
horizontal. Points above the line correspond to losses, whereas points
below the line correspond to winners.

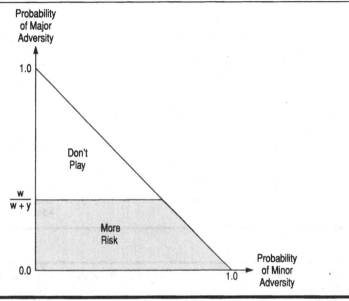

profitable result at point A, and the results stemming from both points
B and C will be negative.

Because we've looked at two conditions, let's put both of them on
the diagram and interpret the result. Combining the two diagrams
shows that there is overlap between the two strategies. This is shown in
Figure 4.8.

There is a region of the diagram where the two strategies overlap.
The region is shaded in Figure 4.8. This overlap is a problem, because
we don't know if we should play More Risk or Less Risk for points lying
in this region. So far we have looked at when it is advantageous to play
Less Risk and when it is advantageous to play More Risk, assuming that
the Less Risk strategy yields a negative result. We still need to determine when it is advantageous to play More Risk, irrespective of the
merit of playing Less Risk. Solving this problem will eliminate the
overlap between the regions.

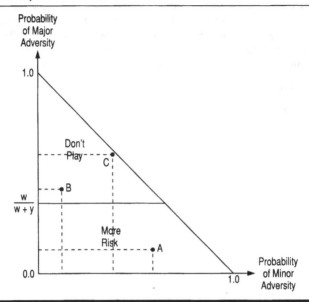

FIGURE 4.7 Once again the coordinates of a point show its profitability. "A" is a winner, and "B" and "C" are losers.

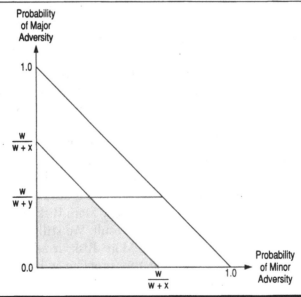

FIGURE 4.8 This figure combines the two analyses done so far. Both the Less Risk and More Risk strategies are shown. Note that there is considerable overlap between the two strategies, as shown by the shaded region. If a point is in the shaded region, which strategy should be used?

SEPARATION OF LESS RISK AND MORE RISK

The above analysis of the More Risk strategy only partially determined when it is advantageous to play More Risk. We need to analyze the situation in which TERM 1 is *always positive* to complete the analysis of the More Risk region.

Let:

TERM 1 > Zero

$$(w + x)\, p_1 - (y - x)\, p_2 > 0$$

Solved:

$$p_2 < \frac{w + x}{y - x}\, p_1$$

or

$$\frac{\text{Probability of}}{\text{Major Adversity}} > \frac{\text{Profit plus Less Risk}}{\text{More Risk minus Less Risk}} \times \frac{\text{Probability of}}{\text{Minor Adversity}}$$

For clarity this will be called Equation C.

If Equation C were expressed as an equality instead of an inequality, it has the familiar $y = mx + b$ formula for the slope of a line. Where does this line fit on the diagram?

Assuming Equation C is an equality, then if the probability of Minor Adversity is equal to zero (i.e., p_1 is equal to zero), then the probability of Major Adversity (p_2) has to be equal to zero as well. If we allow Equation C to remain an inequality, the logic holds true as well: If the probability of Minor Adversity (p_1) is zero, then Major Adversity (p_2) will have to be zero as well. Mathematically one may argue that if p_1 were zero, then p_2 would have to be *less* than zero, but this is in conflict with the parameters of the variables as well as common sense. Probabilities can take values between zero and one. They cannot be negative. Also the probability of Major Adversity occurring in the real world is not less than zero. If it were (or could be), we would all be millionaires.

The formula that expresses the slope of the line $((w + x)/(y - x))$ is always a positive number, as the variables x, w, and y are all positive numbers. Hence whenever p_1 is zero, then p_2 has to be zero and vice versa. From this perspective it is easy to see that the line expressed by

Equation C is a ray that extends out from the origin of the diagram with a slope of $(w + x)/(y - x)$ (Figure 4.9).

The line itself represents the boundary where it is equally advantageous to play the pure strategies of either Less Risk or More Risk. The area under the line defines where it is advantageous to play More Risk, and the area above the line defines where it is advantageous to play Less Risk.

This result is combined with the first two results in Figure 4.10.

The three regions are bounded by the solid lines. These are the Don't Play region, the Less Risk region, and the More Risk region. The dotted lines show the location of the original complete lines. This diagram is drawn so that all of the interior lines intersect at one point. This intersection is called the *locus of strategic separation*. Do the lines necessarily intersect in such a locus?

The vertical coordinate of the locus is easy to see from the diagram. It is $w/(w + y)$, which is the result shown from Equation B. It is somewhat more difficult to determine the horizontal coordinate of the locus.

FIGURE 4.9 The relative attractiveness between the two strategies is described by a ray that extends from the origin. It is better to accept more risk for points above the line and less risk for points below the line. The slope of the line varies according to the choice of risk acceptance levels and profit objective.

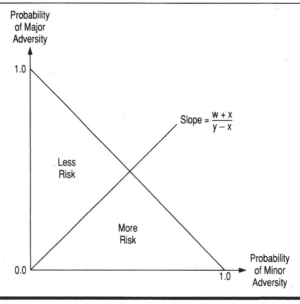

FIGURE 4.10 This figure combines the three prior steps. The triangle is divided into three regions. These are Don't Play, Less Risk, and More Risk. Once again profitability is determined by the coordinates of a point. It appears as if the three lines intersect at a single point.

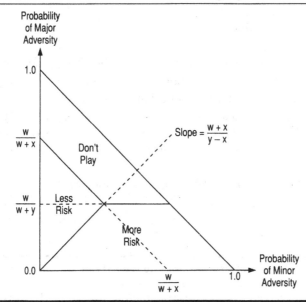

To determine the horizontal coordinate of the locus, it's necessary to set the equation that expresses the upward sloping ray emanating from the origin equal to the equation which expresses the downward sloping line that defines the Less Risk strategy. In other words we need to set Equation A and C equal to each other and solve for p_1.

Let:

Equation A = Equation C

$$\frac{w}{w+x} > p_1 + p_2 = p_2 < \frac{w+x}{y-x} p_1$$

Solved:

$$p_1 = \frac{w(y-x)}{(w+x)(w+y)}$$

This will be called Equation D. It is the horizontal coordinate of the locus of strategic separation. All the lines do in fact intersect at a specific point.

THE COMPLETED MODEL

The complete model, which incorporates all the above calculations and graphic representations, has a general form as shown in Figure 4.11.

Figure 4.11 represents the situation a speculator faces in a financial market. It takes into account the speculator accepting either More Risk or Less Risk, and the market generating conditions of either Zero Adversity, Minor Adversity, or Major Adversity with respect to the speculator's position.

The diagram has Major Adversity and Minor Adversity on its axes, yet it also shows the condition of Zero Adversity. Recall how these terms have been defined. Zero Adversity is the condition that prevails

FIGURE 4.11   The completed model. The lines do in fact intersect at a common point: the *locus of strategic separation*. This model accurately describes the behavior of any financial market, given the risk/reward choices that were selected.

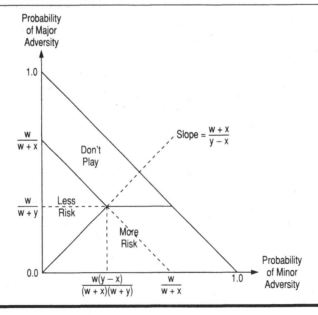

when the market moves *completely favorably* to the speculator's position. It is the complete absence of *both* Major Adversity and Minor Adversity. This condition is represented by the origin on the diagram, because the probabilities of both Major Adversity and Minor Adversity are zero at the origin.

From this perspective the probability triangle has three points that define the speculator's universe: the point of 100% Major Adversity, the point of 100% Minor Adversity, and the point of 0% Major and/or Minor Adversity. This last point can also be defined as 100% Zero Adversity. Because the model was developed explicitly to show the loss producing conditions of Major Adversity and Minor Adversity, the condition of Zero Adversity has been implicit in the diagram as a "background solution."

5

Understanding
the Model

The probability triangle has been divided into three regions. First there is a Don't Play region where playing the game will cause a speculator to lose money. Next there is a region where a speculator should use the pure strategy of Less Risk. Last there is a region where a speculator should follow a pure strategy of More Risk.

The model has been developed in the general case. This means we have not tried to develop a model for some specific risk to reward levels, but we have developed a model using variables. The relationships between these variables apply to any and all players in a market—from a large player to someone who can only afford "one lots."

The highly subjective concepts of "Less Risk" and "More Risk" are used in the model. Similarly the degree of "Adversity" generated by prevailing market conditions only has meaning with respect to each individual's unique circumstances. Because all the parameters are unique to each different player, the model is as applicable to a small investor as it is to a mutual fund manager.

The model has to be interpreted in terms of "if these certain probabilities exist, then I should play a specific strategy." Assume, for example, that the actual probabilities of Major Adversity and Minor Adversity occurring are the coordinates of a point lying in the More Risk region. This implies that the speculator should employ the strategy of More Risk. The model cannot tell you *what* the probabilities are, it only tells you that *if* certain probabilities exist, then a particular strategy should be employed.

This may become clearer if we look at a specific example. Assume you want to take a position in XYZ Corporation. XYZ is currently trading at $50 per share. You will sell out at a profit if the price reaches $57.50 per share. So your profit objective is $7.50 per share. You have also determined that Less Risk is equal to a drop of $2.50 per share, and More Risk is equal to a drop of $5.00 per share.

In terms of the model, $w = 7.50$, $x = 2.50$, and $y = 5.00$.

Substituting these values into the equations in the finished model yields the following result shown in Figure 5.1.

The Don't Play region appears to be pretty small. It appears as if the More Risk strategy is the strategy to use. However, only the shape

FIGURE 5.1   The model as calculated for XYZ Corporation. Point A represents the estimates of the actual probabilities of Major and Minor Adversity (65% chance of Major Adversity and 35% chance of Minor Adversity). The trade is destined to lose money, as it lies in the Don't Play region.

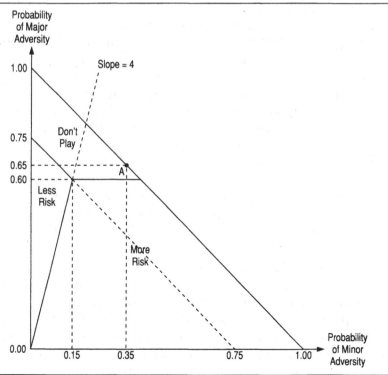

and size of these regions is determined by the speculator's risk/reward parameters: The market is going to determine with what probabilities of Major Adversity and Minor Adversity actually occur.

Let's further assume you have done your homework and have a good estimate of the actual probabilities associated with Major Adversity and Minor Adversity. You think there is a 65% chance that Major Adversity will prevail, and a 35% chance that Minor Adversity will prevail. Mark a point in the triangle with these values as its coordinates. (This has been done with point "A" in the diagram.) Point "A" lies in the Don't Play region. This trade is a money loser.

If you make this trade, you will either make money or lose money. This is because the model reflects the fact that playing the markets is an iterated game. This makes it impossible to predict the result of any *individual* trade, but makes it possible to predict the result of any *class* of trades. In this example, the "class" of trades is: XYZ Corp. with a Profit Objective of $7.50, a Less Risk amount of $2.50, a More Risk amount of $5.00. Also part of the "class" are the market's strategies, or probabilities of the degree of adversity encountered.

So this particular trade is a money loser in an iterated sense. If you make a single trade, it's certainly possible that it may be profitable, but over the long haul this class of trades is unprofitable. Speculators should endeavor to only execute trades that are in a profitable class.

Even though game theory "guarantees" a certain payoff (in this case a negative payoff), this should be interpreted in a probabilistic sense rather than in an absolute sense. If your estimate of a 65% chance of Major Adversity is completely correct, you will still be wrong 35% of the time. From this perspective, playing the markets is akin to playing an iterated game. If you flip a coin there is a 50% probability of heads and a 50% probability of tails. If you flip a coin 10 times, you may get 7 heads and 3 tails. This doesn't mean that the laws of probability are wrong, it means you haven't flipped the coin enough times to get an accurate sample. If you flip the coin 10,000 times, the number of head and tails will be very close to 50% each.

Similarly, if you play the "market game" repeatedly under the circumstances described in this example, the losses will outweigh the wins and the net result of your trading will be unprofitable.

The speculator must estimate with what probability the market will play the strategies of Major Adversity and Minor Adversity. These estimates must be accurate. If they are not, the model will lose its predictive value.

DETERMINING THE PROBABILITY OF ADVERSITY

How can the probabilities of Major Adversity and Minor Adversity be determined? Because playing the markets is an iterated game, measuring past price changes to determine their dispersion should yield a probabilistic result.

Price changes in stock prices (or bond prices or most any other financial instrument) generally pattern themselves in a *normal distribution*. A normal distribution is the familiar bell-shaped curve taught in statistics courses. There are numerous different ways to determine the probability function for a financial instrument. Price changes can be measured and quantified empirically, either by the percent change in the instrument's value over specified time intervals or by the change in the logarithm of the price over the time intervals.

The logarithmic method is well documented. The Black-Scholes formula for option pricing assumes a lognormal dispersion of prices. There is a "theoretical" lognormal distribution that can be inferred from the Black-Scholes formula. This formula is extremely complex. A discussion of the lognormal derivation of price changes is beyond the scope of this book. Readers who are interested in a detailed presentation of lognormal price distributions should consult a financial text. Two excellent sources are *Options as a Strategic Investment* by Lawrence G. McMillan (published by the New York Institute of Finance) and *Stock Market Probability* by Joseph E. Murphy, Jr. (published by Probus Publishing).

Fortunately measuring percentage price changes yields a result nearly equivalent to the lognormal method, especially for price changes less than 15%. This method affords a fair approximation of the real world and is fairly simple to calculate, especially if a spreadsheet program (such as Excel or Lotus) is used.

Let's take a look at a single stock as an example. General Motors (GM) is a fairly good test case. It is an extremely large company, with many shares of stock both traded and outstanding, which allows a sufficiently large sample to work with. It is a widely held and liquid stock. How has GM's stock price fluctuated over time? Can a probability function be derived that describes this behavior? We could take a historical sample of GM's stock prices and examine the degree of price fluctuation. Table 5.1 lists month end prices for GM for 1970, along with the month-to-month price change. These prices are in decimal for the last trading day of the month.

TABLE 5.1 Month-end Data for General Motors for the Year 1970

Date	Close	Previous Month Price Change
1/30/70	$29.30	
2/27/70	$31.75	$ 2.45
3/31/70	$34.03	$ 2.28
4/30/70	$31.75	$(2.28)
5/29/70	$29.69	$(2.06)
6/30/70	$28.45	$(1.24)
7/31/70	$31.11	$ 2.66
8/31/70	$33.77	$ 2.66
9/30/70	$33.00	$(0.77)
10/30/70	$32.20	$(0.80)
11/30/70	$35.06	$ 2.86
12/31/70	$36.83	$ 1.77
Averages	$32.24	$ 0.68

The average price of GM's stock during 1970 was $32.24, and the average monthly change was $0.68. Is this approach useful in measuring price changes? By 1995 the average monthly price had increased to $45.823 and the average monthly price change had increased to $0.955. The analysis will be skewed by the change in the price level if we want to look at a large sample, hence the need for measuring percentage changes in price.

The following Figures illustrate this point. Figure 5.2 shows month-end prices for GM's common stock from January 1970 until December 1995. The prices in the earlier years are markedly lower than the prices in later years. Figure 5.3 shows the monthly changes in price for the same time period.

Any statistical method used to analyze price changes has to be able to account for the increase in the price level of the instrument, as these two figures show. This can be taken care of by looking at the percentage changes in price, rather than the actual price changes.

Figure 5.4 shows the monthly percentage change in price for GM. It is easy to see that the price fluctuations no longer increase in magnitude as the year increases: Rather the percentage changes stay consistent for the entire time frame.

What inferences can be made about Figure 5.4? In general it appears that the majority of monthly price changes fall into a band

FIGURE 5.2 Twenty-five years of historical monthly closing prices for General Motors. Price levels are generally higher in the more recent years.

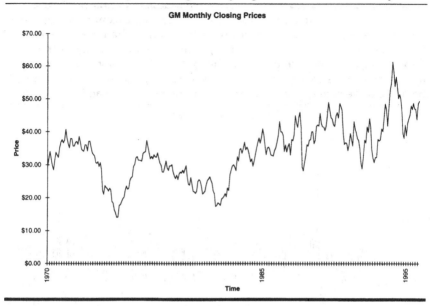

GM Monthly Closing Prices

FIGURE 5.3 This shows the monthly change in GM's closing prices for the same twenty-five-year period. The price swings are much greater in the more recent years, largely because of the higher price level associated with the stock.

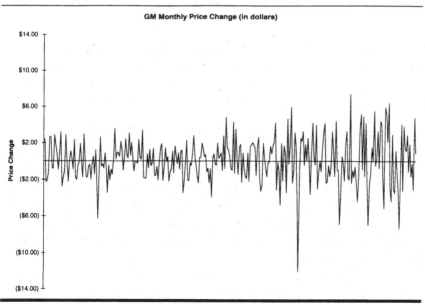

GM Monthly Price Change (in dollars)

FIGURE 5.4   The same twenty-five-year time frame, except now the chart
is of the percentage change in closing prices, rather than the absolute
dollar magnitude. In percentage terms, there is no upward bias in the size
of the changes. Large swings (price changes of 15% or more) occurred in
the earlier years as well as the later years. It seems, however, that most of
the percentage changes are in a band of between 10% up and 10% down.

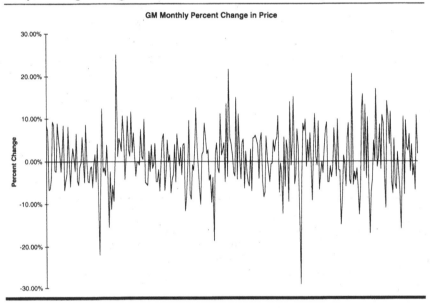

between a 30% rise and a 30% fall. The months that prices changed by
the larger percentages seem to be randomly scattered throughout the
entire period. This is different than the pattern in Figure 5.3 where
the absolute magnitude of the price changes is noticeably greater in the
later years.

The data in Figure 5.4 needs to be further analyzed. Recall that
percent changes in price should follow a normal distribution (theoretically, anyway). Do GM's price fluctuations follow a normal distribution? This can be ascertained by making a histogram of the data in
Figure 5.4. A histogram is a relative frequency distribution of a series
of observations for evenly spaced intervals. Table 5.2 lists the frequency distribution of the data in Figure 5.4 with intervals corresponding to 3% changes in price.

Figure 5.5 is a histogram of the data from Table 5.2. Often patterns
in data can be seen more readily if they are charted: The histogram is
merely a chart of the frequency distribution.

TABLE 5.2 Percent Price Changes Divided into 3% Bands (or "Bins")

% Price Change	Frequency by Number of Months
−30%	0
−27%	1
−24%	0
−21%	1
−18%	1
−15%	3
−12%	3
−9%	9
−6%	27
−3%	57
0%	58
3%	46
6%	45
9%	25
12%	21
15%	7
18%	4
21%	1
24%	1
27%	1
30%	0

We now have a bell-shaped curve, more or less. It is apparent that the monthly percentage changes in GM's stock prices are normally distributed. The curve appears somewhat uneven: It isn't as smooth as a standard normal distribution. In other words it isn't perfectly symmetric on either side of the mean. Most real world measurements of data with a normal distribution vary from the standard normal distribution. They have some "lumpiness" or skewing of the curve. This can be seen in the GM data. Compare the 9% positive price change and the 9% negative price change: There were 9 months of a 9% decrease in price, and there have been 25 months that saw a 9% increase in price.

The "theoretic" lognormal distribution for stock prices has a slight skew to the positive side. This is because there is an inherent upward bias in stock prices. Since the turn of the century, stocks have appreciated at approximately a 5% annual rate. This is partly due to inflation, but it is also due to increases in productivity, or the economic surplus society generates. If prices generally rise at 5% per annum, then there should be more months with positive price changes than negative price

FIGURE 5.5 A histogram of the frequency distribution as calculated in Table 5.2. It has the overall shape of a bell-shaped curve, although it isn't a "standard normal" distribution. Note the upward bias: The positive tail has more frequency than the negative tail. The most likely explanation for this is the inherent upward bias in stock prices. In general, stock prices rise over time. A frequency distribution of their prices reflect this phenomena.

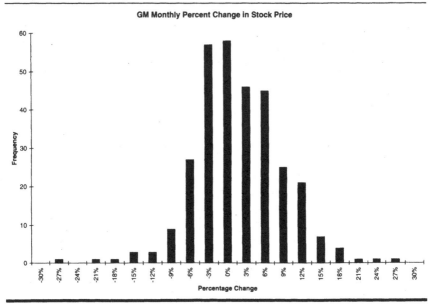

changes. Hence the skewing to the positive side of theoretic lognormal distribution.

The data for GM appear to be skewed in the positive direction: There are fatter tails on the positive side of the price distribution. This is what is to be expected in looking at a common stock, at least for a generally healthy and financially solvent company. In GM's case there have been 45 months of negative price changes, 105 months of positive price changes, and 161 months of neutral price changes where the price didn't fluctuate by more than 3%.

Because the data we are looking at extend from 1970 to 1995, they contain all events that have affected GM's stock price during the time frame. Factors that have a bearing on GM's financial success such as wars, depression, peace and prosperity, oil shortages, foreign competition, stock market crashes, and so forth, are all contained in the data.

This is an important point in doing any kind of a mathematical analysis of a financial instrument: Compare the results obtained with the theoretic result. Do they concur? Do they differ? If they differ, are there logical reasons why? This type of questioning of the "fundamentals" keeps you going in the right direction. If we examine a stock that differed in its price change pattern substantially from the theoretic pattern and we could not come up with plausible reasons for the difference, we should be hesitant about the investment. In other words ask yourself "What's wrong with this picture?" If you can't answer what is wrong (and why it is wrong) perhaps you should put your effort into analyzing something else. There are a lot of stocks, bonds, options, futures, etc. that can be speculated in: Find ones that yield good fundamental results, as well as accurate mathematic results.

So we are satisfied with our results so far. The positive bias in GM's stock price distribution agrees with what we would theoretically expect. We have a large sample to work with (25 years of monthly data). What next?

We need to convert the frequency distribution (i.e., histogram) into probabilities.

The simplest way to do this is convert the frequency histogram into percentages. This is easily done by dividing each category's frequency by the total number of observations. By doing this, we are now looking at relative frequencies; in other words we are looking at how often each data point occurred, expressed as a percent of the total. This shown in tabular form in Table 5.3 and graphically by Figure 5.6.

The height of the bars are proportionally the same for each category in this figure as the corresponding bars were in Figure 5.5. The only difference is the vertical axis: It is now expressed as the percent of each category to the whole.

Generally future price changes are extrapolated from past price changes. An argument can be made that the past has no bearing on the future; that is, GM may invent a new car that runs on sea water tomorrow, so its past price history isn't necessarily reflective of what will transpire in the future. Nevertheless statistical analysis involves measuring the past to predict the future. Statistics are also a much sounder approach than relying on instinct.

The percentage changes in Table 5.3 can serve as proxies for probabilities. In other words we can say there is an 8.68% chance that the price will drop by 6% in the next month. Similarly there is a 14.47% chance of the stock price rising 6% next month.

TABLE 5.3   Relative Frequencies (Previous Distribution)

% Price Change	% Frequency
−30%	0.00%
−27%	0.32%
−24%	0.00%
−21%	0.32%
−18%	0.32%
−15%	0.96%
−12%	0.96%
−9%	2.89%
−6%	8.68%
−3%	18.33%
0%	18.65%
3%	14.79%
6%	14.47%
9%	8.04%
12%	6.75%
15%	2.25%
18%	1.29%
21%	0.32%
24%	0.32%
27%	0.32%
30%	0.00%

Note: The relative frequency of each bin can serve as a proxy for the probability of the bin.

The data used to construct Figure 5.6 extended from January 1970 to December 1995. The month-end closing price in December 1995 was $49.375. Standard theory assumes the current (or latest) stock price will correspond to the mean of the distribution. In this example the mean corresponds to the 0% change category. So if we set $49.375 equal to the mean, we can determine the adjusted prices for the rest of the categories. This has been done in Table 5.4.

Using Table 5.4 as a given, a speculator may make the following risk and reward determinations:

Transaction	Price
Buy GM at:	$49.375
Profit Objective of:	$52.375
Less Risk Amount:	$46.375
More Risk Amount:	$44.875

FIGURE 5.6   A histogram of Table 5.3. The height of each bar corresponds to the relative height of each bar shown in Figure 5.5. The difference is in the Y-axis: We are looking at relative frequencies rather that actual frequencies.

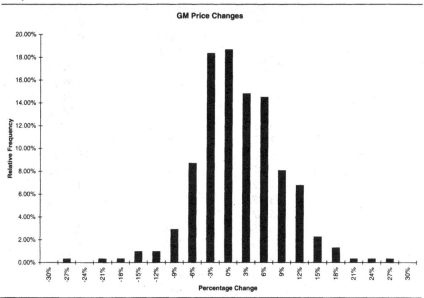

In terms of the game theory model, the amount of a win is $3.00 ($52.375 − $49.375); the amount of a small loss is −$3.00 ($46.375 − $49.375); and a large loss is −$4.50 ($44.875 − $49.375). Substituting these values into the model's equations produces the result shown in Figure 5.7.

Given the likelihood of various price changes as shown in Table 5.4, can we determine if this trade is profitable under these parameters? We need to estimate the probabilities of Major and Minor Adversity using Table 5.4 as a starting point.

AN ESTIMATION OF THE PROBABILITIES OF ADVERSITY

Table 5.4 shows that a price drop of 6% (an amount equal to the less risk amount) has a probability of 8.68%. Once the price drops by at least 6%, it is at the less risk threshold. If the price drops any further than 6%, it will have passed *through* the less risk threshold. If the

TABLE 5.4   Substitution of the Most Recent Month-end Closing Price for the "0% Change" Bin

	Price	% Price Change	% Frequency
	34.500	−30%	0.00%
	36.000	−27%	0.32%
	37.500	−24%	0.00%
	39.000	−21%	0.32%
	40.500	−18%	0.32%
	41.875	−15%	0.96%
	43.500	−12%	0.96%
	44.875	−9%	2.89%
	46.375	−6%	8.68%
	47.875	−3%	18.33%
Last Price ===>	49.375	0%	18.65%
	50.875	3%	14.79%
	52.375	6%	14.47%
	53.875	9%	8.04%
	55.375	12%	6.75%
	56.750	15%	2.25%
	58.250	18%	1.29%
	59.750	21%	0.32%
	61.250	24%	0.32%
	62.750	27%	0.32%
	64.125	30%	0.00%

Note: By this substitution we can estimate the probability of where the price will be one month from now. The prices in the Table don't correspond exactly to the percent change shown, as they have rounded to the nearest eighth.

speculator is playing the less risk strategy, then the trade is a money loser if the price drops by at least 6%.

If the price drops by 9%, obviously it had to pass through −6%. So the probability of incurring a 6% loss is the *sum* of all categories for price drops of 6% *or more*. Similar reasoning applies to the probability of a profit: All the profit yielding categories need to have their probabilities added together to derive the overall probability of profitability.

This method will only develop the probabilities of these events occurring by the end of the month, because the data have been developed from month-end closing prices. It is certainly possible that the price won't have fluctuated enough to reach either the profit objective or the less risk amount during the month. Because the speculator intends to hold the stock until one of these events occur, additional calculations

FIGURE 5.7 The model calculated for these specific risk and reward amounts: buy price at $49.375; profit objective at $52.375; Less Risk amount at $46.375; More Risk amount at $44.875; win amount at $3.00; small loss at $-3.00; and large loss at $-4.50. The prices are all in decimal to make the calculations simpler.

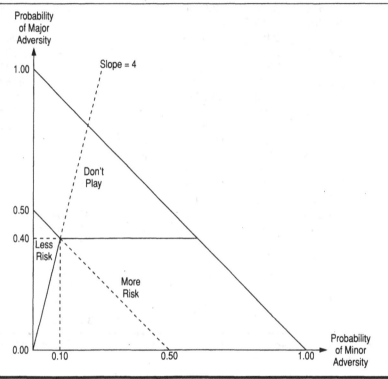

will have to be made to estimate the probabilities for the going forward months. Table 5.5 shows the probability of encountering minor adversity, making a profit, or still holding the trade at the end of the month.

At the end of the first month, there is a 33.76% chance the Profit Objective will be reached and a 14.47% chance that a loss equal to Less Risk will have been incurred. Additionally there is a 51.77% chance that the price won't have fluctuated enough to reach either condition. These numbers are, of course, predicated on playing the Less Risk strategy.

The same analysis needs to be done for the More Risk strategy, because we need the probabilities for both the Less Risk and More Risk

TABLE 5.5 Relative Frequency Distribution Estimating the Probabilities of Profit or Minor Loss by Month End

	Price	Change	% Price % Frequency	Hold	Profit	Minor Adversity
	34.500	−30%	0.00%			0.00%
	36.000	−27%	0.32%			0.32%
	37.500	−24%	0.00%			0.00%
	39.000	−21%	0.32%			0.32%
	40.500	−18%	0.32%			0.32%
	41.875	−15%	0.96%			0.96%
	43.500	−12%	0.96%			0.96%
	44.875	−9%	2.89%			2.89%
	46.375	−6%	8.68%			8.68%
	47.875	−3%	18.33%	18.33%		
Buy Price	49.375	0%	18.65%	18.65%		
	50.875	3%	14.79%	14.79%		
	52.375	6%	14.47%		14.47%	
	53.875	9%	8.04%		8.04%	
	55.375	12%	6.75%		6.75%	
	56.750	15%	2.25%		2.25%	
	58.250	18%	1.29%		1.29%	
	59.750	21%	0.32%		0.32%	
	61.250	24%	0.32%		0.32%	
	62.750	27%	0.32%		0.32%	
	64.125	30%	0.00%		0.00%	
SUM				51.77%	33.76%	14.47%

Note: There is also some probability that the trade won't be closed out, as shown by the "Hold" column.

strategies to evaluate them using the game theory model. Recall that the More Risk strategy exposes the trade to Major Adversity. Table 5.6 calculates the probability table for the More Risk strategy. The analysis indicates a probability of 5.79% that the More Risk amount will be reached. Additionally there is a 60.45% chance that the trade will be open at the end of the month and a 33.76% chance that the trade will have been concluded at a profit.

If these values are plotted as a point in the game theory model, we can see whether we should play the less risk strategy or more risk strategy, given these parameters. For purposes of this example, the coordinates of the less risk and more risk probabilities need to be put into Figure 5.7. This has been done as Figure 5.8.

TABLE 5.6 Relative Frequency Distribution Estimating the Probabilities
of Profit or Major Loss by Month End

	Price	% Price Change	% Frequency	Hold	Profit	Major Adversity
	34.500	-30%	0.00%			0.00%
	36.000	-27%	0.32%			0.32%
	37.500	-24%	0.00%			0.00%
	39.000	-21%	0.32%			0.32%
	40.500	-18%	0.32%			0.32%
	41.875	-15%	0.96%			0.96%
	43.500	-12%	0.96%			0.96%
	44.875	-9%	2.89%			2.89%
	46.375	-6%	8.68%	8.68%		
	47.875	-3%	18.33%	18.33%		
Buy Price	49.375	0%	18.65%	18.65%		
	50.875	3%	14.79%	14.79%		
	52.375	6%	14.47%		14.47%	
	53.875	9%	8.04%		8.04%	
	55.375	12%	6.75%		6.75%	
	56.750	15%	2.25%		2.25%	
	58.250	18%	1.29%		1.29%	
	59.750	21%	0.32%		0.32%	
	61.250	24%	0.32%		0.32%	
	62.750	27%	0.32%		0.32%	
	64.125	30%	0.00%		0.00%	
SUM				60.45%	33.76%	5.79%

Note: There is also some probability that the trade won't be closed out, as shown by the "Hold" column.

The above analysis gives us a good measure of what will happen by the end of the month, but what about the scenarios in which the price hasn't fluctuated enough to complete the trade? Tables 5.5 and 5.6 imply that the most likely scenario is to still be holding the trade at the end of the month.

The stock will still be held at the end of the month if the price hasn't fluctuated by at least 6% in either direction. This corresponds to a price range of between $46.125 and $52.375. To estimate the chance of either making a profit or incurring a loss in Month 2 (for the Less Risk strategy), we need to replicate Table 5.5 three times: once for each price with the "0% change" category equal to the price in question. We will also need to perform the same operation four times for the More Risk strategy.

FIGURE 5.8   The game theory model with the point marked with the estimated probabilities of Major and Minor Adversity occurring by the end of the month. The trade appears to be a winner, although the probability of still holding the trade at month-end hasn't been taken into account.

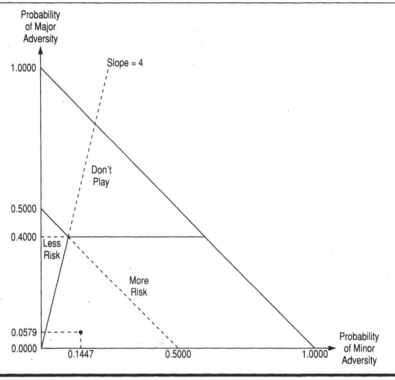

For example let's assume the price has risen to $50.875 by the end of the first month. This isn't enough of a rise to reach the Profit Objective. What is the likelihood of either the Profit Objective or Less Risk amount being reached by the end of the second month? Adjusting the table for the new price of $50.875 yields Table 5.7.

Note that because the price has risen to $50.875, we only need a further 3% rise to reach the profit objective of $52.375. As you can see, the probabilities for profit, loss, and holding have been adjusted. In Table 5.7A the probability of making a profit has increased, and the probability of loss has decreased.

The same procedure needs to be followed for prices of $49.375 and $47.875 as well. If the month end close is $49.375 (i.e., exactly the

TABLES 5.7A   Estimation of Probability of Minor Adversity for Month 2
for Prior Month Close of 50.875

	Price	% Price Change	% Frequency	Hold	Profit	Minor Adversity
	36.000	−30%	0.00%			0.00%
	37.500	−27%	0.32%			0.32%
	39.000	−24%	0.00%			0.00%
	40.500	−21%	0.32%			0.32%
	41.875	−18%	0.32%			0.32%
	43.500	−15%	0.96%			0.96%
	44.875	−12%	0.96%			0.96%
	46.375	−9%	2.89%			2.89%
	47.875	−6%	8.68%	8.68%		
Month 1	49.375	−3%	18.33%	18.33%		
Close }	50.875	0%	18.65%	18.65%		
	52.375	3%	14.79%		14.79%	
	53.875	6%	14.47%		14.47%	
	55.375	9%	8.04%		8.04%	
	56.750	12%	6.75%		6.75%	
	58.250	15%	2.25%		2.25%	
	59.750	18%	1.29%		1.29%	
	61.250	21%	0.32%		0.32%	
	62.750	24%	0.32%		0.32%	
	64.125	27%	0.32%		0.32%	
	66.125	30%	0.00%		0.00%	
SUM				45.66%	48.55%	5.79%

Note: Substitute each of the possible prices that may still be held at month-end into the
"0% change" bin. In this example there are three bins that the price may reside at the
end of the month without an offsetting trade having been made. There are three Tables
that need calculating because there are three open bins. If the analysis were done with
1% price changes (or price changes measured in dollars or eighths, etc.), more bins may
be needed. The results of this operation only show the probability for Month 2, not
Months 1 and 2 combined.

same as where it started), the Table doesn't need to be recalculated. If
the price drops to $47.875, the new Table will show a decreased prob-
ability of profit and an increased probability of loss. These conditions
are shown in Tables 5.7B and 5.7C.

The above process needs to be done for the more risk scenario as
well. The Tables generated by the calculations are not shown, but they
are done exactly the same way.

The probabilities determined in Tables 5.7A, B, and C show the
likelihood of any of these events occurring in Month 2. They don't take

TABLES 5.7B   Estimation of Probability of Minor Adversity for Month 2 for Prior Month Close of 49.375

	Price	% Price Change	% Frequency	Hold	Profit	Minor Adversity
	34.500	−30%	0.00%			0.00%
	36.000	−27%	0.32%			0.32%
	37.500	−24%	0.00%			0.00%
	39.000	−21%	0.32%			0.32%
	40.500	−18%	0.32%			0.32%
	41.875	−15%	0.96%			0.96%
	43.500	−12%	0.96%			0.96%
	44.875	−9%	2.89%			2.89%
	46.375	−6%	8.68%			8.68%
Month 1 Close {	47.875	−3%	18.33%	18.33%		
	49.375	0%	18.65%	18.65%		
	50.875	3%	14.79%	14.79%		
	52.375	6%	14.47%		14.47%	
	53.875	9%	8.04%		8.04%	
	55.375	12%	6.75%		6.75%	
	56.750	15%	2.25%		2.25%	
	58.250	18%	1.29%		1.29%	
	59.750	21%	0.32%		0.32%	
	61.250	24%	0.32%		0.32%	
	62.750	27%	0.32%		0.32%	
	64.125	30%	0.00%		0.00%	
SUM				51.77%	33.76%	14.47%

Note: Substitute each of the possible prices that may still be held at month-end into the "0% change" bin. In this example there are three bins that the price may reside at the end of the month without an offsetting trade having been made. There are three Tables that need calculating because there are three open bins. If the analysis were done with 1% price changes (or price changes measured in dollars or eighths, etc.), more bins may be needed. The results of this operation only show the probability for Month 2, not Months 1 and 2 combined.

into account the probability of still holding the trade at the end of Month 1. The question we are facing is "What is the likelihood of the trade concluding in Month 2, given that it is still held after Month 1?" In other words what is the probability of the first event occurring (still . holding the trade), and the probability that the second event will occur (close the trade out in Month 2)? This answer can be found by multiplying the two probabilities together. This needs to be done for each of the Month 1 events separately. Table 5.8 shows how this is done.

TABLES 5.7C   Estimation of Probability of Minor Adversity for Month 2 for Prior Month Close of 47.875

	Price	% Price Change	% Frequency	Hold	Profit	Minor Adversity
	33.500	−30%	0.00%			0.00%
	34.500	−27%	0.32%			0.32%
	36.000	−24%	0.00%			0.00%
	37.500	−21%	0.32%			0.32%
	39.000	−18%	0.32%			0.32%
	40.500	−15%	0.96%			0.96%
	41.875	−12%	0.96%			0.96%
	43.500	−9%	2.89%			2.89%
	44.875	−6%	8.68%			8.68%
Month 1 Close }	46.375	−3%	18.33%			18.33%
	47.875	0%	18.65%	18.65%		
	49.375	3%	14.79%	14.79%		
	50.875	6%	14.47%	14.47%		
	52.375	9%	8.04%		8.04%	
	53.875	12%	6.75%		6.75%	
	55.375	15%	2.25%		2.25%	
	56.750	18%	1.29%		1.29%	
	58.250	21%	0.32%		0.32%	
	59.750	24%	0.32%		0.32%	
	61.250	27%	0.32%		0.32%	
	62.750	30%	0.00%		0.00%	
SUM				47.91%	19.29%	32.80%

Note: Substitute each of the possible prices that may still be held at month-end into the "0% change" bin. In this example there are three bins that the price may reside at the end of the month without an offsetting trade having been made. There are three Tables that need calculating because there are three open bins. If the analysis were done with 1% price changes (or price changes measured in dollars or eighths, etc.), more bins may be needed. The results of this operation only show the probability for Month 2, not Months 1 and 2 combined.

The final step is to sum all of the probabilities for each scenario. This will yield the actual probabilities of Major and Minor Adversity occurring during the two-month time frame. This is shown in Table 5.9.

There is a 24.04% chance of encountering Minor Adversity and a 12.79% chance of encountering Major Adversity. Armed with these numbers, we can return to the game theory model to see if the trade is still profitable (Figure 5.9).

The trade is still profitable. Note that the coordinate of the point has moved upward and to the right, although it remains in the More

TABLE 5.8   Estimation of Probabilities for Month 2

Price Held at End of Month 1:   50.875
Probability of Holding: 14.79%

	Month 2 Probabilities	
	Minor Adversity	Major Adversity
Probability of Month 2 Event	5.79%	2.89%
× Probability of Holding	14.79%	14.79%
Actual Probability	0.86%	0.43%

Price Held at End of Month 1:   49.375
Probability of Holding: 18.65%

	Minor Adversity	Major Adversity
Probability of Month 2 Event	14.47%	5.79%
× Probability of Holding	18.65%	18.65%
Actual Probability	2.70%	1.08%

Price Held at End of Month 1:   47.875
Probability of Holding: 18.33%

	Minor Adversity	Major Adversity
Probability of Month 2 Event	32.80%	14.47%
× Probability of Holding	18.33%	18.33%
Actual Probability	6.01%	2.65%

Price Held at End of Month 1:   46.375
Probability of Holding: 8.68%

	Minor Adversity	Major Adversity
Probability of Month 2 Event	0.00%	32.80%
× Probability of Holding	8.68%	8.68%
Actual Probability	0.00%	2.85%

Note: The probability of each Month 2 event needs to be multiplied by the probability that the trade is still open at the end of Month 1.

TABLE 5.9   Actual Probability of Major or Minor Adversity Over Two-Month Time Frame

	Probability of Minor Adversity	Probability of Major Adversity
Month 1	14.47%	5.79%
Month 2 (held @ $50.875)	0.86%	0.43%
Month 2 (held @ $49.375)	2.70%	1.08%
Month 2 (held @ $47.875)	6.01%	2.65%
Month 2 (held @ $46.375)	0.00%	2.85%
Total	24.04%	12.79%

Note: The probabilities of all the events need to be added to determine the overall probability.

FIGURE 5.9   The revised probabilities for two months have been plotted as a point in the model. The trade should still be profitable.

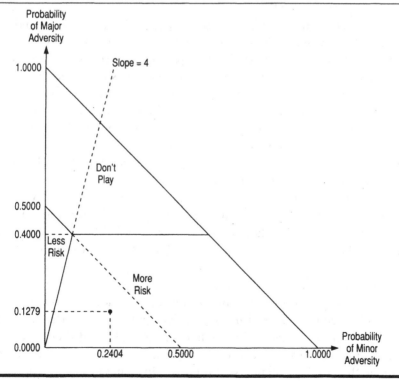

Risk region of the model. Once again the answer is valid for the time frame in question: two months in this case.

For longer time frames, the above process needs to be iterated for Month 3, Month 4, and so on. It isn't possible to actually "solve" for all the probabilities. Statistically there will always be some chance that the price won't fluctuate enough to reach either condition. This can be a problem if the profit objective and risk acceptance levels are set so far away from the current price that the chance of reaching them becomes remote. This isn't a problem in this example, because our levels are only a 6% change in GM's price. Historically GM's price fluctuates by at least 6% within a few months. ·

There are a few other considerations that must be taken into account in evaluating this example. First the price data used to determine the probabilities are based on month-end prices. These figures don't show where the price was at any time during the month, so the price could have fluctuated to either the risk or reward levels *during* the month. The analysis makes no assessment of that probability. A more accurate analysis should incorporate the high and low price for each time period as well.

Second the probabilities were developed by looking at 3% bands in terms of percentage price changes. A more accurate solution will need to examine prices in more detail, perhaps using eighth-point or quarter-point changes instead of percentages. To analyze using actual prices instead of percentage changes, a more rigorous statistical method should be used, such as the lognormal method. This involves taking the natural logarithm of each price change instead of the percentage price change. The resulting data can then be converted to a standard normal distribution using *z-scores,* and the probabilities can be calculated using standard statistical techniques.

There is no "unique" solution for any individual stock. If we had picked different levels of risk and reward in the GM example, the resulting probability calculations would have been different. The best way to make a flexible model is by using a spreadsheet or other computer program. This way you can input various risk and reward levels and see if there is a positive solution set.

Certain types of financial instruments have additional quirks that need to be accounted for. Futures, options, and various other derivatives have a time element that the model hasn't taken into account. Futures and options expire at a certain point in the future. The model assumes that the speculator will *hold* the instrument until either the risk acceptance level or the profit objective is reached. This may not be possible with a future or an option. Great care must be taken in determining the probabilities associated with these instruments: the probabilities calculated will need to take the expiration date into account.

Whether or not a profit is made doesn't depend on an absolute measurement of the probabilities of Major Adversity and Minor Adversity. Profitability is determined by the individual risk/reward values selected by the speculator, with respect to the probabilities determined by the market. Different risk/reward values change whether or not a certain probability function yields a positive payoff. If a certain probability function can be determined for a particular market, the speculator may be able to vary his risk/reward values to find a solution that will yield a positive payoff.

A game theoretic analysis cannot come up with a strategy that will ensure that every single trade will be profitable. There is no "Holy Grail" that can guarantee every trade you make will be a winner. However, game theory does suggest solutions exist in the form of strategies that ensure positive payoffs if the game is repeatedly played over time.

6

Treasury Bond Futures

The U.S. Treasury Bond (T-Bond) futures market is an ideal market to analyze. It is one of the biggest markets in the world in terms of liquidity. Several hundred thousand contracts trade on a typical day. Because of the tremendous volume, it is highly unlikely that any single player can affect prices. In general the bond market will give prices to all participants. There may be times of thin trading where a large speculator may be able to move prices, but these instances are rare and not sustainable in the long term.

The general long-term trend of the bond market is set by macroeconomic forces that are outside the control of any individual player. Bond prices are inversely correlated with interest rates, and no one controls interest rates. Interest rates are set by government policy but are affected by market forces in a complex interaction. So in the long run, the prices observed in the bond market really represent the "state of nature" that exists with respect to interest rates at any given point in time.

In the short run, the bond market experiences daily fluctuations that are not necessarily related to the true direction of interest rates. The government releases statistics on a wide variety of economic indicators on a regular schedule. Often these statistics will contradict each other. For example the latest figures on the Consumer Price Index may suggest rising prices, leading market participants to have inflationary expectations, thereby driving the price of bonds down and interest rates up. Yet a few days later, a weaker than expected employment report may have the opposite effect.

The bond market responds to these events by fluctuating prices; however, the short-term fluctuations caused by the interpretation of these statistics may or may not be indicative of the true direction of interest rates. Only time will tell. But it is the "state of nature" that prevails after the release of a government report that determines the short-term price direction (and profitability to each individual player).

Because we don't know what state of nature will prevail, we don't know whether we should have a long or short position (in the short term) prior to the release of an economic statistic. In the long term, we also don't know whether we should be long or short, as we really don't know what set of inflationary expectations will exist a year from now.

The stock market has a long-term upward bias. This is primarily due to the fact that we live in a dynamic society. Technological advances are made, new products are invented, corporations try and use resources as efficiently as possible, and so on. The above is not true of the bond market. With stocks, prices appreciate in the long run (for the market as whole, anyway, although this isn't necessarily true for any particular stock). Interest rates don't advance over time in the same manner that stock prices increase, because it is their ability to fluctuate higher and lower that represents the force needed to dampen or stimulate the economy.

With stocks it is much riskier to take a short position, primarily due to the long-run price appreciation of the market. Historically the state of nature that typically prevails is one of generally rising prices.

Recall the parlor game discussed in Chapter 3. All the price lines generated by this game are highly random. In the real-life stock market game, prices will have an upward bias. In other words more of the price lines will be rising rather than falling. However, the risk in the stock market is that of sharp price drops. All price shocks are downward, because nearly all traders are long.

Additionally because of the extra margin costs associated with selling short, the game is not truly symmetrical in terms of the payoffs. The parlor game was constructed so that it is as easy to go short as it is to go long, but in the real world shorting a stock is more difficult and expensive than buying one. The payoffs from either shorting or going long are identical in the parlor game (i.e., symmetrical), but in reality the addition of margin costs makes shorting a stock more expensive.

This isn't true of the T-Bond futures market. Because it is a futures contract, the cost of either being long or short are identical, because all positions require the same amount of margin, and the margin is treated as a deposit. This is a big change from the stock market, where shorting the market requires extra financial outlay for margin costs and where any shortfall is treated as a loan. Adding margin costs to the payoffs has the effect of decreasing profit and increasing the magnitude of the losses. In the futures market, margin costs are identical on either side of a trade, so the payoffs from pursuing either strategy are symmetrical.

The futures market gives one of the closest approximations to the parlor game that can be found in the real world. Buying put or call options is another example. Because we want to play this as a game against nature, we need a market that is big enough to give prices to all of the players, and one where price fluctuations are unbiased. The T-Bond futures market certainly fits the bill. The S&P 500 contract also satisfies the first requirement, but falls short on the second, because it has the same inherent upward bias as stocks. So, its price movement isn't quite as unbiased (or random) as bonds.

Let's take a look at a database of T-Bond futures prices between the inception of trading on September 21, 1977 and March 3, 1993. The first contract in the database is US Z77 and the last is US M93. Contract months are coded as H = March, M = June, U = September, and Z = December. The database consists of the expiring contracts only: no statistical adjustment has been made for rollover as each contract expires. The database is structured as follows:

Day Number	Date	Contract	Open	High	Low	Close
1	9/21/77	US Z77	103.06250	103.25000	103.06250	103.21875
2	9/22/77	US Z77	103.09375	103.12500	102.81250	102.84375
3	9/23/77	US Z77	102.78125	102.96875	102.75000	102.96875
4	9/26/77	US Z77	102.87500	102.87500	102.71875	102.78125
5	9/27/77	US Z77	102.78125	103.09375	102.78125	103.06250
⋮	⋮	⋮	⋮	⋮	⋮	⋮
⋮	⋮	⋮	⋮	⋮	⋮	⋮
⋮	⋮	⋮	⋮	⋮	⋮	⋮

This structure continues until March 3, 1993, which is day number 3,902.

When the US Z77 contract expires, the next entry in the database will be for the US H78 contract. As each contract expires, the next entry will be for the unexpired front month contract.

In a manner similar to the GM example, let's chart the closing prices (Figure 6.1).

As can be seen from the chart, bond prices have varied widely during the time frame in question. There is no inherent upward bias in the

FIGURE 6.1 This is a price chart showing the expiring month T-Bond futures contract from September 21, 1977 to March 3, 1993. Prices have fluctuated dramatically over the fifteen-year time frame.

price level, as is the case with common stocks. As interest rates have risen and fallen, bond prices have moved in the opposite direction.

In the GM case, we looked at monthly data. In this situation we are looking at daily data. The daily change in the closing prices needs to be measured to see the distribution pattern.

Recall that we needed to look at the percentage change in GM's stock price rather than the actual change to remove the effect of the increasing price level from the analysis. This isn't necessary with bond prices, so we can just measure the actual change. We need to measure how far each day's close varied from the preceding day's close. This will show us the average daily dispersion of the prices. This has been done in Figure 6.2.

Before proceeding any further, let's take a closer look at Figure 6.2 and see what the data is telling us. First, on the vast majority of days,

FIGURE 6.2   This shows the daily change in price of the bond contract as measured in points. The vast majority of days have experienced price fluctuations of one point or less.

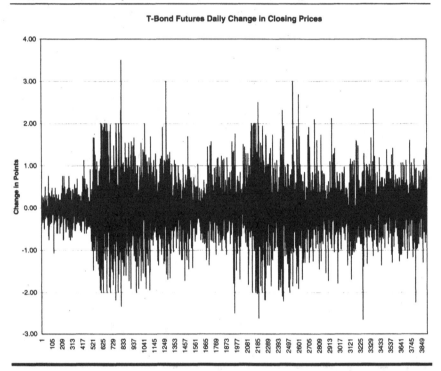

T-Bond Futures Daily Change in Closing Prices

bond prices haven't fluctuated by more than one point either up or down. This is what we should expect, as smaller price fluctuations occur more frequently than large ones. As anticipated the overall pattern appears to be mostly noise, without bias. Also note that prices have never fluctuated more than four points from the preceding day's close. This is also to be expected, as for most of the time period the daily limit was set at two points. However, with the daily limit set at two points, we wouldn't expect that there would be *any* days where there is more than a two-point fluctuation, but there are.

Recall that the data haven't been adjusted for rollover in any way. The occurrences where the price has fluctuated more than two points coincide with contract expiration (at least in the earlier part of the data). The exchange (CBOT) has since raised the daily limit to three points, so wider fluctuations are to be expected in the later part of the time series.

Next, let's plot the relative frequency of the daily changes in histogram format to see if the data are normally distributed. The bins are equal to one tick (1/32 point) each, with the minimum and maximum being a two-point swing in either direction. This has been done in Figure 6.3.

The histogram shows a more or less normal distribution, but it is very ragged. It also has a spike at each tail, which stems from the outliers (i.e., days of high volatility and/or abnormalities in the data due to contract expiration). Although we could construct a probability analysis from the data (similar to the GM analysis), the raggedness of the data will not yield good estimates. The data could be smoothed using larger bars, for example, grouping the data into three tick ranges instead of single tick ranges.

FIGURE 6.3   A histogram of the daily changes price chart. The data has the look of a bell-shaped curve, although it is fairly ragged.

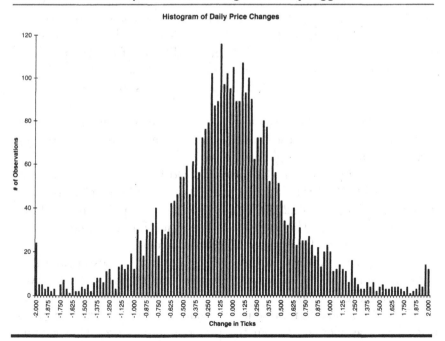

The preceding example using the daily closing price changes is somewhat incomplete. It doesn't take into account the full trading range from high to low each day. If this is analyzed the same way the GM data were analyzed, a profit objective and risk acceptance levels will be set, and the numbers will be run through the game theory model to see the profit and loss regions, given the actual (or estimated) probabilities. Yet this analytic method is incomplete.

Obviously either the profit objective or one of the risk acceptance levels can be reached during any particular day, but this wouldn't be apparent because the data is limited to closing prices only. Because we are looking at daily data, we are really asking ourselves "What will the bond market do tomorrow?": That is, we are attempting to predict intraday price movements. Using closing prices alone isn't sufficient.

Let's expand this example, and this time, take the full range into account. Taking the daily range into account will give us a better estimate of intraday price changes.

INTRADAY T-BOND PRICE MOVEMENTS

Many futures markets have daily limits set on price movements (with certain exceptions). So the largest price movement possible on any given day is either limit up or limit down. Treasury bonds are one of those markets. Limits are set a specified distance from the previous day's closing price for each market. For the bond market, the limit was two basis points for most of the time frame in question; therefore, let's assume that bond prices may fluctuate in a four-point range from limit to limit. Admittedly, this may lead to some distortion in the more recent period because of the increase in the limit to three points, but three-point moves in a single day are very rare.

Referring back to the database, the closing price was 103⁷⁄₃₂ on September 21, 1977. The highest price that could be reached the following day (September 22, 1977) was 105⁷⁄₃₂ or two points higher than the preceding close. The lowest possible price for the same day was 101⁷⁄₃₂ or two points lower than the preceding close.

The bond market also opens at 7:20 A.M. and closes at 2:00 P.M. (Central Time). With this information the "trading box" can be drawn for any day (Figure 6.4).

The horizontal axis represents time, and the vertical axis represents price levels as measured from the previous day's close. The opening

FIGURE 6.4   The "trading box." During most of the analysis period, prices were constrained by a daily range of four points (either two points up or down from the preceding day's closing price). Each day's price movement can be plotted as a series of points within the trading box.

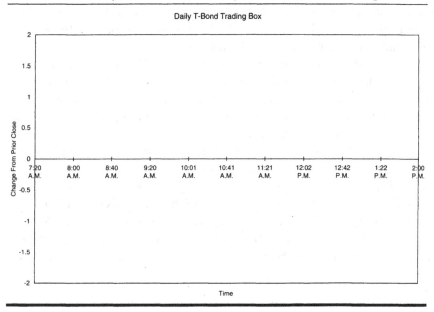

Daily T-Bond Trading Box

price will lie somewhere on the left-most vertical axis. The day's price line will fluctuate from that point forward, extending across the chart to the right, until it is 2:00 P.M. when trading stops. The right-most terminus of the price line will be the day's closing price. All price movements for the day will be inside the box, hence the term "trading box." Please note that this analysis isn't contemplating the evening session.

You can see this for yourself if you have charting software that allows tick-by-tick analysis. Chart a few days of the bond market on a tick-by-tick basis. Each of the price lines generated will be in the daily trading box. They will also look the same as all of the rest of the price lines shown in this book. They will also look the same as the price lines drawn from playing the parlor game.

For each day a profit objective and risk acceptance levels could be chosen and those lines drawn as well. These could be tested by running them through a computer program to see which combinations yield money winners and which combinations yield money losers. Because there are many different profit objectives and risk acceptance levels that can be chosen, this would have to be done repeatedly for many different combinations to find winning solutions.

This method would prove to be very time-consuming, even with the use of a computer to test the various scenarios. What is needed to speed up the analysis is a method of estimating the probability of any individual price being reached during the day.

The bond market trades in ticks. Each tick is $\frac{1}{32}$ of a point. Because we are looking at a maximum change of a two-point swing in either direction, there are 128 (32 ticks times the 4-point range) possible prices that can be reached on a daily basis. What is the likelihood of any of these possible prices being reached?

Because there are 128 potential prices, a table can be constructed showing each price, as measured as a deviation from the prior close (Table 6.1). For clarity not all of the 128 prices are shown. The zero in the middle row represents no change from the previous day's close, and each number ascending or descending from zero represents a single tick.

Let's determine the actual frequency at which each price occurred. For example on September 22, 1977, the high was $103\frac{4}{32}$ and

---

TABLE 6.1 Bins for the T-Bond Market

Prices above prior close (in ticks)

:
:
:
5
4
3
2
1
0
−1
−2
−3
−4
−5
:
:
:

Prices below prior close (in ticks)

the low was 102²⁶/₃₂. The prior close was 103⁷/₃₂. Measuring the high and low as a deviation from the prior close, we see that the high was three ticks below the prior close ($-3/32$), and the low was thirteen ticks below the prior close ($-13/32$).

Let's add another column to the table to indicate whether or not each particular price was reached (Table 6.2).

Observe that the table is only showing what happened on the day in question. In other words it is only recording prices that were actually reached during the day. The market opened lower than the previous day's close and never rose higher than ³/₃₂ below it. So the entries for -1 and -2 are properly filled in with a "N," because those prices didn't trade.

To develop a meaningful database, this process needs to be replicated for every day of the historical sample. In other words for each day a new column needs to be added to the table. It is filled in exactly the same as above, except the Ys and Ns are based on each succeeding day's closing prices. After some time has elapsed, the rows can be summed to see how frequently any price has been reached.

TABLE 6.2   Bin Values for the First Day

Prices above prior close (in ticks)	Occurred (Y or N)
:	N
:	N
:	N
5	N
4	N
3	N
2	N
1	N
0	N
−1	N
−2	N
−3	Y
−4	Y
−5	Y
:	Y
:	Y
:	Y
Prices below prior close (in ticks)	

Observe that for each day, the Ys and Ns show how prices varied *the next day*. So the analysis isn't showing what happened *today* in the market; it is showing what happened *tomorrow*. By doing the statistics this way, we will be able to draw inferences about the likely price activity tomorrow, based on today's close.

For example after five days, we can look at the pattern of Ys and Ns and make some inferences about how frequently individual prices are reached. We may see that after five days, there are three days where the price has varied by positive six ticks. The following table illustrates the procedure. The data used in the table haven't been taken from the bond market database, they are just sample data used to illustrate the idea (Table 6.3).

Of course, five days is too short a time frame to look at. The answers yielded will not be credible. However, the data examined for the bond market extend for 3,902 days, sufficient to get a very good sample. Naturally when automating this process using a computer program, the Ys and Ns are cumbersome. It is more convenient to let a "1" indicate if a price has been reached and a "0" indicate that it has not.

Also note that the method assumes that each and every price between the high and the low traded during the day. Because of the heavy volume of trading in the bond market, this assumption will hold true most of the time. When the market is moving very fast, it is likely

TABLE 6.3   Bin Values for the First Week

Tick Variation	Day 1	Day 2	Day 3	Day 4	Day 5	Sum
7	N	N	Y	N	Y	2
6	N	Y	Y	N	Y	3
5	N	Y	Y	N	Y	3
4	N	Y	Y	N	Y	3
3	N	Y	Y	N	Y	3
2	Y	Y	Y	N	Y	4
1	Y	Y	Y	N	Y	4
0	Y	Y	Y	Y	N	4
−1	Y	Y	N	Y	N	3
−2	Y	Y	N	Y	N	3
−3	Y	N	N	Y	N	2
−4	Y	N	N	Y	N	2
−5	Y	N	N	Y	N	2
−6	Y	N	N	Y	N	2
−7	Y	N	N	Y	N	2

that some prices don't have much volume behind them, but intraday gaps aren't very common in the bond market. If you have access to a tick-by-tick database, you can analyze the numbers more accurately.

A strong argument in favor of assuming continuity is that lack of liquidity with respect to price is not reasonable to predict. The problem of intraday gaps isn't a major one in the bond market, but if the same analysis is applied to a small and thinly traded market such as cocoa, the answer is bound to be somewhat soft (or not as precise as the answer garnered from analyzing a very liquid market like T-Bonds).

The prices are not weighted by volume either. If there is heavy trading at certain prices and light trading at others, each price still gets a single "1" or "0" as its outcome. Readers who have access to historical data that include volume may want to adjust the analysis to a volume-weighted one.

The following table (Table 6.4) shows the actual frequency of prices during the analysis period from September 21, 1977 to March 3, 1993. The entire table hasn't been reproduced here, only the middle of

TABLE 6.4   Bin Values for the Entire Database

Tick Variation	Number of Occurrences
10	1916
9	2061
8	2199
7	2313
6	2424
5	2552
4	2662
3	2716
2	2776
1	2809
0	2812
−1	2812
−2	2805
−3	2711
−4	2618
−5	2496
−6	2367
−7	2229
−8	2097
−9	1958
−10	1823

the range. The entire table is included as Appendix B at the end of the book.

This distribution gives a much more meaningful analysis. The sample is quite large, thus it should yield a very credible answer. Be aware that because the data don't make any statistical adjustment for contract rollover, four days per year are not really based on the same method as the other days. Given the size of this sample, the error is relatively minor.

The last thing that needs to be done to the data before they are ready to be plugged into the game theory model is to express the above table in terms of the relative frequency that each price occurs, not just in terms of the number of occurrences. Because there are 3,902 days in the sample, dividing each price's number of occurrences by the total sample size will yield the relative frequency (Table 6.5). Once again, the entire table isn't shown, just a portion of the middle of the range. The entire table is included as Appendix C.

Plotting the above data as a chart will reveal whether or not the data have a normal distribution (Figure 6.5).

TABLE 6.5   Conversion of Bin Values to Relative Frequencies

Tick Variation	Number of Occurrences	Relative Frequency
8	2199	.5517
7	2313	.5803
6	2424	.6081
5	2552	.6402
4	2662	.6678
3	2716	.6814
2	2776	.6964
1	2809	.7047
0	2812	.7055
−1	2812	.7055
−2	2805	.7037
−3	2711	.6801
−4	2618	.6570
−5	2496	.6262
−6	2367	.5938
−7	2229	.5592
−8	2097	.5261

Our eye tells us that Figure 6.5 is a normal distribution. This is an extremely important point: *the distribution of daily price changes in the bond market is normal.*

Normal distributions arise out of random variables, so the daily fluctuation of bond prices can be described by a random variable. Then even though the daily price lines generated by the bond market are random, statistical inferences can be drawn that have predictive value.

The normal distribution for the bond market for the 15-year test period has the following characteristics (Table 6.6).

The frequency distribution was created using Microsoft QuickBasic. The QuickBasic computer code is included in this book as Appendix D. The basic code is written so that it will work for any market: All that is required is to change a few parameters to fit the different

FIGURE 6.5   This is the distribution of the expiring T-Bond contract for the entire 15-year analysis period, after taking into account the daily price range. It is obviously a bell-shaped curve. We can use this to draw probabilistic inferences about the likelihood of future price changes.

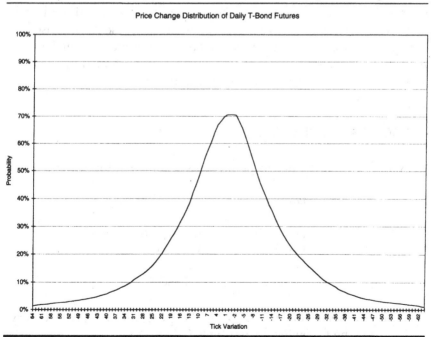

Price Change Distribution of Daily T-Bond Futures

TABLE 6.6   Descriptive Statistics for the T-Bond Markets Bell-Shaped Curve

Descriptive Statistics	
Mean	0.199
Standard Error	0.018
Median	0.098
Mode	0.017
Standard Deviation	0.213
Sample Variance	0.045
Kurtosis	0.072
Skewness	1.170
Range	0.694
Minimum	0.011
Maximum	0.705
Sum	25.689
Count	129
Confidence Level (95.0%)	0.037

market at hand, such as the tick value, the range size expressed in ticks, etc. Anyone with a home computer will be able to re-create this program to analyze whichever market they wish. The analysis will work for any time frame as well: In this example the database is comprised of daily prices. If a weekly analysis is more appropriate, just make sure the database consists of weekly prices. The results yielded by the program will then be for the time frame in question.

A PRACTICAL APPLICATION

An example is in order at this point. Let's assume the following:

Position:	Short
Entry Price:	105.7500
Profit Objective:	8 tick profit
Less Risk:	6 tick loss
More Risk:	14 tick loss
Prior Close:	105.65625

Running these numbers through the program and game theory model yields the following result (Table 6.7).

TABLE 6.7   Relative Frequencies and Game Theory Results for the Trading Example

	Tick	Price	Relative Frequency
	18	106.21875	0.27446
More Risk ⇒	17	106.18750	0.29503
	16	106.15625	0.31786
	15	106.12500	0.33818
	14	106.09375	0.36177
	13	106.06250	0.38736
	12	106.03125	0.42198
	11	106.00000	0.44907
	10	105.96875	0.48068
Less Risk ⇒	9	105.93750	0.51706
	8	105.90625	0.55168
	7	105.87500	0.58028
	6	105.84375	0.60813
	5	105.81250	0.64024
	4	105.78125	0.66784
Sell Price ⇒	3	105.75000	0.68138
	2	105.71875	0.69644
	1	105.68750	0.70472
Prior Close = ➜	0	105.65625	0.70547
	−1	105.62500	0.70547
	−2	105.59375	0.70371
	−3	105.56250	0.68013
	−4	105.53125	0.65680
Buy Price ⇒	−5	105.50000	0.62619
(i.e. Profit Objectivity)	−6	105.46875	0.59383

Entry Price: 105.75000
Profit Objective: 8
Minor Adversity: 6
Major Adversity: 14
Long or Short: Short
Profit Objective: 105.50000
Minor Adversity: 105.93750
Major Adversity: 106.18750

Item	Value
w/(w + x)	0.5714286
w/(w + y)	0.3636364
Slope	1.75
Locus	0.2077922

The prices are in decimal format, as the program needs decimals rather than fractions. The chart of the above table is illustrated as Figure 6.6.

Table 6.7 and Figure 6.6 need to be studied together. The small table at the bottom left hand corner of Table 6.7 contains the expressions that determine the boundaries of the regions. The More Risk and Less Risk relative frequencies are found in the main table of Table 6.7.

FIGURE 6.6 Given the stated risk/reward parameters, this is the completed game theory model for the T-Bond market. The size and shapes of the regions will vary with changes in the risk & reward parameters.

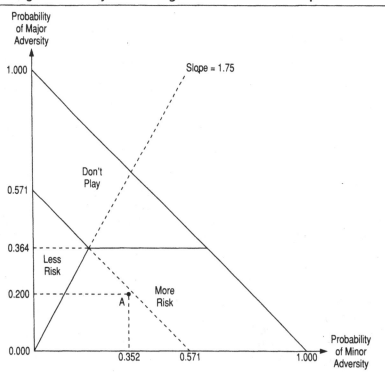

Minor Adversity		Major Adversity	
Prob. of Entry Price Occurring	.681	Prob. of Entry Price Occurring	.681
× Prob. of Less Risk Price Occurring	.517	× Prob. of More Risk Price Occurring	.295
	.352		.200

Coordinates of Point "A"

It is simple to calculate the probabilities associated with Less Risk and More Risk: merely multiply the relative frequency that the entry price occurs by the relative frequency that both Less Risk and More Risk occur. This has been done in Figure 6.6, with the coordinates plotted in the model as Point "A." This point clearly lies in the More Risk region, which indicates that a trade based on the More Risk amount will be successful, if it is iterated over time.

This example suggests that these trading parameters will yield a money winner. This should prove to be true in an iterated sense: the trade must be made repeatedly in order to have success. Some of the trades will make money and some will lose money, but the winners will outweigh the losers by enough magnitude to produce an overall winner.

Since the actual frequency that prices have occurred has been measured, it is a safe assumption to equate the relative frequency with the probability. Mathematical purists might want to convert this probability density function into a standard normal distribution using z-scores, and compute the probabilities using standard statistical techniques. This subject is quite complex in its own right, and is beyond the scope of this book.

Some readers may know that probabilities should sum to one, and obviously the column of relative frequencies sum to a number much greater than one. But this is true only for mutually exclusive events. These are not mutually exclusive events. An entire range of prices occurs every day; the market does not trade at only one price each day.

The relative frequency of each bin can serve as a proxy for its probability. For example, look at Bin +3, which is the entry price. It has occurred 68.138% of the time. This implies it has not occurred 31.862% of the time ($1 - .68138 = .31862$). So the probability of each individual price either occurring or not occurring sums to one; however, it is a mistake to add the probabilities of different prices together looking for the same relationship.

How can an individual speculator take advantage of this model? First, we are looking at intraday price movements, so we are really talking about day-trading the bond market. This will prove very difficult to implement successfully unless you are very close to the market. Even if you were a floor trader or were watching the market on screen all day (and can *rapidly* have an order executed), this particular strategy would be very difficult to pull off in the real world. Delays in placing the order, slippage on the fills, and even the delay in prices reading your quote machine, and so on, will make a strategy that is anticipating profit in minuscule amounts of ticks a poor performer. The profits can evaporate due to bad fills alone, aside from considering the commission costs that have to be paid.

A better way to use this strategy is to call the orders in prior to the opening bell. The buy and the sell are placed, as well as two stop-loss orders. One stop loss is needed in case the buy is executed first, the other is needed in case the sell is executed first. Once the buy or sell has been executed, the other stop loss needs to be immediately canceled so that you don't end up getting filled on both orders. Take the following orders, for example:

Buy Stop	106.06250
Sell	105.90625
Buy	105.71875
Sell Stop	105.53125

If the buy is executed first, immediately cancel the buy stop. If the sell is executed first, immediately cancel the sell stop. Once again you will have to watch the market all day long and have immediate access to be able to implement this scheme.

The use of order-cancels-order (OCO) trades may increase the practicality of this method. In an OCO trade, the execution of the buy causes immediate (you hope) cancellation of the buy stop. It works the same for selling: The execution of the sell causes immediate cancellation of the sell stop. Some brokerage firms don't accept OCO trades, either at all or for certain markets, so research this issue. If the buy and sell are very close, then the broker is at risk, and typically a second set of orders based on which of the first orders is executed won't be allowed.

Alternatively because you are watching the market anyway, place the entries only, then place the appropriate stop after you are in. The bond market doesn't typically move so fast that you won't be able to call the stop in (although it may).

Note that if you place orders as described above, a single game theory analysis is insufficient. It no longer represents your actions in the market. The model needs to be run twice to determine the profitability of the trade: once for the possibility of being short and again for the possibility of being long. Both of the analyses need to show a profit or the trade may be unprofitable. This is because even if you risk the same amount no matter whether you are long or short, the probabilities of the risk amounts actually occurring will be different.

There is another issue that needs to be addressed if we are looking at a day-trading method. The development of the game theory model assumes that a trade will be held *until* either the profit objective or risk acceptance level is reached. Because our statistics are for daily price movements (recall the "trading box"), there is some probability that only one side of the trade will be executed during the day. If we are looking at this as an iterated game that can played each and every day, positions would not be held overnight. Of course a position *can* actually be held overnight, but the probabilities as calculated above will be inaccurate. One method of solving this problem is to iterate the probabilities for each price between the entry price and the risk acceptance level (as was done in the GM example), but this is very cumbersome.

A better way to play is to enter the orders as described above (i.e., a buy, a sell, and a stop-loss order), and then close out your position on the close. Typically this would be done by canceling the stop-loss order near the closing bell and making the unexecuted buy or sell market-on-close (MOC).

Once again this will change the probabilities from what was calculated above. The "real" profit objective will be *any* profitable trade between the entry price and "nominal" profit objective. Similarly the "real" Less Risk level is not just the "nominal" (or stated) price, but *every* price between the entry price and the "nominal" Less Risk level. This doesn't apply to the More Risk amount, as the price first has to cross through the Less Risk amount to get to the More Risk amount.

In the above example, assume that a short position was filled at $105^{24}/_{32}$. The Less Risk amount was set at $105^{30}/_{32}$, and the Profit Objective at $105^{16}/_{32}$, giving you an 8 tick profit with 6 ticks of risk. The Less Risk price is placed as a stop-loss order. If neither the buy nor the stop-loss order has been executed as the day draws to a close, cancel the stop loss and make the buy order MOC. The position may in fact be closed out without actually achieving either original target. It may get closed out somewhere in between. Therefore the actual probability of a profit is overstated in the above calculation, and the probability of losing the Less Risk amount is understated. Table 6.8 illustrates the situation now faced by the trader.

The original parameters of the trade indicated a profit would be made if the price dropped to 105.500 and a loss incurred if the price rose to 105.9375. By making the exit order MOC (in this case the buy, since it is a short trade), the trade may be offset at several different prices. Each of these possibilities will yield either a profit or a loss, as shown in Table 6.8.

TABLE 6.8   Making the Exit Strategy Market on Close (MOC)

	Tick	Price	Relative Frequency	
	18	106.21875	0.27446	
More Risk ⇒	17	106.18750	0.29503	
	16	106.15625	0.31786	
	15	106.12500	0.33818	
	14	106.09375	0.36177	
	13	106.06250	0.38736	
	12	106.03125	0.42198	
	11	106.00000	0.44907	
	10	105.96875	0.48068	
Less Risk ⇒	9	105.93750	0.51706	
	8	105.90625	0.55168	← = Buy is MOC (Loss)
	7	105.87500	0.58028	← = Buy is MOC (Loss)
	6	105.84375	0.60813	← = Buy is MOC (Loss)
	5	105.81250	0.64024	← = Buy is MOC (Loss)
	4	105.78125	0.66784	← = Buy is MOC (Loss)
Sell Price ⇒	3	105.75000	0.68138	← = Buy is MOC (Break Even)
	2	105.71875	0.69644	← = Buy is MOC (Profit)
	1	105.68750	0.70472	← = Buy is MOC (Profit)
Prior Close = →	0	105.65625	0.70547	← = Buy is MOC (Profit)
	−1	105.62500	0.70547	← = Buy is MOC (Profit)
	−2	105.59375	0.70371	← = Buy is MOC (Profit)
	−3	105.56250	0.68013	← = Buy is MOC (Profit)
	−4	105.53125	0.65680	← = Buy is MOC (Profit)
Buy Price ⇒	−5	105.50000	0.62619	
	−6	105.46875	0.59383	

The above discussion illustrates an important point: Although the game theory model accurately describes the behavior of the market, the mechanics of order placement need to be taken into account. The theory cannot be kept apart from the practical usage. In this example the problem stems from violating one of the principles behind the game theory model, namely, that the speculator is prepared to hold a trade until one of the specified levels is reached. By creating a set of rules for order placement in a day-trading scheme, we added MOC orders. This has changed the premise of the argument somewhat.

If the orders are placed as per the above example, there is a buy, a sell, and a stop loss. You can only have a single stop-loss order on any given trade. In game theory terms, the Less Risk amount and the More

Risk amount are exactly the same. Many real-world trades work this way. Actually analyzing markets in terms of a single risk acceptance level (i.e., I'm willing to lose "X $" on this trade) is quite common. The game theory model shows this situation as well.

For example take the following parameters shown in Table 6.9 and graphed using the game theory model as Figure 6.7. Note that the More Risk region has disappeared entirely. This is what is to be expected, because if there is only one risk acceptance level, there is only one region of loss. The x and y intercepts of the demarcation line between profit and loss will correspond to Less Risk result, that is, $w / (w + x)$. Also note that algebraically there is "no slope" associated with the ray from the origin, and the locus of strategic separation is zero.

Bear in mind that adding a time constraint affects the model. This is of more importance to futures or options traders than it is to stock traders. This is because the futures and options deal in instruments that expire. Common stocks do not. Also if you are going to use a trading scheme that incorporates a time limit (such as the example discussed above), the time constraint issue arises as well. Although the method of calculating probabilities in the above example is fairly rigorous, note that the timing issue must be dealt with carefully.

The above analysis can be done for any time frame desired. The example used here has been daily price changes; however, weekly or monthly changes could have been used as well. The use of a longer time

---

TABLE 6.9   The Effect of Having a Single Risk Acceptance Level

Entry Price:	105.75000
Profit Objective:	8
Minor Adversity:	14
Major Adversity:	14
Long or Short:	Short
Profit Objective:	105.50000
Minor Adversity:	106.18750
Major Adversity:	106.18750

Item	Value
$w/(w + x)$	0.3636364
$w/(w + y)$	0.3636364
Slope	No Slope
Locus	0

FIGURE 6.7 This shows the effect of accepting only a single risk level. In mathematic terms Less Risk is equal to More Risk; hence, the More Risk region disappears entirely. Many real-world trading strategies are based on this type of analysis (where there is a single risk level on any given trade).

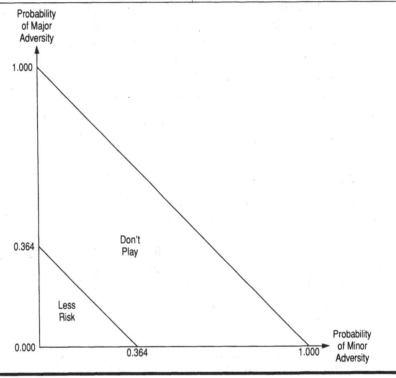

frame greatly decreases the problems associated with the mechanics of day trading and order placement. A longer time frame doesn't require that you scalp a few ticks; you can catch larger moves and be less dependent on the quality of the fills.

There are myriad ways to determine the probabilities. The approach illustrated here is just one of many possible approaches. For example, stochastics or some other technical method can be used to evaluate prices. An historical test could be run comparing changes in prices to changes in the stochastic variable. Probabilistic inferences can be drawn from this, yielding a different way to analyze the probabilities.

There are numerous books available that discuss predicting price movements. Any of these methods can be used to determine the probabilities, although the results of the model will only be as sound as the data.

Make sure you trade the same way you calculate probabilities!!

HOW CHANGES IN THE RISK/REWARD VARIABLES CHANGE THE REGIONS

The size and shape of the various regions in the graph of the model will change based upon the selection of the profit objective and risk acceptance levels. Care must be taken to ensure proper interpretation of the results, otherwise unwise trading decisions may be made.

First by increasing the size of the Profit Objective variable, the Don't Play region of the graph shrinks markedly. It seems the model suggests that a very lucrative strategy is to try for a large amount of profit. This is not necessarily true. Let's look at an example to see this effect.

Assume the speculator makes the following risk/reward criteria (Table 6.10).

Note that the Profit Objective has been increased from eight ticks to 50 ticks. The other parameters have remained the same as in the previous example. Graphically the situation is shown in Figure 6.8.

The More Risk region dominates the graph, and the Don't Play region is quite small. With these parameters the probability of

---

TABLE 6.10   The Effect of Greatly Increasing the Profit Objective

Entry Price:	105.75000
Profit Objective:	50
Minor Adversity:	6
Major Adversity:	14
Long or Short:	Short
Profit Objective:	104.18750
Minor Adversity:	105.93750
Major Adversity:	106.18750

Item	Value
$w/(w + x)$	0.8928571
$w/(w + y)$	0.78125
Slope	7.00
Locus	0.1116071

FIGURE 6.8 This shows the effect of dramatically increasing the Profit Objective. The Don't Play and Less Risk regions shrink substantially. Increasing the Profit Objective excessively may cause your strategy to lose touch with reality: Always ask yourself, "How realistic are these parameters?" when evaluating a trade. The game theory model assumes you are going to hold a trade until one of the offsetting parameters is reached, so if you are trading an instrument with an expiration date such as a future or option, you may not be able to do so.

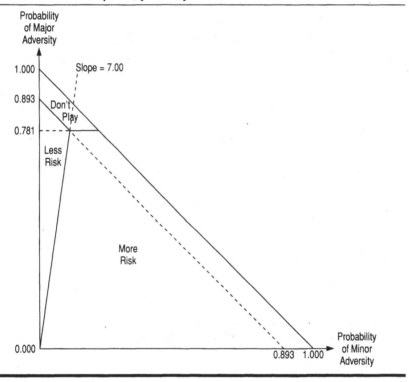

encountering Major Adversity would have to be greater than 78% to lose money. This looks as if it is a great trade.

It is a great trade, provided the real world execution of the trade doesn't violate any of the premises of the model. Can this trade happen in the real world? In the discussion above, the model presumes that you are *willing to hold* the trade until either the Profit Objective or one of the risk acceptance levels is reached. Because the data (and trading scheme) we are analyzing are day trading the bond market, we need to ask: "How realistic is it that this trade can be held until one of the objectives is reached?" The answer is "Not very likely."

The statistical analysis that generated the normal distribution is based on daily data, so the resulting probabilities are in terms of intraday price changes. How often can you hold a day trade in hope of making a 50-tick profit? Not very often. If you could, this trade should make money. If you make the trade and plan to hold until one of the levels is reached, additional analysis is needed. The probabilities as determined above simply don't reflect holding the trade overnight.

This should give a stock trader or someone with a longer time frame food for thought, though. If this were a stock trade with a bullish position, it might not be a bad idea. Most stock prices have an upward bias, as discussed earlier. Hence the probabilities derived from historical data strongly suggest long positions over short positions. Because stocks don't expire, they can be held indefinitely. Holding out for relatively larger profits appears to make sense for stocks. Perhaps the old saw about buying and holding great companies is a winning long-term stock market strategy.

How does the model change if the More Risk amount is increased substantially? The next example shows how. Assume the following parameters (Table 6.11).

These parameters return to the original choices of a Profit Objective of eight ticks and Less Risk of six ticks, but More Risk has been increased to 50 ticks. Graphically the model is shown in Figure 6.9.

TABLE 6.11   The Effect of Greatly Increasing More Risk

Entry Price:	105.75000
Profit Objective:	8
Minor Adversity:	6
Major Adversity:	50
Long or Short:	Short
Profit Objective:	105.50000
Minor Adversity:	105.93750
Major Adversity:	107.31250

Item	Value
$w/(w + x)$	0.5714286
$w/(w + y)$	0.137931
Slope	0.32
Locus	0.4334975

FIGURE 6.9   This shows the effect of having the More Risk parameter markedly increased. The Less Risk region will expand, because at some point the gains from increasing the More Risk amount are offset by the size of the loss when it does occur.

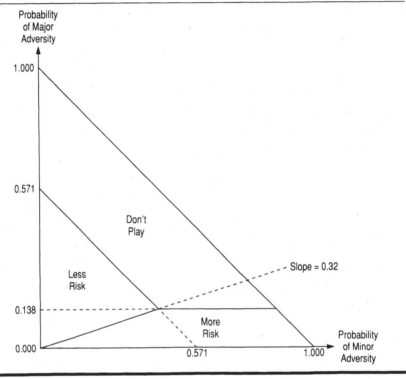

The More Risk region shrinks at the expense of the Don't Play and Less Risk regions. Does this seem logical? Recall how the More Risk region is defined. It represents the universe of trades where the price dips against the position enough to cause a small loss, but the price adversity doesn't go far enough to cause a large loss. By increasing the More Risk variable, we have increased the amount of risk accepted but decreased the likelihood of it occurring. In the above example, the More Risk amount was increased substantially to show the effect that at some point the gains from decreasing the likelihood of a large loss are outweighed by the magnitude of the loss (when it does occur).

Naturally this is a trade-off. If the More Risk amount were only one tick greater than the Less Risk amount, the effect is negligible. You can't get on the road to huge profits by accepting tremendous risk, although the model does suggest that somewhat higher risk acceptance levels can yield somewhat greater profit. All told this is in keeping with traditional economic theory, which says the greater the risk associated with something, the greater the reward has to be to induce you to take the risk.

The main point of the discussion of changing the size and shape of the regions by varying the risk/reward amounts leads to an extremely important point: Once you determine the probabilities for a given market, you can "back in" to a successful strategy by varying the parameters in the model until the proposed trade is in a profitable region. If you have a probability dispersion such as the one calculated for the bond market, you can find a profitable trade by plugging numbers into the model until you find risk/reward parameters that are in a profitable region. Be sure you use enough data, or else you will find that the results are finely tuned to a short period of activity.

A MORE SOPHISTICATED APPROACH: TAKE THE TREND INTO ACCOUNT

Sometimes there is a bull market, other times a bear market. Markets typically move either up, down, or sideways. The probability distribution shown earlier for the bond market did not take the trend into account. The numbers were crunched using the entire period at hand and treating it the same. No distinction was made between up trends or down trends.

The result garnered from just looking at the market as a whole yielded a very smooth, regular, bell-shaped curve. The peak of the bell is very close to zero tick variation, indicating no directional bias, and the tails are very smooth on either side. The shape is a "textbook" example of a bell-shaped curve. This curve is made up of undifferentiated data. When the market generally is rising, prices generally will be higher on a day-to-day basis. When the market is falling, prices generally are lower. In a sideways market, prices will fluctuate around the average, with no discernible trend. If we make a trading decision based on the bell-shaped curve alone, we might be wrong often. For example if we are in a bear market, following a strategy of "playing the middle" probably will yield more losers than winners. We should be playing a somewhat bullish strategy when the market is rising and a somewhat bearish strategy when the market is falling.

How should "bull" and "bear" markets be defined? It is possible to look at a price chart and subjectively decide whether the current conditions represent a bull or bear market, but this is imprecise. Additionally is it a strongly trending market or a weakly trending market? Once again a subjective method can be used, but the result will vary with who does the naming. Analyst "A" may say we are in a bull market, but Analyst "B" may say the market is moving sideways or consolidating. Having several analysts agree on what the market is doing is somewhat problematic (and if they *all* agree, then they are almost certainly wrong).

Various mathematic or analytic techniques are available. For example, periods when prices are above a moving average trend-line may defined as a bull market and vice versa. Price momentum, stochastics, linear regression, and other methods may also be used.

The best method will show not only if the market is rising or falling but the strength of the move. The method should also be completely objective; that is, criteria are established that yield the same result no matter who is doing the analysis.

Moving averages are particularly well suited to showing the trend of a market, especially if several moving averages are used in conjunction with one another. The following discussion uses a moving average approach, but *is not* predicated on "buy when one line crosses another" or some other such mechanical trading rule. Rather the probability dispersion of bond prices will be examined for different moving average conditions. Trading decisions can then be made based on each of the separate probability distributions.

Several moving averages have been calculated for the data in question. A three-, four-, six-, and nine-day moving average will be used. Because the idea is to look at day trading schemes, the use of longer averages begins to lose any practical value.

Additionally instead of using the moving averages themselves, oscillators have been derived from the moving averages. The longer-term oscillator used is the difference between the four-day moving average and the nine-day moving average. Subtracting the nine-day average from the four-day average produces the 4–9 oscillator. Obviously when this number is positive, prices are advancing, and when it is negative, prices are falling. When they equal each other, prices are neutral.

This may be a simplistic interpretation of the oscillator. If it is examined for the course of the data, one finds that it is rarely above 1.5 or below −1.5. These values can equate to "strongly bullish" and "strongly bearish," respectively. The values between these extremes need to be looked at. Certainly the market doesn't turn on a dime from being strongly bullish to being strongly bearish. A graph of the 4–9 oscillator for the 15-year database is shown as Figure 6.10.

What we are going to do is calculate a series of frequency distributions based on the oscillator. Recall that the original distribution was based on undifferentiated data. It did not take the market trend into account. We can use the value of the oscillator to determine the direction of the trend. We can expect that frequency distributions for bullish trends will be skewed to the upside, and bear markets will be skewed

---

FIGURE 6.10 The value of the 4–9 oscillator for the 15-year time frame. It is derived by subtracting nine-day moving average from the four-day moving average. When the oscillator is above zero, it is a bullish sign (because the four-day average is higher than the nine-day average). The converse is true when the oscillator is below zero. Negative values suggest a bearish trend. Using an oscillator gives a convenient, objective, and impartial method of determining the trend of a market.

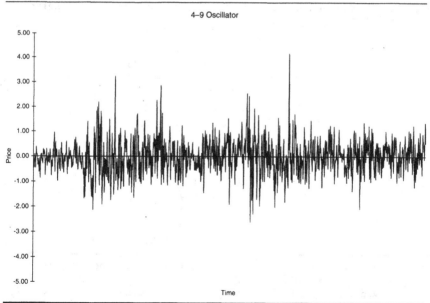

4–9 Oscillator

to the downside. Additionally we may find that for some conditions a range of very high probabilities exists, such as an 80% likelihood of certain prices being reached. Armed with this information, trades can be made with a high probability of success.

A useful way to organize the data (from a statistical perspective) is to put the measurements into regularly spaced bins. Each bin must be discreet; that is, each value of the oscillator should only fit in a single bin.

Fourteen bins have been selected. This bin frequency is in keeping with standard statistical techniques, which generally don't use more than 15 bins for any single variable. Each bin comprises an interval of 0.25 of the value of the oscillator, as shown in Table 6.12.

Bin #1 is the most bullish, Bin #14 the most bearish, and Bins #7 and #8 are the most neutral.

Each day in the historical data series can be classified as belonging to exactly one of these bins. An analysis identical to the earlier example can be done to determine the dispersion of the relative frequencies or probabilities.

TABLE 6.12 Detailed Trend Analyses Using 14 Bins and 4–9 Oscillator

Bin Number	Value of 4–9 Oscillator
1	(4–9) > = 1.50
2	1.50 < (4–9) > = 1.25
3	1.25 < (4–9) > = 1.00
4	1.00 < (4–9) > = 0.75
5	0.75 < (4–9) > = 0.50
6	0.50 < (4–9) > = 0.25
7	0.25 < (4–9) > = 0.00
8	0.00 < (4–9) > = –0.25
9	–0.25 < (4–9) > = –.050
10	–.050 < (4–9) > = –0.75
11	–0.75 < (4–9) > = –1.00
12	–1.00 < (4–9) > = –1.25
13	–1.25 < (4–9) > = –1.50
14	–1.50 < (4–9)

Note: Instead of just considering positive values of the oscillator to be bullish (and negative values bearish), why not divide the range into a series of equal sized bins? These can be ranked from top to bottom, corresponding to "strongly bullish" and "strongly bearish." This is a continuum: Bins in the middle of the range are neutral. Each day of the analysis period can be classified by its bin.

What result would be expected from such an analysis? Logically the bell-shaped curves associated with each of the bins will have their center or midpoint in a different position, as well as vary in height and in the shape of the tails. For example the curve associated with a low-numbered bin (such as Bin #4, a relatively bullish bin) should have the peak of the bell-shaped curve on the bullish part of the daily range. Conversely a high-numbered bearish bin such as Bin #12 will have the distribution skewed to the bearish side.

Let's add the faster term oscillator to the analysis. In a manner identical to how the 4–9 oscillator was compartmentalized, let's do the same thing to the 3–6 oscillator (Table 6.13).

The same reasoning holds for this oscillator: Low bins are bullish and high bins are bearish.

Each day can now be classified by two variables: the 4–9 and 3–6 oscillators. Further let's stipulate that the 4–9 oscillator is the main variable, and the 3–6 oscillator is a secondary variable. Because there are 14 conditions for each classification, there are 196 (14 × 14 = 196) total classifications.

If the data are analyzed this way, and each day is put into one of the discreet 196 classifications, a table showing the dispersion of prices by oscillator can be constructed (Table 6.14).

TABLE 6.13   Detailed Trend Analyses Using 14 Bins and 3–6 Oscillator

Bin Number	Value of 3–6 Oscillator
1	(3–6) >= 1.50
2	1.50 < (3–6) > = 1.25
3	1.25 < (3–6) > = 1.00
4	1.00 < (3–6) > = 0.75
5	0.75 < (3–6) > = 0.50
6	0.50 < (3–6) > = 0.25
7	0.25 < (3–6) > = 0.00
8	0.00 < (3–6) > = –0.25
9	–0.25 < (3–6) > = –.050
10	–.050 < (3–6) > = –0.75
11	–0.75 < (3–6) > = –1.00
12	–1.00 < (3–6) > = –1.25
13	–1.25 < (3–6) > = –1.50
14	–1.50 < (3–6)

Note: Values range from bullish on top to bearish on the bottom.

TABLE 6.14 Frequency by Oscillator Condition

		1	2	3	4	5	6	7	8	9	10	11	12	13	14
							Condition 2 (3–6)								
C	1	19	11	13	16	6	2	0	1	0	0	0	0	0	0
o	2	0	6	11	18	12	4	2	3	0	0	0	0	0	0
n	3	0	2	9	27	31	18	5	3	1	0	0	0	0	0
d	4	0	1	11	31	70	71	27	5	0	0	0	0	0	0
i	5	0	2	6	26	68	134	86	24	4	2	0	0	0	0
t	6	0	0	5	10	58	164	193	71	11	3	0	0	0	0
i	7	0	0	0	6	24	92	303	183	40	9	0	0	0	0
o	8	0	0	0	4	10	39	206	297	118	18	5	0	0	0
n	9	0	0	0	1	3	18	65	206	203	59	8	3	0	0
	10	0	0	0	0	0	1	29	92	115	74	27	6	0	0
	11	0	0	0	0	0	4	4	25	72	70	37	7	1	0
1	12	0	0	0	0	1	0	1	5	21	33	30	12	3	4
	13	0	0	0	0	0	0	1	4	5	8	12	8	2	0
(4–9)	14	0	0	0	0	0	0	1	0	3	5	9	12	11	9

Note: Because each day has a value for both oscillators, each day can be classified by them as well. Condition (1, 1) corresponds to "strongly bullish," and Condition (14, 14) corresponds to "strongly bearish." Basically what we have done is dragged a "comb" through the entire database: The first time was to classify each day by the slower oscillator (4–9), the second time to classify each day by a faster oscillator (3–6). Now instead of an unruly mess, the data is well organized. We can take a detailed look at each condition by measuring the relative frequencies of price fluctuations within each condition. We would expect that bullish conditions will have the distribution skewed to the upside, and bearish conditions are skewed to the downside.

The 4–9 oscillator's value is shown on the vertical axis, and the 3–6 oscillator's value is on the horizontal axis.

Studying the table we see that the largest values are in the middle, with the values tapering off toward either extreme. Interestingly note how the bottom left and top right of the table all have values of zero. Apparently one oscillator is never strongly bullish while the other is strongly bearish. The converse seems to hold true as well: If one oscillator is very bullish, it is likely that the other will be as well. Also note that the top left portion of the table has more values (and values of greater magnitude) than the bottom right portion. If the market is a dynamic between fear and greed, it appears as if greed (or euphoria) reigns more often. The above data have been converted into a chart to better visualize the data (see Figure 6.11).

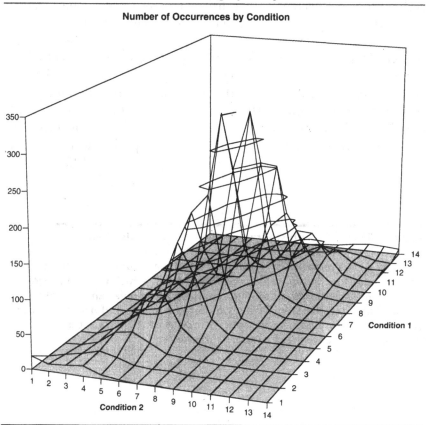

Number of Occurrences by Condition

The data take on the shape of a mountain range: There are two
peaks that dominate the rest, but there are still other substantial
crests, as well as foothills, and so on. The data (and chart) follow what
is to be expected: Prices more often than not cluster in the middle—
only occasionally are there strong moves in one direction or the other.

   Wherein lie the profit potentials? How do we profit from this mass
of numbers? Let's look at a trading example to see how put the system
into operation.

DEVELOPING A TRADING SYSTEM

Each of the 196 bin combinations has had its relative frequency determined. They are all included as Appendix E to the book (studying them will be a well-rewarded exercise), and some are particularly interesting.

Let's look at a bin that lies near to one of the extremes—not so extreme so that there are only a few days of data in the analysis, but far enough in one direction or the other that the market is definitely in a trend. Four–nine condition #10 and 3–6 condition #10 occurred on 74 days during the 15-year analysis period. The relative frequencies for the tick variation are shown in Figure 6.12. The peak is at the mean of the distribution. In this case the peak corresponds to "+ 1 tick."

FIGURE 6.12   This is a histogram of the frequency distribution of Condition (10, 10), a bearish condition. Observe that most of the data points lie to the negative side, which is what we would expect for a bearish condition. Compare this with Figure 6.5 (which is the histogram for the undifferentiated data). Figure 6.5 is very regular and smooth, without bias to either side. This set of data have bias and hence a trading opportunity. Interestingly the peak (or mean) of the data set are at +1 tick. This is where we want to short the market.

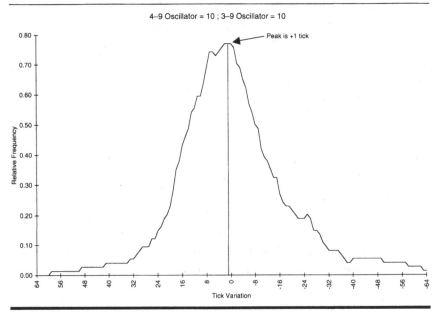

Because this is a bearish condition, we should short the market whenever both oscillators evaluate to condition #10. Let's test this hypothesis using data for 1994. The data between 1977 and 1993 cannot be used for testing purposes because they have been used to create the statistics. If they are used, they will lead to a "curve fitted" answer. If the statistics generated by the 15-year database are valid, we should be able to apply them on a going-forward basis and get positive results.

The risk and reward parameters need to be determined for the test. Assume a Profit Objective of eight ticks, a Less Risk amount of eight ticks, and a More Risk amount of 16 ticks. Running these values through the game theory model yields the following (Figure 6.13).

The model suggests that accepting More Risk will result in a profitable trading series. Let's test this for 1994 and see if it is true.

There were 9 days in 1994 that met the test criteria. The first was February 7, 1994. On that day both oscillators' values fell into condition #10 bins. The close was $114^{26}/_{32}$. The trading strategy for February 8 is to short the market when the price is 1 tick higher than the prior close (short at $114^{27}/_{32}$), offset with a profit at $114^{19}/_{32}$ (down 7 ticks), or accept More Risk at $115^{11}/_{32}$ (up 17 ticks). The same parameters were applied to each day that met the test criteria.

The following table (Table 6.15) summarizes the results of the test. A tick-by-tick database for 1994 was used for accuracy.

Overall the results are positive. There were 9 days when the 2 oscillators both evaluated to bin #10. Trades were made on 7 of those 9 days. There were 4 winners and 3 losers. The strategy yielded 8 ticks in overall profit. This is not a great deal of profit, but bear in mind this was a strictly "mechanical" test.

Figures 6.14A through 6.14I show the results of the test on a day-to-day basis. Please note that the entry price is critical: We want to short the market when the current price corresponds to the peak of the distribution. Typically when a sell order is executed, it is for the sell price or higher (the theory being that selling for a price higher than the order is a better fill), but in our case we want to short the market at a specific price. The statistics have been developed for a specific entry price, so the order needs to be put in for that price exactly. It is all right if the buy is executed at a price lower than the target price. This would be a better fill at a better price.

To implement the strategy successfully, the market will have to be watched all day long. If you are watching the market, you do not necessarily have to exit as soon as the Profit Objective is reached. Once the

FIGURE 6.13 The game theory model for 4–9 condition #10 and 3–6 condition #10. It is a bearish trend, so the market should be shorted.

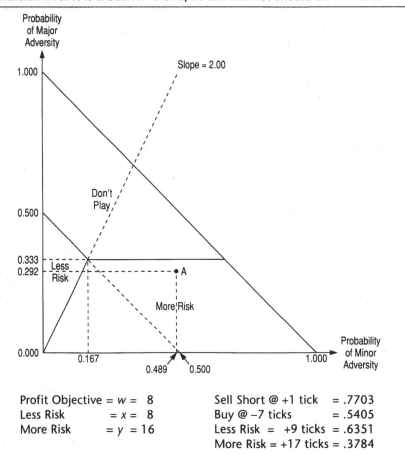

Profit Objective = w =	8	Sell Short @ +1 tick	= .7703
Less Risk	= x = 8	Buy @ –7 ticks	= .5405
More Risk	= y = 16	Less Risk = +9 ticks	= .6351
		More Risk = +17 ticks	= .3784

Minor Adversity		*Major Adversity*	
Prob. of Entry Price Occurring	.7703	Prob. of Entry Price Occurring	.7703
× Prob. of Less Risk Price Occurring	.6351	× Prob. of More Risk Price Occurring	.3784
	.4892		.2915
	↖		↗
		Coordinates of Point "A"	

TABLE 6.15 Test Results for 1994 with Both Oscillators at Condition #10

Date	Close	Next Day Sell Target	Next Day Buy Target	Next Day Risk	Long / Short	Entry Price	Exit Price	Ticks Profit/(Loss)	Dollars Profit/(Loss)
2/7/94[a]	114.81250	114.84375	114.59375	115.34375	NoTrade	—	—	—	—
2/22/94[b]	113.09375	113.12500	112.87500	113.62500	Short	113.12500	112.87500	8	250.00
3/24/94[c]	107.84375	107.87500	107.62500	108.37500	Short	107.87500	107.62500	8	250.00
4/19/94[d]	104.03125	104.06250	103.81250	104.56250	Short	104.06250	103.81250	8	250.00
6/21/94[e]	103.46875	103.50000	103.25000	104.00000	Short	103.50000	103.62500	(4)	(125.00)
6/30/94[f]	101.21875	101.25000	101.00000	101.75000	Short	101.25000	101.37500	(4)	(125.00)
9/26/94[g]	99.28125	99.31250	99.06250	99.81250	NoTrade	—	—	—	—
10/24/94[h]	97.40625	97.43750	97.18750	97.93750	Short	97.43750	97.18750	8	250.00
11/7/94[i]	96.28125	96.31250	96.06250	96.81250	Short	96.31250	96.81250	(16)	(500.00)
								8	250.00

[a] Corresponds to Figure 6.14A
[b] Corresponds to Figure 6.14B
[c] Corresponds to Figure 6.14C
[d] Corresponds to Figure 6.14D
[e] Corresponds to Figure 6.14E
[f] Corresponds to Figure 6.14F
[g] Corresponds to Figure 6.14G
[h] Corresponds to Figure 6.14H
[i] Corresponds to Figure 6.14I

FIGURE 6.14A   No trade, as the sell was never hit.

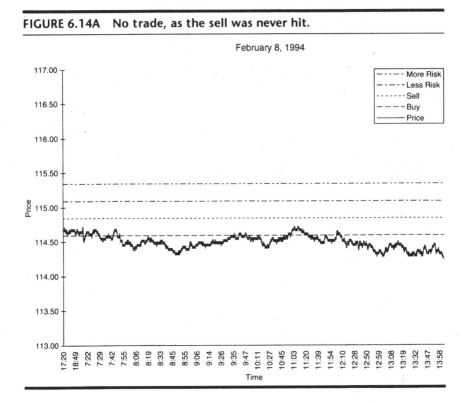

February 8, 1994

Profit Objective is reached, you can continue to ride the trade without fear of loss. The old saying "Cut your losses and let your profits run" was not followed in the mechanical test.

There were several days in which profits could have been allowed to run. Doing this would greatly increase the attractiveness of the results of the test. Allowing profits to run is somewhat subjective: At what point do you exit the trade and bank the dollars? This amount is different for each of us. However, the strategy yields a profit even when it is applied in a purely mechanical sense. If the trader is actively monitoring the position, actual results can be much better.

Profits were not allowed to run for the test because it would violate the premise of the argument, namely, that the game theory model suggests that at the specified risk/reward parameters the trading series will be profitable, without adding in extra profits by letting profits run. If this test is passed, then the game theory model is validated.

FIGURE 6.14B   This day is an example of when to let the profits run. Once the Price passes the exit position (Buy @ 112.875), the trade can be held for greater profit.

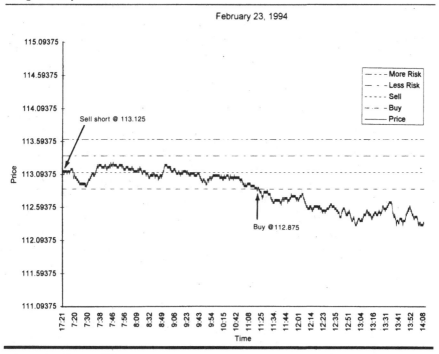

February 23, 1994

Of course the profits that can be garnered by actively monitoring the position should be larger than those predicted by the test.

ANOTHER TEST

Let's look at 4–9 condition #11 and 3–6 condition #9. Once again this is a bearish condition. There were 72 days in which this condition prevailed, as can be seen in Table 6.14.

The first step is to make a histogram or bell-shaped curve from the data (all the data needed to make this chart and analysis are included as Appendix E). This has been done in Figure 6.15. The peak of the graph corresponds to the mean price. In this case it is 4 ticks higher than the previous close. Because the oscillator conditions are bearish,

FIGURE 6.14C This illustrates the trade off between less risk and more risk. Had we accepted less risk, we would have closed the trade for a loss. Accepting more risk yielded a profit.

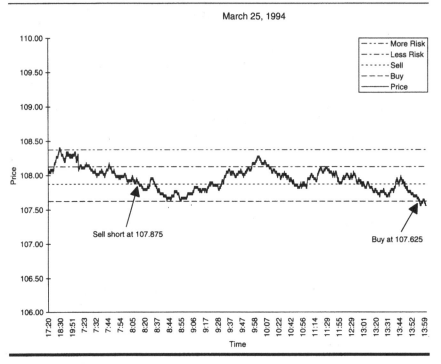

we will want to short the market when the price is 4 ticks higher than the previous close.

The second step is to run the numbers through the game theory model. In this example the risk/reward amounts are the same as in the previous example. Because we are looking to short the market at +4 ticks, the Less Risk amount of 8 ticks now corresponds to a price of 12 ticks up from the prior close. Similarly because More Risk entails 16 ticks of loss, the number we'll trade on is 20 ticks higher than the prior close.

The model has been calculated in Figure 6.16. The relative frequencies for trading parameters were looked up in Appendix E (from the same Table that generated the frequency distribution). The probabilities

FIGURE 6.14D   A profitable trade.

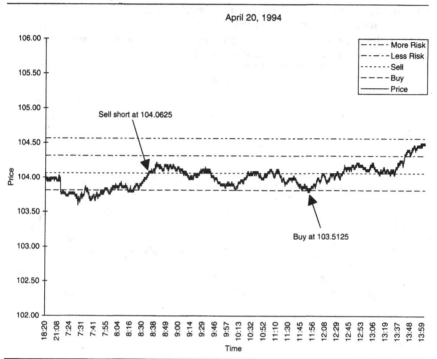

April 20, 1994

of Major and Minor Adversity have been calculated and are plotted in the diagram. The coordinates lie in the More Risk region.

The third step is to go through the data for 1994 and identify on which days the oscillator condition matches the test conditions. The first matching date is February 10, 1994. This means that on February 11, 1994 (the next trading day), we will want to short the market when the price is 4 ticks higher than the February 10 close. We will try and offset at a profit if the price drops to 4 ticks lower than the prior close. We will accept More Risk of 16 ticks, which equates to a price 20 ticks higher than the prior close.

This is then repeated for every day in 1994 that matches the test conditions. The results of the test are shown in Table 6.16, and each day's trading results are shown in Figures 6.17A through 6.17K.

FIGURE 6.14E   After initiating the trade short at 103.50, neither the
profit objective nor the risk acceptance level was reached. The position
was then offset at the close, resulting in a loss. This date is also the first
day that the September contract becomes the expiring contract. There is
a definite problem with rollover on this date.

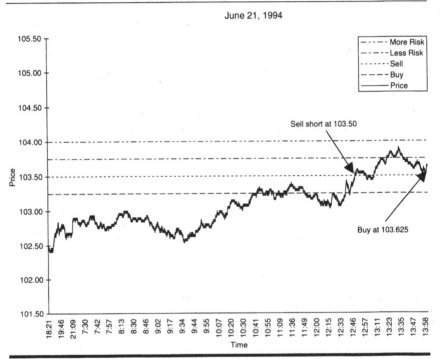

This test yields profitable results. The oscillator conditions were
matched 11 times during 1994. Seven trades were made, of which 5
were profitable. A total of 21 ticks per contract were made. There were
3 days where the price fluctuation didn't hit our targeted short price of
+4 ticks.

As in the previous example, this is just the mathematical result. If
profits were allowed to run, the actual return would have been higher.
I have not tried to estimate what the return might have been, because
if the trade is being held subjectively past the targeted exit price, the
actual results will depend on the skill of the holder. This will vary from
reader to reader.

FIGURE 6.14F   Another day where neither the profit objective or more risk amount was hit. The low for the day *was* the profit objective, but when testing a system, you can't "buy the low."

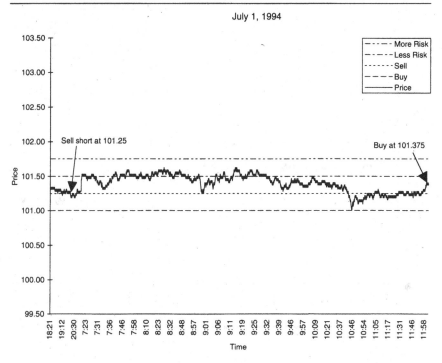

The two test cases we have examined suggest that these strategies are lucrative. Repeatedly playing these strategies (i.e., iterating them over time) is profitable, as has been demonstrated by the tests.

It is important to realize that the risk/reward parameters used in the tests are not the only parameters that may yield a profit. What other parameters may be profitable? It is very easy to determine this. Run the risk/reward parameters you have in mind through the game theory model, then calculate the probabilities as shown. You can tell at a glance whether coordinates lie in a profitable region. I strongly recommend running a test using a tick-by-tick database before committing actual dollars to the trading strategy.

FIGURE 6.14G   No trade, as the sell was never hit.

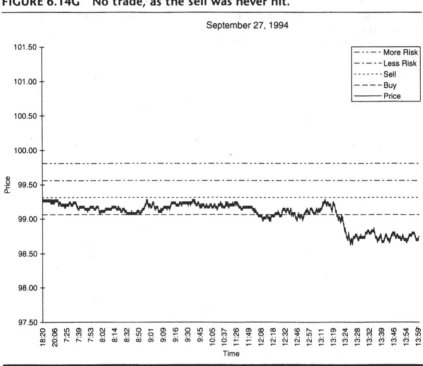

September 27, 1994

Examine the tables shown in Appendix E. There are quite a few different sets of conditions that have relative frequencies *greater than 80%* for part of the daily range.

Naturally there a host of methods that can be used to analyze probabilities. The examples in this book use probability distributions based on price changes (sorted by the magnitude of the oscillator). This is not to say that this is either the best or the only method available. Many technicians undoubtedly see how to apply the game theory within the context of their own analytic techniques. However, to get meaningful results, the best methods will be objective.

The game theory is not the "Holy Grail" that everyone searches for, but it is a method that can offer significant insight into the likelihood of profit or loss on any given trade. Think of it as another "arrow in the quiver," that is, a tool to use to evaluate potential trades. A conservative

FIGURE 6.14H   A profitable trade.

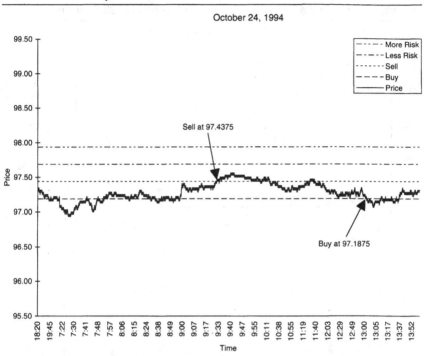

October 24, 1994

approach is to use game theory in conjunction with other methods. For example many systems use multiple indicators to determine when to make a trade. Game theory can be used as one of the indicators. If several indicators all suggest that a trade is profitable, then the comfort level associated with the trade should be markedly increased.

FIGURE 6.14I The trade deteriorated all the way to the More Risk amount. This trade was the biggest money loser of the test period.

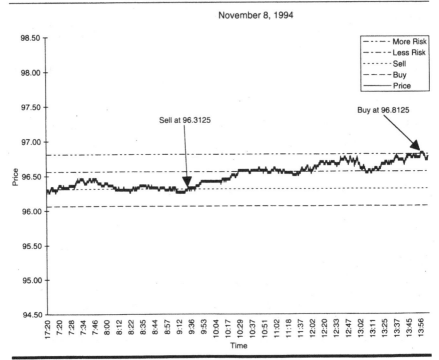

November 8, 1994

FIGURE 6.15 The frequency for Condition (11, 9). Once again, we see bias to the downside. The peak lies at plus 4 ticks, which is where we should short the market.

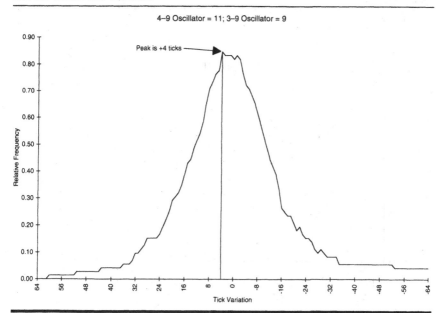

4–9 Oscillator = 11; 3–9 Oscillator = 9

FIGURE 6.16 The game theory model for 4–9 condition #11 and 3–6 condition #9. Once again this is a bearish condition, so the market needs to be shorted.

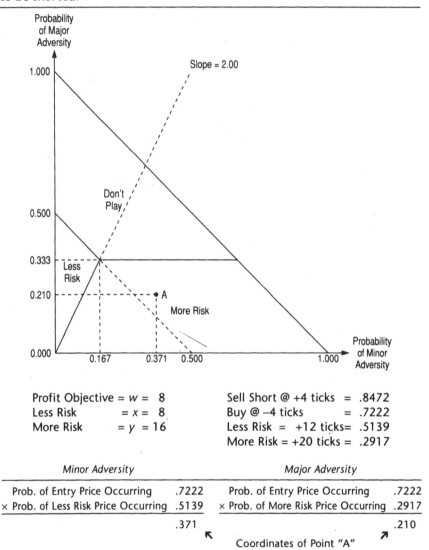

Profit Objective = w = 8	Sell Short @ +4 ticks = .8472
Less Risk = x = 8	Buy @ –4 ticks = .7222
More Risk = y = 16	Less Risk = +12 ticks= .5139
	More Risk = +20 ticks = .2917

Minor Adversity		Major Adversity	
Prob. of Entry Price Occurring	.7222	Prob. of Entry Price Occurring	.7222
× Prob. of Less Risk Price Occurring	.5139	× Prob. of More Risk Price Occurring	.2917
	.371		.210

Coordinates of Point "A"

TABLE 6.16 Test Results for 1994 with 4–9 Oscillators at Condition #11 and the 3–6 Oscillator at Condition #9

Date	Close	Next Day Sell Target	Next Day Buy Target	Next Day Risk	Long / Short	Entry Price	Exit Price	Ticks Profit/(Loss)	Dollars Profit/(Loss)
2/10/94 [a]	114.53125	114.65625	114.40625	115.15625	Short	114.65625	114.40625	8	250.00
2/28/94 [b]	112.40625	112.53125	112.28125	113.03125	Short	112.53125	112.28125	8	250.00
3/1/94 [c]	110.96875	111.09375	110.84375	111.59375	Short	111.09375	110.84375	8	250.00
3/4/94 [d]	110.75000	110.87500	110.62500	111.37500	No Trade	—	—	—	—
5/4/94 [e]	104.31250	104.43750	104.18750	104.93750	Short	104.43750	104.53125	(3)	(93.75)
5/6/94 [f]	102.46875	102.59375	102.34375	103.09375	No Trade	—	—	—	—
7/1/94 [g]	101.34375	101.46875	101.21875	101.96875	Short	101.46875	101.21875	8	250.00
7/6/94 [h]	101.50000	101.62500	101.37500	102.12500	Short	101.62500	101.62500	—	—
8/12/94 [i]	102.78125	102.90625	102.65625	103.40625	No Trade	—	—	—	—
9/27/94 [j]	98.71875	98.84375	98.59375	99.34375	Short	98.84375	99.34375	(16)	(500.00)
10/25/94 [k]	97.28125	97.40625	97.15625	97.90625	Short	97.40625	97.15625	8	250.00
								21	656.25

[a] Corresponds to Figure 6.17A
[b] Corresponds to Figure 6.17B
[c] Corresponds to Figure 6.17C
[d] Corresponds to Figure 6.17D
[e] Corresponds to Figure 6.17E
[f] Corresponds to Figure 6.17F
[g] Corresponds to Figure 6.17G
[h] Corresponds to Figure 6.17H
[i] Corresponds to Figure 6.17I
[j] Corresponds to Figure 6.17J
[k] Corresponds to Figure 6.17K

FIGURE 6.17A   A profitable trade. Perhaps there was some potential to let profits run.

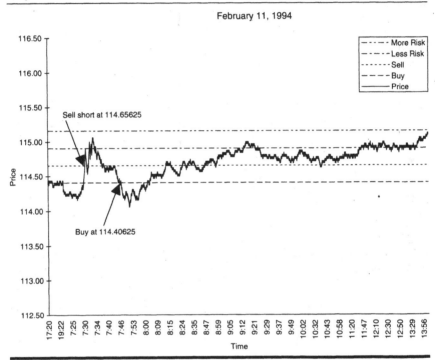

February 11, 1994

FIGURE 6.17B   Another profitable day. With prices falling strongly, the trade could have been held for additional profit.

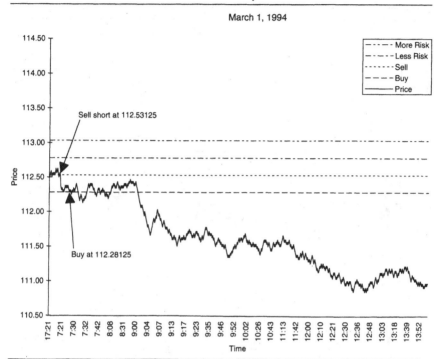

March 1, 1994

FIGURE 6.17C   A profitable day. This chart illustrates the risk in trying to hold out for additional profits: Prices recovered strongly enough to erase the profits.

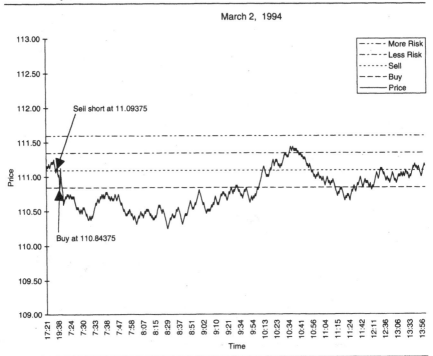

March 2, 1994

FIGURE 6.17D No trade, as the sell was never hit.

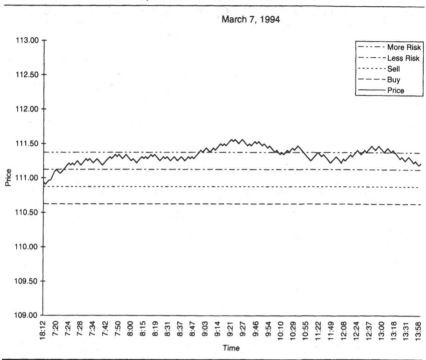

March 7, 1994

FIGURE 6.17E The MOC came into play, as there wasn't enough price volatility to reach either the Profit Objective or the More Risk amount.

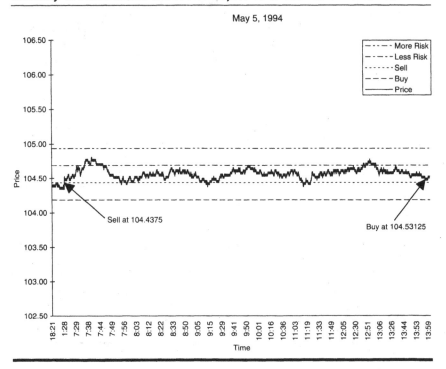

May 5, 1994

Sell at 104.4375

Buy at 104.53125

More Risk
Less Risk
Sell
Buy
Price

Price

Time

FIGURE 6.17F   No trade, as the sell was never hit.

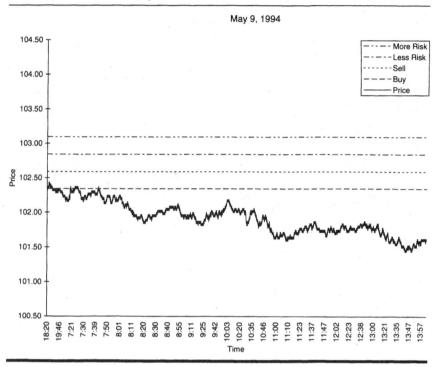

May 9, 1994

FIGURE 6.17G   A profitable day.

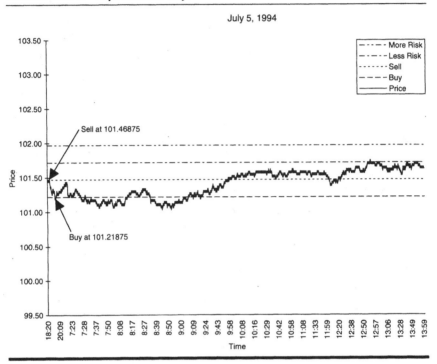

July 5, 1994

FIGURE 6.17H   Another day of low volatility, which caused the trade to close MOC.

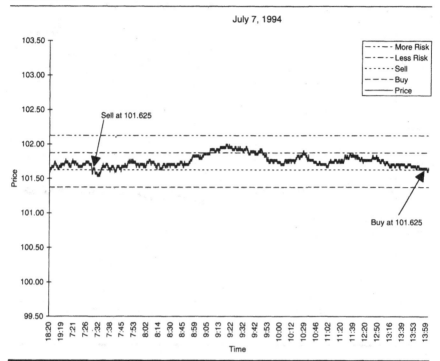

July 7, 1994

FIGURE 6.17I No trade, as the sell was never hit.

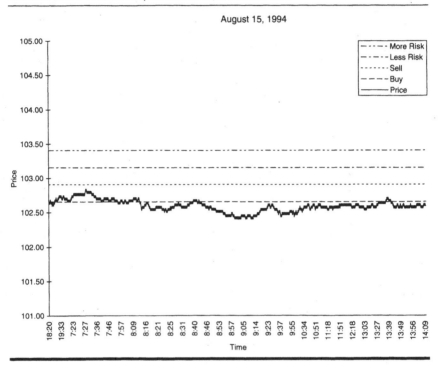

August 15, 1994

FIGURE 6.17J   A losing trade.

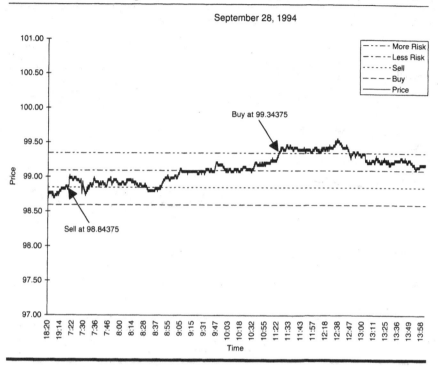

September 28, 1994

FIGURE 6.17K   A winning trade.

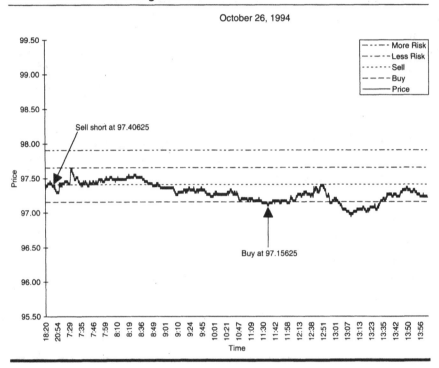

October 26, 1994

Appendix A

Mathematical Representation of the Model

This appendix is for readers who are interested in following the mathematical development of the model. A strong background in math is helpful, but not essential.

The techniques used to develop the model are relatively straightforward although some the equations can be quite long. Fortunately they aren't very complicated.

Let's start with the game table (Figure A.1):

FIGURE A.1 Algebraic representation of the game table.

		SPECULATOR	
		q	$1-q_1$
	$1-p_1-p_2$	w	w
MARKET	p_1	w	$-x$
	p_2	$-y$	$-x$

The variables represented correspond to the market's strategies, the speculator's strategies, and the outcomes to the speculator. These are:

161

Market Strategies

p_1 = the probability the market plays "Minor Adversity"

p_2 = the probability the market plays "Major Adversity"

$1 - p_1 - p_2$ = the probability the market plays "Zero Adversity"

Speculator Strategies

q_1 = the probability the speculator plays "More Risk"

$1 - q_1$ = the probability the speculator plays "Less Risk"

Payoffs to Speculator

w = profit to the speculator (this is a "win")

$-x$ = loss equal to the "Less Risk" amount (this is a "small loss")

$-y$ = loss equal to the "More Risk" amount (this is a "large loss")

Where:

$w > x > y$

Essentially we have three matrices in Figure A.1. The first matrix consists of the market's strategies, the second matrix is payoff table, and the third matrix consists of the speculator's strategies. The matrices have to be multiplied to derive the equations used to construct the model. The first step is to multiply the market strategy matrix by the payoff matrix. Let's structure the market strategy matrix as a one-row vector with three columns. Doing this yields the following vector:

$1 - p_1 - p_2, p_1, p_2$

Each position in the vector is separated by a comma. A vector is really just a matrix of a particular sort: it is a matrix that either has one row or one column. In this case the market's strategies are represented by a vector (i.e., matrix) that has one row and three columns. Its size is (1×3). The payoff matrix has three rows and two columns. Its size is (3×2).

Matrices are multipliable if the number of columns in the first matrix equals the number of rows in the second. In this case the number of columns in market matrix is three, and the number of rows in the payoff matrix is three. Hence these matrices are multipliable. The product of this multiplication is a new matrix with a size of (1×2).

Each market strategy needs to be multiplied by the corresponding payoff, and the results summed. This will be done twice—once for each column in the payoff matrix. Therefore the first position in the new matrix becomes:

Step 1: $(1 - p_1 - p_2)w + p_1 w - p_2 y$

Step 2: $w - p_1 w - p_2 w + p_1 w - p_2 y$

Step 3: $w - p_2 w - p_2 y$

The formula in Step 3 is the first position in the new matrix. The same procedure needs to be done for the second position:

Step 1: $(1 - p_1 - p_2) w - p_1 x - p_2 x$

Step 2: $w - p_1 w - p_2 w - p_1 x - p_2 x$

The formula in Step 2 is the second position of the new matrix. The new matrix has the form:

$$w - p_2 w - p_2 y, \; w - p_1 w - p_2 w - p_1 x - p_2 x$$

Observe this is a matrix with one row and two columns (i.e., has a size of 1 $\times$ 2).

Next we need to multiply the speculator's strategies into the new matrix. This is done fairly easily. First we need to express the speculators strategies as a (2×1) matrix:

q

$1 - q$

The q is the top position in the matrix, and the $1 - q$ is the bottom position.

These values need to be multiplied into the "new" matrix as determined above. Note that when this multiplication is complete, the answer will be a new matrix with a size of (1×1). In other words we will have a single equation that is the product of the speculator's strategies, the market's strategies, and the payoff table. To wit:

Step 1: $(w - p_2 w - p_2 y) q + (w - p_1 w - p_2 w - p_1 x - p_2 x)(1 - q)$

Step 2: $wq - p_2 wq - p_2 yq + w - p_1 w - p_2 w - p_1 x - p_2 x - wq + p_1 wq + p_2 wq + p_1 xq + p_2 xq$

Step 3: (Simplify the above.)

$$p_1 wq + p_1 xq + p_2 xq - p_2 yq + w - p_1 w - p_2 w - p_1 x - p_2 x$$

This equation incorporates all the strategies and payoffs. It is difficult to work with, and it needs to be separated into the two components of interest to the speculator; that is, we need to identify the speculator's More Risk and Less Risk strategies. This is easily done, as the More Risk strategy has been defined in terms of q. All that is required is to factor in terms of q:

More Risk Equation: $(p_1 w + p_1 x + p_2 x - p_2 y) q$

Less Risk Equation: $w - p_1 w - p_2 w - p_1 x - p_2 x$

The next step is to rewrite these two equations in terms of the relevant market strategies; that is, the equations need to be rewritten in terms of p_1 and p_2. In doing so we will drop the q coefficient associated with the More Risk strategy. It isn't needed any longer: it has just allowed us to identify which parts of the equation correspond with More Risk. Rewriting these equations is simple: again all that is required to factor out the p_1 and p_2 from each equation:

More Risk Equation: $(w + x) p_1 - (y - x) p_2$ $\Leftarrow$ Term 1

Less Risk Equation: $w - (w + x) p_1 - (w + x) p_2$ $\Leftarrow$ Term 2

At this point the reader can refer to Chapter 4 for the development of the model.

Appendix B

Frequency Distribution for Expiring Month T-Bond Futures Prices

Data from September 22, 1977 to March 3, 1993

Tick Variation	Number of Observations	Tick Variation	Number of Observations
64	53	45	172
63	61	44	180
62	68	43	190
61	72	42	206
60	75	41	219
59	80	40	231
58	87	39	253
57	92	38	269
56	98	37	284
55	103	36	302
54	108	35	324
53	113	34	343
52	121	33	368
51	125	32	393
50	133	31	432
49	139	30	461
48	147	29	490
47	154	28	516
46	163	27	550

Data from September 22, 1977 to March 3, 1993 *(Continued)*

Tick Variation	Number of Observations	Tick Variation	Number of Observations
26	590	−13	1503
25	632	−14	1416
24	685	−15	1312
23	746	−16	1217
22	805	−17	1128
21	880	−18	1051
20	952	−19	987
19	1030	−20	923
18	1094	−21	863
17	1176	−22	812
16	1267	−23	763
15	1348	−24	721
14	1442	−25	672
13	1544	−26	627
12	1682	−27	590
11	1790	−28	546
10	1916	−29	510
9	2061	−30	468
8	2199	−31	430
7	2313	−32	402
6	2424	−33	379
5	2552	−34	356
4	2662	−35	332
3	2716	−36	298
2	2776	−37	278
1	2809	−38	261
0	2812	−39	240
−1	2812	−40	224
−2	2805	−41	210
−3	2711	−42	193
−4	2618	−43	181
−5	2496	−44	169
−6	2367	−45	159
−7	2229	−46	154
−8	2097	−47	145
−9	1958	−48	135
−10	1823	−49	129
−11	1716	−50	121
−12	1617	−51	114

Data from September 22, 1977 to March 3, 1993 *(Continued)*

Tick Variation	Number of Observations	Tick Variation	Number of Observations
−52	110	−59	77
−53	107	−60	74
−54	101	−61	68
−55	96	−62	63
−56	94	−63	50
−57	87	−64	44
−58	83		

Appendix C

Relative Frequency Distribution for Expiring Month T-Bond Futures Prices

Data from September 22, 1977 to March 1, 1993

Tick Variation	Relative Frequency	Tick Variation	Relative Frequency
64	1.32965%	46	4.08931%
63	1.53036%	45	4.31510%
62	1.70597%	44	4.51581%
61	1.80632%	43	4.76668%
60	1.88159%	42	5.16809%
59	2.00702%	41	5.49423%
58	2.18264%	40	5.79528%
57	2.30808%	39	6.34722%
56	2.45861%	38	6.74862%
55	2.58404%	37	7.12494%
54	2.70948%	36	7.57652%
53	2.83492%	35	8.12845%
52	3.03562%	34	8.60512%
51	3.13598%	33	9.23231%
50	3.33668%	32	9.85951%
49	3.48721%	31	10.83793%
48	3.68791%	30	11.56548%
47	3.86352%	29	12.29303%

Data from September 22, 1977 to March 1, 1993 *(Continued)*

Tick Variation	Relative Frequency	Tick Variation	Relative Frequency
28	12.94531%	−11	43.05068%
27	13.79829%	−12	40.56698%
26	14.80181%	−13	37.70697%
25	15.85549%	−14	35.52434%
24	17.18515%	−15	32.91520%
23	18.71550%	−16	30.53186%
22	20.19568%	−17	28.29905%
21	22.07727%	−18	26.36729%
20	23.88359%	−19	24.76167%
19	25.84044%	−20	23.15605%
18	27.44606%	−21	21.65078%
17	29.50326%	−22	20.37130%
16	31.78625%	−23	19.14200%
15	33.81836%	−24	18.08831%
14	36.17662%	−25	16.85901%
13	38.73557%	−26	15.73006%
12	42.19769%	−27	14.80181%
11	44.90718%	−28	13.69794%
10	48.06824%	−29	12.79478%
9	51.70597%	−30	11.74109%
8	55.16809%	−31	10.78776%
7	58.02810%	−32	10.08530%
6	60.81284%	−33	9.50828%
5	64.02408%	−34	8.93126%
4	66.78374%	−35	8.32915%
3	68.13848%	−36	7.47617%
2	69.64375%	−37	6.97441%
1	70.47165%	−38	6.54792%
0	70.54691%	−39	6.02107%
−1	70.54691%	−40	5.61967%
−2	70.37130%	−41	5.26844%
−3	68.01305%	−42	4.84195%
−4	65.67988%	−43	4.54089%
−5	62.61917%	−44	4.23984%
−6	59.38284%	−45	3.98896%
−7	55.92072%	−46	3.86352%
−8	52.60913%	−47	3.63773%
−9	49.12193%	−48	3.38685%
−10	45.73507%	−49	3.23633%

Data from September 22, 1977 to March 1, 1993 *(Continued)*

Tick Variation	Relative Frequency	Tick Variation	Relative Frequency
−50	3.03562%	−58	2.08229%
−51	2.86001%	−59	1.93176%
−52	2.75966%	−60	1.85650%
−53	2.68440%	−61	1.70597%
−54	2.53387%	−62	1.58053%
−55	2.40843%	−63	1.25439%
−56	2.35825%	−64	1.10386%
−57	2.18264%		

Appendix D

Quick Basic Program for Relative Frequencies

This is a Quick Basic program that will calculate the price dispersion and relative frequencies of any market. The user will have to reset the variables in the next section to fit the market at hand.

Make sure the filenames, directories, and paths are appropriate to your configuration. These are mine; yours will be different.

The data must be in a random access Quick Basic file structured as follows:

DAYNUM, TDATE, CONTRACT, OPENVAL, HIGHVAL, LOWVAL, CLSVAL

Each of the above is a variable. They are defined as follows:

DAYNUM = The day number of each record. Corresponds to each record in the database.
TDATE = The date of each record, that is, 09-22-77.
CONTRACT = The contract designator for the prices, i.e., USZ77.
OPENVAL = The opening price for each day.
HIGHVAL = The high for each day.
LOWVAL = The low for each day
CLSVAL = The closing price for each day.

Furthermore each record has the following characteristics:

DAYNUM is an integer variable that is 2 bytes long.
TDATE is a string variable that is 8 bytes long.
CONTRACT is a string variable that is 6 bytes long.

OPENVAL is a double precision variable that is 8 bytes long.
HIGHVAL is a double precision variable that is 8 bytes long.
LOWVAL is a double precision variable that is 8 bytes long.
CLSVAL is a double precision variable that is 8 bytes long.

Note that the size of each record is 48 bytes.

All providers of historical data have an option to output the data as either text or ASCII. You may be able to output the data exactly as shown. If not, you will have to amend it. Once you have the data in a text or ASCII file, write a Quick Basic program to read it into a random access file structured as shown above.

Tick values must be in decimal format for this program to work.

Examine the output section of the program carefully. It will output to the specified filename. Make sure the filename, directory, and path correspond to your system. The data written will be in text format. It can then be read by Microsoft Excel (or another spreadsheet program).

The following is the program:

Variables to be Changed for the Market Being Analyzed

```
,
TICK# = .03125
RANGE# = TICK# ° 64
,
'
,
```

Unchanging Variables and Program Parameters

```
,
OPTION BASE 1
TYPE DAILYPRICE
   DAYNUM AS INTEGER
   TDATE AS STRING × 8
   CONTRACT AS STRING × 6
   OPENVAL AS DOUBLE
   HIGHVAL AS DOUBLE
   LOWVAL AS DOUBLE
   CLSVAL AS DOUBLE
END TYPE
DIM PRICE AS DAILYPRICE
FIRSTDAY = 1
DIM OCCUR(((RANGE# / TICK#) × 2) + 1)
```

```
DIM PROB((((RANGE# / TICK#) ° 2) + 1)
'
'
'
```

Count the Number of Records in the Database

```
'
OPEN "C:\WINDOWS\DESKTOP\GAMES\BONDRAND.RAN" FOR
    RANDOM AS #1 LEN = 48
RECORDNUMBER = LOF(1) \ 48
MAXDAY = RECORDNUMBER
CLOSE #1
'
'
'
```

Determine How Often Each Price Has Occurred

```
'
OPEN "C:\WINDOWS\DESKTOP\GAMES\BONDRAND.RAN" FOR
    RANDOM AS #2 LEN = 48
FOR I = 1 TO MAXDAY-1
  GET #2, FIRSTDAY, PRICE
  YESCLS# = PRICE.CLSVAL
  FIRSTDAY = FIRSTDAY + 1
  GET #2, FIRSTDAY, PRICE
  HIGHVAL# = PRICE.HIGHVAL
  LOWVAL# = PRICE.LOWVAL
  TOP# = YESCLS# + RANGE# + TICK#
  FOR J = 1 TO (((RANGE# / TICK#) × 2) + 1)
    TOP# = TOP# -TICK#
    IF TOP# < = HIGHVAL# AND TOP# > = LOWVAL# THEN
    OCCUR(J) = OCCUR(J) + 1
    ELSE
    OCCUR(J) = OCCUR(J) + 0
    END IF
  NEXT J
  NEXT I
CLOSE #2
'
'
'
```

Determine the Relative Frequencies

'

```
FOR K = 1 TO (((RANGE# / TICK#) × 2) + 1)
   PROB(K) = OCCUR(K) / MAXDAY
   NEXT K
'
'
'
```

Output the Result to the Screen and/or a File

'

```
OPEN "C:\WINDOWS\DESKTOP\GAMES\BONDPROB.TXT" FOR
   APPEND AS #3
PRINTSTRING$ = "### #.#####"
FOR K = 1 TO (((RANGE# / TICK#) × 2) + 1)
   PRINT USING PRINTSTRING$; ((RANGE# / TICK#) + 1) −K;
      PROB(K)
   WRITE #3, PROB(K)
   NEXT K
CLOSE #3
'
'
'
```

```
END
```

Appendix E

Relative Frequencies by Oscillator Conditions

Main Condition 1

Probabilities

Secondary Conditions

Tick Variation	1	2	3	4	5	6	7	8	9	10	11	12	13	14
64	0.1053	0.1818	0.0000,	0.1250	0.1667	0.0000	0.0000	0.0000	0.0000	0.0000	0.0000	0.0000	0.0000	0.0000
63	0.1053	0.1818	0.0000	0.1250	0.1667	0.0000	0.0000	0.0000	0.0000	0.0000	0.0000	0.0000	0.0000	0.0000
62	0.1053	0.1818	0.0000	0.1250	0.1667	0.0000	0.0000	0.0000	0.0000	0.0000	0.0000	0.0000	0.0000	0.0000
61	0.1053	0.1818	0.0000	0.1250	0.1667	0.0000	0.0000	0.0000	0.0000	0.0000	0.0000	0.0000	0.0000	0.0000
60	0.1053	0.1818	0.0000	0.1250	0.1667	0.0000	0.0000	0.0000	0.0000	0.0000	0.0000	0.0000	0.0000	0.0000
59	0.1053	0.1818	0.0000	0.1250	0.1667	0.0000	0.0000	0.0000	0.0000	0.0000	0.0000	0.0000	0.0000	0.0000
58	0.1579	0.1818	0.0000	0.1875	0.1667	0.0000	0.0000	0.0000	0.0000	0.0000	0.0000	0.0000	0.0000	0.0000
57	0.2105	0.1818	0.0769	0.1875	0.1667	0.0000	0.0000	0.0000	0.0000	0.0000	0.0000	0.0000	0.0000	0.0000
56	0.2105	0.1818	0.0769	0.1875	0.1667	0.0000	0.0000	0.0000	0.0000	0.0000	0.0000	0.0000	0.0000	0.0000
55	0.2105	0.1818	0.1538	0.1875	0.1667	0.0000	0.0000	0.0000	0.0000	0.0000	0.0000	0.0000	0.0000	0.0000
54	0.2105	0.1818	0.1538	0.1875	0.1667	0.0000	0.0000	0.0000	0.0000	0.0000	0.0000	0.0000	0.0000	0.0000
53	0.2105	0.1818	0.1538	0.1875	0.1667	0.0000	0.0000	0.0000	0.0000	0.0000	0.0000	0.0000	0.0000	0.0000
52	0.2632	0.1818	0.1538	0.2500	0.1667	0.0000	0.0000	0.0000	0.0000	0.0000	0.0000	0.0000	0.0000	0.0000
51	0.2632	0.1818	0.1538	0.2500	0.1667	0.0000	0.0000	0.0000	0.0000	0.0000	0.0000	0.0000	0.0000	0.0000
50	0.2632	0.2727	0.1538	0.2500	0.1667	0.0000	0.0000	0.0000	0.0000	0.0000	0.0000	0.0000	0.0000	0.0000
49	0.2632	0.2727	0.1538	0.2500	0.1667	0.0000	0.0000	0.0000	0.0000	0.0000	0.0000	0.0000	0.0000	0.0000
48	0.2632	0.2727	0.1538	0.2500	0.1667	0.0000	0.0000	0.0000	0.0000	0.0000	0.0000	0.0000	0.0000	0.0000
47	0.2632	0.2727	0.1538	0.2500	0.1667	0.0000	0.0000	0.0000	0.0000	0.0000	0.0000	0.0000	0.0000	0.0000
46	0.2632	0.2727	0.1538	0.2500	0.1667	0.0000	0.0000	0.0000	0.0000	0.0000	0.0000	0.0000	0.0000	0.0000
45	0.2632	0.3636	0.1538	0.2500	0.1667	0.0000	0.0000	0.0000	0.0000	0.0000	0.0000	0.0000	0.0000	0.0000
44	0.2632	0.3636	0.1538	0.2500	0.1667	0.0000	0.0000	0.0000	0.0000	0.0000	0.0000	0.0000	0.0000	0.0000
43	0.2632	0.3636	0.1538	0.2500	0.1667	0.0000	0.0000	0.0000	0.0000	0.0000	0.0000	0.0000	0.0000	0.0000
42	0.2632	0.3636	0.1538	0.3125	0.1667	0.0000	0.0000	0.0000	0.0000	0.0000	0.0000	0.0000	0.0000	0.0000
41	0.2632	0.3636	0.1538	0.3125	0.1667	0.0000	0.0000	0.0000	0.0000	0.0000	0.0000	0.0000	0.0000	0.0000
40	0.2632	0.3636	0.1538	0.3125	0.1667	0.0000	0.0000	0.0000	0.0000	0.0000	0.0000	0.0000	0.0000	0.0000
39	0.2632	0.3636	0.1538	0.3125	0.1667	0.5000	0.0000	0.0000	0.0000	0.0000	0.0000	0.0000	0.0000	0.0000
38	0.2632	0.3636	0.1538	0.3125	0.1667	0.5000	0.0000	0.0000	0.0000	0.0000	0.0000	0.0000	0.0000	0.0000
37	0.3158	0.3636	0.1538	0.3750	0.1667	0.5000	0.0000	0.0000	0.0000	0.0000	0.0000	0.0000	0.0000	0.0000
36	0.3684	0.3636	0.1538	0.3750	0.1667	0.5000	0.0000	0.0000	0.0000	0.0000	0.0000	0.0000	0.0000	0.0000
35	0.3684	0.4545	0.1538	0.3750	0.1667	0.5000	0.0000	0.0000	0.0000	0.0000	0.0000	0.0000	0.0000	0.0000
34	0.3684	0.4545	0.1538	0.3750	0.1667	0.5000	0.0000	0.0000	0.0000	0.0000	0.0000	0.0000	0.0000	0.0000
33	0.3684	0.4545	0.1538	0.4375	0.1667	0.5000	0.0000	0.0000	0.0000	0.0000	0.0000	0.0000	0.0000	0.0000
32	0.3684	0.4545	0.1538	0.4375	0.1667	0.5000	0.0000	0.0000	0.0000	0.0000	0.0000	0.0000	0.0000	0.0000
31	0.3684	0.5455	0.2308	0.4375	0.3333	0.5000	0.0000	0.0000	0.0000	0.0000	0.0000	0.0000	0.0000	0.0000
30	0.3684	0.5455	0.2308	0.4375	0.3333	0.5000	0.0000	0.0000	0.0000	0.0000	0.0000	0.0000	0.0000	0.0000
29	0.3684	0.5455	0.2308	0.4375	0.3333	0.5000	0.0000	0.0000	0.0000	0.0000	0.0000	0.0000	0.0000	0.0000
28	0.3684	0.6364	0.2308	0.5625	0.3333	0.5000	0.0000	0.0000	0.0000	0.0000	0.0000	0.0000	0.0000	0.0000
27	0.3684	0.6364	0.3077	0.6250	0.3333	0.5000	0.0000	0.0000	0.0000	0.0000	0.0000	0.0000	0.0000	0.0000
26	0.3684	0.6364	0.3077	0.6250	0.3333	0.5000	0.0000	0.0000	0.0000	0.0000	0.0000	0.0000	0.0000	0.0000
25	0.3684	0.6364	0.3077	0.6250	0.3333	0.5000	0.0000	1.0000	0.0000	0.0000	0.0000	0.0000	0.0000	0.0000
24	0.3684	0.6364	0.3846	0.5625	0.3333	0.5000	0.0000	1.0000	0.0000	0.0000	0.0000	0.0000	0.0000	0.0000
23	0.4211	0.7273	0.3846	0.5625	0.3333	0.5000	0.0000	1.0000	0.0000	0.0000	0.0000	0.0000	0.0000	0.0000
22	0.4737	0.6364	0.3846	0.5625	0.3333	0.5000	0.0000	1.0000	0.0000	0.0000	0.0000	0.0000	0.0000	0.0000
21	0.5263	0.6364	0.3846	0.5625	0.3333	0.5000	0.0000	1.0000	0.0000	0.0000	0.0000	0.0000	0.0000	0.0000
20	0.5263	0.6364	0.3846	0.5625	0.3333	0.5000	0.0000	1.0000	0.0000	0.0000	0.0000	0.0000	0.0000	0.0000
19	0.5263	0.6364	0.3077	0.6250	0.3333	0.5000	0.0000	1.0000	0.0000	0.0000	0.0000	0.0000	0.0000	0.0000
18	0.5263	0.6364	0.3077	0.6250	0.3333	0.5000	0.0000	1.0000	0.0000	0.0000	0.0000	0.0000	0.0000	0.0000
17	0.5263	0.6364	0.3077	0.6250	0.3333	0.5000	0.0000	1.0000	0.0000	0.0000	0.0000	0.0000	0.0000	0.0000
16	0.5263	0.6364	0.3077	0.6250	0.3333	0.5000	0.0000	1.0000	0.0000	0.0000	0.0000	0.0000	0.0000	0.0000
15	0.5789	0.6364	0.3846	0.6875	0.3333	1.0000	0.0000	1.0000	0.0000	0.0000	0.0000	0.0000	0.0000	0.0000
14	0.5789	0.6364	0.3846	0.7500	0.5000	1.0000	0.0000	1.0000	0.0000	0.0000	0.0000	0.0000	0.0000	0.0000
13	0.6842	0.6364	0.3846	0.7500	0.6667	1.0000	0.0000	1.0000	0.0000	0.0000	0.0000	0.0000	0.0000	0.0000
12	0.7895	0.6364	0.3846	0.7500	0.8333	1.0000	0.0000	1.0000	0.0000	0.0000	0.0000	0.0000	0.0000	0.0000
11	0.7895	0.6364	0.4615	0.6875	0.8333	1.0000	0.0000	1.0000	0.0000	0.0000	0.0000	0.0000	0.0000	0.0000
10	0.7895	0.7273	0.4615	0.6875	0.8333	1.0000	0.0000	1.0000	0.0000	0.0000	0.0000	0.0000	0.0000	0.0000
9	0.8421	0.7273	0.5385	0.8125	0.8333	1.0000	0.0000	1.0000	0.0000	0.0000	0.0000	0.0000	0.0000	0.0000
8	0.8421	0.7273	0.5385	0.8125	0.8333	1.0000	0.0000	1.0000	0.0000	0.0000	0.0000	0.0000	0.0000	0.0000
7	0.8421	0.7273	0.5385	0.8125	0.8333	0.5000	0.0000	1.0000	0.0000	0.0000	0.0000	0.0000	0.0000	0.0000
6	0.8421	0.7273	0.6154	0.8125	0.8333	0.5000	0.0000	1.0000	0.0000	0.0000	0.0000	0.0000	0.0000	0.0000
5	0.8421	0.7273	0.7692	0.8125	0.8333	0.5000	0.0000	1.0000	0.0000	0.0000	0.0000	0.0000	0.0000	0.0000
4	0.8421	0.7273	0.7692	0.7500	0.8333	0.5000	0.0000	1.0000	0.0000	0.0000	0.0000	0.0000	0.0000	0.0000
3	0.8421	0.7273	0.7692	0.7500	0.8333	0.5000	0.0000	1.0000	0.0000	0.0000	0.0000	0.0000	0.0000	0.0000
2	0.7895	0.7273	0.7692	0.7500	0.8333	0.5000	0.0000	1.0000	0.0000	0.0000	0.0000	0.0000	0.0000	0.0000
1	0.8421	0.7273	0.7692	0.7500	0.8333	0.5000	0.0000	1.0000	0.0000	0.0000	0.0000	0.0000	0.0000	0.0000
0	0.8421	0.7273	0.7692	0.7500	0.8333	0.5000	0.0000	1.0000	0.0000	0.0000	0.0000	0.0000	0.0000	0.0000
-1	0.8421	0.7273	0.7692	0.7500	0.8333	0.5000	0.0000	1.0000	0.0000	0.0000	0.0000	0.0000	0.0000	0.0000
-2	0.8947	0.7273	0.7692	0.7500	0.8333	0.5000	0.0000	1.0000	0.0000	0.0000	0.0000	0.0000	0.0000	0.0000
-3	0.8947	0.7273	0.7692	0.7500	0.6667	0.5000	0.0000	1.0000	0.0000	0.0000	0.0000	0.0000	0.0000	0.0000
-4	0.8947	0.7273	0.6923	0.7500	0.6667	0.5000	0.0000	1.0000	0.0000	0.0000	0.0000	0.0000	0.0000	0.0000
-5	0.8947	0.7273	0.6923	0.7500	0.6667	0.5000	0.0000	1.0000	0.0000	0.0000	0.0000	0.0000	0.0000	0.0000
-6	0.8947	0.6364	0.7692	0.6250	0.6667	0.5000	0.0000	1.0000	0.0000	0.0000	0.0000	0.0000	0.0000	0.0000
-7	0.8421	0.6364	0.7692	0.5625	0.6667	0.5000	0.0000	1.0000	0.0000	0.0000	0.0000	0.0000	0.0000	0.0000
-8	0.8421	0.6364	0.6923	0.5625	0.6667	0.5000	0.0000	0.0000	0.0000	0.0000	0.0000	0.0000	0.0000	0.0000
-9	0.8421	0.6364	0.6923	0.5000	0.6667	0.5000	0.0000	0.0000	0.0000	0.0000	0.0000	0.0000	0.0000	0.0000
-10	0.8421	0.4545	0.6923	0.4375	0.6667	0.5000	0.0000	0.0000	0.0000	0.0000	0.0000	0.0000	0.0000	0.0000

Main Condition 1 *(Continued)*   **Probabilities**

Tick Variation	\multicolumn{14}{c}{Secondary Conditions}													
	1	2	3	4	5	6	7	8	9	10	11	12	13	14
-11	0.7895	0.4545	0.6923	0.4375	0.6667	0.5000	0.0000	0.0000	0.0000	0.0000	0.0000	0.0000	0.0000	0.0000
-12	0.7895	0.4545	0.6923	0.3750	0.6667	0.5000	0.0000	0.0000	0.0000	0.0000	0.0000	0.0000	0.0000	0.0000
-13	0.7895	0.4545	0.6923	0.3125	0.6667	0.5000	0.0000	0.0000	0.0000	0.0000	0.0000	0.0000	0.0000	0.0000
-14	0.7895	0.6364	0.6923	0.3125	0.6667	0.0000	0.0000	0.0000	0.0000	0.0000	0.0000	0.0000	0.0000	0.0000
-15	0.7368	0.4545	0.6923	0.3125	0.6667	0.0000	0.0000	0.0000	0.0000	0.0000	0.0000	0.0000	0.0000	0.0000
-16	0.7368	0.4545	0.6923	0.3125	0.6667	0.0000	0.0000	0.0000	0.0000	0.0000	0.0000	0.0000	0.0000	0.0000
-17	0.6842	0.4545	0.6923	0.3125	0.6667	0.0000	0.0000	0.0000	0.0000	0.0000	0.0000	0.0000	0.0000	0.0000
-18	0.6316	0.3636	0.6923	0.3750	0.5000	0.0000	0.0000	0.0000	0.0000	0.0000	0.0000	0.0000	0.0000	0.0000
-19	0.6316	0.3636	0.6923	0.3750	0.5000	0.0000	0.0000	0.0000	0.0000	0.0000	0.0000	0.0000	0.0000	0.0000
-20	0.5789	0.3636	0.6923	0.3125	0.5000	0.0000	0.0000	0.0000	0.0000	0.0000	0.0000	0.0000	0.0000	0.0000
-21	0.5789	0.3636	0.6154	0.2500	0.5000	0.0000	0.0000	0.0000	0.0000	0.0000	0.0000	0.0000	0.0000	0.0000
-22	0.5789	0.3636	0.5385	0.2500	0.3333	0.0000	0.0000	0.0000	0.0000	0.0000	0.0000	0.0000	0.0000	0.0000
-23	0.5263	0.3636	0.5385	0.2500	0.3333	0.0000	0.0000	0.0000	0.0000	0.0000	0.0000	0.0000	0.0000	0.0000
-24	0.5263	0.3636	0.5385	0.1875	0.3333	0.0000	0.0000	0.0000	0.0000	0.0000	0.0000	0.0000	0.0000	0.0000
-25	0.5263	0.3636	0.3846	0.1875	0.3333	0.0000	0.0000	0.0000	0.0000	0.0000	0.0000	0.0000	0.0000	0.0000
-26	0.4737	0.3636	0.3077	0.1875	0.3333	0.0000	0.0000	0.0000	0.0000	0.0000	0.0000	0.0000	0.0000	0.0000
-27	0.4737	0.3636	0.2308	0.1875	0.3333	0.0000	0.0000	0.0000	0.0000	0.0000	0.0000	0.0000	0.0000	0.0000
-28	0.3684	0.2727	0.2308	0.1875	0.3333	0.0000	0.0000	0.0000	0.0000	0.0000	0.0000	0.0000	0.0000	0.0000
-29	0.3684	0.2727	0.2308	0.1875	0.3333	0.0000	0.0000	0.0000	0.0000	0.0000	0.0000	0.0000	0.0000	0.0000
-30	0.3684	0.2727	0.2308	0.1875	0.3333	0.0000	0.0000	0.0000	0.0000	0.0000	0.0000	0.0000	0.0000	0.0000
-31	0.3684	0.1818	0.2308	0.1875	0.3333	0.0000	0.0000	0.0000	0.0000	0.0000	0.0000	0.0000	0.0000	0.0000
-32	0.3684	0.1818	0.2308	0.1875	0.3333	0.0000	0.0000	0.0000	0.0000	0.0000	0.0000	0.0000	0.0000	0.0000
-33	0.3684	0.1818	0.2308	0.1875	0.3333	0.0000	0.0000	0.0000	0.0000	0.0000	0.0000	0.0000	0.0000	0.0000
-34	0.3684	0.1818	0.2308	0.1875	0.3333	0.0000	0.0000	0.0000	0.0000	0.0000	0.0000	0.0000	0.0000	0.0000
-35	0.3158	0.1818	0.2308	0.1875	0.3333	0.0000	0.0000	0.0000	0.0000	0.0000	0.0000	0.0000	0.0000	0.0000
-36	0.3158	0.1818	0.2308	0.1875	0.3333	0.0000	0.0000	0.0000	0.0000	0.0000	0.0000	0.0000	0.0000	0.0000
-37	0.3158	0.1818	0.2308	0.1875	0.3333	0.0000	0.0000	0.0000	0.0000	0.0000	0.0000	0.0000	0.0000	0.0000
-38	0.3158	0.0909	0.2308	0.1875	0.3333	0.0000	0.0000	0.0000	0.0000	0.0000	0.0000	0.0000	0.0000	0.0000
-39	0.3158	0.0909	0.1538	0.1875	0.3333	0.0000	0.0000	0.0000	0.0000	0.0000	0.0000	0.0000	0.0000	0.0000
-40	0.2632	0.0909	0.1538	0.1875	0.3333	0.0000	0.0000	0.0000	0.0000	0.0000	0.0000	0.0000	0.0000	0.0000
-41	0.2632	0.0909	0.0769	0.1875	0.1667	0.0000	0.0000	0.0000	0.0000	0.0000	0.0000	0.0000	0.0000	0.0000
-42	0.2632	0.0000	0.0769	0.1875	0.1667	0.0000	0.0000	0.0000	0.0000	0.0000	0.0000	0.0000	0.0000	0.0000
-43	0.2632	0.0000	0.0769	0.1875	0.1667	0.0000	0.0000	0.0000	0.0000	0.0000	0.0000	0.0000	0.0000	0.0000
-44	0.2632	0.0000	0.0769	0.1875	0.1667	0.0000	0.0000	0.0000	0.0000	0.0000	0.0000	0.0000	0.0000	0.0000
-45	0.2105	0.0000	0.0769	0.1875	0.1667	0.0000	0.0000	0.0000	0.0000	0.0000	0.0000	0.0000	0.0000	0.0000
-46	0.2105	0.0000	0.0769	0.1875	0.1667	0.0000	0.0000	0.0000	0.0000	0.0000	0.0000	0.0000	0.0000	0.0000
-47	0.2105	0.0000	0.0769	0.1875	0.1667	0.0000	0.0000	0.0000	0.0000	0.0000	0.0000	0.0000	0.0000	0.0000
-48	0.2105	0.0000	0.0769	0.1875	0.1667	0.0000	0.0000	0.0000	0.0000	0.0000	0.0000	0.0000	0.0000	0.0000
-49	0.2105	0.0000	0.0769	0.1875	0.1667	0.0000	0.0000	0.0000	0.0000	0.0000	0.0000	0.0000	0.0000	0.0000
-50	0.2105	0.0000	0.0000	0.1875	0.1667	0.0000	0.0000	0.0000	0.0000	0.0000	0.0000	0.0000	0.0000	0.0000
-51	0.2105	0.0000	0.0000	0.1875	0.1667	0.0000	0.0000	0.0000	0.0000	0.0000	0.0000	0.0000	0.0000	0.0000
-52	0.2105	0.0000	0.0000	0.1875	0.1667	0.0000	0.0000	0.0000	0.0000	0.0000	0.0000	0.0000	0.0000	0.0000
-53	0.2105	0.0000	0.0000	0.1250	0.1667	0.0000	0.0000	0.0000	0.0000	0.0000	0.0000	0.0000	0.0000	0.0000
-54	0.1579	0.0000	0.0000	0.1250	0.1667	0.0000	0.0000	0.0000	0.0000	0.0000	0.0000	0.0000	0.0000	0.0000
-55	0.1579	0.0000	0.0000	0.1250	0.1667	0.0000	0.0000	0.0000	0.0000	0.0000	0.0000	0.0000	0.0000	0.0000
-56	0.1579	0.0000	0.0000	0.1250	0.1667	0.0000	0.0000	0.0000	0.0000	0.0000	0.0000	0.0000	0.0000	0.0000
-57	0.1579	0.0000	0.0000	0.1250	0.1667	0.0000	0.0000	0.0000	0.0000	0.0000	0.0000	0.0000	0.0000	0.0000
-58	0.1053	0.0000	0.0000	0.1250	0.1667	0.0000	0.0000	0.0000	0.0000	0.0000	0.0000	0.0000	0.0000	0.0000
-59	0.1053	0.0000	0.0000	0.1250	0.1667	0.0000	0.0000	0.0000	0.0000	0.0000	0.0000	0.0000	0.0000	0.0000
-60	0.1053	0.0000	0.0000	0.1250	0.1667	0.0000	0.0000	0.0000	0.0000	0.0000	0.0000	0.0000	0.0000	0.0000
-61	0.1053	0.0000	0.0000	0.1250	0.1667	0.0000	0.0000	0.0000	0.0000	0.0000	0.0000	0.0000	0.0000	0.0000
-62	0.1053	0.0000	0.0000	0.0625	0.1667	0.0000	0.0000	0.0000	0.0000	0.0000	0.0000	0.0000	0.0000	0.0000
-63	0.1053	0.0000	0.0000	0.0625	0.1667	0.0000	0.0000	0.0000	0.0000	0.0000	0.0000	0.0000	0.0000	0.0000
-64	0.1053	0.0000	0.0000	0.0000	0.1667	0.0000	0.0000	0.0000	0.0000	0.0000	0.0000	0.0000	0.0000	0.0000

Main Condition 2   Probabilities

Secondary Conditions

Tick Variation	1	2	3	4	5	6	7	8	9	10	11	12	13	14
64	0.0000	0.0000	0.0909	0.0000	0.0000	0.0000	0.0000	0.0000	0.0000	0.0000	0.0000	0.0000	0.0000	0.0000
63	0.0000	0.0000	0.0909	0.0000	0.0000	0.0000	0.0000	0.0000	0.0000	0.0000	0.0000	0.0000	0.0000	0.0000
62	0.0000	0.0000	0.0909	0.0000	0.0833	0.0000	0.0000	0.0000	0.0000	0.0000	0.0000	0.0000	0.0000	0.0000
61	0.0000	0.0000	0.0909	0.0000	0.0833	0.0000	0.0000	0.0000	0.0000	0.0000	0.0000	0.0000	0.0000	0.0000
60	0.0000	0.0000	0.0909	0.0000	0.0833	0.0000	0.0000	0.0000	0.0000	0.0000	0.0000	0.0000	0.0000	0.0000
59	0.0000	0.0000	0.0909	0.0000	0.0833	0.0000	0.0000	0.0000	0.0000	0.0000	0.0000	0.0000	0.0000	0.0000
58	0.0000	0.0000	0.0909	0.0000	0.0833	0.0000	0.0000	0.0000	0.0000	0.0000	0.0000	0.0000	0.0000	0.0000
57	0.0000	0.0000	0.0909	0.0556	0.0833	0.0000	0.0000	0.0000	0.0000	0.0000	0.0000	0.0000	0.0000	0.0000
56	0.0000	0.0000	0.0909	0.0556	0.0833	0.0000	0.0000	0.0000	0.0000	0.0000	0.0000	0.0000	0.0000	0.0000
55	0.0000	0.0000	0.0909	0.0556	0.0833	0.0000	0.0000	0.0000	0.0000	0.0000	0.0000	0.0000	0.0000	0.0000
54	0.0000	0.0000	0.0909	0.0556	0.0833	0.0000	0.0000	0.0000	0.0000	0.0000	0.0000	0.0000	0.0000	0.0000
53	0.0000	0.0000	0.0909	0.1111	0.0833	0.0000	0.0000	0.0000	0.0000	0.0000	0.0000	0.0000	0.0000	0.0000
52	0.0000	0.0000	0.0909	0.1111	0.0833	0.0000	0.0000	0.0000	0.0000	0.0000	0.0000	0.0000	0.0000	0.0000
51	0.0000	0.0000	0.0909	0.1111	0.0833	0.0000	0.0000	0.0000	0.0000	0.0000	0.0000	0.0000	0.0000	0.0000
50	0.0000	0.0000	0.0909	0.1111	0.0833	0.0000	0.0000	0.0000	0.0000	0.0000	0.0000	0.0000	0.0000	0.0000
49	0.0000	0.0000	0.0909	0.1111	0.0833	0.0000	0.0000	0.0000	0.0000	0.0000	0.0000	0.0000	0.0000	0.0000
48	0.0000	0.0000	0.0909	0.1111	0.1667	0.0000	0.0000	0.0000	0.0000	0.0000	0.0000	0.0000	0.0000	0.0000
47	0.0000	0.0000	0.0909	0.1111	0.1667	0.0000	0.0000	0.0000	0.0000	0.0000	0.0000	0.0000	0.0000	0.0000
46	0.0000	0.0000	0.0909	0.1111	0.1667	0.0000	0.0000	0.0000	0.0000	0.0000	0.0000	0.0000	0.0000	0.0000
45	0.0000	0.0000	0.0909	0.1111	0.1667	0.0000	0.0000	0.0000	0.0000	0.0000	0.0000	0.0000	0.0000	0.0000
44	0.0000	0.0000	0.0909	0.1111	0.1667	0.0000	0.0000	0.0000	0.0000	0.0000	0.0000	0.0000	0.0000	0.0000
43	0.0000	0.0000	0.0909	0.1667	0.1667	0.2500	0.0000	0.0000	0.0000	0.0000	0.0000	0.0000	0.0000	0.0000
42	0.0000	0.0000	0.0909	0.1667	0.1667	0.2500	0.0000	0.0000	0.0000	0.0000	0.0000	0.0000	0.0000	0.0000
41	0.0000	0.0000	0.0909	0.1667	0.1667	0.2500	0.0000	0.0000	0.0000	0.0000	0.0000	0.0000	0.0000	0.0000
40	0.0000	0.1667	0.0909	0.2222	0.1667	0.2500	0.0000	0.0000	0.0000	0.0000	0.0000	0.0000	0.0000	0.0000
39	0.0000	0.1667	0.0909	0.2222	0.1667	0.2500	0.0000	0.0000	0.0000	0.0000	0.0000	0.0000	0.0000	0.0000
38	0.0000	0.1667	0.0909	0.2222	0.1667	0.2500	0.0000	0.0000	0.0000	0.0000	0.0000	0.0000	0.0000	0.0000
37	0.0000	0.1667	0.0909	0.2222	0.1667	0.2500	0.0000	0.0000	0.0000	0.0000	0.0000	0.0000	0.0000	0.0000
36	0.0000	0.1667	0.0909	0.2222	0.1667	0.2500	0.5000	0.0000	0.0000	0.0000	0.0000	0.0000	0.0000	0.0000
35	0.0000	0.1667	0.0909	0.2222	0.2500	0.2500	0.5000	0.0000	0.0000	0.0000	0.0000	0.0000	0.0000	0.0000
34	0.0000	0.1667	0.0909	0.2222	0.2500	0.2500	0.5000	0.0000	0.0000	0.0000	0.0000	0.0000	0.0000	0.0000
33	0.0000	0.1667	0.0909	0.2222	0.2500	0.2500	0.5000	0.0000	0.0000	0.0000	0.0000	0.0000	0.0000	0.0000
32	0.0000	0.1667	0.0909	0.2222	0.2500	0.2500	0.5000	0.0000	0.0000	0.0000	0.0000	0.0000	0.0000	0.0000
31	0.0000	0.1667	0.0909	0.2222	0.2500	0.2500	0.5000	0.0000	0.0000	0.0000	0.0000	0.0000	0.0000	0.0000
30	0.0000	0.1667	0.0909	0.2222	0.2500	0.2500	0.5000	0.0000	0.0000	0.0000	0.0000	0.0000	0.0000	0.0000
29	0.0000	0.3333	0.0909	0.2778	0.2500	0.2500	0.5000	0.0000	0.0000	0.0000	0.0000	0.0000	0.0000	0.0000
28	0.0000	0.3333	0.0909	0.2778	0.2500	0.2500	0.5000	0.3333	0.0000	0.0000	0.0000	0.0000	0.0000	0.0000
27	0.0000	0.3333	0.0909	0.3333	0.2500	0.2500	0.5000	0.3333	0.0000	0.0000	0.0000	0.0000	0.0000	0.0000
26	0.0000	0.5000	0.0909	0.3333	0.2500	0.2500	0.5000	0.3333	0.0000	0.0000	0.0000	0.0000	0.0000	0.0000
25	0.0000	0.5000	0.0909	0.3333	0.2500	0.2500	0.5000	0.3333	0.0000	0.0000	0.0000	0.0000	0.0000	0.0000
24	0.0000	0.5000	0.0909	0.3333	0.2500	0.2500	0.5000	0.6667	0.0000	0.0000	0.0000	0.0000	0.0000	0.0000
23	0.0000	0.5000	0.1818	0.3889	0.2500	0.2500	0.5000	1.0000	0.0000	0.0000	0.0000	0.0000	0.0000	0.0000
22	0.0000	0.5000	0.1818	0.3889	0.2500	0.2500	0.5000	1.0000	0.0000	0.0000	0.0000	0.0000	0.0000	0.0000
21	0.0000	0.5000	0.1818	0.3889	0.2500	0.2500	0.5000	1.0000	0.0000	0.0000	0.0000	0.0000	0.0000	0.0000
20	0.0000	0.5000	0.1818	0.3889	0.3333	0.0000	0.5000	1.0000	0.0000	0.0000	0.0000	0.0000	0.0000	0.0000
19	0.0000	0.5000	0.1818	0.3889	0.2500	0.0000	0.5000	1.0000	0.0000	0.0000	0.0000	0.0000	0.0000	0.0000
18	0.0000	0.8333	0.0909	0.3333	0.2500	0.0000	0.5000	1.0000	0.0000	0.0000	0.0000	0.0000	0.0000	0.0000
17	0.0000	0.8333	0.0909	0.3889	0.2500	0.0000	0.5000	1.0000	0.0000	0.0000	0.0000	0.0000	0.0000	0.0000
16	0.0000	0.8333	0.1818	0.3889	0.2500	0.0000	0.5000	1.0000	0.0000	0.0000	0.0000	0.0000	0.0000	0.0000
15	0.0000	0.8333	0.1818	0.3889	0.1667	0.2500	0.5000	1.0000	0.0000	0.0000	0.0000	0.0000	0.0000	0.0000
14	0.0000	0.8333	0.1818	0.3889	0.1667	0.2500	0.5000	1.0000	0.0000	0.0000	0.0000	0.0000	0.0000	0.0000
13	0.0000	0.8333	0.1818	0.4444	0.2500	0.2500	0.5000	1.0000	0.0000	0.0000	0.0000	0.0000	0.0000	0.0000
12	0.0000	0.8333	0.1818	0.6667	0.2500	0.2500	1.0000	1.0000	0.0000	0.0000	0.0000	0.0000	0.0000	0.0000
11	0.0000	0.8333	0.1818	0.6667	0.3333	0.5000	1.0000	1.0000	0.0000	0.0000	0.0000	0.0000	0.0000	0.0000
10	0.0000	0.8333	0.1818	0.6667	0.4167	0.5000	1.0000	1.0000	0.0000	0.0000	0.0000	0.0000	0.0000	0.0000
9	0.0000	0.8333	0.2727	0.7222	0.4167	0.5000	1.0000	1.0000	0.0000	0.0000	0.0000	0.0000	0.0000	0.0000
8	0.0000	0.8333	0.2727	0.7778	0.4167	0.5000	1.0000	1.0000	0.0000	0.0000	0.0000	0.0000	0.0000	0.0000
7	0.0000	0.8333	0.2727	0.7222	0.5000	0.5000	1.0000	1.0000	0.0000	0.0000	0.0000	0.0000	0.0000	0.0000
6	0.0000	0.8333	0.2727	0.8333	0.5000	0.7500	1.0000	1.0000	0.0000	0.0000	0.0000	0.0000	0.0000	0.0000
5	0.0000	0.8333	0.3636	0.8333	0.5000	0.7500	1.0000	1.0000	0.0000	0.0000	0.0000	0.0000	0.0000	0.0000
4	0.0000	0.8333	0.4545	0.8333	0.5000	0.7500	1.0000	1.0000	0.0000	0.0000	0.0000	0.0000	0.0000	0.0000
3	0.0000	0.8333	0.4545	0.7778	0.5000	0.7500	1.0000	1.0000	0.0000	0.0000	0.0000	0.0000	0.0000	0.0000
2	0.0000	0.8333	0.5455	0.7778	0.5000	0.7500	1.0000	1.0000	0.0000	0.0000	0.0000	0.0000	0.0000	0.0000
1	0.0000	0.8333	0.5455	0.7778	0.5000	0.7500	1.0000	1.0000	0.0000	0.0000	0.0000	0.0000	0.0000	0.0000
0	0.0000	0.8333	0.5455	0.7778	0.5000	0.7500	1.0000	1.0000	0.0000	0.0000	0.0000	0.0000	0.0000	0.0000
−1	0.0000	0.8333	0.5455	0.7778	0.5833	0.7500	1.0000	1.0000	0.0000	0.0000	0.0000	0.0000	0.0000	0.0000
−2	0.0000	0.8333	0.5455	0.7778	0.6667	0.7500	1.0000	1.0000	0.0000	0.0000	0.0000	0.0000	0.0000	0.0000
−3	0.0000	0.8333	0.5455	0.7778	0.5833	0.7500	1.0000	1.0000	0.0000	0.0000	0.0000	0.0000	0.0000	0.0000
−4	0.0000	0.8333	0.6364	0.7222	0.5833	0.7500	1.0000	1.0000	0.0000	0.0000	0.0000	0.0000	0.0000	0.0000
−5	0.0000	0.8333	0.6364	0.7222	0.5833	0.7500	1.0000	1.0000	0.0000	0.0000	0.0000	0.0000	0.0000	0.0000
−6	0.0000	0.6667	0.6364	0.7222	0.5833	0.7500	1.0000	1.0000	0.0000	0.0000	0.0000	0.0000	0.0000	0.0000
−7	0.0000	0.6667	0.6364	0.7222	0.6667	0.5000	1.0000	1.0000	0.0000	0.0000	0.0000	0.0000	0.0000	0.0000
−8	0.0000	0.6667	0.6364	0.7222	0.6667	0.5000	1.0000	1.0000	0.0000	0.0000	0.0000	0.0000	0.0000	0.0000
−9	0.0000	0.6667	0.5455	0.6667	0.6667	0.5000	1.0000	1.0000	0.0000	0.0000	0.0000	0.0000	0.0000	0.0000
−10	0.0000	0.6667	0.5455	0.6111	0.6667	0.5000	1.0000	1.0000	0.0000	0.0000	0.0000	0.0000	0.0000	0.0000

Main Condition 2 *(Continued)*   Probabilities

Tick Variation	1	2	3	4	5	6	7	8	9	10	11	12	13	14
								Secondary Conditions						
−11	0.0000	0.6667	0.4545	0.5556	0.6667	0.5000	1.0000	1.0000	0.0000	0.0000	0.0000	0.0000	0.0000	0.0000
−12	0.0000	0.5000	0.4545	0.5000	0.6667	0.5000	1.0000	1.0000	0.0000	0.0000	0.0000	0.0000	0.0000	0.0000
−13	0.0000	0.3333	0.4545	0.4444	0.6667	0.5000	0.5000	1.0000	0.0000	0.0000	0.0000	0.0000	0.0000	0.0000
−14	0.0000	0.3333	0.4545	0.4444	0.6667	0.5000	0.5000	1.0000	0.0000	0.0000	0.0000	0.0000	0.0000	0.0000
−15	0.0000	0.3333	0.4545	0.3889	0.6667	0.5000	0.0000	1.0000	0.0000	0.0000	0.0000	0.0000	0.0000	0.0000
−16	0.0000	0.3333	0.4545	0.3889	0.6667	0.5000	0.0000	1.0000	0.0000	0.0000	0.0000	0.0000	0.0000	0.0000
−17	0.0000	0.3333	0.4545	0.3333	0.6667	0.5000	0.0000	1.0000	0.0000	0.0000	0.0000	0.0000	0.0000	0.0000
−18	0.0000	0.3333	0.4545	0.3333	0.5833	0.5000	0.0000	1.0000	0.0000	0.0000	0.0000	0.0000	0.0000	0.0000
−19	0.0000	0.3333	0.4545	0.3333	0.5833	0.5000	0.0000	1.0000	0.0000	0.0000	0.0000	0.0000	0.0000	0.0000
−20	0.0000	0.3333	0.4545	0.3333	0.5833	0.2500	0.0000	1.0000	0.0000	0.0000	0.0000	0.0000	0.0000	0.0000
−21	0.0000	0.3333	0.4545	0.3333	0.4167	0.2500	0.0000	1.0000	0.0000	0.0000	0.0000	0.0000	0.0000	0.0000
−22	0.0000	0.3333	0.3636	0.2222	0.3333	0.2500	0.0000	1.0000	0.0000	0.0000	0.0000	0.0000	0.0000	0.0000
−23	0.0000	0.3333	0.3636	0.2222	0.3333	0.2500	0.0000	1.0000	0.0000	0.0000	0.0000	0.0000	0.0000	0.0000
−24	0.0000	0.3333	0.3636	0.2222	0.3333	0.2500	0.0000	1.0000	0.0000	0.0000	0.0000	0.0000	0.0000	0.0000
−25	0.0000	0.3333	0.2727	0.1667	0.3333	0.2500	0.0000	1.0000	0.0000	0.0000	0.0000	0.0000	0.0000	0.0000
−26	0.0000	0.3333	0.2727	0.1667	0.2500	0.2500	0.0000	1.0000	0.0000	0.0000	0.0000	0.0000	0.0000	0.0000
−27	0.0000	0.3333	0.1818	0.1667	0.2500	0.2500	0.0000	1.0000	0.0000	0.0000	0.0000	0.0000	0.0000	0.0000
−28	0.0000	0.3333	0.0909	0.1667	0.0833	0.2500	0.0000	1.0000	0.0000	0.0000	0.0000	0.0000	0.0000	0.0000
−29	0.0000	0.3333	0.0909	0.1667	0.0833	0.2500	0.0000	0.6667	0.0000	0.0000	0.0000	0.0000	0.0000	0.0000
−30	0.0000	0.3333	0.0909	0.0556	0.0833	0.2500	0.0000	0.6667	0.0000	0.0000	0.0000	0.0000	0.0000	0.0000
−31	0.0000	0.3333	0.0909	0.0556	0.0833	0.2500	0.0000	0.6667	0.0000	0.0000	0.0000	0.0000	0.0000	0.0000
−32	0.0000	0.3333	0.0909	0.0556	0.0833	0.2500	0.0000	0.6667	0.0000	0.0000	0.0000	0.0000	0.0000	0.0000
−33	0.0000	0.3333	0.1818	0.0556	0.0833	0.2500	0.0000	0.6667	0.0000	0.0000	0.0000	0.0000	0.0000	0.0000
−34	0.0000	0.3333	0.0909	0.0556	0.0833	0.2500	0.0000	0.3333	0.0000	0.0000	0.0000	0.0000	0.0000	0.0000
−35	0.0000	0.1667	0.0909	0.0556	0.0833	0.2500	0.0000	0.3333	0.0000	0.0000	0.0000	0.0000	0.0000	0.0000
−36	0.0000	0.1667	0.0909	0.0556	0.0000	0.2500	0.0000	0.3333	0.0000	0.0000	0.0000	0.0000	0.0000	0.0000
−37	0.0000	0.1667	0.0909	0.0556	0.0000	0.2500	0.0000	0.3333	0.0000	0.0000	0.0000	0.0000	0.0000	0.0000
−38	0.0000	0.1667	0.0909	0.0556	0.0000	0.2500	0.0000	0.3333	0.0000	0.0000	0.0000	0.0000	0.0000	0.0000
−39	0.0000	0.1667	0.0909	0.0556	0.0000	0.2500	0.0000	0.0000	0.0000	0.0000	0.0000	0.0000	0.0000	0.0000
−40	0.0000	0.1667	0.0909	0.0556	0.0000	0.2500	0.0000	0.0000	0.0000	0.0000	0.0000	0.0000	0.0000	0.0000
−41	0.0000	0.1667	0.0909	0.0556	0.0000	0.2500	0.0000	0.0000	0.0000	0.0000	0.0000	0.0000	0.0000	0.0000
−42	0.0000	0.0000	0.0909	0.0556	0.0000	0.2500	0.0000	0.0000	0.0000	0.0000	0.0000	0.0000	0.0000	0.0000
−43	0.0000	0.0000	0.0909	0.0556	0.0000	0.2500	0.0000	0.0000	0.0000	0.0000	0.0000	0.0000	0.0000	0.0000
−44	0.0000	0.0000	0.0909	0.0000	0.0000	0.2500	0.0000	0.0000	0.0000	0.0000	0.0000	0.0000	0.0000	0.0000
−45	0.0000	0.0000	0.0909	0.0000	0.0000	0.2500	0.0000	0.0000	0.0000	0.0000	0.0000	0.0000	0.0000	0.0000
−46	0.0000	0.0000	0.0909	0.0000	0.0000	0.2500	0.0000	0.0000	0.0000	0.0000	0.0000	0.0000	0.0000	0.0000
−47	0.0000	0.0000	0.0909	0.0000	0.0000	0.2500	0.0000	0.0000	0.0000	0.0000	0.0000	0.0000	0.0000	0.0000
−48	0.0000	0.0000	0.0909	0.0000	0.0000	0.2500	0.0000	0.0000	0.0000	0.0000	0.0000	0.0000	0.0000	0.0000
−49	0.0000	0.0000	0.0909	0.0000	0.0000	0.2500	0.0000	0.0000	0.0000	0.0000	0.0000	0.0000	0.0000	0.0000
−50	0.0000	0.0000	0.0909	0.0000	0.0000	0.2500	0.0000	0.0000	0.0000	0.0000	0.0000	0.0000	0.0000	0.0000
−51	0.0000	0.0000	0.0909	0.0000	0.0000	0.2500	0.0000	0.0000	0.0000	0.0000	0.0000	0.0000	0.0000	0.0000
−52	0.0000	0.0000	0.0909	0.0000	0.0000	0.2500	0.0000	0.0000	0.0000	0.0000	0.0000	0.0000	0.0000	0.0000
−53	0.0000	0.0000	0.0000	0.0000	0.0000	0.2500	0.0000	0.0000	0.0000	0.0000	0.0000	0.0000	0.0000	0.0000
−54	0.0000	0.0000	0.0000	0.0000	0.0000	0.2500	0.0000	0.0000	0.0000	0.0000	0.0000	0.0000	0.0000	0.0000
−55	0.0000	0.0000	0.0000	0.0000	0.0000	0.2500	0.0000	0.0000	0.0000	0.0000	0.0000	0.0000	0.0000	0.0000
−56	0.0000	0.0000	0.0000	0.0000	0.0000	0.2500	0.0000	0.0000	0.0000	0.0000	0.0000	0.0000	0.0000	0.0000
−57	0.0000	0.0000	0.0000	0.0000	0.0000	0.2500	0.0000	0.0000	0.0000	0.0000	0.0000	0.0000	0.0000	0.0000
−58	0.0000	0.0000	0.0000	0.0000	0.0000	0.2500	0.0000	0.0000	0.0000	0.0000	0.0000	0.0000	0.0000	0.0000
−59	0.0000	0.0000	0.0000	0.0000	0.0000	0.2500	0.0000	0.0000	0.0000	0.0000	0.0000	0.0000	0.0000	0.0000
−60	0.0000	0.0000	0.0000	0.0000	0.0000	0.2500	0.0000	0.0000	0.0000	0.0000	0.0000	0.0000	0.0000	0.0000
−61	0.0000	0.0000	0.0000	0.0000	0.0000	0.2500	0.0000	0.0000	0.0000	0.0000	0.0000	0.0000	0.0000	0.0000
−62	0.0000	0.0000	0.0000	0.0000	0.0000	0.2500	0.0000	0.0000	0.0000	0.0000	0.0000	0.0000	0.0000	0.0000
−63	0.0000	0.0000	0.0000	0.0000	0.0000	0.2500	0.0000	0.0000	0.0000	0.0000	0.0000	0.0000	0.0000	0.0000
−64	0.0000	0.0000	0.0000	0.0000	0.0000	0.2500	0.0000	0.0000	0.0000	0.0000	0.0000	0.0000	0.0000	0.0000

Main Condition 3 — **Probabilities**

Tick Variation	Secondary Conditions													
	1	2	3	4	5	6	7	8	9	10	11	12	13	14
64	0.0000	0.0000	0.0000	0.0370	0.0323	0.0556	0.0000	0.0000	0.0000	0.0000	0.0000	0.0000	0.0000	0.0000
63	0.0000	0.0000	0.0000	0.0370	0.0645	0.0556	0.0000	0.0000	0.0000	0.0000	0.0000	0.0000	0.0000	0.0000
62	0.0000	0.0000	0.0000	0.0741	0.0968	0.0556	0.0000	0.0000	0.0000	0.0000	0.0000	0.0000	0.0000	0.0000
61	0.0000	0.0000	0.0000	0.0741	0.0968	0.0556	0.0000	0.0000	0.0000	0.0000	0.0000	0.0000	0.0000	0.0000
60	0.0000	0.0000	0.0000	0.0741	0.0968	0.0556	0.0000	0.0000	0.0000	0.0000	0.0000	0.0000	0.0000	0.0000
59	0.0000	0.0000	0.0000	0.0741	0.0968	0.0556	0.0000	0.0000	0.0000	0.0000	0.0000	0.0000	0.0000	0.0000
58	0.0000	0.0000	0.0000	0.0741	0.0968	0.0556	0.0000	0.0000	0.0000	0.0000	0.0000	0.0000	0.0000	0.0000
57	0.0000	0.0000	0.0000	0.0741	0.0968	0.0556	0.0000	0.0000	0.0000	0.0000	0.0000	0.0000	0.0000	0.0000
56	0.0000	0.0000	0.0000	0.0741	0.0968	0.0556	0.0000	0.0000	0.0000	0.0000	0.0000	0.0000	0.0000	0.0000
55	0.0000	0.0000	0.0000	0.0741	0.0968	0.0556	0.0000	0.0000	0.0000	0.0000	0.0000	0.0000	0.0000	0.0000
54	0.0000	0.0000	0.0000	0.0741	0.0968	0.0556	0.0000	0.0000	0.0000	0.0000	0.0000	0.0000	0.0000	0.0000
53	0.0000	0.0000	0.0000	0.0741	0.0968	0.0556	0.0000	0.0000	0.0000	0.0000	0.0000	0.0000	0.0000	0.0000
52	0.0000	0.0000	0.0000	0.0741	0.0968	0.0556	0.0000	0.0000	0.0000	0.0000	0.0000	0.0000	0.0000	0.0000
51	0.0000	0.0000	0.0000	0.0741	0.0968	0.0556	0.0000	0.0000	0.0000	0.0000	0.0000	0.0000	0.0000	0.0000
50	0.0000	0.0000	0.0000	0.0741	0.0968	0.0556	0.0000	0.0000	0.0000	0.0000	0.0000	0.0000	0.0000	0.0000
49	0.0000	0.0000	0.0000	0.0741	0.0968	0.0556	0.0000	0.0000	0.0000	0.0000	0.0000	0.0000	0.0000	0.0000
48	0.0000	0.0000	0.0000	0.0741	0.0968	0.0556	0.0000	0.0000	0.0000	0.0000	0.0000	0.0000	0.0000	0.0000
47	0.0000	0.0000	0.0000	0.0741	0.0968	0.0556	0.0000	0.0000	0.0000	0.0000	0.0000	0.0000	0.0000	0.0000
46	0.0000	0.0000	0.0000	0.0741	0.0968	0.0556	0.0000	0.0000	0.0000	0.0000	0.0000	0.0000	0.0000	0.0000
45	0.0000	0.0000	0.0000	0.1111	0.0968	0.0556	0.0000	0.0000	0.0000	0.0000	0.0000	0.0000	0.0000	0.0000
44	0.0000	0.0000	0.0000	0.1111	0.0968	0.0556	0.0000	0.0000	0.0000	0.0000	0.0000	0.0000	0.0000	0.0000
43	0.0000	0.0000	0.0000	0.1111	0.0968	0.0556	0.0000	0.0000	0.0000	0.0000	0.0000	0.0000	0.0000	0.0000
42	0.0000	0.0000	0.0000	0.1111	0.1290	0.0556	0.0000	0.0000	0.0000	0.0000	0.0000	0.0000	0.0000	0.0000
41	0.0000	0.5000	0.0000	0.1481	0.1290	0.0556	0.0000	0.0000	0.0000	0.0000	0.0000	0.0000	0.0000	0.0000
40	0.0000	0.5000	0.0000	0.1481	0.1290	0.0556	0.0000	0.0000	0.0000	0.0000	0.0000	0.0000	0.0000	0.0000
39	0.0000	0.5000	0.1111	0.1852	0.1290	0.0556	0.0000	0.0000	0.0000	0.0000	0.0000	0.0000	0.0000	0.0000
38	0.0000	0.5000	0.1111	0.1852	0.1290	0.0556	0.0000	0.0000	0.0000	0.0000	0.0000	0.0000	0.0000	0.0000
37	0.0000	0.5000	0.1111	0.1852	0.1290	0.0556	0.2000	0.0000	0.0000	0.0000	0.0000	0.0000	0.0000	0.0000
36	0.0000	0.5000	0.1111	0.1852	0.1290	0.0556	0.4000	0.0000	0.0000	0.0000	0.0000	0.0000	0.0000	0.0000
35	0.0000	0.5000	0.1111	0.1852	0.1290	0.1667	0.4000	0.0000	1.0000	0.0000	0.0000	0.0000	0.0000	0.0000
34	0.0000	0.5000	0.1111	0.1852	0.1290	0.1667	0.4000	0.0000	1.0000	0.0000	0.0000	0.0000	0.0000	0.0000
33	0.0000	0.5000	0.1111	0.1852	0.1290	0.1667	0.4000	0.0000	1.0000	0.0000	0.0000	0.0000	0.0000	0.0000
32	0.0000	0.5000	0.1111	0.1852	0.1290	0.1667	0.4000	0.0000	1.0000	0.0000	0.0000	0.0000	0.0000	0.0000
31	0.0000	0.5000	0.1111	0.1852	0.1613	0.2778	0.4000	0.0000	1.0000	0.0000	0.0000	0.0000	0.0000	0.0000
30	0.0000	0.5000	0.1111	0.2222	0.1935	0.3333	0.4000	0.0000	1.0000	0.0000	0.0000	0.0000	0.0000	0.0000
29	0.0000	0.5000	0.1111	0.2222	0.1935	0.3333	0.4000	0.0000	1.0000	0.0000	0.0000	0.0000	0.0000	0.0000
28	0.0000	0.5000	0.1111	0.2222	0.1935	0.3333	0.4000	0.0000	1.0000	0.0000	0.0000	0.0000	0.0000	0.0000
27	0.0000	0.5000	0.1111	0.2222	0.1935	0.3333	0.4000	0.0000	1.0000	0.0000	0.0000	0.0000	0.0000	0.0000
26	0.0000	0.5000	0.1111	0.2222	0.1935	0.3333	0.4000	0.0000	1.0000	0.0000	0.0000	0.0000	0.0000	0.0000
25	0.0000	0.5000	0.2222	0.2222	0.1935	0.3333	0.4000	0.0000	1.0000	0.0000	0.0000	0.0000	0.0000	0.0000
24	0.0000	0.5000	0.2222	0.2593	0.1935	0.3333	0.4000	0.0000	1.0000	0.0000	0.0000	0.0000	0.0000	0.0000
23	0.0000	0.5000	0.2222	0.2593	0.1935	0.3333	0.4000	0.0000	1.0000	0.0000	0.0000	0.0000	0.0000	0.0000
22	0.0000	0.5000	0.2222	0.2593	0.1935	0.3333	0.4000	0.0000	1.0000	0.0000	0.0000	0.0000	0.0000	0.0000
21	0.0000	0.5000	0.2222	0.2593	0.1935	0.3889	0.4000	0.0000	1.0000	0.0000	0.0000	0.0000	0.0000	0.0000
20	0.0000	0.5000	0.3333	0.2593	0.1613	0.4444	0.4000	0.0000	1.0000	0.0000	0.0000	0.0000	0.0000	0.0000
19	0.0000	0.5000	0.5556	0.2593	0.1935	0.5000	0.4000	0.0000	1.0000	0.0000	0.0000	0.0000	0.0000	0.0000
18	0.0000	0.5000	0.5556	0.2963	0.2258	0.5556	0.4000	0.0000	1.0000	0.0000	0.0000	0.0000	0.0000	0.0000
17	0.0000	0.5000	0.5556	0.2963	0.2903	0.5556	0.4000	0.3333	1.0000	0.0000	0.0000	0.0000	0.0000	0.0000
16	0.0000	0.5000	0.5556	0.3333	0.2903	0.5000	0.4000	0.3333	1.0000	0.0000	0.0000	0.0000	0.0000	0.0000
15	0.0000	0.5000	0.5556	0.3333	0.2903	0.5000	0.4000	0.3333	1.0000	0.0000	0.0000	0.0000	0.0000	0.0000
14	0.0000	0.5000	0.5556	0.3333	0.3226	0.5000	0.4000	0.6667	1.0000	0.0000	0.0000	0.0000	0.0000	0.0000
13	0.0000	0.5000	0.5556	0.3333	0.3226	0.5000	0.4000	0.6667	1.0000	0.0000	0.0000	0.0000	0.0000	0.0000
12	0.0000	0.5000	0.5556	0.3704	0.3871	0.5000	0.4000	0.6667	1.0000	0.0000	0.0000	0.0000	0.0000	0.0000
11	0.0000	0.5000	0.5556	0.4074	0.4194	0.6111	0.4000	0.6667	1.0000	0.0000	0.0000	0.0000	0.0000	0.0000
10	0.0000	0.5000	0.6667	0.4444	0.4839	0.6111	0.4000	0.6667	1.0000	0.0000	0.0000	0.0000	0.0000	0.0000
9	0.0000	0.5000	0.6667	0.5556	0.5806	0.6111	0.4000	0.6667	1.0000	0.0000	0.0000	0.0000	0.0000	0.0000
8	0.0000	0.5000	0.6667	0.6667	0.5806	0.6667	0.6000	0.6667	1.0000	0.0000	0.0000	0.0000	0.0000	0.0000
7	0.0000	0.5000	0.7778	0.7037	0.5806	0.6111	0.6000	0.6667	1.0000	0.0000	0.0000	0.0000	0.0000	0.0000
6	0.0000	0.5000	0.7778	0.7407	0.6129	0.6111	0.6000	0.6667	1.0000	0.0000	0.0000	0.0000	0.0000	0.0000
5	0.0000	0.5000	0.7778	0.7407	0.6774	0.6667	0.6000	0.6667	1.0000	0.0000	0.0000	0.0000	0.0000	0.0000
4	0.0000	0.5000	0.7778	0.7778	0.7097	0.6667	0.6000	0.6667	1.0000	0.0000	0.0000	0.0000	0.0000	0.0000
3	0.0000	0.5000	0.7778	0.7407	0.7419	0.6667	0.8000	0.6667	1.0000	0.0000	0.0000	0.0000	0.0000	0.0000
2	0.0000	0.5000	0.7778	0.7407	0.8387	0.6667	0.8000	0.6667	1.0000	0.0000	0.0000	0.0000	0.0000	0.0000
1	0.0000	1.0000	0.7778	0.7037	0.8710	0.6667	0.8000	0.6667	1.0000	0.0000	0.0000	0.0000	0.0000	0.0000
0	0.0000	1.0000	0.7778	0.7407	0.8710	0.7222	1.0000	0.6667	1.0000	0.0000	0.0000	0.0000	0.0000	0.0000
−1	0.0000	1.0000	0.6667	0.8148	0.8710	0.7778	1.0000	0.6667	1.0000	0.0000	0.0000	0.0000	0.0000	0.0000
−2	0.0000	1.0000	0.5556	0.8148	0.8710	0.7778	0.8000	0.6667	1.0000	0.0000	0.0000	0.0000	0.0000	0.0000
−3	0.0000	1.0000	0.5556	0.8148	0.8387	0.7222	0.8000	0.6667	1.0000	0.0000	0.0000	0.0000	0.0000	0.0000
−4	0.0000	1.0000	0.5556	0.8148	0.8065	0.7222	0.8000	0.6667	1.0000	0.0000	0.0000	0.0000	0.0000	0.0000
−5	0.0000	1.0000	0.6667	0.7778	0.7742	0.7222	0.8000	0.6667	1.0000	0.0000	0.0000	0.0000	0.0000	0.0000
−6	0.0000	1.0000	0.6667	0.7407	0.7742	0.6667	0.8000	1.0000	1.0000	0.0000	0.0000	0.0000	0.0000	0.0000
−7	0.0000	1.0000	0.6667	0.6296	0.7419	0.5556	0.8000	1.0000	1.0000	0.0000	0.0000	0.0000	0.0000	0.0000
−8	0.0000	1.0000	0.6667	0.6296	0.7419	0.5556	0.8000	1.0000	0.0000	0.0000	0.0000	0.0000	0.0000	0.0000
−9	0.0000	1.0000	0.6667	0.5556	0.6774	0.5000	0.8000	1.0000	0.0000	0.0000	0.0000	0.0000	0.0000	0.0000
−10	0.0000	1.0000	0.6667	0.5556	0.6452	0.4444	0.8000	1.0000	0.0000	0.0000	0.0000	0.0000	0.0000	0.0000

Main Condition 3 *(Continued)* — **Probabilities**

Tick Variation	\t Secondary Conditions													
	1	2	3	4	5	6	7	8	9	10	11	12	13	14
−11	0.0000	1.0000	0.6667	0.5556	0.6129	0.3889	0.8000	1.0000	0.0000	0.0000	0.0000	0.0000	0.0000	0.0000
−12	0.0000	0.5000	0.5556	0.5556	0.5161	0.4444	0.8000	1.0000	0.0000	0.0000	0.0000	0.0000	0.0000	0.0000
−13	0.0000	0.5000	0.4444	0.5185	0.5484	0.3889	0.8000	1.0000	0.0000	0.0000	0.0000	0.0000	0.0000	0.0000
−14	0.0000	0.5000	0.3333	0.4815	0.4839	0.3889	0.6000	1.0000	0.0000	0.0000	0.0000	0.0000	0.0000	0.0000
−15	0.0000	0.5000	0.2222	0.4815	0.4839	0.3889	0.6000	1.0000	0.0000	0.0000	0.0000	0.0000	0.0000	0.0000
−16	0.0000	0.5000	0.2222	0.4815	0.4839	0.3889	0.6000	1.0000	0.0000	0.0000	0.0000	0.0000	0.0000	0.0000
−17	0.0000	0.5000	0.2222	0.4074	0.4839	0.3889	0.6000	1.0000	0.0000	0.0000	0.0000	0.0000	0.0000	0.0000
−18	0.0000	0.0000	0.2222	0.4074	0.4194	0.3333	0.4000	1.0000	0.0000	0.0000	0.0000	0.0000	0.0000	0.0000
−19	0.0000	0.0000	0.2222	0.3333	0.3871	0.3333	0.4000	1.0000	0.0000	0.0000	0.0000	0.0000	0.0000	0.0000
−20	0.0000	0.0000	0.2222	0.3333	0.3871	0.2778	0.4000	0.6667	0.0000	0.0000	0.0000	0.0000	0.0000	0.0000
−21	0.0000	0.0000	0.2222	0.2963	0.3226	0.2778	0.4000	0.6667	0.0000	0.0000	0.0000	0.0000	0.0000	0.0000
−22	0.0000	0.0000	0.2222	0.2963	0.3226	0.2222	0.4000	0.6667	0.0000	0.0000	0.0000	0.0000	0.0000	0.0000
−23	0.0000	0.0000	0.2222	0.2963	0.2581	0.2222	0.2000	0.6667	0.0000	0.0000	0.0000	0.0000	0.0000	0.0000
−24	0.0000	0.0000	0.2222	0.2963	0.2581	0.1667	0.2000	0.6667	0.0000	0.0000	0.0000	0.0000	0.0000	0.0000
−25	0.0000	0.0000	0.2222	0.2222	0.2581	0.1667	0.2000	0.6667	0.0000	0.0000	0.0000	0.0000	0.0000	0.0000
−26	0.0000	0.0000	0.1111	0.2222	0.2258	0.1111	0.2000	0.6667	0.0000	0.0000	0.0000	0.0000	0.0000	0.0000
−27	0.0000	0.0000	0.1111	0.1852	0.1613	0.1111	0.2000	0.6667	0.0000	0.0000	0.0000	0.0000	0.0000	0.0000
−28	0.0000	0.0000	0.1111	0.1481	0.1613	0.0556	0.2000	0.6667	0.0000	0.0000	0.0000	0.0000	0.0000	0.0000
−29	0.0000	0.0000	0.1111	0.1481	0.1613	0.0556	0.2000	0.6667	0.0000	0.0000	0.0000	0.0000	0.0000	0.0000
−30	0.0000	0.0000	0.1111	0.1481	0.1290	0.0556	0.2000	0.6667	0.0000	0.0000	0.0000	0.0000	0.0000	0.0000
−31	0.0000	0.0000	0.0000	0.1481	0.1290	0.0556	0.2000	0.6667	0.0000	0.0000	0.0000	0.0000	0.0000	0.0000
−32	0.0000	0.0000	0.0000	0.1111	0.0968	0.0556	0.2000	0.6667	0.0000	0.0000	0.0000	0.0000	0.0000	0.0000
−33	0.0000	0.0000	0.0000	0.1111	0.0968	0.0556	0.2000	0.6667	0.0000	0.0000	0.0000	0.0000	0.0000	0.0000
−34	0.0000	0.0000	0.0000	0.0741	0.0968	0.0556	0.2000	0.6667	0.0000	0.0000	0.0000	0.0000	0.0000	0.0000
−35	0.0000	0.0000	0.0000	0.0741	0.0645	0.0556	0.2000	0.6667	0.0000	0.0000	0.0000	0.0000	0.0000	0.0000
−36	0.0000	0.0000	0.0000	0.0741	0.0645	0.0556	0.2000	0.3333	0.0000	0.0000	0.0000	0.0000	0.0000	0.0000
−37	0.0000	0.0000	0.0000	0.0741	0.0645	0.0556	0.0000	0.3333	0.0000	0.0000	0.0000	0.0000	0.0000	0.0000
−38	0.0000	0.0000	0.0000	0.0370	0.0645	0.0556	0.0000	0.3333	0.0000	0.0000	0.0000	0.0000	0.0000	0.0000
−39	0.0000	0.0000	0.0000	0.0370	0.0645	0.0556	0.0000	0.3333	0.0000	0.0000	0.0000	0.0000	0.0000	0.0000
−40	0.0000	0.0000	0.0000	0.0370	0.0645	0.0556	0.0000	0.0000	0.0000	0.0000	0.0000	0.0000	0.0000	0.0000
−41	0.0000	0.0000	0.0000	0.0370	0.0645	0.0556	0.0000	0.0000	0.0000	0.0000	0.0000	0.0000	0.0000	0.0000
−42	0.0000	0.0000	0.0000	0.0000	0.0645	0.0556	0.0000	0.0000	0.0000	0.0000	0.0000	0.0000	0.0000	0.0000
−43	0.0000	0.0000	0.0000	0.0000	0.0645	0.0556	0.0000	0.0000	0.0000	0.0000	0.0000	0.0000	0.0000	0.0000
−44	0.0000	0.0000	0.0000	0.0000	0.0645	0.0556	0.0000	0.0000	0.0000	0.0000	0.0000	0.0000	0.0000	0.0000
−45	0.0000	0.0000	0.0000	0.0000	0.0323	0.0556	0.0000	0.0000	0.0000	0.0000	0.0000	0.0000	0.0000	0.0000
−46	0.0000	0.0000	0.0000	0.0000	0.0323	0.0556	0.0000	0.0000	0.0000	0.0000	0.0000	0.0000	0.0000	0.0000
−47	0.0000	0.0000	0.0000	0.0000	0.0323	0.0556	0.0000	0.0000	0.0000	0.0000	0.0000	0.0000	0.0000	0.0000
−48	0.0000	0.0000	0.0000	0.0000	0.0323	0.0556	0.0000	0.0000	0.0000	0.0000	0.0000	0.0000	0.0000	0.0000
−49	0.0000	0.0000	0.0000	0.0000	0.0323	0.0556	0.0000	0.0000	0.0000	0.0000	0.0000	0.0000	0.0000	0.0000
−50	0.0000	0.0000	0.0000	0.0000	0.0323	0.0556	0.0000	0.0000	0.0000	0.0000	0.0000	0.0000	0.0000	0.0000
−51	0.0000	0.0000	0.0000	0.0000	0.0323	0.0556	0.0000	0.0000	0.0000	0.0000	0.0000	0.0000	0.0000	0.0000
−52	0.0000	0.0000	0.0000	0.0000	0.0323	0.0556	0.0000	0.0000	0.0000	0.0000	0.0000	0.0000	0.0000	0.0000
−53	0.0000	0.0000	0.0000	0.0000	0.0323	0.0556	0.0000	0.0000	0.0000	0.0000	0.0000	0.0000	0.0000	0.0000
−54	0.0000	0.0000	0.0000	0.0000	0.0323	0.0556	0.0000	0.0000	0.0000	0.0000	0.0000	0.0000	0.0000	0.0000
−55	0.0000	0.0000	0.0000	0.0000	0.0323	0.0556	0.0000	0.0000	0.0000	0.0000	0.0000	0.0000	0.0000	0.0000
−56	0.0000	0.0000	0.0000	0.0000	0.0323	0.0556	0.0000	0.0000	0.0000	0.0000	0.0000	0.0000	0.0000	0.0000
−57	0.0000	0.0000	0.0000	0.0000	0.0323	0.0556	0.0000	0.0000	0.0000	0.0000	0.0000	0.0000	0.0000	0.0000
−58	0.0000	0.0000	0.0000	0.0000	0.0323	0.0556	0.0000	0.0000	0.0000	0.0000	0.0000	0.0000	0.0000	0.0000
−59	0.0000	0.0000	0.0000	0.0000	0.0323	0.0000	0.0000	0.0000	0.0000	0.0000	0.0000	0.0000	0.0000	0.0000
−60	0.0000	0.0000	0.0000	0.0000	0.0323	0.0000	0.0000	0.0000	0.0000	0.0000	0.0000	0.0000	0.0000	0.0000
−61	0.0000	0.0000	0.0000	0.0000	0.0323	0.0000	0.0000	0.0000	0.0000	0.0000	0.0000	0.0000	0.0000	0.0000
−62	0.0000	0.0000	0.0000	0.0000	0.0323	0.0000	0.0000	0.0000	0.0000	0.0000	0.0000	0.0000	0.0000	0.0000
−63	0.0000	0.0000	0.0000	0.0000	0.0323	0.0000	0.0000	0.0000	0.0000	0.0000	0.0000	0.0000	0.0000	0.0000
−64	0.0000	0.0000	0.0000	0.0000	0.0000	0.0000	0.0000	0.0000	0.0000	0.0000	0.0000	0.0000	0.0000	0.0000

Main Condition 4						Probabilities							
Tick						Secondary Conditions							
Variation	1	2	3	4	5	6	7	8	9	10	11	12	13	14

Tick Variation	1	2	3	4	5	6	7	8	9	10	11	12	13	14
64	0.0000	0.0000	0.1818	0.0000	0.0000	0.0000	0.0370	0.0000	0.0000	0.0000	0.0000	0.0000	0.0000	0.0000
63	0.0000	0.0000	0.1818	0.0000	0.0143	0.0141	0.0370	0.0000	0.0000	0.0000	0.0000	0.0000	0.0000	0.0000
62	0.0000	0.0000	0.1818	0.0000	0.0143	0.0141	0.0370	0.0000	0.0000	0.0000	0.0000	0.0000	0.0000	0.0000
61	0.0000	0.0000	0.1818	0.0323	0.0286	0.0141	0.0370	0.0000	0.0000	0.0000	0.0000	0.0000	0.0000	0.0000
60	0.0000	0.0000	0.1818	0.0323	0.0429	0.0141	0.0370	0.0000	0.0000	0.0000	0.0000	0.0000	0.0000	0.0000
59	0.0000	0.0000	0.1818	0.0323	0.0429	0.0141	0.0370	0.0000	0.0000	0.0000	0.0000	0.0000	0.0000	0.0000
58	0.0000	0.0000	0.1818	0.0323	0.0429	0.0141	0.0370	0.0000	0.0000	0.0000	0.0000	0.0000	0.0000	0.0000
57	0.0000	0.0000	0.1818	0.0323	0.0429	0.0282	0.0370	0.0000	0.0000	0.0000	0.0000	0.0000	0.0000	0.0000
56	0.0000	0.0000	0.1818	0.0323	0.0429	0.0282	0.0741	0.0000	0.0000	0.0000	0.0000	0.0000	0.0000	0.0000
55	0.0000	0.0000	0.1818	0.0323	0.0429	0.0282	0.0741	0.0000	0.0000	0.0000	0.0000	0.0000	0.0000	0.0000
54	0.0000	0.0000	0.1818	0.0323	0.0429	0.0282	0.0741	0.0000	0.0000	0.0000	0.0000	0.0000	0.0000	0.0000
53	0.0000	0.0000	0.1818	0.0323	0.0429	0.0282	0.0741	0.0000	0.0000	0.0000	0.0000	0.0000	0.0000	0.0000
52	0.0000	0.0000	0.1818	0.0323	0.0429	0.0282	0.0741	0.0000	0.0000	0.0000	0.0000	0.0000	0.0000	0.0000
51	0.0000	0.0000	0.1818	0.0323	0.0429	0.0282	0.0741	0.0000	0.0000	0.0000	0.0000	0.0000	0.0000	0.0000
50	0.0000	0.0000	0.1818	0.0323	0.0429	0.0423	0.0741	0.0000	0.0000	0.0000	0.0000	0.0000	0.0000	0.0000
49	0.0000	0.0000	0.1818	0.0645	0.0429	0.0423	0.0741	0.0000	0.0000	0.0000	0.0000	0.0000	0.0000	0.0000
48	0.0000	0.0000	0.1818	0.0968	0.0571	0.0423	0.0741	0.0000	0.0000	0.0000	0.0000	0.0000	0.0000	0.0000
47	0.0000	0.0000	0.1818	0.0968	0.0571	0.0423	0.0741	0.0000	0.0000	0.0000	0.0000	0.0000	0.0000	0.0000
46	0.0000	0.0000	0.1818	0.0968	0.0571	0.0563	0.0741	0.0000	0.0000	0.0000	0.0000	0.0000	0.0000	0.0000
45	0.0000	0.0000	0.2727	0.0968	0.0571	0.0563	0.0741	0.0000	0.0000	0.0000	0.0000	0.0000	0.0000	0.0000
44	0.0000	0.0000	0.2727	0.0968	0.0571	0.0563	0.0741	0.0000	0.0000	0.0000	0.0000	0.0000	0.0000	0.0000
43	0.0000	0.0000	0.3636	0.0968	0.0571	0.0563	0.0741	0.0000	0.0000	0.0000	0.0000	0.0000	0.0000	0.0000
42	0.0000	0.0000	0.3636	0.1290	0.0571	0.0563	0.1111	0.0000	0.0000	0.0000	0.0000	0.0000	0.0000	0.0000
41	0.0000	0.0000	0.2727	0.1290	0.0571	0.0563	0.1111	0.0000	0.0000	0.0000	0.0000	0.0000	0.0000	0.0000
40	0.0000	0.0000	0.2727	0.1290	0.0571	0.0845	0.1111	0.0000	0.0000	0.0000	0.0000	0.0000	0.0000	0.0000
39	0.0000	0.0000	0.2727	0.1290	0.0571	0.0986	0.1111	0.0000	0.0000	0.0000	0.0000	0.0000	0.0000	0.0000
38	0.0000	0.0000	0.2727	0.1290	0.0571	0.0986	0.0741	0.2000	0.0000	0.0000	0.0000	0.0000	0.0000	0.0000
37	0.0000	0.0000	0.1818	0.1290	0.0429	0.1127	0.1111	0.2000	0.0000	0.0000	0.0000	0.0000	0.0000	0.0000
36	0.0000	0.0000	0.1818	0.1290	0.0429	0.1268	0.1111	0.2000	0.0000	0.0000	0.0000	0.0000	0.0000	0.0000
35	0.0000	0.0000	0.1818	0.1290	0.0429	0.1268	0.1481	0.2000	0.0000	0.0000	0.0000	0.0000	0.0000	0.0000
34	0.0000	0.0000	0.1818	0.1613	0.0429	0.1268	0.1481	0.2000	0.0000	0.0000	0.0000	0.0000	0.0000	0.0000
33	0.0000	0.0000	0.1818	0.1613	0.0571	0.1408	0.1481	0.2000	0.0000	0.0000	0.0000	0.0000	0.0000	0.0000
32	0.0000	0.0000	0.1818	0.1613	0.0714	0.1549	0.1481	0.2000	0.0000	0.0000	0.0000	0.0000	0.0000	0.0000
31	0.0000	0.0000	0.1818	0.1935	0.0714	0.1831	0.1481	0.2000	0.0000	0.0000	0.0000	0.0000	0.0000	0.0000
30	0.0000	0.0000	0.1818	0.1935	0.0857	0.2113	0.1481	0.2000	0.0000	0.0000	0.0000	0.0000	0.0000	0.0000
29	0.0000	0.0000	0.2727	0.1935	0.1000	0.2254	0.1481	0.2000	0.0000	0.0000	0.0000	0.0000	0.0000	0.0000
28	0.0000	0.0000	0.2727	0.1935	0.1000	0.2254	0.1481	0.2000	0.0000	0.0000	0.0000	0.0000	0.0000	0.0000
27	0.0000	0.0000	0.2727	0.1935	0.1143	0.2254	0.1481	0.4000	0.0000	0.0000	0.0000	0.0000	0.0000	0.0000
26	0.0000	0.0000	0.2727	0.2258	0.1571	0.2254	0.1481	0.4000	0.0000	0.0000	0.0000	0.0000	0.0000	0.0000
25	0.0000	0.0000	0.2727	0.2258	0.1714	0.2676	0.1481	0.4000	0.0000	0.0000	0.0000	0.0000	0.0000	0.0000
24	0.0000	0.0000	0.2727	0.2258	0.1857	0.2676	0.1481	0.4000	0.0000	0.0000	0.0000	0.0000	0.0000	0.0000
23	0.0000	0.0000	0.2727	0.2581	0.2000	0.2817	0.1481	0.4000	0.0000	0.0000	0.0000	0.0000	0.0000	0.0000
22	0.0000	0.0000	0.3636	0.2903	0.2143	0.3099	0.1481	0.4000	0.0000	0.0000	0.0000	0.0000	0.0000	0.0000
21	0.0000	0.0000	0.3636	0.2903	0.2429	0.3239	0.1852	0.4000	0.0000	0.0000	0.0000	0.0000	0.0000	0.0000
20	0.0000	0.0000	0.3636	0.3226	0.2714	0.3239	0.1852	0.4000	0.0000	0.0000	0.0000	0.0000	0.0000	0.0000
19	0.0000	0.0000	0.4545	0.3226	0.2857	0.3380	0.1852	0.6000	0.0000	0.0000	0.0000	0.0000	0.0000	0.0000
18	0.0000	0.0000	0.4545	0.3226	0.3000	0.3521	0.2222	0.6000	0.0000	0.0000	0.0000	0.0000	0.0000	0.0000
17	0.0000	0.0000	0.4545	0.3226	0.3000	0.3944	0.1852	0.8000	0.0000	0.0000	0.0000	0.0000	0.0000	0.0000
16	0.0000	0.0000	0.4545	0.3226	0.3000	0.4225	0.2593	0.8000	0.0000	0.0000	0.0000	0.0000	0.0000	0.0000
15	0.0000	0.0000	0.4545	0.3226	0.3143	0.4366	0.3333	0.8000	0.0000	0.0000	0.0000	0.0000	0.0000	0.0000
14	0.0000	0.0000	0.4545	0.3548	0.3429	0.4507	0.3333	0.8000	0.0000	0.0000	0.0000	0.0000	0.0000	0.0000
13	0.0000	0.0000	0.4545	0.3226	0.3857	0.4930	0.3333	0.8000	0.0000	0.0000	0.0000	0.0000	0.0000	0.0000
12	0.0000	0.0000	0.5455	0.3548	0.4143	0.5634	0.2963	0.8000	0.0000	0.0000	0.0000	0.0000	0.0000	0.0000
11	0.0000	0.0000	0.4545	0.3548	0.4286	0.5775	0.2963	0.8000	0.0000	0.0000	0.0000	0.0000	0.0000	0.0000
10	0.0000	0.0000	0.5455	0.3871	0.4286	0.6056	0.3333	0.8000	0.0000	0.0000	0.0000	0.0000	0.0000	0.0000
9	0.0000	0.0000	0.5455	0.4516	0.4714	0.6761	0.3333	0.8000	0.0000	0.0000	0.0000	0.0000	0.0000	0.0000
8	0.0000	0.0000	0.6364	0.5161	0.5000	0.7324	0.4444	0.8000	0.0000	0.0000	0.0000	0.0000	0.0000	0.0000
7	0.0000	0.0000	0.6364	0.6452	0.5571	0.7465	0.4815	0.8000	0.0000	0.0000	0.0000	0.0000	0.0000	0.0000
6	0.0000	0.0000	0.6364	0.7097	0.5857	0.7324	0.5185	0.8000	0.0000	0.0000	0.0000	0.0000	0.0000	0.0000
5	0.0000	0.0000	0.6364	0.7419	0.6286	0.7183	0.5185	0.8000	0.0000	0.0000	0.0000	0.0000	0.0000	0.0000
4	0.0000	0.0000	0.6364	0.7419	0.6571	0.6901	0.5185	0.8000	0.0000	0.0000	0.0000	0.0000	0.0000	0.0000
3	0.0000	0.0000	0.6364	0.7097	0.6571	0.6761	0.5185	0.8000	0.0000	0.0000	0.0000	0.0000	0.0000	0.0000
2	0.0000	0.0000	0.6364	0.7097	0.7000	0.6761	0.6296	0.8000	0.0000	0.0000	0.0000	0.0000	0.0000	0.0000
1	0.0000	0.0000	0.6364	0.6774	0.7000	0.6479	0.6296	0.8000	0.0000	0.0000	0.0000	0.0000	0.0000	0.0000
0	0.0000	0.0000	0.6364	0.7097	0.7143	0.6338	0.7037	0.8000	0.0000	0.0000	0.0000	0.0000	0.0000	0.0000
-1	0.0000	0.0000	0.6364	0.7097	0.6857	0.6620	0.7407	0.8000	0.0000	0.0000	0.0000	0.0000	0.0000	0.0000
-2	0.0000	0.0000	0.6364	0.6774	0.7000	0.6479	0.6667	0.8000	0.0000	0.0000	0.0000	0.0000	0.0000	0.0000
-3	0.0000	0.0000	0.6364	0.6774	0.7143	0.6761	0.6667	0.8000	0.0000	0.0000	0.0000	0.0000	0.0000	0.0000
-4	0.0000	0.0000	0.6364	0.7097	0.6857	0.6479	0.6667	0.8000	0.0000	0.0000	0.0000	0.0000	0.0000	0.0000
-5	0.0000	0.0000	0.6364	0.6452	0.6714	0.6338	0.6667	0.8000	0.0000	0.0000	0.0000	0.0000	0.0000	0.0000
-6	0.0000	0.0000	0.6364	0.6452	0.6571	0.6056	0.6296	0.8000	0.0000	0.0000	0.0000	0.0000	0.0000	0.0000
-7	0.0000	0.0000	0.6364	0.6452	0.5857	0.5493	0.6667	0.8000	0.0000	0.0000	0.0000	0.0000	0.0000	0.0000
-8	0.0000	0.0000	0.6364	0.6452	0.5286	0.4789	0.6296	0.6000	0.0000	0.0000	0.0000	0.0000	0.0000	0.0000
-9	0.0000	0.0000	0.6364	0.5484	0.5286	0.4789	0.5185	0.6000	0.0000	0.0000	0.0000	0.0000	0.0000	0.0000
-10	0.0000	0.0000	0.6364	0.4839	0.5143	0.4366	0.4444	0.6000	0.0000	0.0000	0.0000	0.0000	0.0000	0.0000

Main Condition 4 *(Continued)*   **Probabilities**

Secondary Conditions

Tick Variation	1	2	3	4	5	6	7	8	9	10	11	12	13	14
−11	0.0000	0.0000	0.6364	0.4516	0.4714	0.3944	0.4444	0.6000	0.0000	0.0000	0.0000	0.0000	0.0000	0.0000
−12	0.0000	0.0000	0.6364	0.4194	0.4286	0.3662	0.4444	0.6000	0.0000	0.0000	0.0000	0.0000	0.0000	0.0000
−13	0.0000	0.0000	0.5455	0.3871	0.3857	0.3662	0.4444	0.6000	0.0000	0.0000	0.0000	0.0000	0.0000	0.0000
−14	0.0000	0.0000	0.5455	0.3226	0.3714	0.3521	0.4074	0.6000	0.0000	0.0000	0.0000	0.0000	0.0000	0.0000
−15	0.0000	0.0000	0.4545	0.3226	0.3571	0.3380	0.4074	0.4000	0.0000	0.0000	0.0000	0.0000	0.0000	0.0000
−16	0.0000	0.0000	0.3636	0.2581	0.3286	0.2958	0.4074	0.4000	0.0000	0.0000	0.0000	0.0000	0.0000	0.0000
−17	0.0000	1.0000	0.2727	0.2903	0.2714	0.2817	0.3333	0.4000	0.0000	0.0000	0.0000	0.0000	0.0000	0.0000
−18	0.0000	1.0000	0.2727	0.2581	0.2286	0.2817	0.3333	0.4000	0.0000	0.0000	0.0000	0.0000	0.0000	0.0000
−19	0.0000	1.0000	0.2727	0.2581	0.2286	0.2676	0.3333	0.4000	0.0000	0.0000	0.0000	0.0000	0.0000	0.0000
−20	0.0000	1.0000	0.2727	0.2258	0.2286	0.2394	0.2222	0.4000	0.0000	0.0000	0.0000	0.0000	0.0000	0.0000
−21	0.0000	1.0000	0.2727	0.2258	0.2000	0.2254	0.1852	0.4000	0.0000	0.0000	0.0000	0.0000	0.0000	0.0000
−22	0.0000	1.0000	0.1818	0.2258	0.2143	0.2113	0.1852	0.4000	0.0000	0.0000	0.0000	0.0000	0.0000	0.0000
−23	0.0000	1.0000	0.1818	0.1935	0.2143	0.1972	0.1481	0.4000	0.0000	0.0000	0.0000	0.0000	0.0000	0.0000
−24	0.0000	1.0000	0.0909	0.1935	0.2000	0.1408	0.1481	0.4000	0.0000	0.0000	0.0000	0.0000	0.0000	0.0000
−25	0.0000	1.0000	0.0909	0.1935	0.1857	0.1127	0.1481	0.4000	0.0000	0.0000	0.0000	0.0000	0.0000	0.0000
−26	0.0000	1.0000	0.0000	0.1935	0.1857	0.0986	0.1481	0.4000	0.0000	0.0000	0.0000	0.0000	0.0000	0.0000
−27	0.0000	1.0000	0.0000	0.1613	0.1714	0.0986	0.1481	0.4000	0.0000	0.0000	0.0000	0.0000	0.0000	0.0000
−28	0.0000	1.0000	0.0000	0.0968	0.1429	0.0845	0.1481	0.4000	0.0000	0.0000	0.0000	0.0000	0.0000	0.0000
−29	0.0000	1.0000	0.0000	0.0645	0.1286	0.0845	0.1481	0.4000	0.0000	0.0000	0.0000	0.0000	0.0000	0.0000
−30	0.0000	1.0000	0.0000	0.0645	0.1286	0.0845	0.1481	0.4000	0.0000	0.0000	0.0000	0.0000	0.0000	0.0000
−31	0.0000	1.0000	0.0000	0.0645	0.1286	0.0704	0.1481	0.4000	0.0000	0.0000	0.0000	0.0000	0.0000	0.0000
−32	0.0000	1.0000	0.0000	0.0645	0.1000	0.0704	0.1481	0.4000	0.0000	0.0000	0.0000	0.0000	0.0000	0.0000
−33	0.0000	1.0000	0.0000	0.0645	0.1143	0.0704	0.1481	0.4000	0.0000	0.0000	0.0000	0.0000	0.0000	0.0000
−34	0.0000	1.0000	0.0000	0.0645	0.1143	0.0563	0.1481	0.4000	0.0000	0.0000	0.0000	0.0000	0.0000	0.0000
−35	0.0000	1.0000	0.0000	0.0645	0.1143	0.0423	0.1481	0.4000	0.0000	0.0000	0.0000	0.0000	0.0000	0.0000
−36	0.0000	1.0000	0.0000	0.0645	0.1000	0.0423	0.1111	0.4000	0.0000	0.0000	0.0000	0.0000	0.0000	0.0000
−37	0.0000	1.0000	0.0000	0.0645	0.1000	0.0423	0.0741	0.4000	0.0000	0.0000	0.0000	0.0000	0.0000	0.0000
−38	0.0000	1.0000	0.0000	0.0645	0.1000	0.0423	0.0741	0.2000	0.0000	0.0000	0.0000	0.0000	0.0000	0.0000
−39	0.0000	1.0000	0.0000	0.0645	0.1000	0.0423	0.0741	0.2000	0.0000	0.0000	0.0000	0.0000	0.0000	0.0000
−40	0.0000	1.0000	0.0000	0.0645	0.1000	0.0423	0.0741	0.2000	0.0000	0.0000	0.0000	0.0000	0.0000	0.0000
−41	0.0000	1.0000	0.0000	0.0645	0.0857	0.0423	0.0741	0.2000	0.0000	0.0000	0.0000	0.0000	0.0000	0.0000
−42	0.0000	1.0000	0.0000	0.0645	0.0857	0.0423	0.0741	0.0000	0.0000	0.0000	0.0000	0.0000	0.0000	0.0000
−43	0.0000	1.0000	0.0000	0.0645	0.0714	0.0423	0.0741	0.0000	0.0000	0.0000	0.0000	0.0000	0.0000	0.0000
−44	0.0000	1.0000	0.0000	0.0645	0.0714	0.0423	0.0370	0.0000	0.0000	0.0000	0.0000	0.0000	0.0000	0.0000
−45	0.0000	1.0000	0.0000	0.0645	0.0714	0.0282	0.0370	0.0000	0.0000	0.0000	0.0000	0.0000	0.0000	0.0000
−46	0.0000	1.0000	0.0000	0.0645	0.0714	0.0282	0.0370	0.0000	0.0000	0.0000	0.0000	0.0000	0.0000	0.0000
−47	0.0000	1.0000	0.0000	0.0645	0.0714	0.0282	0.0370	0.0000	0.0000	0.0000	0.0000	0.0000	0.0000	0.0000
−48	0.0000	1.0000	0.0000	0.0645	0.0571	0.0141	0.0370	0.0000	0.0000	0.0000	0.0000	0.0000	0.0000	0.0000
−49	0.0000	1.0000	0.0000	0.0645	0.0571	0.0141	0.0370	0.0000	0.0000	0.0000	0.0000	0.0000	0.0000	0.0000
−50	0.0000	1.0000	0.0000	0.0645	0.0571	0.0141	0.0370	0.0000	0.0000	0.0000	0.0000	0.0000	0.0000	0.0000
−51	0.0000	1.0000	0.0000	0.0645	0.0571	0.0141	0.0370	0.0000	0.0000	0.0000	0.0000	0.0000	0.0000	0.0000
−52	0.0000	1.0000	0.0000	0.0645	0.0571	0.0141	0.0370	0.0000	0.0000	0.0000	0.0000	0.0000	0.0000	0.0000
−53	0.0000	1.0000	0.0000	0.0645	0.0571	0.0141	0.0370	0.0000	0.0000	0.0000	0.0000	0.0000	0.0000	0.0000
−54	0.0000	1.0000	0.0000	0.0323	0.0714	0.0141	0.0370	0.0000	0.0000	0.0000	0.0000	0.0000	0.0000	0.0000
−55	0.0000	1.0000	0.0000	0.0323	0.0714	0.0141	0.0370	0.0000	0.0000	0.0000	0.0000	0.0000	0.0000	0.0000
−56	0.0000	1.0000	0.0000	0.0323	0.0714	0.0141	0.0370	0.0000	0.0000	0.0000	0.0000	0.0000	0.0000	0.0000
−57	0.0000	1.0000	0.0000	0.0000	0.0571	0.0000	0.0370	0.0000	0.0000	0.0000	0.0000	0.0000	0.0000	0.0000
−58	0.0000	1.0000	0.0000	0.0000	0.0571	0.0000	0.0370	0.0000	0.0000	0.0000	0.0000	0.0000	0.0000	0.0000
−59	0.0000	1.0000	0.0000	0.0000	0.0286	0.0000	0.0370	0.0000	0.0000	0.0000	0.0000	0.0000	0.0000	0.0000
−60	0.0000	0.0000	0.0000	0.0000	0.0286	0.0000	0.0370	0.0000	0.0000	0.0000	0.0000	0.0000	0.0000	0.0000
−61	0.0000	0.0000	0.0000	0.0000	0.0286	0.0000	0.0000	0.0000	0.0000	0.0000	0.0000	0.0000	0.0000	0.0000
−62	0.0000	0.0000	0.0000	0.0000	0.0286	0.0000	0.0000	0.0000	0.0000	0.0000	0.0000	0.0000	0.0000	0.0000
−63	0.0000	0.0000	0.0000	0.0000	0.0286	0.0000	0.0000	0.0000	0.0000	0.0000	0.0000	0.0000	0.0000	0.0000
−64	0.0000	0.0000	0.0000	0.0000	0.0286	0.0000	0.0000	0.0000	0.0000	0.0000	0.0000	0.0000	0.0000	0.0000

Main Condition 5   **Probabilities**

Tick Variation	1	2	3	4	5	6	7	8	9	10	11	12	13	14
						Secondary Conditions								
64	0.0000	0.0000	0.0000	0.0385	0.0147	0.0075	0.0116	0.0000	0.2500	0.5000	0.0000	0.0000	0.0000	0.0000
63	0.0000	0.0000	0.0000	0.0385	0.0147	0.0075	0.0116	0.0000	0.2500	0.5000	0.0000	0.0000	0.0000	0.0000
62	0.0000	0.0000	0.0000	0.0385	0.0147	0.0075	0.0116	0.0000	0.2500	0.5000	0.0000	0.0000	0.0000	0.0000
61	0.0000	0.0000	0.0000	0.0385	0.0147	0.0075	0.0116	0.0000	0.2500	0.5000	0.0000	0.0000	0.0000	0.0000
60	0.0000	0.0000	0.0000	0.0385	0.0147	0.0075	0.0116	0.0000	0.2500	0.5000	0.0000	0.0000	0.0000	0.0000
59	0.0000	0.0000	0.0000	0.0385	0.0147	0.0075	0.0116	0.0000	0.2500	0.5000	0.0000	0.0000	0.0000	0.0000
58	0.0000	0.0000	0.0000	0.0385	0.0147	0.0075	0.0116	0.0000	0.2500	0.5000	0.0000	0.0000	0.0000	0.0000
57	0.0000	0.0000	0.0000	0.0385	0.0147	0.0075	0.0116	0.0000	0.2500	0.5000	0.0000	0.0000	0.0000	0.0000
56	0.0000	0.0000	0.0000	0.0385	0.0147	0.0075	0.0116	0.0000	0.2500	0.5000	0.0000	0.0000	0.0000	0.0000
55	0.0000	0.0000	0.0000	0.0385	0.0147	0.0075	0.0116	0.0000	0.2500	0.5000	0.0000	0.0000	0.0000	0.0000
54	0.0000	0.0000	0.0000	0.0385	0.0147	0.0075	0.0233	0.0000	0.2500	0.5000	0.0000	0.0000	0.0000	0.0000
53	0.0000	0.0000	0.0000	0.0385	0.0147	0.0075	0.0349	0.0000	0.2500	0.5000	0.0000	0.0000	0.0000	0.0000
52	0.0000	0.0000	0.0000	0.0385	0.0147	0.0075	0.0349	0.0000	0.2500	0.5000	0.0000	0.0000	0.0000	0.0000
51	0.0000	0.0000	0.0000	0.0385	0.0147	0.0075	0.0349	0.0000	0.2500	0.5000	0.0000	0.0000	0.0000	0.0000
50	0.0000	0.0000	0.0000	0.0385	0.0147	0.0149	0.0349	0.0000	0.2500	0.5000	0.0000	0.0000	0.0000	0.0000
49	0.0000	0.0000	0.0000	0.0385	0.0294	0.0149	0.0349	0.0000	0.2500	0.5000	0.0000	0.0000	0.0000	0.0000
48	0.0000	0.0000	0.0000	0.0385	0.0294	0.0149	0.0349	0.0000	0.2500	0.5000	0.0000	0.0000	0.0000	0.0000
47	0.0000	0.0000	0.0000	0.0385	0.0294	0.0149	0.0349	0.0000	0.2500	0.5000	0.0000	0.0000	0.0000	0.0000
46	0.0000	0.0000	0.0000	0.0385	0.0588	0.0224	0.0349	0.0000	0.2500	0.5000	0.0000	0.0000	0.0000	0.0000
45	0.0000	0.0000	0.0000	0.0385	0.0588	0.0224	0.0349	0.0000	0.2500	0.5000	0.0000	0.0000	0.0000	0.0000
44	0.0000	0.0000	0.0000	0.0385	0.0735	0.0224	0.0349	0.0000	0.2500	0.5000	0.0000	0.0000	0.0000	0.0000
43	0.0000	0.0000	0.0000	0.0385	0.0735	0.0224	0.0349	0.0000	0.2500	0.5000	0.0000	0.0000	0.0000	0.0000
42	0.0000	0.0000	0.0000	0.0385	0.0882	0.0224	0.0349	0.0000	0.2500	0.5000	0.0000	0.0000	0.0000	0.0000
41	0.0000	0.0000	0.0000	0.0385	0.0882	0.0224	0.0349	0.0000	0.2500	0.5000	0.0000	0.0000	0.0000	0.0000
40	0.0000	0.0000	0.0000	0.0385	0.1029	0.0224	0.0349	0.0000	0.2500	0.5000	0.0000	0.0000	0.0000	0.0000
39	0.0000	0.0000	0.0000	0.0385	0.1029	0.0224	0.0349	0.0000	0.2500	0.5000	0.0000	0.0000	0.0000	0.0000
38	0.0000	0.0000	0.0000	0.0385	0.1029	0.0299	0.0465	0.0417	0.2500	0.5000	0.0000	0.0000	0.0000	0.0000
37	0.0000	0.0000	0.0000	0.0385	0.1029	0.0299	0.0698	0.0417	0.2500	0.5000	0.0000	0.0000	0.0000	0.0000
36	0.0000	0.0000	0.0000	0.0385	0.1176	0.0373	0.0930	0.0417	0.2500	0.5000	0.0000	0.0000	0.0000	0.0000
35	0.0000	0.0000	0.0000	0.0385	0.1176	0.0522	0.0930	0.0417	0.2500	0.5000	0.0000	0.0000	0.0000	0.0000
34	0.0000	0.0000	0.0000	0.0385	0.1324	0.0522	0.1047	0.0417	0.2500	0.5000	0.0000	0.0000	0.0000	0.0000
33	0.0000	0.0000	0.0000	0.0385	0.1324	0.0597	0.1047	0.0417	0.2500	0.5000	0.0000	0.0000	0.0000	0.0000
32	0.0000	0.0000	0.0000	0.0385	0.1324	0.0672	0.1047	0.0417	0.2500	0.5000	0.0000	0.0000	0.0000	0.0000
31	0.0000	0.0000	0.0000	0.0385	0.1324	0.0970	0.1163	0.0417	0.2500	0.5000	0.0000	0.0000	0.0000	0.0000
30	0.0000	0.0000	0.0000	0.0385	0.1471	0.0970	0.1163	0.0417	0.2500	0.5000	0.0000	0.0000	0.0000	0.0000
29	0.0000	0.0000	0.1667	0.0385	0.1471	0.0896	0.1395	0.0833	0.2500	1.0000	0.0000	0.0000	0.0000	0.0000
28	0.0000	0.0000	0.1667	0.0385	0.1618	0.1045	0.1395	0.0833	0.2500	1.0000	0.0000	0.0000	0.0000	0.0000
27	0.0000	0.0000	0.1667	0.0385	0.1765	0.1045	0.1395	0.0833	0.2500	1.0000	0.0000	0.0000	0.0000	0.0000
26	0.0000	0.0000	0.1667	0.0769	0.1912	0.1194	0.1512	0.0833	0.2500	1.0000	0.0000	0.0000	0.0000	0.0000
25	0.0000	0.0000	0.1667	0.0769	0.2353	0.1269	0.1744	0.1667	0.2500	1.0000	0.0000	0.0000	0.0000	0.0000
24	0.0000	0.0000	0.3333	0.1154	0.2500	0.1642	0.1977	0.1667	0.5000	1.0000	0.0000	0.0000	0.0000	0.0000
23	0.0000	0.0000	0.3333	0.1154	0.2647	0.1866	0.2093	0.1667	0.5000	1.0000	0.0000	0.0000	0.0000	0.0000
22	0.0000	0.0000	0.3333	0.1538	0.2647	0.2015	0.2093	0.1667	0.5000	1.0000	0.0000	0.0000	0.0000	0.0000
21	0.0000	0.0000	0.3333	0.1538	0.2941	0.2313	0.2442	0.2083	0.5000	1.0000	0.0000	0.0000	0.0000	0.0000
20	0.0000	0.0000	0.3333	0.1538	0.3088	0.2388	0.2674	0.2083	0.5000	1.0000	0.0000	0.0000	0.0000	0.0000
19	0.0000	0.0000	0.3333	0.2308	0.3382	0.2612	0.3256	0.2083	0.5000	1.0000	0.0000	0.0000	0.0000	0.0000
18	0.0000	0.0000	0.3333	0.2308	0.3529	0.2836	0.3488	0.2083	0.5000	1.0000	0.0000	0.0000	0.0000	0.0000
17	0.0000	0.0000	0.3333	0.2308	0.3676	0.3134	0.3605	0.2083	0.5000	1.0000	0.0000	0.0000	0.0000	0.0000
16	0.0000	0.0000	0.3333	0.2692	0.4412	0.3134	0.3953	0.2083	0.5000	1.0000	0.0000	0.0000	0.0000	0.0000
15	0.0000	0.0000	0.3333	0.2692	0.4265	0.3209	0.4186	0.2083	0.5000	1.0000	0.0000	0.0000	0.0000	0.0000
14	0.0000	0.5000	0.3333	0.3077	0.4412	0.3433	0.4419	0.2917	0.5000	1.0000	0.0000	0.0000	0.0000	0.0000
13	0.0000	0.5000	0.5000	0.3846	0.4559	0.3507	0.4535	0.3333	0.5000	1.0000	0.0000	0.0000	0.0000	0.0000
12	0.0000	0.5000	0.5000	0.4615	0.4853	0.3657	0.4767	0.3333	0.5000	0.5000	0.0000	0.0000	0.0000	0.0000
11	0.0000	1.0000	0.5000	0.4615	0.5441	0.3731	0.5000	0.4167	0.5000	0.5000	0.0000	0.0000	0.0000	0.0000
10	0.0000	1.0000	0.5000	0.4615	0.5588	0.4104	0.5465	0.4167	0.5000	0.5000	0.0000	0.0000	0.0000	0.0000
9	0.0000	1.0000	0.5000	0.4615	0.5588	0.4552	0.5465	0.5417	0.5000	0.5000	0.0000	0.0000	0.0000	0.0000
8	0.0000	1.0000	0.5000	0.4615	0.6029	0.4925	0.6047	0.5833	0.5000	0.5000	0.0000	0.0000	0.0000	0.0000
7	0.0000	1.0000	0.5000	0.4615	0.6176	0.5224	0.6512	0.5833	0.5000	0.5000	0.0000	0.0000	0.0000	0.0000
6	0.0000	1.0000	0.5000	0.5385	0.6765	0.5672	0.6860	0.6250	0.2500	0.5000	0.0000	0.0000	0.0000	0.0000
5	0.0000	1.0000	0.5000	0.6154	0.7206	0.5970	0.6860	0.6250	0.2500	0.5000	0.0000	0.0000	0.0000	0.0000
4	0.0000	1.0000	0.5000	0.6154	0.7206	0.6269	0.6977	0.5833	0.2500	0.5000	0.0000	0.0000	0.0000	0.0000
3	0.0000	1.0000	0.5000	0.7308	0.7647	0.6493	0.7209	0.5833	0.2500	0.5000	0.0000	0.0000	0.0000	0.0000
2	0.0000	1.0000	0.5000	0.7308	0.7647	0.7015	0.7326	0.6250	0.2500	0.5000	0.0000	0.0000	0.0000	0.0000
1	0.0000	1.0000	0.5000	0.6538	0.8088	0.7090	0.6977	0.5833	0.2500	0.5000	0.0000	0.0000	0.0000	0.0000
0	0.0000	1.0000	0.5000	0.6538	0.7794	0.7164	0.6977	0.6250	0.2500	0.5000	0.0000	0.0000	0.0000	0.0000
-1	0.0000	1.0000	0.5000	0.6923	0.7647	0.7015	0.6977	0.6667	0.2500	0.5000	0.0000	0.0000	0.0000	0.0000
-2	0.0000	1.0000	0.1667	0.7308	0.7794	0.7164	0.6512	0.6667	0.2500	0.5000	0.0000	0.0000	0.0000	0.0000
-3	0.0000	1.0000	0.3333	0.8077	0.7206	0.6940	0.6279	0.6250	0.2500	0.5000	0.0000	0.0000	0.0000	0.0000
-4	0.0000	1.0000	0.3333	0.8077	0.6471	0.6866	0.6047	0.6667	0.2500	0.5000	0.0000	0.0000	0.0000	0.0000
-5	0.0000	1.0000	0.3333	0.8462	0.6324	0.6642	0.5814	0.6667	0.2500	0.5000	0.0000	0.0000	0.0000	0.0000
-6	0.0000	1.0000	0.3333	0.8462	0.6176	0.5970	0.5465	0.6250	0.2500	0.5000	0.0000	0.0000	0.0000	0.0000
-7	0.0000	1.0000	0.3333	0.7308	0.6029	0.5672	0.5349	0.5833	0.2500	0.5000	0.0000	0.0000	0.0000	0.0000
-8	0.0000	1.0000	0.3333	0.7308	0.5441	0.5149	0.5233	0.5833	0.2500	0.5000	0.0000	0.0000	0.0000	0.0000
-9	0.0000	1.0000	0.3333	0.6538	0.5147	0.4851	0.4767	0.5833	0.2500	0.5000	0.0000	0.0000	0.0000	0.0000
-10	0.0000	1.0000	0.6667	0.6538	0.4559	0.4701	0.4419	0.6250	0.5000	0.5000	0.0000	0.0000	0.0000	0.0000

Main Condition 5 *(Continued)*   **Probabilities**

Tick Variation	*1*	*2*	*3*	*4*	*5*	*6*	*7*	*8*	*9*	*10*	*11*	*12*	*13*	*14*
−11	0.0000	1.0000	0.6667	0.6154	0.4118	0.4403	0.4070	0.5417	0.5000	0.5000	0.0000	0.0000	0.0000	0.0000
−12	0.0000	1.0000	0.6667	0.5769	0.4118	0.4104	0.3953	0.5417	0.5000	0.5000	0.0000	0.0000	0.0000	0.0000
−13	0.0000	1.0000	0.6667	0.4615	0.3824	0.4030	0.3953	0.5000	0.5000	0.5000	0.0000	0.0000	0.0000	0.0000
−14	0.0000	1.0000	0.6667	0.4231	0.3676	0.3881	0.3721	0.5000	0.5000	0.5000	0.0000	0.0000	0.0000	0.0000
−15	0.0000	1.0000	0.6667	0.3462	0.3529	0.3507	0.3372	0.5000	0.5000	0.5000	0.0000	0.0000	0.0000	0.0000
−16	0.0000	1.0000	0.6667	0.3462	0.3529	0.3209	0.3023	0.4167	0.5000	0.5000	0.0000	0.0000	0.0000	0.0000
−17	0.0000	1.0000	0.6667	0.2692	0.3235	0.2836	0.2674	0.3750	0.5000	0.5000	0.0000	0.0000	0.0000	0.0000
−18	0.0000	1.0000	0.6667	0.2692	0.3088	0.2612	0.2326	0.3333	0.5000	0.5000	0.0000	0.0000	0.0000	0.0000
−19	0.0000	1.0000	0.6667	0.1923	0.3088	0.2313	0.1860	0.2917	0.5000	0.5000	0.0000	0.0000	0.0000	0.0000
−20	0.0000	1.0000	0.6667	0.2308	0.3088	0.1940	0.1744	0.2917	0.5000	0.5000	0.0000	0.0000	0.0000	0.0000
−21	0.0000	1.0000	0.6667	0.1923	0.2941	0.1716	0.1628	0.3333	0.5000	0.5000	0.0000	0.0000	0.0000	0.0000
−22	0.0000	0.5000	0.6667	0.1923	0.2794	0.1567	0.1628	0.3333	0.5000	0.5000	0.0000	0.0000	0.0000	0.0000
−23	0.0000	0.5000	0.6667	0.1538	0.2647	0.1194	0.1628	0.3333	0.5000	0.5000	0.0000	0.0000	0.0000	0.0000
−24	0.0000	0.5000	0.6667	0.1538	0.2500	0.1194	0.1628	0.3333	0.5000	0.5000	0.0000	0.0000	0.0000	0.0000
−25	0.0000	0.5000	0.6667	0.1538	0.2353	0.1119	0.1395	0.3333	0.5000	0.5000	0.0000	0.0000	0.0000	0.0000
−26	0.0000	0.5000	0.6667	0.1538	0.2206	0.1119	0.1279	0.2917	0.5000	0.5000	0.0000	0.0000	0.0000	0.0000
−27	0.0000	0.5000	0.5000	0.1538	0.1912	0.1119	0.1279	0.2500	0.5000	0.5000	0.0000	0.0000	0.0000	0.0000
−28	0.0000	0.5000	0.5000	0.1538	0.1765	0.1119	0.1163	0.2500	0.5000	0.5000	0.0000	0.0000	0.0000	0.0000
−29	0.0000	0.5000	0.5000	0.1538	0.1618	0.1045	0.1047	0.2500	0.5000	0.5000	0.0000	0.0000	0.0000	0.0000
−30	0.0000	0.0000	0.5000	0.1538	0.1471	0.0896	0.0814	0.2500	0.5000	0.5000	0.0000	0.0000	0.0000	0.0000
−31	0.0000	0.0000	0.5000	0.1538	0.1324	0.0746	0.0814	0.2500	0.5000	0.5000	0.0000	0.0000	0.0000	0.0000
−32	0.0000	0.0000	0.5000	0.1538	0.1324	0.0597	0.0814	0.2500	0.2500	0.5000	0.0000	0.0000	0.0000	0.0000
−33	0.0000	0.0000	0.5000	0.1538	0.1324	0.0522	0.0698	0.2500	0.2500	0.5000	0.0000	0.0000	0.0000	0.0000
−34	0.0000	0.0000	0.5000	0.1538	0.1324	0.0522	0.0581	0.2083	0.2500	0.5000	0.0000	0.0000	0.0000	0.0000
−35	0.0000	0.0000	0.5000	0.1538	0.1176	0.0597	0.0581	0.2083	0.2500	0.5000	0.0000	0.0000	0.0000	0.0000
−36	0.0000	0.0000	0.5000	0.1538	0.1176	0.0597	0.0465	0.2083	0.2500	0.0000	0.0000	0.0000	0.0000	0.0000
−37	0.0000	0.0000	0.5000	0.1154	0.1176	0.0448	0.0349	0.2083	0.2500	0.0000	0.0000	0.0000	0.0000	0.0000
−38	0.0000	0.0000	0.5000	0.1154	0.1176	0.0448	0.0349	0.2083	0.2500	0.0000	0.0000	0.0000	0.0000	0.0000
−39	0.0000	0.0000	0.5000	0.1154	0.0882	0.0373	0.0349	0.2083	0.2500	0.0000	0.0000	0.0000	0.0000	0.0000
−40	0.0000	0.0000	0.5000	0.1154	0.0735	0.0373	0.0349	0.2083	0.2500	0.0000	0.0000	0.0000	0.0000	0.0000
−41	0.0000	0.0000	0.5000	0.1154	0.0588	0.0299	0.0349	0.1667	0.2500	0.0000	0.0000	0.0000	0.0000	0.0000
−42	0.0000	0.0000	0.5000	0.1154	0.0588	0.0224	0.0349	0.0833	0.2500	0.0000	0.0000	0.0000	0.0000	0.0000
−43	0.0000	0.0000	0.5000	0.1154	0.0588	0.0224	0.0349	0.0833	0.2500	0.0000	0.0000	0.0000	0.0000	0.0000
−44	0.0000	0.0000	0.5000	0.1154	0.0588	0.0224	0.0349	0.0833	0.2500	0.0000	0.0000	0.0000	0.0000	0.0000
−45	0.0000	0.0000	0.5000	0.1154	0.0588	0.0224	0.0349	0.0833	0.2500	0.0000	0.0000	0.0000	0.0000	0.0000
−46	0.0000	0.0000	0.5000	0.1154	0.0441	0.0224	0.0349	0.0417	0.2500	0.0000	0.0000	0.0000	0.0000	0.0000
−47	0.0000	0.0000	0.1667	0.1154	0.0441	0.0224	0.0349	0.0417	0.2500	0.0000	0.0000	0.0000	0.0000	0.0000
−48	0.0000	0.0000	0.1667	0.0769	0.0294	0.0224	0.0349	0.0417	0.2500	0.0000	0.0000	0.0000	0.0000	0.0000
−49	0.0000	0.0000	0.1667	0.0769	0.0147	0.0224	0.0349	0.0417	0.2500	0.0000	0.0000	0.0000	0.0000	0.0000
−50	0.0000	0.0000	0.1667	0.0769	0.0000	0.0224	0.0349	0.0000	0.2500	0.0000	0.0000	0.0000	0.0000	0.0000
−51	0.0000	0.0000	0.1667	0.0769	0.0000	0.0224	0.0349	0.0000	0.2500	0.0000	0.0000	0.0000	0.0000	0.0000
−52	0.0000	0.0000	0.1667	0.0769	0.0000	0.0224	0.0233	0.0000	0.2500	0.0000	0.0000	0.0000	0.0000	0.0000
−53	0.0000	0.0000	0.1667	0.0769	0.0000	0.0224	0.0233	0.0000	0.2500	0.0000	0.0000	0.0000	0.0000	0.0000
−54	0.0000	0.0000	0.0000	0.0769	0.0000	0.0224	0.0233	0.0000	0.2500	0.0000	0.0000	0.0000	0.0000	0.0000
−55	0.0000	0.0000	0.0000	0.0769	0.0000	0.0224	0.0233	0.0000	0.2500	0.0000	0.0000	0.0000	0.0000	0.0000
−56	0.0000	0.0000	0.0000	0.0769	0.0000	0.0224	0.0233	0.0000	0.2500	0.0000	0.0000	0.0000	0.0000	0.0000
−57	0.0000	0.0000	0.0000	0.0769	0.0000	0.0224	0.0233	0.0000	0.2500	0.0000	0.0000	0.0000	0.0000	0.0000
−58	0.0000	0.0000	0.0000	0.0769	0.0000	0.0224	0.0233	0.0000	0.2500	0.0000	0.0000	0.0000	0.0000	0.0000
−59	0.0000	0.0000	0.0000	0.0769	0.0000	0.0224	0.0233	0.0000	0.2500	0.0000	0.0000	0.0000	0.0000	0.0000
−60	0.0000	0.0000	0.0000	0.0769	0.0000	0.0224	0.0233	0.0000	0.2500	0.0000	0.0000	0.0000	0.0000	0.0000
−61	0.0000	0.0000	0.0000	0.0769	0.0000	0.0149	0.0233	0.0000	0.2500	0.0000	0.0000	0.0000	0.0000	0.0000
−62	0.0000	0.0000	0.0000	0.0769	0.0000	0.0149	0.0233	0.0000	0.2500	0.0000	0.0000	0.0000	0.0000	0.0000
−63	0.0000	0.0000	0.0000	0.0000	0.0000	0.0075	0.0116	0.0000	0.2500	0.0000	0.0000	0.0000	0.0000	0.0000
−64	0.0000	0.0000	0.0000	0.0000	0.0000	0.0075	0.0116	0.0000	0.2500	0.0000	0.0000	0.0000	0.0000	0.0000

Main Condition 6						Probabilities							
Tick						Secondary Conditions							
Variation	1	2	3	4	5	6	7	8	9	10	11	12	13	14

Tick Variation	1	2	3	4	5	6	7	8	9	10	11	12	13	14
64	0.0000	0.0000	0.2000	0.0000	0.0172	0.0000	0.0104	0.0282	0.0000	0.3333	0.0000	0.0000	0.0000	0.0000
63	0.0000	0.0000	0.4000	0.0000	0.0172	0.0061	0.0104	0.0282	0.0000	0.3333	0.0000	0.0000	0.0000	0.0000
62	0.0000	0.0000	0.4000	0.0000	0.0172	0.0061	0.0104	0.0282	0.0000	0.3333	0.0000	0.0000	0.0000	0.0000
61	0.0000	0.0000	0.4000	0.0000	0.0172	0.0061	0.0104	0.0282	0.0000	0.3333	0.0000	0.0000	0.0000	0.0000
60	0.0000	0.0000	0.4000	0.0000	0.0172	0.0061	0.0104	0.0282	0.0000	0.3333	0.0000	0.0000	0.0000	0.0000
59	0.0000	0.0000	0.4000	0.0000	0.0172	0.0122	0.0104	0.0282	0.0000	0.3333	0.0000	0.0000	0.0000	0.0000
58	0.0000	0.0000	0.4000	0.0000	0.0172	0.0122	0.0104	0.0282	0.0000	0.3333	0.0000	0.0000	0.0000	0.0000
57	0.0000	0.0000	0.4000	0.0000	0.0172	0.0122	0.0104	0.0282	0.0000	0.3333	0.0000	0.0000	0.0000	0.0000
56	0.0000	0.0000	0.4000	0.0000	0.0172	0.0183	0.0104	0.0282	0.0000	0.3333	0.0000	0.0000	0.0000	0.0000
55	0.0000	0.0000	0.4000	0.0000	0.0172	0.0183	0.0104	0.0282	0.0000	0.3333	0.0000	0.0000	0.0000	0.0000
54	0.0000	0.0000	0.4000	0.0000	0.0172	0.0244	0.0155	0.0282	0.0000	0.3333	0.0000	0.0000	0.0000	0.0000
53	0.0000	0.0000	0.4000	0.0000	0.0172	0.0305	0.0155	0.0282	0.0000	0.3333	0.0000	0.0000	0.0000	0.0000
52	0.0000	0.0000	0.4000	0.0000	0.0172	0.0305	0.0155	0.0282	0.0000	0.3333	0.0000	0.0000	0.0000	0.0000
51	0.0000	0.0000	0.4000	0.0000	0.0172	0.0366	0.0207	0.0282	0.0000	0.3333	0.0000	0.0000	0.0000	0.0000
50	0.0000	0.0000	0.4000	0.0000	0.0172	0.0366	0.0207	0.0282	0.0000	0.3333	0.0000	0.0000	0.0000	0.0000
49	0.0000	0.0000	0.4000	0.0000	0.0172	0.0366	0.0207	0.0282	0.0000	0.3333	0.0000	0.0000	0.0000	0.0000
48	0.0000	0.0000	0.4000	0.0000	0.0345	0.0366	0.0207	0.0282	0.0000	0.3333	0.0000	0.0000	0.0000	0.0000
47	0.0000	0.0000	0.4000	0.0000	0.0345	0.0366	0.0207	0.0423	0.0000	0.3333	0.0000	0.0000	0.0000	0.0000
46	0.0000	0.0000	0.4000	0.0000	0.0345	0.0366	0.0259	0.0423	0.0000	0.3333	0.0000	0.0000	0.0000	0.0000
45	0.0000	0.0000	0.4000	0.0000	0.0345	0.0366	0.0259	0.0423	0.0909	0.3333	0.0000	0.0000	0.0000	0.0000
44	0.0000	0.0000	0.4000	0.0000	0.0345	0.0366	0.0259	0.0423	0.0909	0.3333	0.0000	0.0000	0.0000	0.0000
43	0.0000	0.0000	0.4000	0.0000	0.0345	0.0427	0.0311	0.0423	0.0909	0.3333	0.0000	0.0000	0.0000	0.0000
42	0.0000	0.0000	0.4000	0.0000	0.0345	0.0427	0.0311	0.0423	0.0909	0.3333	0.0000	0.0000	0.0000	0.0000
41	0.0000	0.0000	0.4000	0.0000	0.0517	0.0427	0.0311	0.0423	0.0909	0.3333	0.0000	0.0000	0.0000	0.0000
40	0.0000	0.0000	0.4000	0.0000	0.0517	0.0427	0.0311	0.0423	0.0909	0.3333	0.0000	0.0000	0.0000	0.0000
39	0.0000	0.0000	0.4000	0.0000	0.0690	0.0488	0.0415	0.0423	0.0909	0.3333	0.0000	0.0000	0.0000	0.0000
38	0.0000	0.0000	0.4000	0.0000	0.0862	0.0488	0.0466	0.0704	0.0909	0.3333	0.0000	0.0000	0.0000	0.0000
37	0.0000	0.0000	0.4000	0.0000	0.0862	0.0488	0.0518	0.0704	0.0909	0.3333	0.0000	0.0000	0.0000	0.0000
36	0.0000	0.0000	0.4000	0.0000	0.1207	0.0488	0.0518	0.0845	0.0909	0.0000	0.0000	0.0000	0.0000	0.0000
35	0.0000	0.0000	0.4000	0.0000	0.1379	0.0488	0.0518	0.0845	0.0909	0.0000	0.0000	0.0000	0.0000	0.0000
34	0.0000	0.0000	0.4000	0.0000	0.1379	0.0549	0.0674	0.0986	0.0909	0.0000	0.0000	0.0000	0.0000	0.0000
33	0.0000	0.0000	0.4000	0.0000	0.1379	0.0610	0.0725	0.0986	0.0909	0.0000	0.0000	0.0000	0.0000	0.0000
32	0.0000	0.0000	0.4000	0.0000	0.1552	0.0732	0.0725	0.0986	0.0909	0.0000	0.0000	0.0000	0.0000	0.0000
31	0.0000	0.0000	0.4000	0.0000	0.1552	0.0854	0.0829	0.1408	0.0909	0.0000	0.0000	0.0000	0.0000	0.0000
30	0.0000	0.0000	0.4000	0.0000	0.1552	0.0854	0.0829	0.1690	0.0909	0.0000	0.0000	0.0000	0.0000	0.0000
29	0.0000	0.0000	0.4000	0.0000	0.1379	0.0854	0.0881	0.1831	0.0909	0.0000	0.0000	0.0000	0.0000	0.0000
28	0.0000	0.0000	0.6000	0.1000	0.1379	0.0854	0.0881	0.1972	0.1818	0.0000	0.0000	0.0000	0.0000	0.0000
27	0.0000	0.0000	0.6000	0.1000	0.1379	0.1037	0.0881	0.1972	0.1818	0.0000	0.0000	0.0000	0.0000	0.0000
26	0.0000	0.0000	0.6000	0.1000	0.1379	0.1341	0.0933	0.1972	0.1818	0.0000	0.0000	0.0000	0.0000	0.0000
25	0.0000	0.0000	0.6000	0.2000	0.1379	0.1524	0.0984	0.2113	0.2727	0.0000	0.0000	0.0000	0.0000	0.0000
24	0.0000	0.0000	0.6000	0.2000	0.1379	0.1707	0.1192	0.1972	0.2727	0.0000	0.0000	0.0000	0.0000	0.0000
23	0.0000	0.0000	0.8000	0.2000	0.1379	0.1890	0.1399	0.1972	0.2727	0.0000	0.0000	0.0000	0.0000	0.0000
22	0.0000	0.0000	0.8000	0.2000	0.1724	0.2012	0.1399	0.2394	0.2727	0.0000	0.0000	0.0000	0.0000	0.0000
21	0.0000	0.0000	0.8000	0.2000	0.2069	0.2134	0.1658	0.2817	0.2727	0.0000	0.0000	0.0000	0.0000	0.0000
20	0.0000	0.0000	0.8000	0.3000	0.2414	0.2195	0.1917	0.3380	0.2727	0.0000	0.0000	0.0000	0.0000	0.0000
19	0.0000	0.0000	0.8000	0.3000	0.2414	0.2317	0.2073	0.3380	0.2727	0.0000	0.0000	0.0000	0.0000	0.0000
18	0.0000	0.0000	0.8000	0.4000	0.2759	0.2439	0.2176	0.3803	0.3636	0.0000	0.0000	0.0000	0.0000	0.0000
17	0.0000	0.0000	1.0000	0.5000	0.2759	0.2500	0.2332	0.3944	0.3636	0.0000	0.0000	0.0000	0.0000	0.0000
16	0.0000	0.0000	1.0000	0.5000	0.2931	0.2500	0.2539	0.3944	0.3636	0.0000	0.0000	0.0000	0.0000	0.0000
15	0.0000	0.0000	1.0000	0.5000	0.3276	0.2988	0.2798	0.3944	0.4545	0.0000	0.0000	0.0000	0.0000	0.0000
14	0.0000	0.0000	1.0000	0.5000	0.3276	0.3171	0.3212	0.4507	0.4545	0.0000	0.0000	0.0000	0.0000	0.0000
13	0.0000	0.0000	1.0000	0.5000	0.3448	0.3354	0.3679	0.4648	0.4545	0.0000	0.0000	0.0000	0.0000	0.0000
12	0.0000	0.0000	1.0000	0.5000	0.3621	0.3841	0.3990	0.5070	0.4545	0.3333	0.0000	0.0000	0.0000	0.0000
11	0.0000	0.0000	1.0000	0.5000	0.3793	0.3841	0.4301	0.5352	0.5455	0.3333	0.0000	0.0000	0.0000	0.0000
10	0.0000	0.0000	1.0000	0.5000	0.4310	0.4085	0.4508	0.5634	0.6364	0.3333	0.0000	0.0000	0.0000	0.0000
9	0.0000	0.0000	1.0000	0.5000	0.4310	0.4512	0.4974	0.5775	0.7273	0.3333	0.0000	0.0000	0.0000	0.0000
8	0.0000	0.0000	1.0000	0.6000	0.4310	0.4695	0.5130	0.5915	0.7273	0.3333	0.0000	0.0000	0.0000	0.0000
7	0.0000	0.0000	1.0000	0.6000	0.4655	0.5061	0.5440	0.6197	0.7273	0.3333	0.0000	0.0000	0.0000	0.0000
6	0.0000	0.0000	1.0000	0.6000	0.5000	0.5915	0.5751	0.6620	0.7273	0.3333	0.0000	0.0000	0.0000	0.0000
5	0.0000	0.0000	1.0000	0.7000	0.5345	0.6402	0.6166	0.6761	0.7273	0.3333	0.0000	0.0000	0.0000	0.0000
4	0.0000	0.0000	1.0000	0.7000	0.6034	0.6829	0.6425	0.6761	0.8182	0.3333	0.0000	0.0000	0.0000	0.0000
3	0.0000	0.0000	1.0000	0.7000	0.6034	0.7073	0.6736	0.7324	0.8182	0.3333	0.0000	0.0000	0.0000	0.0000
2	0.0000	0.0000	1.0000	0.8000	0.6207	0.7500	0.6839	0.7042	0.8182	0.3333	0.0000	0.0000	0.0000	0.0000
1	0.0000	0.0000	1.0000	0.9000	0.6552	0.7805	0.7047	0.6901	0.8182	0.3333	0.0000	0.0000	0.0000	0.0000
0	0.0000	0.0000	1.0000	0.9000	0.7069	0.8171	0.6839	0.6901	0.8182	0.3333	0.0000	0.0000	0.0000	0.0000
−1	0.0000	0.0000	1.0000	0.9000	0.7069	0.8110	0.6684	0.7183	0.8182	0.3333	0.0000	0.0000	0.0000	0.0000
−2	0.0000	0.0000	1.0000	0.9000	0.7069	0.8171	0.6788	0.7042	0.8182	0.3333	0.0000	0.0000	0.0000	0.0000
−3	0.0000	0.0000	1.0000	0.8000	0.6552	0.8110	0.6477	0.7042	0.9091	0.3333	0.0000	0.0000	0.0000	0.0000
−4	0.0000	0.0000	1.0000	0.8000	0.6207	0.7683	0.6373	0.6901	0.9091	0.3333	0.0000	0.0000	0.0000	0.0000
−5	0.0000	0.0000	1.0000	0.8000	0.6034	0.6646	0.6166	0.6620	0.9091	0.3333	0.0000	0.0000	0.0000	0.0000
−6	0.0000	0.0000	1.0000	0.8000	0.6034	0.6341	0.5855	0.6056	0.9091	0.3333	0.0000	0.0000	0.0000	0.0000
−7	0.0000	0.0000	1.0000	0.8000	0.5517	0.6220	0.5648	0.5634	0.9091	0.3333	0.0000	0.0000	0.0000	0.0000
−8	0.0000	0.0000	0.8000	0.8000	0.5172	0.5671	0.5181	0.4930	0.8182	0.3333	0.0000	0.0000	0.0000	0.0000
−9	0.0000	0.0000	0.8000	0.8000	0.5345	0.5183	0.4611	0.4789	0.7273	0.3333	0.0000	0.0000	0.0000	0.0000
−10	0.0000	0.0000	0.8000	0.8000	0.5172	0.4939	0.4145	0.4648	0.5455	0.3333	0.0000	0.0000	0.0000	0.0000

Main Condition 6 (*Continued*)   Probabilities

Tick Variation	*1*	*2*	*3*	*4*	*5*	*6*	*7*	*8*	*9*	*10*	*11*	*12*	*13*	*14*
−11	0.0000	0.0000	0.8000	0.7000	0.5000	0.4512	0.3938	0.4085	0.5455	0.3333	0.0000	0.0000	0.0000	0.0000
−12	0.0000	0.0000	0.8000	0.7000	0.4655	0.3963	0.3627	0.4085	0.5455	0.6667	0.0000	0.0000	0.0000	0.0000
−13	0.0000	0.0000	0.8000	0.7000	0.3621	0.3659	0.3212	0.3944	0.5455	0.6667	0.0000	0.0000	0.0000	0.0000
−14	0.0000	0.0000	0.8000	0.8000	0.3448	0.3171	0.2902	0.4085	0.5455	0.6667	0.0000	0.0000	0.0000	0.0000
−15	0.0000	0.0000	0.8000	0.8000	0.2931	0.2744	0.2591	0.4085	0.5455	0.6667	0.0000	0.0000	0.0000	0.0000
−16	0.0000	0.0000	0.8000	0.8000	0.2586	0.2744	0.2383	0.3803	0.5455	0.6667	0.0000	0.0000	0.0000	0.0000
−17	0.0000	0.0000	0.8000	0.8000	0.2414	0.2622	0.2124	0.3521	0.5455	0.6667	0.0000	0.0000	0.0000	0.0000
−18	0.0000	0.0000	0.6000	0.6000	0.2241	0.2500	0.1813	0.3380	0.5455	0.6667	0.0000	0.0000	0.0000	0.0000
−19	0.0000	0.0000	0.4000	0.5000	0.2069	0.2134	0.1710	0.3380	0.5455	0.6667	0.0000	0.0000	0.0000	0.0000
−20	0.0000	0.0000	0.4000	0.5000	0.2069	0.2073	0.1606	0.3239	0.5455	0.6667	0.0000	0.0000	0.0000	0.0000
−21	0.0000	0.0000	0.4000	0.5000	0.2069	0.1890	0.1347	0.2958	0.5455	0.6667	0.0000	0.0000	0.0000	0.0000
−22	0.0000	0.0000	0.4000	0.4000	0.1897	0.1707	0.1244	0.2676	0.5455	0.6667	0.0000	0.0000	0.0000	0.0000
−23	0.0000	0.0000	0.4000	0.3000	0.1379	0.1585	0.1192	0.2254	0.5455	0.6667	0.0000	0.0000	0.0000	0.0000
−24	0.0000	0.0000	0.4000	0.3000	0.1379	0.1585	0.1088	0.2113	0.4545	0.6667	0.0000	0.0000	0.0000	0.0000
−25	0.0000	0.0000	0.4000	0.3000	0.1379	0.1524	0.1036	0.1831	0.4545	0.6667	0.0000	0.0000	0.0000	0.0000
−26	0.0000	0.0000	0.4000	0.3000	0.1034	0.1402	0.1036	0.1831	0.3636	0.6667	0.0000	0.0000	0.0000	0.0000
−27	0.0000	0.0000	0.4000	0.3000	0.1034	0.1280	0.0933	0.1831	0.3636	0.6667	0.0000	0.0000	0.0000	0.0000
−28	0.0000	0.0000	0.4000	0.3000	0.1034	0.1280	0.0881	0.1690	0.2727	0.6667	0.0000	0.0000	0.0000	0.0000
−29	0.0000	0.0000	0.4000	0.3000	0.1034	0.1159	0.0725	0.1408	0.2727	0.6667	0.0000	0.0000	0.0000	0.0000
−30	0.0000	0.0000	0.4000	0.3000	0.1034	0.1159	0.0674	0.1127	0.1818	0.6667	0.0000	0.0000	0.0000	0.0000
−31	0.0000	0.0000	0.4000	0.2000	0.1034	0.0976	0.0674	0.0845	0.0909	0.6667	0.0000	0.0000	0.0000	0.0000
−32	0.0000	0.0000	0.4000	0.2000	0.0690	0.0854	0.0622	0.0845	0.0909	0.6667	0.0000	0.0000	0.0000	0.0000
−33	0.0000	0.0000	0.4000	0.1000	0.0690	0.0854	0.0518	0.0986	0.0909	0.6667	0.0000	0.0000	0.0000	0.0000
−34	0.0000	0.0000	0.2000	0.1000	0.0690	0.0610	0.0466	0.0986	0.0909	0.6667	0.0000	0.0000	0.0000	0.0000
−35	0.0000	0.0000	0.2000	0.1000	0.0690	0.0610	0.0415	0.0986	0.0909	0.6667	0.0000	0.0000	0.0000	0.0000
−36	0.0000	0.0000	0.2000	0.1000	0.0690	0.0610	0.0259	0.0845	0.0909	0.6667	0.0000	0.0000	0.0000	0.0000
−37	0.0000	0.0000	0.0000	0.1000	0.0690	0.0610	0.0259	0.0845	0.0909	0.6667	0.0000	0.0000	0.0000	0.0000
−38	0.0000	0.0000	0.0000	0.1000	0.0517	0.0610	0.0259	0.0845	0.0000	0.0000	0.0000	0.0000	0.0000	0.0000
−39	0.0000	0.0000	0.0000	0.1000	0.0517	0.0427	0.0259	0.0845	0.0000	0.0000	0.0000	0.0000	0.0000	0.0000
−40	0.0000	0.0000	0.0000	0.1000	0.0345	0.0427	0.0259	0.0845	0.0000	0.0000	0.0000	0.0000	0.0000	0.0000
−41	0.0000	0.0000	0.0000	0.1000	0.0345	0.0305	0.0259	0.0845	0.0000	0.0000	0.0000	0.0000	0.0000	0.0000
−42	0.0000	0.0000	0.0000	0.1000	0.0345	0.0305	0.0259	0.0704	0.0000	0.0000	0.0000	0.0000	0.0000	0.0000
−43	0.0000	0.0000	0.0000	0.1000	0.0345	0.0305	0.0259	0.0704	0.0000	0.0000	0.0000	0.0000	0.0000	0.0000
−44	0.0000	0.0000	0.0000	0.1000	0.0345	0.0305	0.0259	0.0704	0.0000	0.0000	0.0000	0.0000	0.0000	0.0000
−45	0.0000	0.0000	0.0000	0.0000	0.0345	0.0305	0.0259	0.0704	0.0000	0.0000	0.0000	0.0000	0.0000	0.0000
−46	0.0000	0.0000	0.0000	0.0000	0.0345	0.0305	0.0207	0.0704	0.0000	0.0000	0.0000	0.0000	0.0000	0.0000
−47	0.0000	0.0000	0.0000	0.0000	0.0172	0.0305	0.0207	0.0563	0.0000	0.0000	0.0000	0.0000	0.0000	0.0000
−48	0.0000	0.0000	0.0000	0.0000	0.0172	0.0244	0.0207	0.0563	0.0000	0.0000	0.0000	0.0000	0.0000	0.0000
−49	0.0000	0.0000	0.0000	0.0000	0.0172	0.0244	0.0104	0.0563	0.0000	0.0000	0.0000	0.0000	0.0000	0.0000
−50	0.0000	0.0000	0.0000	0.0000	0.0000	0.0244	0.0104	0.0563	0.0000	0.0000	0.0000	0.0000	0.0000	0.0000
−51	0.0000	0.0000	0.0000	0.0000	0.0000	0.0244	0.0155	0.0563	0.0000	0.0000	0.0000	0.0000	0.0000	0.0000
−52	0.0000	0.0000	0.0000	0.0000	0.0000	0.0244	0.0104	0.0563	0.0000	0.0000	0.0000	0.0000	0.0000	0.0000
−53	0.0000	0.0000	0.0000	0.0000	0.0000	0.0244	0.0104	0.0563	0.0000	0.0000	0.0000	0.0000	0.0000	0.0000
−54	0.0000	0.0000	0.0000	0.0000	0.0000	0.0183	0.0052	0.0563	0.0000	0.0000	0.0000	0.0000	0.0000	0.0000
−55	0.0000	0.0000	0.0000	0.0000	0.0000	0.0122	0.0052	0.0563	0.0000	0.0000	0.0000	0.0000	0.0000	0.0000
−56	0.0000	0.0000	0.0000	0.0000	0.0000	0.0122	0.0052	0.0563	0.0000	0.0000	0.0000	0.0000	0.0000	0.0000
−57	0.0000	0.0000	0.0000	0.0000	0.0000	0.0122	0.0052	0.0563	0.0000	0.0000	0.0000	0.0000	0.0000	0.0000
−58	0.0000	0.0000	0.0000	0.0000	0.0000	0.0122	0.0052	0.0563	0.0000	0.0000	0.0000	0.0000	0.0000	0.0000
−59	0.0000	0.0000	0.0000	0.0000	0.0000	0.0122	0.0052	0.0563	0.0000	0.0000	0.0000	0.0000	0.0000	0.0000
−60	0.0000	0.0000	0.0000	0.0000	0.0000	0.0061	0.0052	0.0563	0.0000	0.0000	0.0000	0.0000	0.0000	0.0000
−61	0.0000	0.0000	0.0000	0.0000	0.0000	0.0061	0.0052	0.0423	0.0000	0.0000	0.0000	0.0000	0.0000	0.0000
−62	0.0000	0.0000	0.0000	0.0000	0.0000	0.0061	0.0052	0.0423	0.0000	0.0000	0.0000	0.0000	0.0000	0.0000
−63	0.0000	0.0000	0.0000	0.0000	0.0000	0.0061	0.0052	0.0423	0.0000	0.0000	0.0000	0.0000	0.0000	0.0000
−64	0.0000	0.0000	0.0000	0.0000	0.0000	0.0061	0.0052	0.0423	0.0000	0.0000	0.0000	0.0000	0.0000	0.0000

Main Condition 7						Probabilities							
Tick						Secondary Conditions							
Variation	1	2	3	4	5	6	7	8	9	10	11	12	13	14
64	0.0000	0.0000	0.0000	0.1667	0.0000	0.0000	0.0066	0.0055	0.0000	0.2222	0.0000	0.0000	0.0000	0.0000
63	0.0000	0.0000	0.0000	0.1667	0.0000	0.0000	0.0066	0.0055	0.0000	0.2222	0.0000	0.0000	0.0000	0.0000
62	0.0000	0.0000	0.0000	0.1667	0.0000	0.0000	0.0066	0.0109	0.0000	0.2222	0.0000	0.0000	0.0000	0.0000
61	0.0000	0.0000	0.0000	0.1667	0.0000	0.0000	0.0066	0.0109	0.0000	0.2222	0.0000	0.0000	0.0000	0.0000
60	0.0000	0.0000	0.0000	0.1667	0.0000	0.0000	0.0066	0.0109	0.0000	0.2222	0.0000	0.0000	0.0000	0.0000
59	0.0000	0.0000	0.0000	0.1667	0.0000	0.0000	0.0066	0.0109	0.0000	0.2222	0.0000	0.0000	0.0000	0.0000
58	0.0000	0.0000	0.0000	0.1667	0.0000	0.0000	0.0099	0.0109	0.0000	0.2222	0.0000	0.0000	0.0000	0.0000
57	0.0000	0.0000	0.0000	0.1667	0.0000	0.0000	0.0132	0.0109	0.0000	0.2222	0.0000	0.0000	0.0000	0.0000
56	0.0000	0.0000	0.0000	0.1667	0.0000	0.0000	0.0165	0.0109	0.0000	0.2222	0.0000	0.0000	0.0000	0.0000
55	0.0000	0.0000	0.0000	0.1667	0.0000	0.0000	0.0165	0.0109	0.0000	0.2222	0.0000	0.0000	0.0000	0.0000
54	0.0000	0.0000	0.0000	0.3333	0.0000	0.0000	0.0165	0.0109	0.0000	0.2222	0.0000	0.0000	0.0000	0.0000
53	0.0000	0.0000	0.0000	0.3333	0.0000	0.0000	0.0165	0.0109	0.0000	0.2222	0.0000	0.0000	0.0000	0.0000
52	0.0000	0.0000	0.0000	0.3333	0.0000	0.0000	0.0231	0.0109	0.0000	0.2222	0.0000	0.0000	0.0000	0.0000
51	0.0000	0.0000	0.0000	0.3333	0.0000	0.0109	0.0231	0.0109	0.0000	0.2222	0.0000	0.0000	0.0000	0.0000
50	0.0000	0.0000	0.0000	0.3333	0.0000	0.0109	0.0231	0.0164	0.0000	0.2222	0.0000	0.0000	0.0000	0.0000
49	0.0000	0.0000	0.0000	0.3333	0.0000	0.0109	0.0231	0.0164	0.0000	0.2222	0.0000	0.0000	0.0000	0.0000
48	0.0000	0.0000	0.0000	0.3333	0.0000	0.0109	0.0231	0.0164	0.0000	0.2222	0.0000	0.0000	0.0000	0.0000
47	0.0000	0.0000	0.0000	0.3333	0.0000	0.0109	0.0231	0.0164	0.0000	0.2222	0.0000	0.0000	0.0000	0.0000
46	0.0000	0.0000	0.0000	0.3333	0.0000	0.0109	0.0231	0.0164	0.0000	0.2222	0.0000	0.0000	0.0000	0.0000
45	0.0000	0.0000	0.0000	0.3333	0.0000	0.0109	0.0231	0.0164	0.0000	0.2222	0.0000	0.0000	0.0000	0.0000
44	0.0000	0.0000	0.0000	0.3333	0.0417	0.0109	0.0264	0.0164	0.0000	0.2222	0.0000	0.0000	0.0000	0.0000
43	0.0000	0.0000	0.0000	0.3333	0.0417	0.0109	0.0264	0.0164	0.0000	0.2222	0.0000	0.0000	0.0000	0.0000
42	0.0000	0.0000	0.0000	0.3333	0.0417	0.0109	0.0297	0.0273	0.0000	0.2222	0.0000	0.0000	0.0000	0.0000
41	0.0000	0.0000	0.0000	0.3333	0.0417	0.0109	0.0363	0.0273	0.0000	0.2222	0.0000	0.0000	0.0000	0.0000
40	0.0000	0.0000	0.0000	0.3333	0.0417	0.0109	0.0429	0.0328	0.0000	0.2222	0.0000	0.0000	0.0000	0.0000
39	0.0000	0.0000	0.0000	0.3333	0.0833	0.0109	0.0462	0.0328	0.0500	0.3333	0.0000	0.0000	0.0000	0.0000
38	0.0000	0.0000	0.0000	0.3333	0.1250	0.0109	0.0528	0.0328	0.0500	0.3333	0.0000	0.0000	0.0000	0.0000
37	0.0000	0.0000	0.0000	0.3333	0.1667	0.0109	0.0528	0.0328	0.0750	0.3333	0.0000	0.0000	0.0000	0.0000
36	0.0000	0.0000	0.0000	0.3333	0.1667	0.0109	0.0528	0.0383	0.0750	0.3333	0.0000	0.0000	0.0000	0.0000
35	0.0000	0.0000	0.0000	0.3333	0.1667	0.0109	0.0660	0.0383	0.0750	0.3333	0.0000	0.0000	0.0000	0.0000
34	0.0000	0.0000	0.0000	0.3333	0.1667	0.0109	0.0693	0.0383	0.1000	0.3333	0.0000	0.0000	0.0000	0.0000
33	0.0000	0.0000	0.0000	0.3333	0.1667	0.0326	0.0726	0.0546	0.1000	0.3333	0.0000	0.0000	0.0000	0.0000
32	0.0000	0.0000	0.0000	0.3333	0.1667	0.0435	0.0825	0.0601	0.1000	0.3333	0.0000	0.0000	0.0000	0.0000
31	0.0000	0.0000	0.0000	0.3333	0.1667	0.0652	0.0858	0.0601	0.1000	0.3333	0.0000	0.0000	0.0000	0.0000
30	0.0000	0.0000	0.0000	0.3333	0.1667	0.0761	0.0924	0.0601	0.1250	0.3333	0.0000	0.0000	0.0000	0.0000
29	0.0000	0.0000	0.0000	0.3333	0.1667	0.0761	0.0957	0.0656	0.1500	0.3333	0.0000	0.0000	0.0000	0.0000
28	0.0000	0.0000	0.0000	0.3333	0.1667	0.0761	0.1023	0.0710	0.1750	0.4444	0.0000	0.0000	0.0000	0.0000
27	0.0000	0.0000	0.0000	0.3333	0.1667	0.0870	0.1122	0.0765	0.1750	0.4444	0.0000	0.0000	0.0000	0.0000
26	0.0000	0.0000	0.0000	0.3333	0.1667	0.0870	0.1188	0.0820	0.1750	0.5556	0.0000	0.0000	0.0000	0.0000
25	0.0000	0.0000	0.0000	0.3333	0.1667	0.0978	0.1221	0.0929	0.1750	0.5556	0.0000	0.0000	0.0000	0.0000
24	0.0000	0.0000	0.0000	0.3333	0.1667	0.1196	0.1353	0.0984	0.1750	0.5556	0.0000	0.0000	0.0000	0.0000
23	0.0000	0.0000	0.0000	0.5000	0.1667	0.1413	0.1353	0.1093	0.2000	0.5556	0.0000	0.0000	0.0000	0.0000
22	0.0000	0.0000	0.0000	0.5000	0.1667	0.1522	0.1452	0.1148	0.2500	0.5556	0.0000	0.0000	0.0000	0.0000
21	0.0000	0.0000	0.0000	0.5000	0.2083	0.1739	0.1485	0.1421	0.2750	0.6667	0.0000	0.0000	0.0000	0.0000
20	0.0000	0.0000	0.0000	0.5000	0.2083	0.1848	0.1617	0.1639	0.2750	0.6667	0.0000	0.0000	0.0000	0.0000
19	0.0000	0.0000	0.0000	0.5000	0.2917	0.2065	0.1749	0.1803	0.3250	0.6667	0.0000	0.0000	0.0000	0.0000
18	0.0000	0.0000	0.0000	0.6667	0.2917	0.2283	0.1881	0.1803	0.3500	0.6667	0.0000	0.0000	0.0000	0.0000
17	0.0000	0.0000	0.0000	0.8333	0.2500	0.2500	0.2178	0.2077	0.3500	0.6667	0.0000	0.0000	0.0000	0.0000
16	0.0000	0.0000	0.0000	0.8333	0.2500	0.2826	0.2376	0.2459	0.3500	0.6667	0.0000	0.0000	0.0000	0.0000
15	0.0000	0.0000	0.0000	0.8333	0.2500	0.2826	0.2541	0.2568	0.3750	0.6667	0.0000	0.0000	0.0000	0.0000
14	0.0000	0.0000	0.0000	0.6667	0.2500	0.3478	0.2739	0.2787	0.4000	0.6667	0.0000	0.0000	0.0000	0.0000
13	0.0000	0.0000	0.0000	0.6667	0.3333	0.3587	0.2970	0.2951	0.4250	0.6667	0.0000	0.0000	0.0000	0.0000
12	0.0000	0.0000	0.0000	0.6667	0.3750	0.3804	0.3300	0.3279	0.4250	0.6667	0.0000	0.0000	0.0000	0.0000
11	0.0000	0.0000	0.0000	0.6667	0.4167	0.4239	0.3663	0.3661	0.5000	0.6667	0.0000	0.0000	0.0000	0.0000
10	0.0000	0.0000	0.0000	0.6667	0.4583	0.4674	0.4125	0.3989	0.5000	0.6667	0.0000	0.0000	0.0000	0.0000
9	0.0000	0.0000	0.0000	0.6667	0.4583	0.4891	0.4323	0.4317	0.5750	0.7778	0.0000	0.0000	0.0000	0.0000
8	0.0000	0.0000	0.0000	0.6667	0.5417	0.5326	0.4851	0.4645	0.5750	0.7778	0.0000	0.0000	0.0000	0.0000
7	0.0000	0.0000	0.0000	0.6667	0.5417	0.5652	0.5116	0.5191	0.6250	0.7778	0.0000	0.0000	0.0000	0.0000
6	0.0000	0.0000	0.0000	0.6667	0.5833	0.6087	0.5215	0.5355	0.6750	0.7778	0.0000	0.0000	0.0000	0.0000
5	0.0000	0.0000	0.0000	0.6667	0.5833	0.6630	0.5644	0.6066	0.7000	0.7778	0.0000	0.0000	0.0000	0.0000
4	0.0000	0.0000	0.0000	0.6667	0.5833	0.6957	0.6040	0.6284	0.6750	0.7778	0.0000	0.0000	0.0000	0.0000
3	0.0000	0.0000	0.0000	0.6667	0.6667	0.6957	0.6205	0.6667	0.6750	0.8889	0.0000	0.0000	0.0000	0.0000
2	0.0000	0.0000	0.0000	0.6667	0.6667	0.7500	0.6469	0.6885	0.7000	0.8889	0.0000	0.0000	0.0000	0.0000
1	0.0000	0.0000	0.0000	0.6667	0.5833	0.7500	0.6766	0.7049	0.7000	0.8889	0.0000	0.0000	0.0000	0.0000
0	0.0000	0.0000	0.0000	0.6667	0.5417	0.6957	0.6964	0.6940	0.7250	0.8889	0.0000	0.0000	0.0000	0.0000
-1	0.0000	0.0000	0.0000	0.5000	0.5833	0.6848	0.6964	0.6612	0.7250	0.8889	0.0000	0.0000	0.0000	0.0000
-2	0.0000	0.0000	0.0000	0.5000	0.6667	0.6739	0.7030	0.6776	0.7250	0.7778	0.0000	0.0000	0.0000	0.0000
-3	0.0000	0.0000	0.0000	0.5000	0.7083	0.6630	0.6766	0.6776	0.7500	0.7778	0.0000	0.0000	0.0000	0.0000
-4	0.0000	0.0000	0.0000	0.5000	0.7083	0.6522	0.6337	0.6667	0.7500	0.7778	0.0000	0.0000	0.0000	0.0000
-5	0.0000	0.0000	0.0000	0.5000	0.7500	0.5978	0.5875	0.6284	0.7000	0.6667	0.0000	0.0000	0.0000	0.0000
-6	0.0000	0.0000	0.0000	0.5000	0.7500	0.5217	0.5479	0.5847	0.6500	0.6667	0.0000	0.0000	0.0000	0.0000
-7	0.0000	0.0000	0.0000	0.5000	0.7500	0.4891	0.4950	0.5519	0.6500	0.6667	0.0000	0.0000	0.0000	0.0000
-8	0.0000	0.0000	0.0000	0.5000	0.7500	0.4674	0.4587	0.5082	0.6250	0.6667	0.0000	0.0000	0.0000	0.0000
-9	0.0000	0.0000	0.0000	0.5000	0.7083	0.4022	0.3960	0.4918	0.6000	0.6667	0.0000	0.0000	0.0000	0.0000
-10	0.0000	0.0000	0.0000	0.5000	0.6667	0.3587	0.3465	0.4317	0.6000	0.6667	0.0000	0.0000	0.0000	0.0000

Main Condition 7 *(Continued)*   Probabilities

Tick							Secondary Conditions							
Variation	*1*	*2*	*3*	*4*	*5*	*6*	*7*	*8*	*9*	*10*	*11*	*12*	*13*	*14*
−11	0.0000	0.0000	0.0000	0.5000	0.5417	0.3478	0.3201	0.4044	0.5500	0.6667	0.0000	0.0000	0.0000	0.0000
−12	0.0000	0.0000	0.0000	0.5000	0.4583	0.3152	0.3036	0.3661	0.5250	0.6667	0.0000	0.0000	0.0000	0.0000
−13	0.0000	0.0000	0.0000	0.5000	0.4167	0.2826	0.2673	0.3443	0.4750	0.5556	0.0000	0.0000	0.0000	0.0000
−14	0.0000	0.0000	0.0000	0.5000	0.3750	0.2826	0.2508	0.3115	0.4500	0.5556	0.0000	0.0000	0.0000	0.0000
−15	0.0000	0.0000	0.0000	0.3333	0.3750	0.2717	0.2277	0.2732	0.4250	0.4444	0.0000	0.0000	0.0000	0.0000
−16	0.0000	0.0000	0.0000	0.3333	0.3333	0.2717	0.1947	0.2404	0.4250	0.4444	0.0000	0.0000	0.0000	0.0000
−17	0.0000	0.0000	0.0000	0.3333	0.2917	0.2500	0.1617	0.2240	0.4000	0.4444	0.0000	0.0000	0.0000	0.0000
−18	0.0000	0.0000	0.0000	0.3333	0.2917	0.2391	0.1419	0.2022	0.3500	0.4444	0.0000	0.0000	0.0000	0.0000
−19	0.0000	0.0000	0.0000	0.3333	0.2917	0.2174	0.1320	0.1967	0.3500	0.4444	0.0000	0.0000	0.0000	0.0000
−20	0.0000	0.0000	0.0000	0.5000	0.2083	0.2174	0.1254	0.1694	0.3000	0.4444	0.0000	0.0000	0.0000	0.0000
−21	0.0000	0.0000	0.0000	0.5000	0.2083	0.2174	0.1155	0.1530	0.2750	0.4444	0.0000	0.0000	0.0000	0.0000
−22	0.0000	0.0000	0.0000	0.5000	0.2083	0.2283	0.1155	0.1421	0.2750	0.4444	0.0000	0.0000	0.0000	0.0000
−23	0.0000	0.0000	0.0000	0.5000	0.2083	0.2174	0.1122	0.1257	0.3000	0.4444	0.0000	0.0000	0.0000	0.0000
−24	0.0000	0.0000	0.0000	0.5000	0.2083	0.2065	0.1089	0.1202	0.3000	0.3333	0.0000	0.0000	0.0000	0.0000
−25	0.0000	0.0000	0.0000	0.3333	0.1667	0.1739	0.0990	0.1148	0.2750	0.3333	0.0000	0.0000	0.0000	0.0000
−26	0.0000	0.0000	0.0000	0.3333	0.1250	0.1630	0.0924	0.0984	0.2750	0.3333	0.0000	0.0000	0.0000	0.0000
−27	0.0000	0.0000	0.0000	0.3333	0.1250	0.1630	0.0858	0.0929	0.2500	0.3333	0.0000	0.0000	0.0000	0.0000
−28	0.0000	0.0000	0.0000	0.3333	0.1250	0.1630	0.0825	•0.0820	0.2000	0.3333	0.0000	0.0000	0.0000	0.0000
−29	0.0000	0.0000	0.0000	0.3333	0.1250	0.1630	0.0726	0.0820	0.1750	0.3333	0.0000	0.0000	0.0000	0.0000
−30	0.0000	0.0000	0.0000	0.3333	0.0833	0.1522	0.0627	0.0765	0.1500	0.3333	0.0000	0.0000	0.0000	0.0000
−31	0.0000	0.0000	0.0000	0.3333	0.0833	0.1196	0.0594	0.0765	0.1500	0.3333	0.0000	0.0000	0.0000	0.0000
−32	0.0000	0.0000	0.0000	0.3333	0.0833	0.1196	0.0561	0.0601	0.1500	0.3333	0.0000	0.0000	0.0000	0.0000
−33	0.0000	0.0000	0.0000	0.3333	0.0833	0.1196	0.0495	0.0601	0.1500	0.2222	0.0000	0.0000	0.0000	0.0000
−34	0.0000	0.0000	0.0000	0.3333	0.0417	0.1087	0.0462	0.0546	0.1500	0.2222	0.0000	0.0000	0.0000	0.0000
−35	0.0000	0.0000	0.0000	0.3333	0.0417	0.1087	0.0462	0.0492	0.1500	0.2222	0.0000	0.0000	0.0000	0.0000
−36	0.0000	0.0000	0.0000	0.3333	0.0417	0.1087	0.0330	0.0437	0.1250	0.2222	0.0000	0.0000	0.0000	0.0000
−37	0.0000	0.0000	0.0000	0.3333	0.0417	0.0978	0.0330	0.0383	0.1250	0.2222	0.0000	0.0000	0.0000	0.0000
−38	0.0000	0.0000	0.0000	0.3333	0.0417	0.0978	0.0297	0.0383	0.1250	0.2222	0.0000	0.0000	0.0000	0.0000
−39	0.0000	0.0000	0.0000	0.3333	0.0417	0.0978	0.0264	0.0328	0.1250	0.2222	0.0000	0.0000	0.0000	0.0000
−40	0.0000	0.0000	0.0000	0.3333	0.0417	0.0761	0.0264	0.0273	0.1250	0.2222	0.0000	0.0000	0.0000	0.0000
−41	0.0000	0.0000	0.0000	0.3333	0.0417	0.0761	0.0231	0.0273	0.1250	0.2222	0.0000	0.0000	0.0000	0.0000
−42	0.0000	0.0000	0.0000	0.3333	0.0000	0.0761	0.0231	0.0273	0.1000	0.2222	0.0000	0.0000	0.0000	0.0000
−43	0.0000	0.0000	0.0000	0.3333	0.0000	0.0435	0.0198	0.0109	0.1000	0.2222	0.0000	0.0000	0.0000	0.0000
−44	0.0000	0.0000	0.0000	0.3333	0.0000	0.0217	0.0165	0.0109	0.1000	0.2222	0.0000	0.0000	0.0000	0.0000
−45	0.0000	0.0000	0.0000	0.3333	0.0000	0.0217	0.0165	0.0109	0.1000	0.2222	0.0000	0.0000	0.0000	0.0000
−46	0.0000	0.0000	0.0000	0.3333	0.0000	0.0217	0.0132	0.0109	0.1000	0.2222	0.0000	0.0000	0.0000	0.0000
−47	0.0000	0.0000	0.0000	0.3333	0.0000	0.0217	0.0132	0.0109	0.1000	0.2222	0.0000	0.0000	0.0000	0.0000
−48	0.0000	0.0000	0.0000	0.3333	0.0000	0.0217	0.0132	0.0109	0.0750	0.2222	0.0000	0.0000	0.0000	0.0000
−49	0.0000	0.0000	0.0000	0.1667	0.0000	0.0109	0.0132	0.0109	0.0750	0.2222	0.0000	0.0000	0.0000	0.0000
−50	0.0000	0.0000	0.0000	0.1667	0.0000	0.0109	0.0132	0.0055	0.0750	0.2222	0.0000	0.0000	0.0000	0.0000
−51	0.0000	0.0000	0.0000	0.1667	0.0000	0.0109	0.0132	0.0055	0.0750	0.2222	0.0000	0.0000	0.0000	0.0000
−52	0.0000	0.0000	0.0000	0.1667	0.0000	0.0109	0.0099	0.0055	0.0750	0.2222	0.0000	0.0000	0.0000	0.0000
−53	0.0000	0.0000	0.0000	0.1667	0.0000	0.0109	0.0099	0.0055	0.0750	0.2222	0.0000	0.0000	0.0000	0.0000
−54	0.0000	0.0000	0.0000	0.0000	0.0000	0.0109	0.0099	0.0055	0.0750	0.2222	0.0000	0.0000	0.0000	0.0000
−55	0.0000	0.0000	0.0000	0.0000	0.0000	0.0109	0.0099	0.0055	0.0750	0.2222	0.0000	0.0000	0.0000	0.0000
−56	0.0000	0.0000	0.0000	0.0000	0.0000	0.0109	0.0099	0.0055	0.0750	0.2222	0.0000	0.0000	0.0000	0.0000
−57	0.0000	0.0000	0.0000	0.0000	0.0000	0.0109	0.0099	0.0055	0.0500	0.2222	0.0000	0.0000	0.0000	0.0000
−58	0.0000	0.0000	0.0000	0.0000	0.0000	0.0109	0.0099	0.0055	0.0500	0.2222	0.0000	0.0000	0.0000	0.0000
−59	0.0000	0.0000	0.0000	0.0000	0.0000	0.0109	0.0099	0.0055	0.0500	0.2222	0.0000	0.0000	0.0000	0.0000
−60	0.0000	0.0000	0.0000	0.0000	0.0000	0.0109	0.0099	0.0055	0.0500	0.2222	0.0000	0.0000	0.0000	0.0000
−61	0.0000	0.0000	0.0000	0.0000	0.0000	0.0109	0.0066	0.0055	0.0500	0.2222	0.0000	0.0000	0.0000	0.0000
−62	0.0000	0.0000	0.0000	0.0000	0.0000	0.0000	0.0066	0.0055	0.0500	0.2222	0.0000	0.0000	0.0000	0.0000
−63	0.0000	0.0000	0.0000	0.0000	0.0000	0.0000	0.0033	0.0000	0.0500	0.2222	0.0000	0.0000	0.0000	0.0000
−64	0.0000	0.0000	0.0000	0.0000	0.0000	0.0000	0.0033	0.0000	0.0500	0.1111	0.0000	0.0000	0.0000	0.0000

Main Condition 8   Probabilities

Tick Variation	*Secondary Conditions*													
	1	2	3	4	5	6	7	8	9	10	11	12	13	14
64	0.0000	0.0000	0.0000	0.0000	0.0000	0.0000	0.0000	0.0000	0.0085	0.0556	0.0000	0.0000	0.0000	0.0000
63	0.0000	0.0000	0.0000	0.2500	0.0000	0.0000	0.0000	0.0000	0.0085	0.0556	0.0000	0.0000	0.0000	0.0000
62	0.0000	0.0000	0.0000	0.2500	0.0000	0.0000	0.0000	0.0000	0.0085	0.0556	0.0000	0.0000	0.0000	0.0000
61	0.0000	0.0000	0.0000	0.2500	0.0000	0.0000	0.0000	0.0000	0.0085	0.1111	0.0000	0.0000	0.0000	0.0000
60	0.0000	0.0000	0.0000	0.2500	0.0000	0.0000	0.0000	0.0000	0.0085	0.1111	0.0000	0.0000	0.0000	0.0000
59	0.0000	0.0000	0.0000	0.2500	0.0000	0.0000	0.0000	0.0000	0.0085	0.1111	0.0000	0.0000	0.0000	0.0000
58	0.0000	0.0000	0.0000	0.2500	0.0000	0.0000	0.0000	0.0034	0.0085	0.1111	0.0000	0.0000	0.0000	0.0000
57	0.0000	0.0000	0.0000	0.2500	0.0000	0.0000	0.0000	0.0034	0.0085	0.1111	0.0000	0.0000	0.0000	0.0000
56	0.0000	0.0000	0.0000	0.2500	0.0000	0.0000	0.0000	0.0034	0.0085	0.1667	0.0000	0.0000	0.0000	0.0000
55	0.0000	0.0000	0.0000	0.2500	0.0000	0.0000	0.0049	0.0034	0.0085	0.1667	0.0000	0.0000	0.0000	0.0000
54	0.0000	0.0000	0.0000	0.2500	0.0000	0.0000	0.0049	0.0034	0.0085	0.2222	0.0000	0.0000	0.0000	0.0000
53	0.0000	0.0000	0.0000	0.2500	0.0000	0.0000	0.0049	0.0034	0.0085	0.2222	0.0000	0.0000	0.0000	0.0000
52	0.0000	0.0000	0.0000	0.2500	0.0000	0.0000	0.0049	0.0034	0.0085	0.2222	0.0000	0.0000	0.0000	0.0000
51	0.0000	0.0000	0.0000	0.2500	0.0000	0.0000	0.0049	0.0034	0.0085	0.2222	0.0000	0.0000	0.0000	0.0000
50	0.0000	0.0000	0.0000	0.2500	0.0000	0.0000	0.0049	0.0034	0.0085	0.2222	0.0000	0.0000	0.0000	0.0000
49	0.0000	0.0000	0.0000	0.2500	0.0000	0.0000	0.0049	0.0067	0.0085	0.2222	0.0000	0.0000	0.0000	0.0000
48	0.0000	0.0000	0.0000	0.2500	0.0000	0.0000	0.0097	0.0067	0.0085	0.2222	0.0000	0.0000	0.0000	0.0000
47	0.0000	0.0000	0.0000	0.2500	0.0000	0.0000	0.0097	0.0067	0.0085	0.2222	0.0000	0.0000	0.0000	0.0000
46	0.0000	0.0000	0.0000	0.2500	0.0000	0.0000	0.0097	0.0101	0.0085	0.2222	0.0000	0.0000	0.0000	0.0000
45	0.0000	0.0000	0.0000	0.2500	0.0000	0.0256	0.0146	0.0101	0.0085	0.2222	0.0000	0.0000	0.0000	0.0000
44	0.0000	0.0000	0.0000	0.2500	0.0000	0.0256	0.0146	0.0101	0.0085	0.2222	0.0000	0.0000	0.0000	0.0000
43	0.0000	0.0000	0.0000	0.2500	0.1000	0.0256	0.0146	0.0101	0.0169	0.2222	0.0000	0.0000	0.0000	0.0000
42	0.0000	0.0000	0.0000	0.2500	0.1000	0.0256	0.0146	0.0101	0.0254	0.2222	0.0000	0.0000	0.0000	0.0000
41	0.0000	0.0000	0.0000	0.2500	0.1000	0.0513	0.0146	0.0135	0.0254	0.2222	0.0000	0.0000	0.0000	0.0000
40	0.0000	0.0000	0.0000	0.2500	0.1000	0.0513	0.0194	0.0135	0.0254	0.2222	0.0000	0.0000	0.0000	0.0000
39	0.0000	0.0000	0.0000	0.2500	0.1000	0.0513	0.0243	0.0135	0.0339	0.2222	0.0000	0.0000	0.0000	0.0000
38	0.0000	0.0000	0.0000	0.2500	0.1000	0.0513	0.0243	0.0135	0.0339	0.2222	0.0000	0.0000	0.0000	0.0000
37	0.0000	0.0000	0.0000	0.2500	0.1000	0.0769	0.0243	0.0135	0.0424	0.1667	0.0000	0.0000	0.0000	0.0000
36	0.0000	0.0000	0.0000	0.2500	0.1000	0.0769	0.0291	0.0168	0.0424	0.2222	0.0000	0.0000	0.0000	0.0000
35	0.0000	0.0000	0.0000	0.2500	0.1000	0.0769	0.0340	0.0236	0.0424	0.2222	0.0000	0.0000	0.0000	0.0000
34	0.0000	0.0000	0.0000	0.2500	0.1000	0.0769	0.0388	0.0303	0.0424	0.2222	0.0000	0.0000	0.0000	0.0000
33	0.0000	0.0000	0.0000	0.5000	0.1000	0.0769	0.0485	0.0303	0.0593	0.2222	0.0000	0.0000	0.0000	0.0000
32	0.0000	0.0000	0.0000	0.5000	0.1000	0.1282	0.0485	0.0303	0.0593	0.2222	0.0000	0.0000	0.0000	0.0000
31	0.0000	0.0000	0.0000	0.5000	0.1000	0.1282	0.0583	0.0337	0.0678	0.2222	0.0000	0.0000	0.0000	0.0000
30	0.0000	0.0000	0.0000	0.5000	0.1000	0.1282	0.0728	0.0337	0.0678	0.2778	0.0000	0.0000	0.0000	0.0000
29	0.0000	0.0000	0.0000	0.5000	0.1000	0.1538	0.0922	0.0370	0.0763	0.2778	0.0000	0.0000	0.0000	0.0000
28	0.0000	0.0000	0.0000	0.5000	0.1000	0.1538	0.0922	0.0471	0.0932	0.2778	0.0000	0.0000	0.0000	0.0000
27	0.0000	0.0000	0.0000	0.5000	0.1000	0.1795	0.1068	0.0539	0.1102	0.2778	0.0000	0.0000	0.0000	0.0000
26	0.0000	0.0000	0.0000	0.5000	0.2000	0.1795	0.1214	0.0640	0.1102	0.2778	0.0000	0.0000	0.0000	0.0000
25	0.0000	0.0000	0.0000	0.5000	0.2000	0.1795	0.1214	0.0808	0.1186	0.2778	0.0000	0.0000	0.0000	0.0000
24	0.0000	0.0000	0.0000	0.5000	0.2000	0.1795	0.1262	0.0909	0.1271	0.2778	0.0000	0.0000	0.0000	0.0000
23	0.0000	0.0000	0.0000	0.5000	0.2000	0.2051	0.1456	0.1010	0.1441	0.2778	0.0000	0.0000	0.0000	0.0000
22	0.0000	0.0000	0.0000	0.5000	0.2000	0.2308	0.1602	0.1178	0.1525	0.3333	0.0000	0.0000	0.0000	0.0000
21	0.0000	0.0000	0.0000	0.5000	0.2000	0.2308	0.1748	0.1347	0.2034	0.3333	0.0000	0.0000	0.0000	0.0000
20	0.0000	0.0000	0.0000	0.5000	0.3000	0.2308	0.1845	0.1582	0.2034	0.4444	0.0000	0.0000	0.0000	0.0000
19	0.0000	0.0000	0.0000	0.5000	0.3000	0.2564	0.1893	0.1751	0.2288	0.4444	0.0000	0.0000	0.0000	0.0000
18	0.0000	0.0000	0.0000	0.5000	0.3000	0.2821	0.1942	0.1919	0.2373	0.4444	0.0000	0.0000	0.0000	0.0000
17	0.0000	0.0000	0.0000	0.5000	0.4000	0.3077	0.2184	0.2020	0.2797	0.5000	0.0000	0.0000	0.0000	0.0000
16	0.0000	0.0000	0.0000	0.5000	0.5000	0.3077	0.2427	0.2323	0.2881	0.5000	0.2000	0.0000	0.0000	0.0000
15	0.0000	0.0000	0.0000	0.5000	0.5000	0.3077	0.2670	0.2391	0.3136	0.5000	0.2000	0.0000	0.0000	0.0000
14	0.0000	0.0000	0.0000	0.5000	0.5000	0.3077	0.3058	0.2694	0.3305	0.5000	0.2000	0.0000	0.0000	0.0000
13	0.0000	0.0000	0.0000	0.5000	0.5000	0.3590	0.3350	0.2828	0.3729	0.5000	0.2000	0.0000	0.0000	0.0000
12	0.0000	0.0000	0.0000	0.5000	0.5000	0.3590	0.3835	0.3131	0.4068	0.5556	0.6000	0.0000	0.0000	0.0000
11	0.0000	0.0000	0.0000	0.5000	0.5000	0.3590	0.4126	0.3434	0.4492	0.5556	0.6000	0.0000	0.0000	0.0000
10	0.0000	0.0000	0.0000	0.5000	0.5000	0.3333	0.4515	0.3872	0.4576	0.6111	0.6000	0.0000	0.0000	0.0000
9	0.0000	0.0000	0.0000	0.7500	0.5000	0.4615	0.4951	0.4108	0.5169	0.7222	0.6000	0.0000	0.0000	0.0000
8	0.0000	0.0000	0.0000	0.7500	0.5000	0.4615	0.5388	0.4545	0.5424	0.7778	0.6000	0.0000	0.0000	0.0000
7	0.0000	0.0000	0.0000	0.7500	0.5000	0.4615	0.5631	0.4815	0.5593	0.8333	0.6000	0.0000	0.0000	0.0000
6	0.0000	0.0000	0.0000	0.7500	0.7000	0.4615	0.5971	0.5084	0.6017	0.7778	0.6000	0.0000	0.0000	0.0000
5	0.0000	0.0000	0.0000	0.7500	0.7000	0.4872	0.6262	0.5556	0.6695	0.7778	0.6000	0.0000	0.0000	0.0000
4	0.0000	0.0000	0.0000	0.7500	0.7000	0.4872	0.6748	0.5926	0.7288	0.7778	0.6000	0.0000	0.0000	0.0000
3	0.0000	0.0000	0.0000	0.7500	0.8000	0.4872	0.6796	0.6094	0.7288	0.8333	0.6000	0.0000	0.0000	0.0000
2	0.0000	0.0000	0.0000	0.5000	0.8000	0.5641	0.7039	0.6296	0.7288	0.7778	0.6000	0.0000	0.0000	0.0000
1	0.0000	0.0000	0.0000	0.5000	0.8000	0.5897	0.7330	0.6498	0.7288	0.7778	0.8000	0.0000	0.0000	0.0000
0	0.0000	0.0000	0.0000	0.5000	0.8000	0.6410	0.7379	0.6633	0.6949	0.7778	0.8000	0.0000	0.0000	0.0000
-1	0.0000	0.0000	0.0000	0.5000	0.8000	0.6923	0.7379	0.6599	0.7119	0.7222	1.0000	0.0000	0.0000	0.0000
-2	0.0000	0.0000	0.0000	0.5000	0.9000	0.6923	0.6845	0.6801	0.6949	0.7222	1.0000	0.0000	0.0000	0.0000
-3	0.0000	0.0000	0.0000	0.5000	0.9000	0.6923	0.6408	0.6397	0.6610	0.6667	0.8000	0.0000	0.0000	0.0000
-4	0.0000	0.0000	0.0000	0.5000	0.9000	0.6117	0.5993	0.6102	0.6525	0.6111	0.8000	0.0000	0.0000	0.0000
-5	0.0000	0.0000	0.0000	0.5000	0.9000	0.6667	0.5680	0.5589	0.6102	0.6111	0.8000	0.0000	0.0000	0.0000
-6	0.0000	0.0000	0.0000	0.5000	0.9000	0.6667	0.5437	0.5185	0.5678	0.5556	0.8000	0.0000	0.0000	0.0000
-7	0.0000	0.0000	0.0000	0.5000	0.9000	0.5897	0.4757	0.4916	0.5169	0.5556	0.8000	0.0000	0.0000	0.0000
-8	0.0000	0.0000	0.0000	0.5000	0.8000	0.5641	0.4272	0.4646	0.4915	0.5556	0.8000	0.0000	0.0000	0.0000
-9	0.0000	0.0000	0.0000	0.5000	0.6000	0.5385	0.3932	0.4108	0.4576	0.5556	0.8000	0.0000	0.0000	0.0000
-10	0.0000	0.0000	0.0000	0.2500	0.5000	0.5128	0.3544	0.3872	0.3983	0.5000	0.8000	0.0000	0.0000	0.0000

Main Condition 8 *(Continued)*   Probabilities

Secondary Conditions

Tick Variation	1	2	3	4	5	6	7	8	9	10	11	12	13	14
−11	0.0000	0.0000	0.0000	0.2500	0.5000	0.4872	0.3155	0.3603	0.3898	0.3333	0.8000	0.0000	0.0000	0.0000
−12	0.0000	0.0000	0.0000	0.2500	0.5000	0.4615	0.3010	0.3199	0.3559	0.2222	0.8000	0.0000	0.0000	0.0000
−13	0.0000	0.0000	0.0000	0.5000	0.5000	0.4615	0.2816	0.2761	0.3390	0.2222	0.8000	0.0000	0.0000	0.0000
−14	0.0000	0.0000	0.0000	0.5000	0.4000	0.4615	0.2573	0.2593	0.3136	0.2222	0.8000	0.0000	0.0000	0.0000
−15	0.0000	0.0000	0.0000	0.5000	0.4000	0.4615	0.2282	0.2492	0.2712	0.2222	0.8000	0.0000	0.0000	0.0000
−16	0.0000	0.0000	0.0000	0.5000	0.3000	0.4103	0.2087	0.2155	0.2458	0.2222	0.6000	0.0000	0.0000	0.0000
−17	0.0000	0.0000	0.0000	0.5000	0.3000	0.4103	0.1893	0.1987	0.2458	0.2222	0.6000	0.0000	0.0000	0.0000
−18	0.0000	0.0000	0.0000	0.2500	0.3000	0.4103	0.1845	0.1886	0.2458	0.2222	0.4000	0.0000	0.0000	0.0000
−19	0.0000	0.0000	0.0000	0.2500	0.3000	0.3077	0.1796	0.1717	0.2458	0.2222	0.2000	0.0000	0.0000	0.0000
−20	0.0000	0.0000	0.0000	0.2500	0.3000	0.2308	0.1650	0.1549	0.2203	0.1667	0.2000	0.0000	0.0000	0.0000
−21	0.0000	0.0000	0.0000	0.2500	0.3000	0.2308	0.1602	0.1448	0.2034	0.1667	0.2000	0.0000	0.0000	0.0000
−22	0.0000	0.0000	0.0000	0.2500	0.3000	0.1795	0.1553	0.1212	0.1864	0.1111	0.2000	0.0000	0.0000	0.0000
−23	0.0000	0.0000	0.0000	0.2500	0.3000	0.1795	0.1456	0.1145	0.1864	0.1111	0.2000	0.0000	0.0000	0.0000
−24	0.0000	0.0000	0.0000	0.2500	0.3000	0.1795	0.1214	0.1044	0.1610	0.1111	0.2000	0.0000	0.0000	0.0000
−25	0.0000	0.0000	0.0000	0.2500	0.3000	0.1538	0.1117	0.0875	0.1441	0.1111	0.2000	0.0000	0.0000	0.0000
−26	0.0000	0.0000	0.0000	0.2500	0.3000	0.1282	0.1068	0.0909	0.1102	0.1111	0.2000	0.0000	0.0000	0.0000
−27	0.0000	0.0000	0.0000	0.2500	0.3000	0.1282	0.1068	0.0909	0.1017	0.1111	0.2000	0.0000	0.0000	0.0000
−28	0.0000	0.0000	0.0000	0.2500	0.3000	0.1282	0.0825	0.0842	0.0932	0.1111	0.2000	0.0000	0.0000	0.0000
−29	0.0000	0.0000	0.0000	0.2500	0.3000	0.1282	0.0680	0.0842	0.0847	0.1111	0.2000	0.0000	0.0000	0.0000
−30	0.0000	0.0000	0.0000	0.2500	0.2000	0.1538	0.0680	0.0808	0.0763	0.1111	0.2000	0.0000	0.0000	0.0000
−31	0.0000	0.0000	0.0000	0.2500	0.2000	0.1538	0.0631	0.0673	0.0678	0.1111	0.2000	0.0000	0.0000	0.0000
−32	0.0000	0.0000	0.0000	0.2500	0.1000	0.1538	0.0631	0.0606	0.0508	0.1111	0.2000	0.0000	0.0000	0.0000
−33	0.0000	0.0000	0.0000	0.2500	0.1000	0.1538	0.0583	0.0606	0.0508	0.1111	0.2000	0.0000	0.0000	0.0000
−34	0.0000	0.0000	0.0000	0.2500	0.1000	0.1538	0.0534	0.0572	0.0508	0.1111	0.2000	0.0000	0.0000	0.0000
−35	0.0000	0.0000	0.0000	0.2500	0.1000	0.1282	0.0534	0.0471	0.0424	0.1111	0.2000	0.0000	0.0000	0.0000
−36	0.0000	0.0000	0.0000	0.2500	0.1000	0.1026	0.0437	0.0471	0.0339	0.1111	0.2000	0.0000	0.0000	0.0000
−37	0.0000	0.0000	0.0000	0.2500	0.1000	0.1026	0.0437	0.0404	0.0254	0.1111	0.2000	0.0000	0.0000	0.0000
−38	0.0000	0.0000	0.0000	0.2500	0.1000	0.1282	0.0437	0.0370	0.0254	0.1111	0.2000	0.0000	0.0000	0.0000
−39	0.0000	0.0000	0.0000	0.2500	0.1000	0.0769	0.0388	0.0438	0.0254	0.1111	0.2000	0.0000	0.0000	0.0000
−40	0.0000	0.0000	0.0000	0.0000	0.1000	0.0769	0.0340	0.0404	0.0254	0.1111	0.2000	0.0000	0.0000	0.0000
−41	0.0000	0.0000	0.0000	0.0000	0.1000	0.0769	0.0340	0.0370	0.0254	0.1111	0.2000	0.0000	0.0000	0.0000
−42	0.0000	0.0000	0.0000	0.0000	0.1000	0.0769	0.0340	0.0370	0.0169	0.1111	0.0000	0.0000	0.0000	0.0000
−43	0.0000	0.0000	0.0000	0.0000	0.1000	0.0769	0.0340	0.0370	0.0169	0.0556	0.0000	0.0000	0.0000	0.0000
−44	0.0000	0.0000	0.0000	0.0000	0.1000	0.0769	0.0194	0.0337	0.0169	0.0556	0.0000	0.0000	0.0000	0.0000
−45	0.0000	0.0000	0.0000	0.0000	0.1000	0.0769	0.0194	0.0236	0.0169	0.0556	0.0000	0.0000	0.0000	0.0000
−46	0.0000	0.0000	0.0000	0.0000	0.1000	0.0769	0.0194	0.0202	0.0169	0.0556	0.0000	0.0000	0.0000	0.0000
−47	0.0000	0.0000	0.0000	0.0000	0.1000	0.0769	0.0194	0.0168	0.0169	0.0556	0.0000	0.0000	0.0000	0.0000
−48	0.0000	0.0000	0.0000	0.0000	0.1000	0.0769	0.0194	0.0135	0.0169	0.0556	0.0000	0.0000	0.0000	0.0000
−49	0.0000	0.0000	0.0000	0.0000	0.1000	0.0769	0.0194	0.0135	0.0169	0.0556	0.0000	0.0000	0.0000	0.0000
−50	0.0000	0.0000	0.0000	0.0000	0.1000	0.0769	0.0146	0.0135	0.0169	0.0556	0.0000	0.0000	0.0000	0.0000
−51	0.0000	0.0000	0.0000	0.0000	0.1000	0.0769	0.0097	0.0135	0.0085	0.0556	0.0000	0.0000	0.0000	0.0000
−52	0.0000	0.0000	0.0000	0.0000	0.1000	0.0769	0.0097	0.0135	0.0085	0.0556	0.0000	0.0000	0.0000	0.0000
−53	0.0000	0.0000	0.0000	0.0000	0.1000	0.0769	0.0097	0.0135	0.0085	0.0556	0.0000	0.0000	0.0000	0.0000
−54	0.0000	0.0000	0.0000	0.0000	0.1000	0.0769	0.0097	0.0135	0.0085	0.0556	0.0000	0.0000	0.0000	0.0000
−55	0.0000	0.0000	0.0000	0.0000	0.0000	0.0513	0.0097	0.0135	0.0085	0.0000	0.0000	0.0000	0.0000	0.0000
−56	0.0000	0.0000	0.0000	0.0000	0.0000	0.0513	0.0097	0.0135	0.0085	0.0000	0.0000	0.0000	0.0000	0.0000
−57	0.0000	0.0000	0.0000	0.0000	0.0000	0.0513	0.0097	0.0135	0.0085	0.0000	0.0000	0.0000	0.0000	0.0000
−58	0.0000	0.0000	0.0000	0.0000	0.0000	0.0513	0.0097	0.0101	0.0085	0.0000	0.0000	0.0000	0.0000	0.0000
−59	0.0000	0.0000	0.0000	0.0000	0.0000	0.0513	0.0097	0.0101	0.0085	0.0000	0.0000	0.0000	0.0000	0.0000
−60	0.0000	0.0000	0.0000	0.0000	0.0000	0.0513	0.0097	0.0101	0.0085	0.0000	0.0000	0.0000	0.0000	0.0000
−61	0.0000	0.0000	0.0000	0.0000	0.0000	0.0513	0.0097	0.0101	0.0085	0.0000	0.0000	0.0000	0.0000	0.0000
−62	0.0000	0.0000	0.0000	0.0000	0.0000	0.0256	0.0049	0.0101	0.0085	0.0000	0.0000	0.0000	0.0000	0.0000
−63	0.0000	0.0000	0.0000	0.0000	0.0000	0.0256	0.0000	0.0101	0.0085	0.0000	0.0000	0.0000	0.0000	0.0000
−64	0.0000	0.0000	0.0000	0.0000	0.0000	0.0256	0.0000	0.0101	0.0085	0.0000	0.0000	0.0000	0.0000	0.0000

Main Condition 9						Probabilities							
Tick						Secondary Conditions							
Variation	1	2	3	4	5	6	7	8	9	10	11	12	13	14

Tick Variation	1	2	3	4	5	6	7	8	9	10	11	12	13	14
64	0.0000	0.0000	0.0000	1.0000	0.0000	0.0556	0.0154	0.0049	0.0000	0.0169	0.0000	0.0000	0.0000	0.0000
63	0.0000	0.0000	0.0000	1.0000	0.0000	0.0556	0.0154	0.0049	0.0000	0.0169	0.0000	0.0000	0.0000	0.0000
62	0.0000	0.0000	0.0000	1.0000	0.0000	0.0556	0.0154	0.0049	0.0049	0.0169	0.1250	0.0000	0.0000	0.0000
61	0.0000	0.0000	0.0000	1.0000	0.0000	0.0556	0.0154	0.0049	0.0049	0.0169	0.1250	0.0000	0.0000	0.0000
60	0.0000	0.0000	0.0000	1.0000	0.0000	0.0556	0.0154	0.0049	0.0049	0.0169	0.1250	0.0000	0.0000	0.0000
59	0.0000	0.0000	0.0000	1.0000	0.0000	0.0556	0.0308	0.0049	0.0049	0.0169	0.1250	0.0000	0.0000	0.0000
58	0.0000	0.0000	0.0000	1.0000	0.0000	0.0556	0.0308	0.0049	0.0049	0.0169	0.1250	0.3333	0.0000	0.0000
57	0.0000	0.0000	0.0000	1.0000	0.0000	0.0556	0.0308	0.0049	0.0049	0.0169	0.1250	0.3333	0.0000	0.0000
56	0.0000	0.0000	0.0000	1.0000	0.3333	0.0556	0.0308	0.0049	0.0049	0.0169	0.1250	0.3333	0.0000	0.0000
55	0.0000	0.0000	0.0000	1.0000	0.3333	0.0556	0.0308	0.0049	0.0049	0.0169	0.1250	0.3333	0.0000	0.0000
54	0.0000	0.0000	0.0000	1.0000	0.3333	0.0556	0.0308	0.0049	0.0049	0.0169	0.1250	0.3333	0.0000	0.0000
53	0.0000	0.0000	0.0000	1.0000	0.3333	0.0556	0.0308	0.0049	0.0049	0.0169	0.1250	0.3333	0.0000	0.0000
52	0.0000	0.0000	0.0000	1.0000	0.3333	0.0556	0.0308	0.0097	0.0049	0.0169	0.2500	0.3333	0.0000	0.0000
51	0.0000	0.0000	0.0000	1.0000	0.3333	0.0556	0.0308	0.0097	0.0049	0.0169	0.2500	0.3333	0.0000	0.0000
50	0.0000	0.0000	0.0000	1.0000	0.3333	0.0556	0.0308	0.0194	0.0049	0.0169	0.2500	0.3333	0.0000	0.0000
49	0.0000	0.0000	0.0000	1.0000	0.3333	0.0556	0.0308	0.0194	0.0049	0.0169	0.2500	0.3333	0.0000	0.0000
48	0.0000	0.0000	0.0000	1.0000	0.3333	0.0556	0.0615	0.0194	0.0049	0.0169	0.2500	0.3333	0.0000	0.0000
47	0.0000	0.0000	0.0000	1.0000	0.3333	0.0556	0.0923	0.0194	0.0049	0.0169	0.2500	0.3333	0.0000	0.0000
46	0.0000	0.0000	0.0000	1.0000	0.3333	0.0556	0.0923	0.0194	0.0049	0.0169	0.2500	0.3333	0.0000	0.0000
45	0.0000	0.0000	0.0000	1.0000	0.3333	0.1111	0.0923	0.0194	0.0049	0.0169	0.2500	0.3333	0.0000	0.0000
44	0.0000	0.0000	0.0000	1.0000	0.3333	0.1111	0.0923	0.0243	0.0099	0.0169	0.2500	0.3333	0.0000	0.0000
43	0.0000	0.0000	0.0000	1.0000	0.3333	0.1111	0.0923	0.0243	0.0148	0.0169	0.2500	0.3333	0.0000	0.0000
42	0.0000	0.0000	0.0000	1.0000	0.3333	0.1111	0.0923	0.0291	0.0148	0.0169	0.2500	0.3333	0.0000	0.0000
41	0.0000	0.0000	0.0000	1.0000	0.3333	0.1111	0.0923	0.0340	0.0148	0.0169	0.2500	0.3333	0.0000	0.0000
40	0.0000	0.0000	0.0000	1.0000	0.3333	0.1111	0.0923	0.0388	0.0148	0.0169	0.2500	0.3333	0.0000	0.0000
39	0.0000	0.0000	0.0000	1.0000	0.3333	0.1111	0.0923	0.0485	0.0148	0.0169	0.2500	0.3333	0.0000	0.0000
38	0.0000	0.0000	0.0000	1.0000	0.3333	0.1111	0.0923	0.0485	0.0148	0.0339	0.2500	0.3333	0.0000	0.0000
37	0.0000	0.0000	0.0000	0.0000	0.3333	0.1667	0.1077	0.0583	0.0148	0.0508	0.2500	0.3333	0.0000	0.0000
36	0.0000	0.0000	0.0000	0.0000	0.3333	0.1667	0.1231	0.0583	0.0197	0.0508	0.2500	0.3333	0.0000	0.0000
35	0.0000	0.0000	0.0000	0.0000	0.3333	0.1667	0.1385	0.0583	0.0296	0.0678	0.2500	0.3333	0.0000	0.0000
34	0.0000	0.0000	0.0000	0.0000	0.3333	0.1667	0.1538	0.0583	0.0394	0.0847	0.1250	0.3333	0.0000	0.0000
33	0.0000	0.0000	0.0000	0.0000	0.3333	0.1667	0.1538	0.0631	0.0394	0.0847	0.1250	0.3333	0.0000	0.0000
32	0.0000	0.0000	0.0000	0.0000	0.3333	0.1667	0.1692	0.0680	0.0443	0.1017	0.1250	0.3333	0.0000	0.0000
31	0.0000	0.0000	0.0000	0.0000	0.3333	0.1667	0.2000	0.0728	0.0493	0.1017	0.1250	0.3333	0.0000	0.0000
30	0.0000	0.0000	0.0000	0.0000	0.3333	0.1667	0.2154	0.0777	0.0493	0.1017	0.1250	0.6667	0.0000	0.0000
29	0.0000	0.0000	0.0000	0.0000	0.3333	0.1667	0.2154	0.0777	0.0493	0.1017	0.1250	0.6667	0.0000	0.0000
28	0.0000	0.0000	0.0000	0.0000	0.3333	0.1667	0.2154	0.0777	0.0591	0.1017	0.1250	0.6667	0.0000	0.0000
27	0.0000	0.0000	0.0000	0.0000	0.3333	0.1667	0.2308	0.0922	0.0640	0.1186	0.1250	0.6667	0.0000	0.0000
26	0.0000	0.0000	0.0000	0.0000	0.3333	0.1667	0.2462	0.1019	0.0640	0.1356	0.1250	0.6667	0.0000	0.0000
25	0.0000	0.0000	0.0000	0.0000	0.3333	0.1667	0.2615	0.1068	0.0690	0.1695	0.1250	0.6667	0.0000	0.0000
24	0.0000	0.0000	0.0000	0.0000	0.3333	0.1667	0.2769	0.1165	0.0788	0.1695	0.1250	0.6667	0.0000	0.0000
23	0.0000	0.0000	0.0000	0.0000	0.3333	0.2222	0.2769	0.1311	0.0887	0.1695	0.2500	0.6667	0.0000	0.0000
22	0.0000	0.0000	0.0000	0.0000	0.6667	0.2222	0.2769	0.1456	0.1084	0.2203	0.2500	0.6667	0.0000	0.0000
21	0.0000	0.0000	0.0000	0.0000	0.6667	0.2778	0.2923	0.1505	0.1182	0.2203	0.2500	0.6667	0.0000	0.0000
20	0.0000	0.0000	0.0000	0.0000	0.6667	0.2778	0.2923	0.1602	0.1330	0.2542	0.2500	0.6667	0.0000	0.0000
19	0.0000	0.0000	0.0000	0.0000	0.6667	0.2778	0.3231	0.1748	0.1527	0.2712	0.2500	0.6667	0.0000	0.0000
18	0.0000	0.0000	0.0000	0.0000	0.6667	0.3333	0.3385	0.1796	0.1576	0.3051	0.2500	0.6667	0.0000	0.0000
17	0.0000	0.0000	0.0000	0.0000	0.6667	0.3889	0.3538	0.1942	0.1724	0.3051	0.2500	0.6667	0.0000	0.0000
16	0.0000	0.0000	0.0000	0.0000	0.6667	0.5000	0.3692	0.2136	0.1872	0.3220	0.2500	0.6667	0.0000	0.0000
15	0.0000	0.0000	0.0000	0.0000	0.6667	0.5000	0.3846	0.2282	0.2266	0.3390	0.2500	0.6667	0.0000	0.0000
14	0.0000	0.0000	0.0000	0.0000	0.6667	0.5556	0.3846	0.2427	0.2660	0.3559	0.2500	0.6667	0.0000	0.0000
13	0.0000	0.0000	0.0000	0.0000	0.6667	0.5556	0.4308	0.2767	0.2906	0.3898	0.2500	0.6667	0.0000	0.0000
12	0.0000	0.0000	0.0000	0.0000	0.6667	0.5556	0.4923	0.3301	0.3596	0.3898	0.2500	0.6667	0.0000	0.0000
11	0.0000	0.0000	0.0000	0.0000	1.0000	0.5556	0.5077	0.3447	0.4089	0.3898	0.2500	0.6667	0.0000	0.0000
10	0.0000	0.0000	0.0000	0.0000	1.0000	0.6111	0.5077	0.4126	0.4483	0.4237	0.5000	0.6667	0.0000	0.0000
9	0.0000	0.0000	0.0000	0.0000	1.0000	0.6111	0.5077	0.4660	0.4975	0.4746	0.5000	0.6667	0.0000	0.0000
8	0.0000	0.0000	0.0000	0.0000	1.0000	0.6111	0.5385	0.5000	0.5369	0.5254	0.3750	0.6667	0.0000	0.0000
7	0.0000	0.0000	0.0000	0.0000	1.0000	0.6667	0.5538	0.5194	0.5911	0.6441	0.3750	0.6667	0.0000	0.0000
6	0.0000	0.0000	0.0000	0.0000	1.0000	0.6667	0.5846	0.5437	0.6355	0.6949	0.3750	0.6667	0.0000	0.0000
5	0.0000	0.0000	0.0000	0.0000	1.0000	0.7778	0.6154	0.5777	0.6749	0.7458	0.5000	0.6667	0.0000	0.0000
4	0.0000	0.0000	0.0000	0.0000	1.0000	0.7778	0.6462	0.5922	0.6995	0.7966	0.5000	0.6667	0.0000	0.0000
3	0.0000	0.0000	0.0000	0.0000	1.0000	0.7778	0.7077	0.6165	0.6995	0.8136	0.5000	0.6667	0.0000	0.0000
2	0.0000	0.0000	0.0000	0.0000	1.0000	0.7778	0.6769	0.6359	0.7192	0.8305	0.5000	0.6667	0.0000	0.0000
1	0.0000	0.0000	0.0000	0.0000	1.0000	0.7778	0.6769	0.6456	0.7192	0.7966	0.5000	0.6667	0.0000	0.0000
0	0.0000	0.0000	0.0000	0.0000	1.0000	0.7222	0.6923	0.6262	0.7044	0.7797	0.5000	0.6667	0.0000	0.0000
−1	0.0000	0.0000	0.0000	0.0000	1.0000	0.6667	0.7077	0.6214	0.7094	0.7797	0.5000	0.6667	0.0000	0.0000
−2	0.0000	0.0000	0.0000	0.0000	1.0000	0.6667	0.6615	0.6408	0.6897	0.7966	0.5000	0.3333	0.0000	0.0000
−3	0.0000	0.0000	0.0000	0.0000	1.0000	0.6667	0.6462	0.6214	0.6256	0.7288	0.5000	0.3333	0.0000	0.0000
−4	0.0000	0.0000	0.0000	0.0000	1.0000	0.6667	0.6000	0.5971	0.6059	0.6780	0.5000	0.3333	0.0000	0.0000
−5	0.0000	0.0000	0.0000	0.0000	1.0000	0.6111	0.5385	0.5680	0.5567	0.6441	0.5000	0.3333	0.0000	0.0000
−6	0.0000	0.0000	0.0000	0.0000	1.0000	0.5556	0.5077	0.5194	0.5567	0.6441	0.5000	0.3333	0.0000	0.0000
−7	0.0000	0.0000	0.0000	0.0000	1.0000	0.5556	0.4923	0.4612	0.4828	0.6271	0.3750	0.6667	0.0000	0.0000
−8	0.0000	0.0000	0.0000	0.0000	1.0000	0.5556	0.4615	0.4223	0.4631	0.6102	0.3750	0.6667	0.0000	0.0000
−9	0.0000	0.0000	0.0000	0.0000	1.0000	0.5000	0.4462	0.3981	0.4581	0.5593	0.3750	0.6667	0.0000	0.0000
−10	0.0000	0.0000	0.0000	0.0000	1.0000	0.5000	0.4308	0.3592	0.4384	0.5254	0.3750	0.6667	0.0000	0.0000

Main Condition 9 *(Continued)*   Probabilities

Secondary Conditions

Tick Variation	1	2	3	4	5	6	7	8	9	10	11	12	13	14
−11	0.0000	0.0000	0.0000	0.0000	1.0000	0.5000	0.4308	0.3544	0.4138	0.4915	0.3750	0.6667	0.0000	0.0000
−12	0.0000	0.0000	0.0000	0.0000	1.0000	0.5000	0.4308	0.3495	0.3892	0.4915	0.2500	0.6667	0.0000	0.0000
−13	0.0000	0.0000	0.0000	0.0000	1.0000	0.5000	0.4154	0.3204	0.3498	0.4915	0.2500	0.6667	0.0000	0.0000
−14	0.0000	0.0000	0.0000	0.0000	0.6667	0.5000	0.4000	0.2816	0.3153	0.4576	0.2500	0.6667	0.0000	0.0000
−15	0.0000	0.0000	0.0000	0.0000	0.6667	0.4444	0.3846	0.2524	0.2956	0.4576	0.2500	0.6667	0.0000	0.0000
−16	0.0000	0.0000	0.0000	0.0000	0.6667	0.3889	0.3846	0.2330	0.2759	0.4576	0.2500	0.6667	0.0000	0.0000
−17	0.0000	0.0000	0.0000	0.0000	0.6667	0.3889	0.3538	0.2136	0.2562	0.4237	0.2500	0.6667	0.0000	0.0000
−18	0.0000	0.0000	0.0000	0.0000	0.6667	0.3889	0.3231	0.1845	0.2414	0.4068	0.3750	0.6667	0.0000	0.0000
−19	0.0000	0.0000	0.0000	0.0000	0.6667	0.2778	0.3231	0.1650	0.2365	0.3898	0.3750	0.6667	0.0000	0.0000
−20	0.0000	0.0000	0.0000	0.0000	0.3333	0.2778	0.3077	0.1505	0.2118	0.3729	0.2500	0.6667	0.0000	0.0000
−21	0.0000	0.0000	0.0000	0.0000	0.3333	0.2222	0.2923	0.1408	0.2069	0.3220	0.2500	0.6667	0.0000	0.0000
−22	0.0000	0.0000	0.0000	0.0000	0.3333	0.2222	0.2769	0.1262	0.1921	0.3051	0.2500	0.6667	0.0000	0.0000
−23	0.0000	0.0000	0.0000	0.0000	0.3333	0.2222	0.2769	0.1165	0.1773	0.2712	0.2500	0.6667	0.0000	0.0000
−24	0.0000	0.0000	0.0000	0.0000	0.3333	0.2222	0.2769	0.1117	0.1576	0.2712	0.2500	0.6667	0.0000	0.0000
−25	0.0000	0.0000	0.0000	0.0000	0.3333	0.2222	0.2615	0.0971	0.1429	0.2542	0.2500	0.3333	0.0000	0.0000
−26	0.0000	0.0000	0.0000	0.0000	0.3333	0.1111	0.2615	0.0874	0.1232	0.2542	0.2500	0.3333	0.0000	0.0000
−27	0.0000	0.0000	0.0000	0.0000	0.3333	0.1111	0.2308	0.0777	0.1232	0.2373	0.2500	0.3333	0.0000	0.0000
−28	0.0000	0.0000	0.0000	0.0000	0.3333	0.1111	0.2308	0.0728	0.1133	0.2373	0.2500	0.3333	0.0000	0.0000
−29	0.0000	0.0000	0.0000	0.0000	0.3333	0.1111	0.2000	0.0583	0.1034	0.2034	0.2500	0.3333	0.0000	0.0000
−30	0.0000	0.0000	0.0000	0.0000	0.0000	0.1111	0.2000	0.0534	0.0837	0.1695	0.2500	0.3333	0.0000	0.0000
−31	0.0000	0.0000	0.0000	0.0000	0.0000	0.1111	0.1846	0.0485	0.0788	0.1525	0.3750	0.0000	0.0000	0.0000
−32	0.0000	0.0000	0.0000	0.0000	0.0000	0.1111	0.1692	0.0534	0.0640	0.1356	0.3750	0.0000	0.0000	0.0000
−33	0.0000	0.0000	0.0000	0.0000	0.0000	0.1111	0.1538	0.0388	0.0591	0.1186	0.2500	0.0000	0.0000	0.0000
−34	0.0000	0.0000	0.0000	0.0000	0.0000	0.1111	0.1385	0.0340	0.0542	0.1186	0.2500	0.0000	0.0000	0.0000
−35	0.0000	0.0000	0.0000	0.0000	0.0000	0.1111	0.1385	0.0340	0.0542	0.1017	0.2500	0.0000	0.0000	0.0000
−36	0.0000	0.0000	0.0000	0.0000	0.0000	0.0556	0.1077	0.0340	0.0443	0.0847	0.2500	0.0000	0.0000	0.0000
−37	0.0000	0.0000	0.0000	0.0000	0.0000	0.0556	0.0923	0.0291	0.0394	0.0847	0.2500	0.0000	0.0000	0.0000
−38	0.0000	0.0000	0.0000	0.0000	0.0000	0.0556	0.0923	0.0243	0.0394	0.0847	0.2500	0.0000	0.0000	0.0000
−39	0.0000	0.0000	0.0000	0.0000	0.0000	0.0556	0.0769	0.0243	0.0296	0.0847	0.2500	0.0000	0.0000	0.0000
−40	0.0000	0.0000	0.0000	0.0000	0.0000	0.0556	0.0769	0.0194	0.0296	0.0847	0.2500	0.0000	0.0000	0.0000
−41	0.0000	0.0000	0.0000	0.0000	0.0000	0.0000	0.0769	0.0146	0.0296	0.0847	0.2500	0.0000	0.0000	0.0000
−42	0.0000	0.0000	0.0000	0.0000	0.0000	0.0000	0.0615	0.0146	0.0296	0.0678	0.2500	0.0000	0.0000	0.0000
−43	0.0000	0.0000	0.0000	0.0000	0.0000	0.0000	0.0615	0.0146	0.0246	0.0678	0.2500	0.0000	0.0000	0.0000
−44	0.0000	0.0000	0.0000	0.0000	0.0000	0.0000	0.0615	0.0146	0.0246	0.0508	0.2500	0.0000	0.0000	0.0000
−45	0.0000	0.0000	0.0000	0.0000	0.0000	0.0000	0.0615	0.0146	0.0197	0.0508	0.1250	0.0000	0.0000	0.0000
−46	0.0000	0.0000	0.0000	0.0000	0.0000	0.0000	0.0615	0.0146	0.0197	0.0508	0.1250	0.0000	0.0000	0.0000
−47	0.0000	0.0000	0.0000	0.0000	0.0000	0.0000	0.0615	0.0146	0.0148	0.0508	0.1250	0.0000	0.0000	0.0000
−48	0.0000	0.0000	0.0000	0.0000	0.0000	0.0000	0.0615	0.0146	0.0099	0.0508	0.1250	0.0000	0.0000	0.0000
−49	0.0000	0.0000	0.0000	0.0000	0.0000	0.0000	0.0462	0.0146	0.0099	0.0508	0.1250	0.0000	0.0000	0.0000
−50	0.0000	0.0000	0.0000	0.0000	0.0000	0.0000	0.0462	0.0146	0.0099	0.0339	0.1250	0.0000	0.0000	0.0000
−51	0.0000	0.0000	0.0000	0.0000	0.0000	0.0000	0.0462	0.0146	0.0099	0.0339	0.1250	0.0000	0.0000	0.0000
−52	0.0000	0.0000	0.0000	0.0000	0.0000	0.0000	0.0462	0.0146	0.0099	0.0339	0.1250	0.0000	0.0000	0.0000
−53	0.0000	0.0000	0.0000	0.0000	0.0000	0.0000	0.0462	0.0146	0.0099	0.0339	0.1250	0.0000	0.0000	0.0000
−54	0.0000	0.0000	0.0000	0.0000	0.0000	0.0000	0.0462	0.0146	0.0099	0.0339	0.1250	0.0000	0.0000	0.0000
−55	0.0000	0.0000	0.0000	0.0000	0.6667	0.0000	0.0308	0.0146	0.0099	0.0339	0.1250	0.0000	0.0000	0.0000
−56	0.0000	0.0000	0.0000	0.0000	0.0000	0.0000	0.0308	0.0146	0.0049	0.0339	0.1250	0.0000	0.0000	0.0000
−57	0.0000	0.0000	0.0000	0.0000	0.0000	0.0000	0.0308	0.0146	0.0049	0.0339	0.1250	0.0000	0.0000	0.0000
−58	0.0000	0.0000	0.0000	0.0000	0.0000	0.0000	0.0308	0.0146	0.0049	0.0339	0.1250	0.0000	0.0000	0.0000
−59	0.0000	0.0000	0.0000	0.0000	0.0000	0.0000	0.0308	0.0097	0.0049	0.0339	0.1250	0.0000	0.0000	0.0000
−60	0.0000	0.0000	0.0000	0.0000	0.0000	0.0000	0.0308	0.0097	0.0049	0.0339	0.1250	0.0000	0.0000	0.0000
−61	0.0000	0.0000	0.0000	0.0000	0.0000	0.0000	0.0308	0.0097	0.0049	0.0339	0.1250	0.0000	0.0000	0.0000
−62	0.0000	0.0000	0.0000	0.0000	0.0000	0.0000	0.0308	0.0097	0.0049	0.0339	0.1250	0.0000	0.0000	0.0000
−63	0.0000	0.0000	0.0000	0.0000	0.0000	0.0000	0.0308	0.0049	0.0049	0.0339	0.1250	0.0000	0.0000	0.0000
−64	0.0000	0.0000	0.0000	0.0000	0.0000	0.0000	0.0154	0.0049	0.0049	0.0000	0.1250	0.0000	0.0000	0.0000

Main Condition 10 — **Probabilities**

Secondary Conditions

Tick Variation	1	2	3	4	5	6	7	8	9	10	11	12	13	14
64	0.0000	0.0000	0.0000	0.0000	0.0000	0.0000	0.0000	0.0109	0.0087	0.0000	0.0000	0.0000	0.0000	0.0000
63	0.0000	0.0000	0.0000	0.0000	0.0000	0.0000	0.0000	0.0109	0.0087	0.0000	0.0000	0.0000	0.0000	0.0000
62	0.0000	0.0000	0.0000	0.0000	0.0000	0.0000	0.0000	0.0109	0.0087	0.0000	0.0000	0.0000	0.0000	0.0000
61	0.0000	0.0000	0.0000	0.0000	0.0000	0.0000	0.0000	0.0109	0.0087	0.0000	0.0000	0.0000	0.0000	0.0000
60	0.0000	0.0000	0.0000	0.0000	0.0000	0.0000	0.0000	0.0109	0.0087	0.0000	0.0000	0.0000	0.0000	0.0000
59	0.0000	0.0000	0.0000	0.0000	0.0000	0.0000	0.0000	0.0109	0.0087	0.0135	0.0000	0.0000	0.0000	0.0000
58	0.0000	0.0000	0.0000	0.0000	0.0000	0.0000	0.0000	0.0109	0.0087	0.0135	0.0000	0.0000	0.0000	0.0000
57	0.0000	0.0000	0.0000	0.0000	0.0000	0.0000	0.0000	0.0109	0.0087	0.0135	0.0000	0.0000	0.0000	0.0000
56	0.0000	0.0000	0.0000	0.0000	0.0000	0.0000	0.0000	0.0109	0.0174	0.0135	0.0000	0.0000	0.0000	0.0000
55	0.0000	0.0000	0.0000	0.0000	0.0000	0.0000	0.0000	0.0109	0.0174	0.0135	0.0000	0.0000	0.0000	0.0000
54	0.0000	0.0000	0.0000	0.0000	0.0000	0.0000	0.0000	0.0109	0.0174	0.0135	0.0000	0.0000	0.0000	0.0000
53	0.0000	0.0000	0.0000	0.0000	0.0000	0.0000	0.0000	0.0109	0.0174	0.0135	0.0000	0.0000	0.0000	0.0000
52	0.0000	0.0000	0.0000	0.0000	0.0000	0.0000	0.0000	0.0109	0.0174	0.0135	0.0000	0.0000	0.0000	0.0000
51	0.0000	0.0000	0.0000	0.0000	0.0000	0.0000	0.0000	0.0109	0.0174	0.0135	0.0000	0.0000	0.0000	0.0000
50	0.0000	0.0000	0.0000	0.0000	0.0000	0.0000	0.0345	0.0109	0.0261	0.0135	0.0000	0.0000	0.0000	0.0000
49	0.0000	0.0000	0.0000	0.0000	0.0000	0.0000	0.0345	0.0000	0.0261	0.0270	0.0000	0.0000	0.0000	0.0000
48	0.0000	0.0000	0.0000	0.0000	0.0000	0.0000	0.0345	0.0000	0.0261	0.0270	0.0000	0.0000	0.0000	0.0000
47	0.0000	0.0000	0.0000	0.0000	0.0000	0.0000	0.0690	0.0000	0.0348	0.0270	0.0000	0.0000	0.0000	0.0000
46	0.0000	0.0000	0.0000	0.0000	0.0000	0.0000	0.0690	0.0000	0.0348	0.0270	0.0000	0.0000	0.0000	0.0000
45	0.0000	0.0000	0.0000	0.0000	0.0000	0.0000	0.0690	0.0000	0.0348	0.0270	0.0000	0.0000	0.0000	0.0000
44	0.0000	0.0000	0.0000	0.0000	0.0000	0.0000	0.0690	0.0000	0.0348	0.0270	0.0000	0.0000	0.0000	0.0000
43	0.0000	0.0000	0.0000	0.0000	0.0000	0.0000	0.0690	0.0000	0.0348	0.0270	0.0000	0.0000	0.0000	0.0000
42	0.0000	0.0000	0.0000	0.0000	0.0000	0.0000	0.0690	0.0109	0.0522	0.0270	0.0000	0.0000	0.0000	0.0000
41	0.0000	0.0000	0.0000	0.0000	0.0000	0.0000	0.1034	0.0109	0.0522	0.0405	0.0000	0.0000	0.0000	0.0000
40	0.0000	0.0000	0.0000	0.0000	0.0000	0.0000	0.1034	0.0109	0.0609	0.0405	0.0000	0.0000	0.0000	0.0000
39	0.0000	0.0000	0.0000	0.0000	0.0000	0.0000	0.1034	0.0109	0.0783	0.0405	0.0000	0.0000	0.0000	0.0000
38	0.0000	0.0000	0.0000	0.0000	0.0000	0.0000	0.1034	0.0217	0.0783	0.0405	0.0370	0.0000	0.0000	0.0000
37	0.0000	0.0000	0.0000	0.0000	0.0000	0.0000	0.1034	0.0217	0.0696	0.0405	0.0370	0.0000	0.0000	0.0000
36	0.0000	0.0000	0.0000	0.0000	0.0000	0.0000	0.1034	0.0217	0.0783	0.0405	0.0370	0.0000	0.0000	0.0000
35	0.0000	0.0000	0.0000	0.0000	0.0000	0.0000	0.1034	0.0326	0.0783	0.0405	0.0370	0.0000	0.0000	0.0000
34	0.0000	0.0000	0.0000	0.0000	0.0000	0.0000	0.1034	0.0326	0.0696	0.0405	0.0370	0.0000	0.0000	0.0000
33	0.0000	0.0000	0.0000	0.0000	0.0000	0.0000	0.1034	0.0326	0.0783	0.0541	0.0741	0.0000	0.0000	0.0000
32	0.0000	0.0000	0.0000	0.0000	0.0000	0.0000	0.1379	0.0543	0.0870	0.0541	0.0741	0.0000	0.0000	0.0000
31	0.0000	0.0000	0.0000	0.0000	0.0000	0.0000	0.1379	0.0543	0.0870	0.0676	0.1481	0.3333	0.0000	0.0000
30	0.0000	0.0000	0.0000	0.0000	0.0000	0.0000	0.1379	0.0652	0.0957	0.0811	0.1481	0.3333	0.0000	0.0000
29	0.0000	0.0000	0.0000	0.0000	0.0000	1.0000	0.1379	0.0652	0.1130	0.0946	0.1481	0.3333	0.0000	0.0000
28	0.0000	0.0000	0.0000	0.0000	0.0000	1.0000	0.1379	0.0761	0.1130	0.0946	0.1481	0.3333	0.0000	0.0000
27	0.0000	0.0000	0.0000	0.0000	0.0000	1.0000	0.1379	0.0870	0.1130	0.0946	0.1852	0.3333	0.0000	0.0000
26	0.0000	0.0000	0.0000	0.0000	0.0000	1.0000	0.1379	0.0978	0.1130	0.1216	0.1852	0.3333	0.0000	0.0000
25	0.0000	0.0000	0.0000	0.0000	0.0000	1.0000	0.1379	0.1196	0.1217	0.1216	0.2222	0.3333	0.0000	0.0000
24	0.0000	0.0000	0.0000	0.0000	0.0000	1.0000	0.2069	0.1304	0.1478	0.1486	0.2593	0.3333	0.0000	0.0000
23	0.0000	0.0000	0.0000	0.0000	0.0000	1.0000	0.2414	0.1522	0.1652	0.1622	0.2593	0.3333	0.0000	0.0000
22	0.0000	0.0000	0.0000	0.0000	0.0000	1.0000	0.2759	0.1630	0.1826	0.1892	0.2593	0.3333	0.0000	0.0000
21	0.0000	0.0000	0.0000	0.0000	0.0000	1.0000	0.3793	0.1848	0.1826	0.2027	0.2963	0.3333	0.0000	0.0000
20	0.0000	0.0000	0.0000	0.0000	0.0000	1.0000	0.4138	0.1848	0.2087	0.2297	0.4074	0.3333	0.0000	0.0000
19	0.0000	0.0000	0.0000	0.0000	0.0000	1.0000	0.4138	0.2283	0.2348	0.2838	0.4815	0.3333	0.0000	0.0000
18	0.0000	0.0000	0.0000	0.0000	0.0000	1.0000	0.4138	0.2391	0.2609	0.3514	0.5185	0.3333	0.0000	0.0000
17	0.0000	0.0000	0.0000	0.0000	0.0000	1.0000	0.4138	0.2826	0.2957	0.3784	0.5556	0.3333	0.0000	0.0000
16	0.0000	0.0000	0.0000	0.0000	0.0000	1.0000	0.4828	0.3261	0.3217	0.4324	0.5926	0.3333	0.0000	0.0000
15	0.0000	0.0000	0.0000	0.0000	0.0000	1.0000	0.5172	0.3478	0.3304	0.4595	0.6667	0.3333	0.0000	0.0000
14	0.0000	0.0000	0.0000	0.0000	0.0000	1.0000	0.5172	0.3696	0.3391	0.4865	0.6667	0.3333	0.0000	0.0000
13	0.0000	0.0000	0.0000	0.0000	0.0000	1.0000	0.5517	0.4348	0.3478	0.5405	0.7037	0.3333	0.0000	0.0000
12	0.0000	0.0000	0.0000	0.0000	0.0000	1.0000	0.5862	0.4565	0.3913	0.5541	0.7407	0.3333	0.0000	0.0000
11	0.0000	0.0000	0.0000	0.0000	0.0000	1.0000	0.6207	0.4674	0.4435	0.5946	0.7407	0.3333	0.0000	0.0000
10	0.0000	0.0000	0.0000	0.0000	0.0000	1.0000	0.6207	0.4891	0.4696	0.5946	0.7407	0.3333	0.0000	0.0000
9	0.0000	0.0000	0.0000	0.0000	0.0000	1.0000	0.6207	0.5000	0.5130	0.6351	0.7778	0.3333	0.0000	0.0000
8	0.0000	0.0000	0.0000	0.0000	0.0000	1.0000	0.6207	0.5217	0.5652	0.6892	0.7778	0.5000	0.0000	0.0000
7	0.0000	0.0000	0.0000	0.0000	0.0000	1.0000	0.6552	0.5652	0.6087	0.7432	0.7778	0.5000	0.0000	0.0000
6	0.0000	0.0000	0.0000	0.0000	0.0000	1.0000	0.6897	0.5761	0.6000	0.7432	0.8148	0.5000	0.0000	0.0000
5	0.0000	0.0000	0.0000	0.0000	0.0000	1.0000	0.7241	0.6196	0.5913	0.7297	0.8148	0.5000	0.0000	0.0000
4	0.0000	0.0000	0.0000	0.0000	0.0000	1.0000	0.7241	0.6630	0.6000	0.7568	0.8889	0.5000	0.0000	0.0000
3	0.0000	0.0000	0.0000	0.0000	0.0000	1.0000	0.7586	0.6739	0.5913	0.7568	0.8148	0.5000	0.0000	0.0000
2	0.0000	0.0000	0.0000	0.0000	0.0000	1.0000	0.7931	0.6630	0.5826	0.7703	0.8148	0.5000	0.0000	0.0000
1	0.0000	0.0000	0.0000	0.0000	0.0000	1.0000	0.8276	0.6739	0.5826	0.7703	0.8148	0.6667	0.0000	0.0000
0	0.0000	0.0000	0.0000	0.0000	0.0000	1.0000	0.7931	0.6630	0.6000	0.7703	0.8519	0.6667	0.0000	0.0000
-1	0.0000	0.0000	0.0000	0.0000	0.0000	1.0000	0.7586	0.6739	0.6261	0.7568	0.8148	0.6667	0.0000	0.0000
-2	0.0000	0.0000	0.0000	0.0000	0.0000	1.0000	0.7586	0.7065	0.6522	0.7027	0.7778	0.6667	0.0000	0.0000
-3	0.0000	0.0000	0.0000	0.0000	0.0000	1.0000	0.7586	0.6848	0.5913	0.6892	0.7778	0.6667	0.0000	0.0000
-4	0.0000	0.0000	0.0000	0.0000	0.0000	1.0000	0.7241	0.6630	0.6087	0.6486	0.7407	0.6667	0.0000	0.0000
-5	0.0000	0.0000	0.0000	0.0000	0.0000	1.0000	0.6897	0.6630	0.6087	0.6216	0.7407	0.6667	0.0000	0.0000
-6	0.0000	0.0000	0.0000	0.0000	0.0000	1.0000	0.6552	0.6413	0.5304	0.5676	0.7407	0.6667	0.0000	0.0000
-7	0.0000	0.0000	0.0000	0.0000	0.0000	1.0000	0.6552	0.6087	0.5304	0.5405	0.7037	0.6667	0.0000	0.0000
-8	0.0000	0.0000	0.0000	0.0000	0.0000	0.0000	0.6207	0.6087	0.5043	0.5000	0.7037	0.6667	0.0000	0.0000
-9	0.0000	0.0000	0.0000	0.0000	0.0000	0.0000	0.5862	0.5870	0.4696	0.4865	0.6667	0.6667	0.0000	0.0000
-10	0.0000	0.0000	0.0000	0.0000	0.0000	0.0000	0.5862	0.5435	0.4522	0.4189	0.5926	0.6667	0.0000	0.0000

Main Condition 10 *(Continued)*   Probabilities

Tick Variation	1	2	3	4	5	6	7	8	9	10	11	12	13	14
								Secondary Conditions						
−11	0.0000	0.0000	0.0000	0.0000	0.0000	0.0000	0.5862	0.5109	0.4087	0.3919	0.5556	0.6667	0.0000	0.0000
−12	0.0000	0.0000	0.0000	0.0000	0.0000	0.0000	0.5517	0.5000	0.3826	0.3784	0.4815	0.6667	0.0000	0.0000
−13	0.0000	0.0000	0.0000	0.0000	0.0000	0.0000	0.4138	0.4457	0.3826	0.3514	0.4815	0.6667	0.0000	0.0000
−14	0.0000	0.0000	0.0000	0.0000	0.0000	0.0000	0.4138	0.4239	0.3739	0.3243	0.4444	0.6667	0.0000	0.0000
−15	0.0000	0.0000	0.0000	0.0000	0.0000	0.0000	0.3103	0.3478	0.3739	0.3243	0.4444	0.6667	0.0000	0.0000
−16	0.0000	0.0000	0.0000	0.0000	0.0000	0.0000	0.2759	0.3043	0.3478	0.2703	0.4074	0.6667	0.0000	0.0000
−17	0.0000	0.0000	0.0000	0.0000	0.0000	0.0000	0.2759	0.2609	0.3391	0.2432	0.3333	0.5000	0.0000	0.0000
−18	0.0000	0.0000	0.0000	0.0000	0.0000	0.0000	0.2759	0.2500	0.3130	0.2297	0.2963	0.3333	0.0000	0.0000
−19	0.0000	0.0000	0.0000	0.0000	0.0000	0.0000	0.2069	0.2283	0.2870	0.2297	0.2593	0.3333	0.0000	0.0000
−20	0.0000	0.0000	0.0000	0.0000	0.0000	0.0000	0.2069	0.2391	0.2783	0.2162	0.2593	0.3333	0.0000	0.0000
−21	0.0000	0.0000	0.0000	0.0000	0.0000	0.0000	0.2069	0.2283	0.2696	0.2027	0.1852	0.3333	0.0000	0.0000
−22	0.0000	0.0000	0.0000	0.0000	0.0000	0.0000	0.2069	0.2065	0.2609	0.1892	0.1852	0.5000	0.0000	0.0000
−23	0.0000	0.0000	0.0000	0.0000	0.0000	0.0000	0.2069	0.1957	0.2522	0.1892	0.1852	0.5000	0.0000	0.0000
−24	0.0000	0.0000	0.0000	0.0000	0.0000	0.0000	0.2069	0.1739	0.2348	0.1892	0.1852	0.5000	0.0000	0.0000
−25	0.0000	0.0000	0.0000	0.0000	0.0000	0.0000	0.2069	0.1522	0.2348	0.2027	0.1852	0.5000	0.0000	0.0000
−26	0.0000	0.0000	0.0000	0.0000	0.0000	0.0000	0.1724	0.1413	0.2261	0.1892	0.1852	0.5000	0.0000	0.0000
−27	0.0000	0.0000	0.0000	0.0000	0.0000	0.0000	0.1724	0.1304	0.2261	0.1486	0.1481	0.5000	0.0000	0.0000
−28	0.0000	0.0000	0.0000	0.0000	0.0000	0.0000	0.1379	0.1196	0.2174	0.1486	0.1111	0.3333	0.0000	0.0000
−29	0.0000	0.0000	0.0000	0.0000	0.0000	0.0000	0.1379	0.1087	0.2087	0.1351	0.1111	0.3333	0.0000	0.0000
−30	0.0000	0.0000	0.0000	0.0000	0.0000	0.0000	0.1379	0.1087	0.2000	0.1081	0.0741	0.3333	0.0000	0.0000
−31	0.0000	0.0000	0.0000	0.0000	0.0000	0.0000	0.1034	0.1087	0.1739	0.0946	0.0741	0.3333	0.0000	0.0000
−32	0.0000	0.0000	0.0000	0.0000	0.0000	0.0000	0.1034	0.1196	0.1565	0.0811	0.0370	0.3333	0.0000	0.0000
−33	0.0000	0.0000	0.0000	0.0000	0.0000	0.0000	0.0690	0.0978	0.1478	0.0811	0.0370	0.3333	0.0000	0.0000
−34	0.0000	0.0000	0.0000	0.0000	0.0000	0.0000	0.0690	0.0978	0.1478	0.0811	0.0370	0.3333	0.0000	0.0000
−35	0.0000	0.0000	0.0000	0.0000	0.0000	0.0000	0.0690	0.0978	0.1217	0.0811	0.0370	0.3333	0.0000	0.0000
−36	0.0000	0.0000	0.0000	0.0000	0.0000	0.0000	0.0345	0.0978	0.1130	0.0676	0.0370	0.3333	0.0000	0.0000
−37	0.0000	0.0000	0.0000	0.0000	0.0000	0.0000	0.0345	0.0870	0.1043	0.0541	0.0370	0.3333	0.0000	0.0000
−38	0.0000	0.0000	0.0000	0.0000	0.0000	0.0000	0.0345	0.0652	0.0870	0.0405	0.0370	0.3333	0.0000	0.0000
−39	0.0000	0.0000	0.0000	0.0000	0.0000	0.0000	0.0345	0.0435	0.0870	0.0405	0.0000	0.3333	0.0000	0.0000
−40	0.0000	0.0000	0.0000	0.0000	0.0000	0.0000	0.0000	0.0435	0.0609	0.0541	0.0000	0.3333	0.0000	0.0000
−41	0.0000	0.0000	0.0000	0.0000	0.0000	0.0000	0.0000	0.0435	0.0609	0.0541	0.0000	0.3333	0.0000	0.0000
−42	0.0000	0.0000	0.0000	0.0000	0.0000	0.0000	0.0000	0.0326	0.0522	0.0541	0.0000	0.3333	0.0000	0.0000
−43	0.0000	0.0000	0.0000	0.0000	0.0000	0.0000	0.0000	0.0326	0.0522	0.0541	0.0000	0.3333	0.0000	0.0000
−44	0.0000	0.0000	0.0000	0.0000	0.0000	0.0000	0.0000	0.0326	0.0435	0.0541	0.0000	0.3333	0.0000	0.0000
−45	0.0000	0.0000	0.0000	0.0000	0.0000	0.0000	0.0000	0.0326	0.0435	0.0541	0.0000	0.3333	0.0000	0.0000
−46	0.0000	0.0000	0.0000	0.0000	0.0000	0.0000	0.0000	0.0326	0.0435	0.0541	0.0000	0.3333	0.0000	0.0000
−47	0.0000	0.0000	0.0000	0.0000	0.0000	0.0000	0.0000	0.0326	0.0435	0.0541	0.0000	0.3333	0.0000	0.0000
−48	0.0000	0.0000	0.0000	0.0000	0.0000	0.0000	0.0000	0.0326	0.0348	0.0541	0.0000	0.3333	0.0000	0.0000
−49	0.0000	0.0000	0.0000	0.0000	0.0000	0.0000	0.0000	0.0326	0.0348	0.0541	0.0000	0.3333	0.0000	0.0000
−50	0.0000	0.0000	0.0000	0.0000	0.0000	0.0000	0.0000	0.0326	0.0261	0.0405	0.0000	0.3333	0.0000	0.0000
−51	0.0000	0.0000	0.0000	0.0000	0.0000	0.0000	0.0000	0.0217	0.0174	0.0405	0.0000	0.3333	0.0000	0.0000
−52	0.0000	0.0000	0.0000	0.0000	0.0000	0.0000	0.0000	0.0109	0.0174	0.0405	0.0000	0.3333	0.0000	0.0000
−53	0.0000	0.0000	0.0000	0.0000	0.0000	0.0000	0.0000	0.0109	0.0174	0.0405	0.0000	0.3333	0.0000	0.0000
−54	0.0000	0.0000	0.0000	0.0000	0.0000	0.0000	0.0000	0.0109	0.0174	0.0405	0.0000	0.3333	0.0000	0.0000
−55	0.0000	0.0000	0.0000	0.0000	0.0000	0.0000	0.0000	0.0109	0.0174	0.0405	0.0000	0.3333	0.0000	0.0000
−56	0.0000	0.0000	0.0000	0.0000	0.0000	0.0000	0.0000	0.0109	0.0174	0.0405	0.0000	0.3333	0.0000	0.0000
−57	0.0000	0.0000	0.0000	0.0000	0.0000	0.0000	0.0000	0.0109	0.0174	0.0405	0.0000	0.3333	0.0000	0.0000
−58	0.0000	0.0000	0.0000	0.0000	0.0000	0.0000	0.0000	0.0109	0.0174	0.0270	0.0000	0.3333	0.0000	0.0000
−59	0.0000	0.0000	0.0000	0.0000	0.0000	0.0000	0.0000	0.0109	0.0174	0.0270	0.0000	0.0000	0.0000	0.0000
−60	0.0000	0.0000	0.0000	0.0000	0.0000	0.0000	0.0000	0.0109	0.0174	0.0270	0.0000	0.0000	0.0000	0.0000
−61	0.0000	0.0000	0.0000	0.0000	0.0000	0.0000	0.0000	0.0109	0.0174	0.0270	0.0000	0.0000	0.0000	0.0000
−62	0.0000	0.0000	0.0000	0.0000	0.0000	0.0000	0.0000	0.0109	0.0174	0.0270	0.0000	0.0000	0.0000	0.0000
−63	0.0000	0.0000	0.0000	0.0000	0.0000	0.0000	0.0000	0.0109	0.0087	0.0135	0.0000	0.0000	0.0000	0.0000
−64	0.0000	0.0000	0.0000	0.0000	0.0000	0.0000	0.0000	0.0109	0.0087	0.0135	0.0000	0.0000	0.0000	0.0000

Main Condition 11   **Probabilities**

Tick Variation	1	2	3	4	5	6	7	8	9	10	11	12	13	14
						Secondary Conditions								
64	0.0000	0.0000	0.0000	0.0000	0.0000	0.2500	0.0000	0.0400	0.0000	0.0143	0.0000	0.0000	0.0000	0.0000
63	0.0000	0.0000	0.0000	0.0000	0.0000	0.2500	0.0000	0.0400	0.0000	0.0143	0.0000	0.0000	0.0000	0.0000
62	0.0000	0.0000	0.0000	0.0000	0.0000	0.2500	0.0000	0.0400	0.0000	0.0143	0.0000	0.0000	0.0000	0.0000
61	0.0000	0.0000	0.0000	0.0000	0.0000	0.2500	0.0000	0.0400	0.0000	0.0143	0.0000	0.1429	0.0000	0.0000
60	0.0000	0.0000	0.0000	0.0000	0.0000	0.2500	0.0000	0.0400	0.0139	0.0143	0.0270	0.1429	0.0000	0.0000
59	0.0000	0.0000	0.0000	0.0000	0.0000	0.2500	0.0000	0.0400	0.0139	0.0143	0.0270	0.1429	0.0000	0.0000
58	0.0000	0.0000	0.0000	0.0000	0.0000	0.2500	0.0000	0.0400	0.0139	0.0143	0.0541	0.1429	0.0000	0.0000
57	0.0000	0.0000	0.0000	0.0000	0.0000	0.2500	0.0000	0.0400	0.0139	0.0143	0.0541	0.1429	0.0000	0.0000
56	0.0000	0.0000	0.0000	0.0000	0.0000	0.2500	0.0000	0.0400	0.0139	0.0143	0.0541	0.1429	0.0000	0.0000
55	0.0000	0.0000	0.0000	0.0000	0.0000	0.2500	0.0000	0.0400	0.0139	0.0143	0.0541	0.1429	0.0000	0.0000
54	0.0000	0.0000	0.0000	0.0000	0.0000	0.2500	0.0000	0.0400	0.0139	0.0143	0.0541	0.1429	0.0000	0.0000
53	0.0000	0.0000	0.0000	0.0000	0.0000	0.2500	0.0000	0.0400	0.0139	0.0143	0.0541	0.1429	0.0000	0.0000
52	0.0000	0.0000	0.0000	0.0000	0.0000	0.2500	0.0000	0.0400	0.0139	0.0286	0.0541	0.1429	0.0000	0.0000
51	0.0000	0.0000	0.0000	0.0000	0.0000	0.2500	0.0000	0.0400	0.0278	0.0286	0.0541	0.1429	0.0000	0.0000
50	0.0000	0.0000	0.0000	0.0000	0.0000	0.2500	0.0000	0.0400	0.0278	0.0286	0.0541	0.1429	0.0000	0.0000
49	0.0000	0.0000	0.0000	0.0000	0.0000	0.2500	0.0000	0.0400	0.0278	0.0286	0.0541	0.1429	0.0000	0.0000
48	0.0000	0.0000	0.0000	0.0000	0.0000	0.2500	0.0000	0.0400	0.0278	0.0286	0.0541	0.1429	0.0000	0.0000
47	0.0000	0.0000	0.0000	0.0000	0.0000	0.2500	0.0000	0.0400	0.0278	0.0286	0.0811	0.1429	0.0000	0.0000
46	0.0000	0.0000	0.0000	0.0000	0.0000	0.2500	0.0000	0.0400	0.0278	0.0286	0.0811	0.1429	0.0000	0.0000
45	0.0000	0.0000	0.0000	0.0000	0.0000	0.2500	0.2500	0.0400	0.0278	0.0286	0.0811	0.1429	0.0000	0.0000
44	0.0000	0.0000	0.0000	0.0000	0.0000	0.2500	0.2500	0.0400	0.0278	0.0429	0.1081	0.1429	0.0000	0.0000
43	0.0000	0.0000	0.0000	0.0000	0.0000	0.2500	0.2500	0.0400	0.0417	0.0429	0.1081	0.1429	0.0000	0.0000
42	0.0000	0.0000	0.0000	0.0000	0.0000	0.2500	0.2500	0.0400	0.0417	0.0429	0.1081	0.1429	0.0000	0.0000
41	0.0000	0.0000	0.0000	0.0000	0.0000	0.2500	0.2500	0.0400	0.0417	0.0429	0.1622	0.1429	0.0000	0.0000
40	0.0000	0.0000	0.0000	0.0000	0.0000	0.2500	0.2500	0.0400	0.0417	0.0571	0.1622	0.1429	0.0000	0.0000
39	0.0000	0.0000	0.0000	0.0000	0.0000	0.2500	0.2500	0.0800	0.0417	0.0571	0.1622	0.1429	0.0000	0.0000
38	0.0000	0.0000	0.0000	0.0000	0.0000	0.2500	0.2500	0.0800	0.0417	0.0571	0.1892	0.1429	0.0000	0.0000
37	0.0000	0.0000	0.0000	0.0000	0.0000	0.2500	0.2500	0.0800	0.0417	0.0714	0.1892	0.1429	0.0000	0.0000
36	0.0000	0.0000	0.0000	0.0000	0.0000	0.2500	0.2500	0.0800	0.0556	0.0714	0.1892	0.1429	0.0000	0.0000
35	0.0000	0.0000	0.0000	0.0000	0.0000	0.2500	0.2500	0.0800	0.0556	0.0714	0.1892	0.1429	0.0000	0.0000
34	0.0000	0.0000	0.0000	0.0000	0.0000	0.2500	0.2500	0.0800	0.0556	0.0714	0.2162	0.2857	0.0000	0.0000
33	0.0000	0.0000	0.0000	0.0000	0.0000	0.2500	0.2500	0.0800	0.0694	0.0714	0.2162	0.2857	0.0000	0.0000
32	0.0000	0.0000	0.0000	0.0000	0.0000	0.2500	0.2500	0.0800	0.0972	0.0714	0.2162	0.2857	0.0000	0.0000
31	0.0000	0.0000	0.0000	0.0000	0.0000	0.2500	0.2500	0.0800	0.0972	0.0714	0.2162	0.2857	0.0000	0.0000
30	0.0000	0.0000	0.0000	0.0000	0.0000	0.2500	0.2500	0.0800	0.1111	0.0714	0.2432	0.2857	0.0000	0.0000
29	0.0000	0.0000	0.0000	0.0000	0.0000	0.2500	0.2500	0.0800	0.1250	0.0714	0.2703	0.2857	0.0000	0.0000
28	0.0000	0.0000	0.0000	0.0000	0.0000	0.2500	0.2500	0.0800	0.1528	0.0714	0.2703	0.2857	0.0000	0.0000
27	0.0000	0.0000	0.0000	0.0000	0.0000	0.2500	0.5000	0.0800	0.1528	0.0714	0.2973	0.2857	0.0000	0.0000
26	0.0000	0.0000	0.0000	0.0000	0.0000	0.2500	0.5000	0.0800	0.1528	0.0857	0.2973	0.4286	0.0000	0.0000
25	0.0000	0.0000	0.0000	0.0000	0.0000	0.2500	0.5000	0.0800	0.1528	0.0857	0.3514	0.4286	0.0000	0.0000
24	0.0000	0.0000	0.0000	0.0000	0.0000	0.7500	0.5000	0.0800	0.1667	0.0857	0.3784	0.4286	0.0000	0.0000
23	0.0000	0.0000	0.0000	0.0000	0.0000	0.7500	0.5000	0.1200	0.1944	0.1714	0.3784	0.4286	0.0000	0.0000
22	0.0000	0.0000	0.0000	0.0000	0.0000	0.7500	0.5000	0.1600	0.2222	0.1857	0.4324	0.4286	0.0000	0.0000
21	0.0000	0.0000	0.0000	0.0000	0.0000	0.7500	0.5000	0.1600	0.2500	0.2571	0.4595	0.4286	0.0000	0.0000
20	0.0000	0.0000	0.0000	0.0000	0.0000	0.7500	0.5000	0.1600	0.2917	0.2571	0.4595	0.4286	0.0000	0.0000
19	0.0000	0.0000	0.0000	0.0000	0.0000	0.7500	0.5000	0.2000	0.3056	0.2714	0.4865	0.4286	0.0000	0.0000
18	0.0000	0.0000	0.0000	0.0000	0.0000	0.7500	0.5000	0.2400	0.3194	0.2857	0.5135	0.5714	0.0000	0.0000
17	0.0000	0.0000	0.0000	0.0000	0.0000	0.7500	0.5000	0.3200	0.3472	0.3143	0.5135	0.5714	0.0000	0.0000
16	0.0000	0.0000	0.0000	0.0000	0.0000	0.7500	0.5000	0.4000	0.3889	0.3714	0.5405	0.5714	0.0000	0.0000
15	0.0000	0.0000	0.0000	0.0000	0.0000	0.7500	1.0000	0.4000	0.4306	0.4143	0.5405	0.5714	0.0000	0.0000
14	0.0000	0.0000	0.0000	0.0000	0.0000	0.7500	1.0000	0.5200	0.4444	0.4286	0.5676	0.7143	0.0000	0.0000
13	0.0000	0.0000	0.0000	0.0000	0.0000	0.7500	1.0000	0.5200	0.4861	0.5000	0.6486	0.7143	1.0000	0.0000
12	0.0000	0.0000	0.0000	0.0000	0.0000	0.7500	1.0000	0.6000	0.5139	0.5286	0.6486	0.7143	1.0000	0.0000
11	0.0000	0.0000	0.0000	0.0000	0.0000	0.7500	1.0000	0.6400	0.5417	0.5429	0.6486	0.8571	1.0000	0.0000
10	0.0000	0.0000	0.0000	0.0000	0.0000	0.7500	1.0000	0.6400	0.5833	0.5857	0.7027	0.8571	1.0000	0.0000
9	0.0000	0.0000	0.0000	0.0000	0.0000	1.0000	1.0000	0.6400	0.6528	0.6143	0.7027	0.7143	1.0000	0.0000
8	0.0000	0.0000	0.0000	0.0000	0.0000	1.0000	1.0000	0.6800	0.7083	0.6286	0.7568	0.7143	1.0000	0.0000
7	0.0000	0.0000	0.0000	0.0000	0.0000	1.0000	1.0000	0.7200	0.7361	0.6429	0.7838	0.5714	1.0000	0.0000
6	0.0000	0.0000	0.0000	0.0000	0.0000	1.0000	0.7500	0.7200	0.7639	0.7000	0.7838	0.5714	1.0000	0.0000
5	0.0000	0.0000	0.0000	0.0000	0.0000	0.7500	0.5000	0.7200	0.7778	0.7000	0.8378	0.5714	1.0000	0.0000
4	0.0000	0.0000	0.0000	0.0000	0.0000	0.7500	0.5000	0.8400	0.8472	0.7571	0.9189	0.4286	1.0000	0.0000
3	0.0000	0.0000	0.0000	0.0000	0.0000	0.7500	0.5000	0.8400	0.8333	0.8000	0.9189	0.4286	1.0000	0.0000
2	0.0000	0.0000	0.0000	0.0000	0.0000	0.7500	0.5000	0.7600	0.8333	0.8000	0.8649	0.4286	1.0000	0.0000
1	0.0000	0.0000	0.0000	0.0000	0.0000	0.7500	0.5000	0.7600	0.8333	0.7571	0.8108	0.5714	1.0000	0.0000
0	0.0000	0.0000	0.0000	0.0000	0.0000	0.7500	0.5000	0.8000	0.8194	0.7571	0.7838	0.5714	0.0000	0.0000
-1	0.0000	0.0000	0.0000	0.0000	0.0000	0.7500	0.5000	0.8000	0.8333	0.7571	0.7838	0.5714	0.0000	0.0000
-2	0.0000	0.0000	0.0000	0.0000	0.0000	0.7500	0.5000	0.8000	0.8194	0.7429	0.7838	0.5714	0.0000	0.0000
-3	0.0000	0.0000	0.0000	0.0000	0.0000	0.7500	0.5000	0.7600	0.7639	0.7571	0.7297	0.5714	0.0000	0.0000
-4	0.0000	0.0000	0.0000	0.0000	0.0000	0.7500	0.5000	0.7200	0.7222	0.7286	0.6757	0.4286	0.0000	0.0000
-5	0.0000	0.0000	0.0000	0.0000	0.0000	0.7500	0.5000	0.6800	0.7083	0.7143	0.6216	0.4286	0.0000	0.0000
-6	0.0000	0.0000	0.0000	0.0000	0.0000	0.7500	0.5000	0.6800	0.6806	0.6571	0.6216	0.4286	0.0000	0.0000
-7	0.0000	0.0000	0.0000	0.0000	0.0000	0.7500	0.5000	0.6400	0.6528	0.6143	0.6216	0.4286	0.0000	0.0000
-8	0.0000	0.0000	0.0000	0.0000	0.0000	0.7500	0.5000	0.6000	0.6111	0.5571	0.5676	0.4286	0.0000	0.0000
-9	0.0000	0.0000	0.0000	0.0000	0.0000	0.7500	0.5000	0.5600	0.5694	0.5143	0.5676	0.4286	0.0000	0.0000
-10	0.0000	0.0000	0.0000	0.0000	0.0000	0.7500	0.5000	0.5200	0.5278	0.4857	0.4865	0.4286	0.0000	0.0000

Main Condition 11 *(Continued)*   **Probabilities**

Secondary Conditions

Tick Variation	1	2	3	4	5	6	7	8	9	10	11	12	13	14
−11	0.0000	0.0000	0.0000	0.0000	0.0000	0.7500	0.5000	0.5200	0.4861	0.4857	0.4865	0.4286	0.0000	0.0000
−12	0.0000	0.0000	0.0000	0.0000	0.0000	0.7500	0.5000	0.5200	0.4444	0.4571	0.4324	0.2857	0.0000	0.0000
−13	0.0000	0.0000	0.0000	0.0000	0.0000	0.7500	0.5000	0.4400	0.4167	0.4143	0.4324	0.2857	0.0000	0.0000
−14	0.0000	0.0000	0.0000	0.0000	0.0000	0.7500	0.5000	0.4400	0.3889	0.4000	0.4324	0.2857	0.0000	0.0000
−15	0.0000	0.0000	0.0000	0.0000	0.0000	0.5000	0.5000	0.4400	0.3333	0.3714	0.3514	0.2857	0.0000	0.0000
−16	0.0000	0.0000	0.0000	0.0000	0.0000	0.5000	0.5000	0.4400	0.2639	0.3429	0.3243	0.2857	0.0000	0.0000
−17	0.0000	0.0000	0.0000	0.0000	0.0000	0.5000	0.5000	0.4400	0.2500	0.3429	0.2973	0.2857	0.0000	0.0000
−18	0.0000	0.0000	0.0000	0.0000	0.0000	0.5000	0.5000	0.4400	0.2361	0.3429	0.2703	0.2857	0.0000	0.0000
−19	0.0000	0.0000	0.0000	0.0000	0.0000	0.5000	0.5000	0.4000	0.2361	0.3429	0.2703	0.2857	0.0000	0.0000
−20	0.0000	0.0000	0.0000	0.0000	0.0000	0.5000	0.5000	0.4000	0.2083	0.3429	0.2432	0.2857	0.0000	0.0000
−21	0.0000	0.0000	0.0000	0.0000	0.0000	0.5000	0.5000	0.3600	0.1806	0.3286	0.2162	0.2857	0.0000	0.0000
−22	0.0000	0.0000	0.0000	0.0000	0.0000	0.5000	0.2500	0.3600	0.1944	0.3143	0.1892	0.2857	0.0000	0.0000
−23	0.0000	0.0000	0.0000	0.0000	0.0000	0.5000	0.5000	0.3600	0.1667	0.3143	0.1892	0.2857	0.0000	0.0000
−24	0.0000	0.0000	0.0000	0.0000	0.0000	0.5000	0.0000	0.3200	0.1528	0.2857	0.1892	0.2857	0.0000	0.0000
−25	0.0000	0.0000	0.0000	0.0000	0.0000	0.5000	0.0000	0.2800	0.1528	0.2857	0.1892	0.2857	0.0000	0.0000
−26	0.0000	0.0000	0.0000	0.0000	0.0000	0.2500	0.0000	0.2800	0.1389	0.2429	0.1892	0.2857	0.0000	0.0000
−27	0.0000	0.0000	0.0000	0.0000	0.0000	0.2500	0.0000	0.2400	0.1111	0.2286	0.1622	0.2857	0.0000	0.0000
−28	0.0000	0.0000	0.0000	0.0000	0.0000	0.2500	0.0000	0.2400	0.0972	0.2143	0.1351	0.2857	0.0000	0.0000
−29	0.0000	0.0000	0.0000	0.0000	0.0000	0.2500	0.0000	0.2400	0.1111	0.2000	0.1351	0.2857	0.0000	0.0000
−30	0.0000	0.0000	0.0000	0.0000	0.0000	0.2500	0.0000	0.2000	0.0972	0.1714	0.1351	0.1429	0.0000	0.0000
−31	0.0000	0.0000	0.0000	0.0000	0.0000	0.0000	0.0000	0.1600	0.0833	0.1571	0.1351	0.1429	0.0000	0.0000
−32	0.0000	0.0000	0.0000	0.0000	0.0000	0.0000	0.0000	0.1600	0.0833	0.1571	0.1351	0.1429	0.0000	0.0000
−33	0.0000	0.0000	0.0000	0.0000	0.0000	0.0000	0.0000	0.1200	0.0833	0.1429	0.1081	0.1429	0.0000	0.0000
−34	0.0000	0.0000	0.0000	0.0000	0.0000	0.0000	0.0000	0.1200	0.0833	0.1286	0.1081	0.1429	0.0000	0.0000
−35	0.0000	0.0000	0.0000	0.0000	0.0000	0.0000	0.0000	0.0800	0.0556	0.1143	0.1081	0.1429	0.0000	0.0000
−36	0.0000	0.0000	0.0000	0.0000	0.0000	0.0000	0.0000	0.0400	0.0556	0.1000	0.1081	0.1429	0.0000	0.0000
−37	0.0000	0.0000	0.0000	0.0000	0.0000	0.0000	0.0000	0.0400	0.0556	0.0857	0.1081	0.1429	0.0000	0.0000
−38	0.0000	0.0000	0.0000	0.0000	0.0000	0.0000	0.0000	0.0400	0.0556	0.0857	0.1081	0.0000	0.0000	0.0000
−39	0.0000	0.0000	0.0000	0.0000	0.0000	0.0000	0.0000	0.0400	0.0556	0.0857	0.1081	0.0000	0.0000	0.0000
−40	0.0000	0.0000	0.0000	0.0000	0.0000	0.0000	0.0000	0.0400	0.0556	0.0714	0.1081	0.0000	0.0000	0.0000
−41	0.0000	0.0000	0.0000	0.0000	0.0000	0.0000	0.0000	0.0400	0.0556	0.0571	0.1081	0.0000	0.0000	0.0000
−42	0.0000	0.0000	0.0000	0.0000	0.0000	0.0000	0.0000	0.0400	0.0556	0.0571	0.1081	0.0000	0.0000	0.0000
−43	0.0000	0.0000	0.0000	0.0000	0.0000	0.0000	0.0000	0.0400	0.0556	0.0571	0.0811	0.0000	0.0000	0.0000
−44	0.0000	0.0000	0.0000	0.0000	0.0000	0.0000	0.0000	0.0400	0.0556	0.0571	0.0811	0.0000	0.0000	0.0000
−45	0.0000	0.0000	0.0000	0.0000	0.0000	0.0000	0.0000	0.0400	0.0556	0.0571	0.0811	0.0000	0.0000	0.0000
−46	0.0000	0.0000	0.0000	0.0000	0.0000	0.0000	0.0000	0.0400	0.0556	0.0571	0.0811	0.0000	0.0000	0.0000
−47	0.0000	0.0000	0.0000	0.0000	0.0000	0.0000	0.0000	0.0400	0.0556	0.0571	0.0811	0.0000	0.0000	0.0000
−48	0.0000	0.0000	0.0000	0.0000	0.0000	0.0000	0.0000	0.0400	0.0556	0.0571	0.0811	0.0000	0.0000	0.0000
−49	0.0000	0.0000	0.0000	0.0000	0.0000	0.0000	0.0000	0.0400	0.0556	0.0571	0.0811	0.0000	0.0000	0.0000
−50	0.0000	0.0000	0.0000	0.0000	0.0000	0.0000	0.0000	0.0400	0.0556	0.0571	0.0811	0.0000	0.0000	0.0000
−51	0.0000	0.0000	0.0000	0.0000	0.0000	0.0000	0.0000	0.0400	0.0556	0.0571	0.0541	0.0000	0.0000	0.0000
−52	0.0000	0.0000	0.0000	0.0000	0.0000	0.0000	0.0000	0.0400	0.0556	0.0571	0.0541	0.0000	0.0000	0.0000
−53	0.0000	0.0000	0.0000	0.0000	0.0000	0.0000	0.0000	0.0400	0.0417	0.0571	0.0541	0.0000	0.0000	0.0000
−54	0.0000	0.0000	0.0000	0.0000	0.0000	0.0000	0.0000	0.0400	0.0417	0.0571	0.0541	0.0000	0.0000	0.0000
−55	0.0000	0.0000	0.0000	0.0000	0.0000	0.0000	0.0000	0.0400	0.0417	0.0571	0.0541	0.0000	0.0000	0.0000
−56	0.0000	0.0000	0.0000	0.0000	0.0000	0.0000	0.0000	0.0400	0.0417	0.0571	0.0270	0.0000	0.0000	0.0000
−57	0.0000	0.0000	0.0000	0.0000	0.0000	0.0000	0.0000	0.0000	0.0417	0.0429	0.0270	0.0000	0.0000	0.0000
−58	0.0000	0.0000	0.0000	0.0000	0.0000	0.0000	0.0000	0.0000	0.0417	0.0429	0.0270	0.0000	0.0000	0.0000
−59	0.0000	0.0000	0.0000	0.0000	0.0000	0.0000	0.0000	0.0000	0.0417	0.0429	0.0270	0.0000	0.0000	0.0000
−60	0.0000	0.0000	0.0000	0.0000	0.0000	0.0000	0.0000	0.0000	0.0417	0.0429	0.0270	0.0000	0.0000	0.0000
−61	0.0000	0.0000	0.0000	0.0000	0.0000	0.0000	0.0000	0.0000	0.0417	0.0429	0.0270	0.0000	0.0000	0.0000
−62	0.0000	0.0000	0.0000	0.0000	0.0000	0.0000	0.0000	0.0000	0.0417	0.0429	0.0270	0.0000	0.0000	0.0000
−63	0.0000	0.0000	0.0000	0.0000	0.0000	0.0000	0.0000	0.0000	0.0417	0.0143	0.0270	0.0000	0.0000	0.0000
−64	0.0000	0.0000	0.0000	0.0000	0.0000	0.0000	0.0000	0.0000	0.0417	0.0143	0.0270	0.0000	0.0000	0.0000

Main Condition 12 — Probabilities

Secondary Conditions

Tick Variation	1	2	3	4	5	6	7	8	9	10	11	12	13	14
64	0.0000	0.0000	0.0000	0.0000	0.0000	0.0000	0.0000	0.2000	0.0000	0.0000	0.0000	0.1667	0.0000	0.2500
63	0.0000	0.0000	0.0000	0.0000	0.0000	0.0000	0.0000	0.2000	0.0000	0.0000	0.0000	0.1667	0.3333	0.2500
62	0.0000	0.0000	0.0000	0.0000	0.0000	0.0000	0.0000	0.2000	0.0000	0.0000	0.0000	0.1667	0.3333	0.2500
61	0.0000	0.0000	0.0000	0.0000	0.0000	0.0000	0.0000	0.2000	0.0000	0.0000	0.0000	0.1667	0.3333	0.2500
60	0.0000	0.0000	0.0000	0.0000	0.0000	0.0000	0.0000	0.2000	0.0000	0.0000	0.0000	0.1667	0.3333	0.2500
59	0.0000	0.0000	0.0000	0.0000	0.0000	0.0000	0.0000	0.2000	0.0000	0.0000	0.0000	0.1667	0.3333	0.2500
58	0.0000	0.0000	0.0000	0.0000	0.0000	0.0000	0.0000	0.2000	0.0000	0.0303	0.0000	0.1667	0.3333	0.2500
57	0.0000	0.0000	0.0000	0.0000	0.0000	0.0000	0.0000	0.2000	0.0000	0.0303	0.0000	0.1667	0.3333	0.2500
56	0.0000	0.0000	0.0000	0.0000	0.0000	0.0000	0.0000	0.2000	0.0000	0.0303	0.0000	0.1667	0.3333	0.2500
55	0.0000	0.0000	0.0000	0.0000	0.0000	0.0000	0.0000	0.2000	0.0000	0.0303	0.0667	0.1667	0.3333	0.2500
54	0.0000	0.0000	0.0000	0.0000	0.0000	0.0000	0.0000	0.2000	0.0000	0.0303	0.0667	0.1667	0.3333	0.2500
53	0.0000	0.0000	0.0000	0.0000	0.0000	0.0000	0.0000	0.2000	0.0476	0.0303	0.0667	0.1667	0.3333	0.2500
52	0.0000	0.0000	0.0000	0.0000	0.0000	0.0000	0.0000	0.2000	0.0476	0.0303	0.1000	0.1667	0.3333	0.2500
51	0.0000	0.0000	0.0000	0.0000	0.0000	0.0000	0.0000	0.2000	0.0476	0.0303	0.1000	0.1667	0.3333	0.2500
50	0.0000	0.0000	0.0000	0.0000	0.0000	0.0000	0.0000	0.2000	0.0476	0.0303	0.1000	0.1667	0.3333	0.2500
49	0.0000	0.0000	0.0000	0.0000	0.0000	0.0000	0.0000	0.2000	0.0476	0.0303	0.1000	0.1667	0.3333	0.5000
48	0.0000	0.0000	0.0000	0.0000	0.0000	0.0000	0.0000	0.2000	0.0476	0.0303	0.1000	0.1667	0.3333	0.5000
47	0.0000	0.0000	0.0000	0.0000	0.0000	0.0000	0.0000	0.2000	0.0476	0.0303	0.1000	0.1667	0.3333	0.5000
46	0.0000	0.0000	0.0000	0.0000	0.0000	0.0000	0.0000	0.2000	0.0476	0.0303	0.1000	0.1667	0.3333	0.5000
45	0.0000	0.0000	0.0000	0.0000	0.0000	0.0000	0.0000	0.2000	0.0476	0.0303	0.1000	0.1667	0.3333	0.5000
44	0.0000	0.0000	0.0000	0.0000	0.0000	0.0000	0.0000	0.2000	0.0476	0.0606	0.1000	0.1667	0.3333	0.5000
43	0.0000	0.0000	0.0000	0.0000	0.0000	0.0000	0.0000	0.2000	0.0476	0.0606	0.1333	0.1667	0.3333	0.5000
42	0.0000	0.0000	0.0000	0.0000	0.0000	0.0000	0.0000	0.2000	0.0952	0.0606	0.1333	0.1667	0.3333	0.5000
41	0.0000	0.0000	0.0000	0.0000	0.0000	0.0000	0.0000	0.2000	0.0952	0.0606	0.1667	0.1667	0.3333	0.5000
40	0.0000	0.0000	0.0000	0.0000	0.0000	0.0000	0.0000	0.2000	0.0952	0.0606	0.1667	0.1667	0.3333	0.5000
39	0.0000	0.0000	0.0000	0.0000	0.0000	0.0000	0.0000	0.2000	0.0952	0.0606	0.2000	0.1667	0.3333	0.5000
38	0.0000	0.0000	0.0000	0.0000	0.0000	0.0000	0.0000	0.2000	0.0952	0.0606	0.2000	0.1667	0.3333	0.5000
37	0.0000	0.0000	0.0000	0.0000	0.0000	0.0000	0.0000	0.2000	0.0952	0.0909	0.2000	0.1667	0.3333	0.5000
36	0.0000	0.0000	0.0000	0.0000	0.0000	0.0000	0.0000	0.2000	0.0952	0.0909	0.2000	0.1667	0.3333	0.5000
35	0.0000	0.0000	0.0000	0.0000	0.0000	0.0000	0.0000	0.2000	0.0952	0.0909	0.2333	0.1667	0.3333	0.5000
34	0.0000	0.0000	0.0000	0.0000	0.0000	0.0000	0.0000	0.2000	0.0952	0.0909	0.2667	0.1667	0.3333	0.5000
33	0.0000	0.0000	0.0000	0.0000	0.0000	0.0000	0.0000	0.2000	0.1429	0.0909	0.2667	0.1667	0.3333	0.5000
32	0.0000	0.0000	0.0000	0.0000	0.0000	0.0000	0.0000	0.2000	0.1429	0.0909	0.2667	0.1667	0.3333	0.5000
31	0.0000	0.0000	0.0000	0.0000	0.0000	0.0000	0.0000	0.2000	0.1905	0.1212	0.2667	0.1667	0.3333	0.5000
30	0.0000	0.0000	0.0000	0.0000	0.0000	0.0000	0.0000	0.0000	0.2857	0.1212	0.2667	0.1667	0.6667	0.5000
29	0.0000	0.0000	0.0000	0.0000	0.0000	0.0000	0.0000	0.0000	0.2857	0.1515	0.2667	0.2500	0.6667	0.5000
28	0.0000	0.0000	0.0000	0.0000	0.0000	0.0000	0.0000	0.0000	0.2857	0.1515	0.2667	0.2500	0.6667	0.5000
27	0.0000	0.0000	0.0000	0.0000	0.0000	0.0000	0.0000	0.0000	0.3333	0.1515	0.2667	0.2500	0.6667	0.5000
26	0.0000	0.0000	0.0000	0.0000	0.0000	0.0000	0.0000	0.0000	0.3333	0.1515	0.3000	0.2500	0.6667	0.5000
25	0.0000	0.0000	0.0000	0.0000	0.0000	0.0000	0.0000	0.0000	0.3333	0.1515	0.3000	0.2500	0.6667	0.5000
24	0.0000	0.0000	0.0000	0.0000	0.0000	0.0000	0.0000	0.0000	0.4286	0.1818	0.3333	0.1667	0.6667	0.5000
23	0.0000	0.0000	0.0000	0.0000	0.0000	0.0000	0.0000	0.0000	0.4286	0.2121	0.3333	0.1667	0.6667	0.5000
22	0.0000	0.0000	0.0000	0.0000	0.0000	0.0000	0.0000	0.0000	0.4286	0.2424	0.3333	0.2500	0.6667	0.5000
21	0.0000	0.0000	0.0000	0.0000	0.0000	0.0000	0.0000	0.2000	0.4286	0.2424	0.3333	0.2500	0.6667	0.5000
20	0.0000	0.0000	0.0000	0.0000	0.0000	0.0000	0.0000	0.2000	0.4286	0.3333	0.3667	0.4167	0.6667	0.7500
19	0.0000	0.0000	0.0000	0.0000	0.0000	0.0000	0.0000	0.2000	0.4286	0.3636	0.4000	0.4167	0.6667	0.7500
18	0.0000	0.0000	0.0000	0.0000	0.0000	0.0000	0.0000	0.2000	0.5238	0.3939	0.4333	0.4167	0.6667	0.7500
17	0.0000	0.0000	0.0000	0.0000	0.0000	0.0000	0.0000	0.2000	0.5714	0.4545	0.4667	0.4167	0.6667	0.7500
16	0.0000	0.0000	0.0000	0.0000	0.0000	0.0000	1.0000	0.2000	0.5714	0.4545	0.4667	0.4167	0.6667	0.7500
15	0.0000	0.0000	0.0000	0.0000	0.0000	0.0000	1.0000	0.2000	0.5714	0.5152	0.5000	0.5000	0.6667	0.7500
14	0.0000	0.0000	0.0000	0.0000	0.0000	0.0000	1.0000	0.2000	0.6190	0.5758	0.5000	0.5000	0.6667	0.7500
13	0.0000	0.0000	0.0000	0.0000	0.0000	0.0000	1.0000	0.2000	0.6190	0.5758	0.5000	0.5000	0.6667	0.7500
12	0.0000	0.0000	0.0000	0.0000	0.0000	0.0000	1.0000	0.2000	0.6190	0.6364	0.5000	0.5000	0.6667	0.7500
11	0.0000	0.0000	0.0000	0.0000	0.0000	0.0000	1.0000	0.2000	0.5714	0.6364	0.5000	0.5833	0.6667	0.7500
10	0.0000	0.0000	0.0000	0.0000	0.0000	0.0000	1.0000	0.2000	0.6190	0.6364	0.5333	0.5833	0.6667	0.7500
9	0.0000	0.0000	0.0000	0.0000	0.0000	0.0000	1.0000	0.2000	0.6190	0.6970	0.5667	0.6667	0.6667	0.7500
8	0.0000	0.0000	0.0000	0.0000	0.0000	0.0000	1.0000	0.6000	0.6190	0.7273	0.6333	0.6667	0.6667	0.7500
7	0.0000	0.0000	0.0000	0.0000	0.0000	0.0000	1.0000	0.6000	0.6667	0.7576	0.6000	0.6667	0.6667	0.7500
6	0.0000	0.0000	0.0000	0.0000	0.0000	0.0000	1.0000	0.6000	0.7143	0.7879	0.5667	0.7500	0.6667	0.7500
5	0.0000	0.0000	0.0000	0.0000	1.0000	0.0000	1.0000	0.6000	0.7143	0.7879	0.5333	0.8333	0.6667	0.7500
4	0.0000	0.0000	0.0000	0.0000	1.0000	0.0000	1.0000	0.6000	0.7143	0.7576	0.6000	0.9167	0.6667	1.0000
3	0.0000	0.0000	0.0000	0.0000	1.0000	0.0000	1.0000	0.6000	0.7619	0.7576	0.6333	0.8333	0.6667	1.0000
2	0.0000	0.0000	0.0000	0.0000	1.0000	0.0000	1.0000	0.6000	0.7143	0.6970	0.6333	0.8333	0.6667	1.0000
1	0.0000	0.0000	0.0000	0.0000	1.0000	0.0000	1.0000	0.6000	0.7143	0.7273	0.6000	0.8333	0.6667	1.0000
0	0.0000	0.0000	0.0000	0.0000	1.0000	0.0000	1.0000	0.8000	0.7143	0.6970	0.5667	0.8333	0.6667	0.7500
−1	0.0000	0.0000	0.0000	0.0000	1.0000	0.0000	1.0000	0.8000	0.7143	0.6970	0.6333	0.8333	0.6667	0.7500
−2	0.0000	0.0000	0.0000	0.0000	1.0000	0.0000	1.0000	0.8000	0.7143	0.6970	0.6333	0.8333	0.6667	0.7500
−3	0.0000	0.0000	0.0000	0.0000	1.0000	0.0000	1.0000	0.8000	0.6667	0.6364	0.6000	0.8333	0.6667	0.7500
−4	0.0000	0.0000	0.0000	0.0000	1.0000	0.0000	1.0000	0.8000	0.6667	0.6364	0.5667	0.8333	0.6667	0.7500
−5	0.0000	0.0000	0.0000	0.0000	1.0000	0.0000	1.0000	0.8000	0.6667	0.6061	0.5667	0.6667	0.6667	0.7500
−6	0.0000	0.0000	0.0000	0.0000	1.0000	0.0000	1.0000	0.8000	0.6190	0.5758	0.5667	0.6667	0.6667	0.7500
−7	0.0000	0.0000	0.0000	0.0000	1.0000	0.0000	1.0000	0.8000	0.6190	0.5455	0.5333	0.6667	0.6667	0.7500
−8	0.0000	0.0000	0.0000	0.0000	1.0000	0.0000	1.0000	0.8000	0.5714	0.5152	0.5000	0.6667	0.6667	0.7500
−9	0.0000	0.0000	0.0000	0.0000	1.0000	0.0000	1.0000	0.8000	0.4762	0.5152	0.5000	0.6667	0.6667	0.7500
−10	0.0000	0.0000	0.0000	0.0000	1.0000	0.0000	1.0000	0.8000	0.4762	0.4545	0.4667	0.6667	0.6667	0.7500

Main Condition 12 *(Continued)*   Probabilities

Tick Variation	1	2	3	4	5	6	7	8	9	10	11	12	13	14
−11	0.0000	0.0000	0.0000	0.0000	1.0000	0.0000	0.0000	0.8000	0.4286	0.4545	0.4667	0.6667	0.6667	0.7500
−12	0.0000	0.0000	0.0000	0.0000	1.0000	0.0000	0.0000	0.6000	0.4286	0.4242	0.5000	0.6667	0.6667	0.7500
−13	0.0000	0.0000	0.0000	0.0000	1.0000	0.0000	0.0000	0.6000	0.4286	0.4242	0.5000	0.6667	0.6667	0.5000
−14	0.0000	0.0000	0.0000	0.0000	1.0000	0.0000	0.0000	0.6000	0.3333	0.3636	0.4667	0.6667	0.6667	0.5000
−15	0.0000	0.0000	0.0000	0.0000	1.0000	0.0000	0.0000	0.6000	0.2381	0.3636	0.4667	0.6667	0.6667	0.5000
−16	0.0000	0.0000	0.0000	0.0000	1.0000	0.0000	0.0000	0.6000	0.2381	0.3636	0.4333	0.5833	0.6667	0.5000
−17	0.0000	0.0000	0.0000	0.0000	1.0000	0.0000	0.0000	0.6000	0.2381	0.3030	0.4000	0.5833	0.6667	0.5000
−18	0.0000	0.0000	0.0000	0.0000	1.0000	0.0000	0.0000	0.6000	0.2381	0.3030	0.3667	0.5833	0.6667	0.2500
−19	0.0000	0.0000	0.0000	0.0000	1.0000	0.0000	0.0000	0.6000	0.1905	0.2727	0.3667	0.5833	0.6667	0.2500
−20	0.0000	0.0000	0.0000	0.0000	1.0000	0.0000	0.0000	0.6000	0.1905	0.2727	0.3667	0.5833	0.6667	0.0000
−21	0.0000	0.0000	0.0000	0.0000	1.0000	0.0000	0.0000	0.6000	0.1905	0.2121	0.3667	0.5833	0.6667	0.0000
−22	0.0000	0.0000	0.0000	0.0000	1.0000	0.0000	0.0000	0.6000	0.1905	0.1818	0.3667	0.5833	0.6667	0.0000
−23	0.0000	0.0000	0.0000	0.0000	1.0000	0.0000	0.0000	0.6000	0.1905	0.1212	0.3667	0.5833	0.6667	0.0000
−24	0.0000	0.0000	0.0000	0.0000	1.0000	0.0000	0.0000	0.6000	0.1905	0.1212	0.3667	0.5833	0.6667	0.0000
−25	0.0000	0.0000	0.0000	0.0000	1.0000	0.0000	0.0000	0.6000	0.1905	0.1212	0.3667	0.5833	0.3333	0.0000
−26	0.0000	0.0000	0.0000	0.0000	1.0000	0.0000	0.0000	0.6000	0.1429	0.1212	0.3667	0.5833	0.3333	0.0000
−27	0.0000	0.0000	0.0000	0.0000	1.0000	0.0000	0.0000	0.6000	0.1429	0.1212	0.3667	0.5000	0.3333	0.0000
−28	0.0000	0.0000	0.0000	0.0000	1.0000	0.0000	0.0000	0.6000	0.1429	0.1212	0.3000	0.5000	0.3333	0.0000
−29	0.0000	0.0000	0.0000	0.0000	1.0000	0.0000	0.0000	0.6000	0.0952	0.1212	0.3000	0.5000	0.3333	0.0000
−30	0.0000	0.0000	0.0000	0.0000	1.0000	0.0000	0.0000	0.4000	0.0952	0.1212	0.3000	0.4167	0.3333	0.0000
−31	0.0000	0.0000	0.0000	0.0000	1.0000	0.0000	0.0000	0.2000	0.0952	0.1212	0.2667	0.4167	0.3333	0.0000
−32	0.0000	0.0000	0.0000	0.0000	1.0000	0.0000	0.0000	0.2000	0.1429	0.0909	0.2667	0.4167	0.3333	0.0000
−33	0.0000	0.0000	0.0000	0.0000	1.0000	0.0000	0.0000	0.2000	0.1429	0.0909	0.2333	0.4167	0.3333	0.0000
−34	0.0000	0.0000	0.0000	0.0000	1.0000	0.0000	0.0000	0.2000	0.1429	0.0909	0.2000	0.4167	0.3333	0.0000
−35	0.0000	0.0000	0.0000	0.0000	1.0000	0.0000	0.0000	0.2000	0.0476	0.0909	0.1667	0.3333	0.3333	0.0000
−36	0.0000	0.0000	0.0000	0.0000	1.0000	0.0000	0.0000	0.2000	0.0476	0.0909	0.1667	0.2500	0.3333	0.0000
−37	0.0000	0.0000	0.0000	0.0000	1.0000	0.0000	0.0000	0.2000	0.0476	0.0909	0.1667	0.2500	0.3333	0.0000
−38	0.0000	0.0000	0.0000	0.0000	1.0000	0.0000	0.0000	0.2000	0.0476	0.0909	0.1667	0.1667	0.3333	0.0000
−39	0.0000	0.0000	0.0000	0.0000	0.0000	0.0000	0.0000	0.2000	0.0476	0.0909	0.1667	0.0833	0.3333	0.0000
−40	0.0000	0.0000	0.0000	0.0000	0.0000	0.0000	0.0000	0.2000	0.0476	0.0909	0.1667	0.0833	0.3333	0.0000
−41	0.0000	0.0000	0.0000	0.0000	0.0000	0.0000	0.0000	0.2000	0.0476	0.0909	0.1667	0.0833	0.3333	0.0000
−42	0.0000	0.0000	0.0000	0.0000	0.0000	0.0000	0.0000	0.2000	0.0476	0.0909	0.1667	0.0833	0.3333	0.0000
−43	0.0000	0.0000	0.0000	0.0000	0.0000	0.0000	0.0000	0.2000	0.0476	0.0909	0.1667	0.0833	0.3333	0.0000
−44	0.0000	0.0000	0.0000	0.0000	0.0000	0.0000	0.0000	0.2000	0.0476	0.0909	0.1667	0.0833	0.3333	0.0000
−45	0.0000	0.0000	0.0000	0.0000	0.0000	0.0000	0.0000	0.2000	0.0476	0.0909	0.1667	0.0833	0.3333	0.0000
−46	0.0000	0.0000	0.0000	0.0000	0.0000	0.0000	0.0000	0.2000	0.0476	0.0909	0.1667	0.0833	0.3333	0.0000
−47	0.0000	0.0000	0.0000	0.0000	0.0000	0.0000	0.0000	0.0000	0.0476	0.0909	0.1000	0.0833	0.3333	0.0000
−48	0.0000	0.0000	0.0000	0.0000	0.0000	0.0000	0.0000	0.0000	0.0476	0.0909	0.1000	0.0833	0.3333	0.0000
−49	0.0000	0.0000	0.0000	0.0000	0.0000	0.0000	0.0000	0.0000	0.0476	0.0909	0.1000	0.0833	0.3333	0.0000
−50	0.0000	0.0000	0.0000	0.0000	0.0000	0.0000	0.0000	0.0000	0.0476	0.0909	0.1000	0.0833	0.3333	0.0000
−51	0.0000	0.0000	0.0000	0.0000	0.0000	0.0000	0.0000	0.0000	0.0476	0.0909	0.1000	0.0833	0.3333	0.0000
−52	0.0000	0.0000	0.0000	0.0000	0.0000	0.0000	0.0000	0.0000	0.0476	0.0909	0.1000	0.0833	0.3333	0.0000
−53	0.0000	0.0000	0.0000	0.0000	0.0000	0.0000	0.0000	0.0000	0.0476	0.0909	0.1000	0.0833	0.3333	0.0000
−54	0.0000	0.0000	0.0000	0.0000	0.0000	0.0000	0.0000	0.0000	0.0476	0.0606	0.1000	0.0833	0.3333	0.0000
−55	0.0000	0.0000	0.0000	0.0000	0.0000	0.0000	0.0000	0.0000	0.0476	0.0606	0.1000	0.0833	0.3333	0.0000
−56	0.0000	0.0000	0.0000	0.0000	0.0000	0.0000	0.0000	0.0000	0.0476	0.0606	0.1000	0.0833	0.3333	0.0000
−57	0.0000	0.0000	0.0000	0.0000	0.0000	0.0000	0.0000	0.0000	0.0476	0.0606	0.1000	0.0833	0.3333	0.0000
−58	0.0000	0.0000	0.0000	0.0000	0.0000	0.0000	0.0000	0.0000	0.0476	0.0606	0.0667	0.0833	0.3333	0.0000
−59	0.0000	0.0000	0.0000	0.0000	0.0000	0.0000	0.0000	0.0000	0.0476	0.0303	0.0667	0.0833	0.3333	0.0000
−60	0.0000	0.0000	0.0000	0.0000	0.0000	0.0000	0.0000	0.0000	0.0476	0.0303	0.0333	0.0833	0.3333	0.0000
−61	0.0000	0.0000	0.0000	0.0000	0.0000	0.0000	0.0000	0.0000	0.0476	0.0303	0.0333	0.0833	0.3333	0.0000
−62	0.0000	0.0000	0.0000	0.0000	0.0000	0.0000	0.0000	0.0000	0.0476	0.0303	0.0333	0.0833	0.3333	0.0000
−63	0.0000	0.0000	0.0000	0.0000	0.0000	0.0000	0.0000	0.0000	0.0476	0.0303	0.0333	0.0833	0.3333	0.0000
−64	0.0000	0.0000	0.0000	0.0000	0.0000	0.0000	0.0000	0.0000	0.0476	0.0303	0.0333	0.0833	0.3333	0.0000

Main Condition 13						Probabilities							
Tick						Secondary Conditions							
Variation	1	2	3	4	5	6	7	8.	9	10	11	12	13	14

Tick Variation	1	2	3	4	5	6	7	8	9	10	11	12	13	14
64	0.0000	0.0000	0.0000	0.0000	0.0000	0.0000	0.0000	0.0000	0.2000	0.1250	0.0000	0.0000	0.0000	0.0000
63	0.0000	0.0000	0.0000	0.0000	0.0000	0.0000	0.0000	0.0000	0.2000	0.1250	0.0000	0.0000	0.0000	0.0000
62	0.0000	0.0000	0.0000	0.0000	0.0000	0.0000	0.0000	0.0000	0.2000	0.1250	0.0833	0.0000	0.0000	0.0000
61	0.0000	0.0000	0.0000	0.0000	0.0000	0.0000	0.0000	0.0000	0.2000	0.1250	0.0833	0.0000	0.0000	0.0000
60	0.0000	0.0000	0.0000	0.0000	0.0000	0.0000	0.0000	0.0000	0.2000	0.1250	0.0833	0.0000	0.0000	0.0000
59	0.0000	0.0000	0.0000	0.0000	0.0000	0.0000	1.0000	0.0000	0.4000	0.1250	0.0833	0.0000	0.0000	0.0000
58	0.0000	0.0000	0.0000	0.0000	0.0000	0.0000	1.0000	0.0000	0.4000	0.1250	0.0833	0.0000	0.0000	0.0000
57	0.0000	0.0000	0.0000	0.0000	0.0000	0.0000	1.0000	0.0000	0.4000	0.1250	0.0833	0.0000	0.0000	0.0000
56	0.0000	0.0000	0.0000	0.0000	0.0000	0.0000	1.0000	0.0000	0.4000	0.1250	0.0833	0.0000	0.0000	0.0000
55	0.0000	0.0000	0.0000	0.0000	0.0000	0.0000	1.0000	0.0000	0.4000	0.2500	0.0833	0.0000	0.0000	0.0000
54	0.0000	0.0000	0.0000	0.0000	0.0000	0.0000	1.0000	0.0000	0.4000	0.2500	0.0833	0.0000	0.0000	0.0000
53	0.0000	0.0000	0.0000	0.0000	0.0000	0.0000	1.0000	0.0000	0.4000	0.2500	0.0833	0.0000	0.0000	0.0000
52	0.0000	0.0000	0.0000	0.0000	0.0000	0.0000	1.0000	0.0000	0.4000	0.2500	0.0833	0.0000	0.0000	0.0000
51	0.0000	0.0000	0.0000	0.0000	0.0000	0.0000	1.0000	0.0000	0.4000	0.2500	0.0833	0.0000	0.0000	0.0000
50	0.0000	0.0000	0.0000	0.0000	0.0000	0.0000	1.0000	0.0000	0.4000	0.2500	0.0833	0.0000	0.0000	0.0000
49	0.0000	0.0000	0.0000	0.0000	0.0000	0.0000	1.0000	0.0000	0.4000	0.2500	0.0833	0.0000	0.0000	0.0000
48	0.0000	0.0000	0.0000	0.0000	0.0000	0.0000	1.0000	0.0000	0.4000	0.2500	0.0833	0.0000	0.0000	0.0000
47	0.0000	0.0000	0.0000	0.0000	0.0000	0.0000	1.0000	0.0000	0.4000	0.2500	0.0833	0.0000	0.0000	0.0000
46	0.0000	0.0000	0.0000	0.0000	0.0000	0.0000	1.0000	0.0000	0.4000	0.3750	0.0833	0.0000	0.0000	0.0000
45	0.0000	0.0000	0.0000	0.0000	0.0000	0.0000	1.0000	0.0000	0.4000	0.3750	0.0833	0.0000	0.0000	0.0000
44	0.0000	0.0000	0.0000	0.0000	0.0000	0.0000	1.0000	0.0000	0.4000	0.3750	0.0833	0.0000	0.0000	0.0000
43	0.0000	0.0000	0.0000	0.0000	0.0000	0.0000	1.0000	0.0000	0.4000	0.3750	0.0833	0.0000	0.0000	0.0000
42	0.0000	0.0000	0.0000	0.0000	0.0000	0.0000	1.0000	0.0000	0.4000	0.3750	0.1667	0.0000	0.5000	0.0000
41	0.0000	0.0000	0.0000	0.0000	0.0000	0.0000	1.0000	0.0000	0.4000	0.3750	0.1667	0.0000	0.5000	0.0000
40	0.0000	0.0000	0.0000	0.0000	0.0000	0.0000	1.0000	0.0000	0.4000	0.3750	0.1667	0.0000	0.5000	0.0000
39	0.0000	0.0000	0.0000	0.0000	0.0000	0.0000	1.0000	0.0000	0.4000	0.3750	0.1667	0.0000	0.5000	0.0000
38	0.0000	0.0000	0.0000	0.0000	0.0000	0.0000	1.0000	0.0000	0.4000	0.3750	0.1667	0.0000	0.5000	0.0000
37	0.0000	0.0000	0.0000	0.0000	0.0000	0.0000	1.0000	0.0000	0.4000	0.3750	0.1667	0.0000	0.5000	0.0000
36	0.0000	0.0000	0.0000	0.0000	0.0000	0.0000	1.0000	0.0000	0.4000	0.3750	0.1667	0.0000	0.5000	0.0000
35	0.0000	0.0000	0.0000	0.0000	0.0000	0.0000	1.0000	0.0000	0.4000	0.3750	0.1667	0.0000	0.5000	0.0000
34	0.0000	0.0000	0.0000	0.0000	0.0000	0.0000	1.0000	0.0000	0.4000	0.3750	0.1667	0.0000	0.5000	0.0000
33	0.0000	0.0000	0.0000	0.0000	0.0000	0.0000	1.0000	0.0000	0.4000	0.3750	0.1667	0.1250	0.5000	0.0000
32	0.0000	0.0000	0.0000	0.0000	0.0000	0.0000	1.0000	0.0000	0.4000	0.3750	0.3333	0.1250	0.5000	0.0000
31	0.0000	0.0000	0.0000	0.0000	0.0000	0.0000	1.0000	0.0000	0.4000	0.3750	0.3333	0.1250	0.5000	0.0000
30	0.0000	0.0000	0.0000	0.0000	0.0000	0.0000	1.0000	0.0000	0.4000	0.3750	0.4167	0.2500	0.5000	0.0000
29	0.0000	0.0000	0.0000	0.0000	0.0000	0.0000	1.0000	0.0000	0.4000	0.3750	0.4167	0.2500	0.5000	0.0000
28	0.0000	0.0000	0.0000	0.0000	0.0000	0.0000	1.0000	0.0000	0.4000	0.3750	0.4167	0.2500	0.5000	0.0000
27	0.0000	0.0000	0.0000	0.0000	0.0000	0.0000	1.0000	0.2500	0.6000	0.3750	0.4167	0.2500	0.5000	0.0000
26	0.0000	0.0000	0.0000	0.0000	0.0000	0.0000	1.0000	0.2500	0.6000	0.2500	0.5000	0.2500	0.5000	0.0000
25	0.0000	0.0000	0.0000	0.0000	0.0000	0.0000	1.0000	0.2500	0.6000	0.2500	0.5000	0.2500	0.5000	0.0000
24	0.0000	0.0000	0.0000	0.0000	0.0000	0.0000	1.0000	0.2500	0.6000	0.2500	0.5000	0.2500	0.5000	0.0000
23	0.0000	0.0000	0.0000	0.0000	0.0000	0.0000	1.0000	0.2500	0.6000	0.2500	0.5000	0.3750	0.5000	0.0000
22	0.0000	0.0000	0.0000	0.0000	0.0000	0.0000	1.0000	0.2500	0.6000	0.3750	0.5000	0.3750	0.5000	0.0000
21	0.0000	0.0000	0.0000	0.0000	0.0000	0.0000	1.0000	0.2500	0.6000	0.5000	0.6667	0.3750	0.5000	0.0000
20	0.0000	0.0000	0.0000	0.0000	0.0000	0.0000	1.0000	0.2500	0.6000	0.5000	0.6667	0.3750	0.5000	0.0000
19	0.0000	0.0000	0.0000	0.0000	0.0000	0.0000	1.0000	0.2500	0.6000	0.5000	0.7500	0.5000	0.5000	0.0000
18	0.0000	0.0000	0.0000	0.0000	0.0000	0.0000	1.0000	0.2500	0.6000	0.5000	0.6667	0.5000	0.5000	0.0000
17	0.0000	0.0000	0.0000	0.0000	0.0000	0.0000	1.0000	0.2500	0.6000	0.6250	0.6667	0.5000	0.5000	0.0000
16	0.0000	0.0000	0.0000	0.0000	0.0000	0.0000	1.0000	0.2500	0.6000	0.7500	0.6667	0.5000	0.5000	0.0000
15	0.0000	0.0000	0.0000	0.0000	0.0000	0.0000	1.0000	0.2500	0.6000	0.8750	0.6667	0.6250	0.5000	0.0000
14	0.0000	0.0000	0.0000	0.0000	0.0000	0.0000	1.0000	0.2500	0.6000	0.8750	0.6667	0.6250	0.5000	0.0000
13	0.0000	0.0000	0.0000	0.0000	0.0000	0.0000	1.0000	0.2500	0.6000	0.7500	0.6667	0.6250	0.5000	0.0000
12	0.0000	0.0000	0.0000	0.0000	0.0000	0.0000	1.0000	0.2500	0.6000	0.7500	0.7500	0.6250	0.5000	0.0000
11	0.0000	0.0000	0.0000	0.0000	0.0000	0.0000	1.0000	0.2500	0.6000	0.7500	0.7500	0.7500	0.5000	0.0000
10	0.0000	0.0000	0.0000	0.0000	0.0000	0.0000	1.0000	0.2500	0.6000	0.7500	0.7500	0.7500	0.5000	0.0000
9	0.0000	0.0000	0.0000	0.0000	0.0000	0.0000	1.0000	0.0000	0.6000	0.7500	0.7500	0.7500	0.5000	0.0000
8	0.0000	0.0000	0.0000	0.0000	0.0000	0.0000	1.0000	0.0000	0.6000	0.6250	0.7500	0.7500	0.5000	0.0000
7	0.0000	0.0000	0.0000	0.0000	0.0000	0.0000	0.0000	0.2500	0.6000	0.6250	0.7500	0.7500	0.5000	0.0000
6	0.0000	0.0000	0.0000	0.0000	0.0000	0.0000	0.0000	0.2500	0.6000	0.6250	0.7500	0.7500	1.0000	0.0000
5	0.0000	0.0000	0.0000	0.0000	0.0000	0.0000	0.0000	0.2500	0.6000	0.6250	0.7500	0.7500	1.0000	0.0000
4	0.0000	0.0000	0.0000	0.0000	0.0000	0.0000	0.0000	0.2500	0.4000	0.6250	0.6667	0.7500	1.0000	0.0000
3	0.0000	0.0000	0.0000	0.0000	0.0000	0.0000	0.0000	0.2500	0.4000	0.6250	0.6667	0.7500	1.0000	0.0000
2	0.0000	0.0000	0.0000	0.0000	0.0000	0.0000	0.0000	0.5000	0.4000	0.6250	0.6667	0.7500	1.0000	0.0000
1	0.0000	0.0000	0.0000	0.0000	0.0000	0.0000	0.0000	0.5000	0.4000	0.6250	0.7500	0.7500	0.8750	0.0000
0	0.0000	0.0000	0.0000	0.0000	0.0000	0.0000	0.0000	0.7500	0.4000	0.3750	0.7500	0.8750	1.0000	0.0000
-1	0.0000	0.0000	0.0000	0.0000	0.0000	0.0000	0.0000	0.7500	0.4000	0.3750	0.7500	0.8750	1.0000	0.0000
-2	0.0000	0.0000	0.0000	0.0000	0.0000	0.0000	0.0000	0.7500	0.4000	0.3750	0.7500	0.8750	1.0000	0.0000
-3	0.0000	0.0000	0.0000	0.0000	0.0000	0.0000	0.0000	0.7500	0.4000	0.3750	0.7500	0.7500	1.0000	0.0000
-4	0.0000	0.0000	0.0000	0.0000	0.0000	0.0000	0.0000	0.7500	0.4000	0.3750	0.6667	0.7500	1.0000	0.0000
-5	0.0000	0.0000	0.0000	0.0000	0.0000	0.0000	0.0000	0.7500	0.6000	0.3750	0.5833	0.7500	1.0000	0.0000
-6	0.0000	0.0000	0.0000	0.0000	0.0000	0.0000	0.0000	0.7500	0.6000	0.3750	0.5000	0.7500	1.0000	0.0000
-7	0.0000	0.0000	0.0000	0.0000	0.0000	0.0000	0.0000	0.7500	0.6000	0.3750	0.5000	0.7500	1.0000	0.0000
-8	0.0000	0.0000	0.0000	0.0000	0.0000	0.0000	0.0000	0.7500	0.6000	0.3750	0.5000	0.7500	1.0000	0.0000
-9	0.0000	0.0000	0.0000	0.0000	0.0000	0.0000	0.0000	0.7500	0.6000	0.3750	0.5000	0.6250	1.0000	0.0000
-10	0.0000	0.0000	0.0000	0.0000	0.0000	0.0000	0.0000	0.7500	0.4000	0.3750	0.5000	0.6250	1.0000	0.0000

Main Condition 13 *(Continued)*   Probabilities

Tick Variation	1	2	3	4	5	6	7	8	9	10	11	12	13	14
						Secondary Conditions								
−11	0.0000	0.0000	0.0000	0.0000	0.0000	0.0000	0.0000	0.7500	0.4000	0.3750	0.5000	0.6250	1.0000	0.0000
−12	0.0000	0.0000	0.0000	0.0000	0.0000	0.0000	0.0000	0.7500	0.4000	0.3750	0.5000	0.6250	1.0000	0.0000
−13	0.0000	0.0000	0.0000	0.0000	0.0000	0.0000	0.0000	0.7500	0.4000	0.2500	0.4167	0.5000	1.0000	0.0000
−14	0.0000	0.0000	0.0000	0.0000	0.0000	0.0000	0.0000	0.7500	0.6000	0.2500	0.5000	0.3750	1.0000	0.0000
−15	0.0000	0.0000	0.0000	0.0000	0.0000	0.0000	0.0000	0.7500	0.6000	0.2500	0.4167	0.3750	1.0000	0.0000
−16	0.0000	0.0000	0.0000	0.0000	0.0000	0.0000	0.0000	0.7500	0.6000	0.2500	0.4167	0.3750	1.0000	0.0000
−17	0.0000	0.0000	0.0000	0.0000	0.0000	0.0000	0.0000	0.7500	0.6000	0.2500	0.3333	0.3750	1.0000	0.0000
−18	0.0000	0.0000	0.0000	0.0000	0.0000	0.0000	0.0000	0.7500	0.6000	0.2500	0.2500	0.3750	1.0000	0.0000
−19	0.0000	0.0000	0.0000	0.0000	0.0000	0.0000	0.0000	0.7500	0.6000	0.2500	0.1667	0.3750	1.0000	0.0000
−20	0.0000	0.0000	0.0000	0.0000	0.0000	0.0000	0.0000	0.7500	0.6000	0.2500	0.1667	0.3750	1.0000	0.0000
−21	0.0000	0.0000	0.0000	0.0000	0.0000	0.0000	0.0000	0.7500	0.6000	0.2500	0.1667	0.3750	1.0000	0.0000
−22	0.0000	0.0000	0.0000	0.0000	0.0000	0.0000	0.0000	0.7500	0.6000	0.2500	0.1667	0.3750	0.5000	0.0000
−23	0.0000	0.0000	0.0000	0.0000	0.0000	0.0000	0.0000	0.7500	0.6000	0.1250	0.1667	0.3750	0.5000	0.0000
−24	0.0000	0.0000	0.0000	0.0000	0.0000	0.0000	0.0000	0.7500	0.6000	0.1250	0.1667	0.3750	0.5000	0.0000
−25	0.0000	0.0000	0.0000	0.0000	0.0000	0.0000	0.0000	0.7500	0.6000	0.1250	0.1667	0.3750	0.5000	0.0000
−26	0.0000	0.0000	0.0000	0.0000	0.0000	0.0000	0.0000	0.7500	0.6000	0.1250	0.1667	0.3750	0.5000	0.0000
−27	0.0000	0.0000	0.0000	0.0000	0.0000	0.0000	0.0000	0.7500	0.6000	0.0000	0.1667	0.3750	0.5000	0.0000
−28	0.0000	0.0000	0.0000	0.0000	0.0000	0.0000	0.0000	0.7500	0.6000	0.0000	0.1667	0.3750	0.5000	0.0000
−29	0.0000	0.0000	0.0000	0.0000	0.0000	0.0000	0.0000	0.7500	0.4000	0.0000	0.1667	0.3750	0.5000	0.0000
−30	0.0000	0.0000	0.0000	0.0000	0.0000	0.0000	0.0000	0.7500	0.4000	0.0000	0.0833	0.3750	0.5000	0.0000
−31	0.0000	0.0000	0.0000	0.0000	0.0000	0.0000	0.0000	0.7500	0.4000	0.0000	0.0833	0.3750	0.5000	0.0000
−32	0.0000	0.0000	0.0000	0.0000	0.0000	0.0000	0.0000	0.7500	0.4000	0.0000	0.0833	0.3750	0.5000	0.0000
−33	0.0000	0.0000	0.0000	0.0000	0.0000	0.0000	0.0000	0.7500	0.2000	0.0000	0.0000	0.3750	0.5000	0.0000
−34	0.0000	0.0000	0.0000	0.0000	0.0000	0.0000	0.0000	0.7500	0.2000	0.0000	0.0000	0.3750	0.5000	0.0000
−35	0.0000	0.0000	0.0000	0.0000	0.0000	0.0000	0.0000	0.7500	0.2000	0.0000	0.0000	0.3750	0.5000	0.0000
−36	0.0000	0.0000	0.0000	0.0000	0.0000	0.0000	0.0000	0.7500	0.2000	0.0000	0.0000	0.3750	0.0000	0.0000
−37	0.0000	0.0000	0.0000	0.0000	0.0000	0.0000	0.0000	0.5000	0.2000	0.0000	0.0000	0.3750	0.0000	0.0000
−38	0.0000	0.0000	0.0000	0.0000	0.0000	0.0000	0.0000	0.5000	0.2000	0.0000	0.0000	0.2500	0.0000	0.0000
−39	0.0000	0.0000	0.0000	0.0000	0.0000	0.0000	0.0000	0.5000	0.2000	0.0000	0.0000	0.2500	0.0000	0.0000
−40	0.0000	0.0000	0.0000	0.0000	0.0000	0.0000	0.0000	0.5000	0.2000	0.0000	0.0000	0.2500	0.0000	0.0000
−41	0.0000	0.0000	0.0000	0.0000	0.0000	0.0000	0.0000	0.5000	0.2000	0.0000	0.0000	0.2500	0.0000	0.0000
−42	0.0000	0.0000	0.0000	0.0000	0.0000	0.0000	0.0000	0.5000	0.2000	0.0000	0.0000	0.2500	0.0000	0.0000
−43	0.0000	0.0000	0.0000	0.0000	0.0000	0.0000	0.0000	0.5000	0.2000	0.0000	0.0000	0.2500	0.0000	0.0000
−44	0.0000	0.0000	0.0000	0.0000	0.0000	0.0000	0.0000	0.5000	0.2000	0.0000	0.0000	0.2500	0.0000	0.0000
−45	0.0000	0.0000	0.0000	0.0000	0.0000	0.0000	0.0000	0.5000	0.2000	0.0000	0.0000	0.1250	0.0000	0.0000
−46	0.0000	0.0000	0.0000	0.0000	0.0000	0.0000	0.0000	0.5000	0.2000	0.0000	0.0000	0.1250	0.0000	0.0000
−47	0.0000	0.0000	0.0000	0.0000	0.0000	0.0000	0.0000	0.5000	0.2000	0.0000	0.0000	0.1250	0.0000	0.0000
−48	0.0000	0.0000	0.0000	0.0000	0.0000	0.0000	0.0000	0.5000	0.2000	0.0000	0.0000	0.1250	0.0000	0.0000
−49	0.0000	0.0000	0.0000	0.0000	0.0000	0.0000	0.0000	0.5000	0.2000	0.0000	0.0000	0.1250	0.0000	0.0000
−50	0.0000	0.0000	0.0000	0.0000	0.0000	0.0000	0.0000	0.5000	0.2000	0.0000	0.0000	0.1250	0.0000	0.0000
−51	0.0000	0.0000	0.0000	0.0000	0.0000	0.0000	0.0000	0.5000	0.0000	0.0000	0.0000	0.1250	0.0000	0.0000
−52	0.0000	0.0000	0.0000	0.0000	0.0000	0.0000	0.0000	0.5000	0.0000	0.0000	0.0000	0.1250	0.0000	0.0000
−53	0.0000	0.0000	0.0000	0.0000	0.0000	0.0000	0.0000	0.5000	0.0000	0.0000	0.0000	0.1250	0.0000	0.0000
−54	0.0000	0.0000	0.0000	0.0000	0.0000	0.0000	0.0000	0.5000	0.0000	0.0000	0.0000	0.1250	0.0000	0.0000
−55	0.0000	0.0000	0.0000	0.0000	0.0000	0.0000	0.0000	0.5000	0.0000	0.0000	0.0000	0.1250	0.0000	0.0000
−56	0.0000	0.0000	0.0000	0.0000	0.0000	0.0000	0.0000	0.5000	0.0000	0.0000	0.0000	0.1250	0.0000	0.0000
−57	0.0000	0.0000	0.0000	0.0000	0.0000	0.0000	0.0000	0.5000	0.0000	0.0000	0.0000	0.1250	0.0000	0.0000
−58	0.0000	0.0000	0.0000	0.0000	0.0000	0.0000	0.0000	0.5000	0.0000	0.0000	0.0000	0.1250	0.0000	0.0000
−59	0.0000	0.0000	0.0000	0.0000	0.0000	0.0000	0.0000	0.5000	0.0000	0.0000	0.0000	0.1250	0.0000	0.0000
−60	0.0000	0.0000	0.0000	0.0000	0.0000	0.0000	0.0000	0.5000	0.0000	0.0000	0.0000	0.1250	0.0000	0.0000
−61	0.0000	0.0000	0.0000	0.0000	0.0000	0.0000	0.0000	0.2500	0.0000	0.0000	0.0000	0.1250	0.0000	0.0000
−62	0.0000	0.0000	0.0000	0.0000	0.0000	0.0000	0.0000	0.2500	0.0000	0.0000	0.0000	0.1250	0.0000	0.0000
−63	0.0000	0.0000	0.0000	0.0000	0.0000	0.0000	0.0000	0.2500	0.0000	0.0000	0.0000	0.1250	0.0000	0.0000
−64	0.0000	0.0000	0.0000	0.0000	0.0000	0.0000	0.0000	0.2500	0.0000	0.0000	0.0000	0.1250	0.0000	0.0000

| Main Condition 14 | | | | | | Probabilities | | | | | | | |
| Tick Variation | | | | | | Secondary Conditions | | | | | | | |
	1	2	3	4	5	6	7	8	9	10	11	12	13	14
64	0.0000	0.0000	0.0000	0.0000	0.0000	0.0000	0.0000	0.0000	0.0000	0.2000	0.0000	0.0000	0.0000	0.1111
63	0.0000	0.0000	0.0000	0.0000	0.0000	0.0000	0.0000	0.0000	0.0000	0.2000	0.0000	0.0833	0.0000	0.1111
62	0.0000	0.0000	0.0000	0.0000	0.0000	0.0000	0.0000	0.0000	0.0000	0.2000	0.0000	0.0833	0.0000	0.1111
61	0.0000	0.0000	0.0000	0.0000	0.0000	0.0000	0.0000	0.0000	0.0000	0.2000	0.0000	0.0833	0.0000	0.1111
60	0.0000	0.0000	0.0000	0.0000	0.0000	0.0000	0.0000	0.0000	0.0000	0.2000	0.0000	0.0833	0.0000	0.1111
59	0.0000	0.0000	0.0000	0.0000	0.0000	0.0000	0.0000	0.0000	0.0000	0.2000	0.0000	0.0833	0.0000	0.1111
58	0.0000	0.0000	0.0000	0.0000	0.0000	0.0000	0.0000	0.0000	0.0000	0.2000	0.0000	0.0833	0.0000	0.1111
57	0.0000	0.0000	0.0000	0.0000	0.0000	0.0000	0.0000	0.0000	0.0000	0.2000	0.0000	0.0833	0.0000	0.1111
56	0.0000	0.0000	0.0000	0.0000	0.0000	0.0000	0.0000	0.0000	0.0000	0.2000	0.0000	0.0833	0.0000	0.1111
55	0.0000	0.0000	0.0000	0.0000	0.0000	0.0000	0.0000	0.0000	0.0000	0.2000	0.0000	0.0833	0.0000	0.1111
54	0.0000	0.0000	0.0000	0.0000	0.0000	0.0000	0.0000	0.0000	0.0000	0.2000	0.0000	0.0833	0.0000	0.1111
53	0.0000	0.0000	0.0000	0.0000	0.0000	0.0000	0.0000	0.0000	0.0000	0.2000	0.0000	0.0833	0.0909	0.1111
52	0.0000	0.0000	0.0000	0.0000	0.0000	0.0000	0.0000	0.0000	0.0000	0.2000	0.0000	0.0833	0.0909	0.1111
51	0.0000	0.0000	0.0000	0.0000	0.0000	0.0000	0.0000	0.0000	0.0000	0.2000	0.0000	0.0833	0.0909	0.1111
50	0.0000	0.0000	0.0000	0.0000	0.0000	0.0000	0.0000	0.0000	0.0000	0.2000	0.0000	0.0833	0.0909	0.2222
49	0.0000	0.0000	0.0000	0.0000	0.0000	0.0000	0.0000	0.0000	0.0000	0.2000	0.0000	0.0833	0.0909	0.3333
48	0.0000	0.0000	0.0000	0.0000	0.0000	0.0000	0.0000	0.0000	0.0000	0.2000	0.0000	0.0833	0.1818	0.3333
47	0.0000	0.0000	0.0000	0.0000	0.0000	0.0000	0.0000	0.0000	0.0000	0.2000	0.0000	0.0833	0.1818	0.4444
46	0.0000	0.0000	0.0000	0.0000	0.0000	0.0000	0.0000	0.0000	0.0000	0.2000	0.1111	0.1667	0.1818	0.4444
45	0.0000	0.0000	0.0000	0.0000	0.0000	0.0000	0.0000	0.0000	0.3333	0.2000	0.1111	0.1667	0.1818	0.4444
44	0.0000	0.0000	0.0000	0.0000	0.0000	0.0000	0.0000	0.0000	0.3333	0.2000	0.1111	0.1667	0.1818	0.4444
43	0.0000	0.0000	0.0000	0.0000	0.0000	0.0000	0.0000	0.0000	0.3333	0.2000	0.1111	0.1667	0.1818	0.4444
42	0.0000	0.0000	0.0000	0.0000	0.0000	0.0000	0.0000	0.0000	0.3333	0.2000	0.1111	0.1667	0.1818	0.4444
41	0.0000	0.0000	0.0000	0.0000	0.0000	0.0000	1.0000	0.0000	0.3333	0.2000	0.1111	0.1667	0.1818	0.4444
40	0.0000	0.0000	0.0000	0.0000	0.0000	0.0000	1.0000	0.0000	0.3333	0.2000	0.1111	0.1667	0.1818	0.4444
39	0.0000	0.0000	0.0000	0.0000	0.0000	0.0000	1.0000	0.0000	0.3333	0.2000	0.1111	0.1667	0.2727	0.4444
38	0.0000	0.0000	0.0000	0.0000	0.0000	0.0000	1.0000	0.0000	0.3333	0.2000	0.1111	0.2500	0.2727	0.5556
37	0.0000	0.0000	0.0000	0.0000	0.0000	0.0000	1.0000	0.0000	0.3333	0.2000	0.1111	0.2500	0.3636	0.5556
36	0.0000	0.0000	0.0000	0.0000	0.0000	0.0000	1.0000	0.0000	0.3333	0.2000	0.1111	0.2500	0.3636	0.5556
35	0.0000	0.0000	0.0000	0.0000	0.0000	0.0000	1.0000	0.0000	0.3333	0.2000	0.1111	0.2500	0.3636	0.5556
34	0.0000	0.0000	0.0000	0.0000	0.0000	0.0000	1.0000	0.0000	0.3333	0.2000	0.2222	0.2500	0.3636	0.5556
33	0.0000	0.0000	0.0000	0.0000	0.0000	0.0000	1.0000	0.0000	0.3333	0.2000	0.2222	0.2500	0.3636	0.6667
32	0.0000	0.0000	0.0000	0.0000	0.0000	0.0000	1.0000	0.0000	0.3333	0.2000	0.2222	0.2500	0.3636	0.6667
31	0.0000	0.0000	0.0000	0.0000	0.0000	0.0000	1.0000	0.0000	0.3333	0.2000	0.2222	0.2500	0.4545	0.6667
30	0.0000	0.0000	0.0000	0.0000	0.0000	0.0000	1.0000	0.0000	0.3333	0.2000	0.3333	0.2500	0.4545	0.6667
29	0.0000	0.0000	0.0000	0.0000	0.0000	0.0000	1.0000	0.0000	0.3333	0.0000	0.3333	0.2500	0.4545	0.7778
28	0.0000	0.0000	0.0000	0.0000	0.0000	0.0000	1.0000	0.0000	0.3333	0.0000	0.3333	0.2500	0.4545	0.7778
27	0.0000	0.0000	0.0000	0.0000	0.0000	0.0000	1.0000	0.0000	0.3333	0.0000	0.3333	0.2500	0.4545	0.7778
26	0.0000	0.0000	0.0000	0.0000	0.0000	0.0000	1.0000	0.0000	0.3333	0.0000	0.4444	0.2500	0.4545	0.8889
25	0.0000	0.0000	0.0000	0.0000	0.0000	0.0000	1.0000	0.0000	0.3333	0.0000	0.4444	0.2500	0.4545	0.8889
24	0.0000	0.0000	0.0000	0.0000	0.0000	0.0000	1.0000	0.0000	0.3333	0.0000	0.4444	0.2500	0.4545	0.8889
23	0.0000	0.0000	0.0000	0.0000	0.0000	0.0000	1.0000	0.0000	0.3333	0.0000	0.4444	0.2500	0.4545	0.8889
22	0.0000	0.0000	0.0000	0.0000	0.0000	0.0000	1.0000	0.0000	0.3333	0.0000	0.4444	0.2500	0.3636	0.8889
21	0.0000	0.0000	0.0000	0.0000	0.0000	0.0000	1.0000	0.0000	0.3333	0.0000	0.4444	0.2500	0.3636	0.8889
20	0.0000	0.0000	0.0000	0.0000	0.0000	0.0000	1.0000	0.0000	0.3333	0.0000	0.5556	0.5000	0.3636	0.8889
19	0.0000	0.0000	0.0000	0.0000	0.0000	0.0000	1.0000	0.0000	0.3333	0.0000	0.5556	0.5000	0.3636	0.8889
18	0.0000	0.0000	0.0000	0.0000	0.0000	0.0000	1.0000	0.0000	0.3333	0.0000	0.5556	0.5833	0.3636	0.8889
17	0.0000	0.0000	0.0000	0.0000	0.0000	0.0000	1.0000	0.0000	0.3333	0.0000	0.5556	0.5833	0.3636	0.8889
16	0.0000	0.0000	0.0000	0.0000	0.0000	0.0000	1.0000	0.0000	0.3333	0.0000	0.5556	0.6667	0.3636	0.8889
15	0.0000	0.0000	0.0000	0.0000	0.0000	0.0000	1.0000	0.0000	0.3333	0.0000	0.6667	0.6667	0.4545	1.0000
14	0.0000	0.0000	0.0000	0.0000	0.0000	0.0000	1.0000	0.0000	0.3333	0.0000	0.6667	0.6667	0.4545	1.0000
13	0.0000	0.0000	0.0000	0.0000	0.0000	0.0000	1.0000	0.0000	1.0000	0.0000	0.6667	0.5833	0.3636	1.0000
12	0.0000	0.0000	0.0000	0.0000	0.0000	0.0000	1.0000	0.0000	1.0000	0.2000	0.6667	0.5833	0.4545	1.0000
11	0.0000	0.0000	0.0000	0.0000	0.0000	0.0000	1.0000	0.0000	1.0000	0.2000	0.6667	0.5833	0.5455	1.0000
10	0.0000	0.0000	0.0000	0.0000	0.0000	0.0000	1.0000	0.0000	1.0000	0.4000	0.6667	0.6667	0.5455	1.0000
9	0.0000	0.0000	0.0000	0.0000	0.0000	0.0000	1.0000	0.0000	1.0000	0.4000	0.7778	0.6667	0.6364	1.0000
8	0.0000	0.0000	0.0000	0.0000	0.0000	0.0000	1.0000	0.0000	1.0000	0.4000	0.7778	0.6667	0.6364	1.0000
7	0.0000	0.0000	0.0000	0.0000	0.0000	0.0000	1.0000	0.0000	1.0000	0.4000	0.7778	0.6667	0.6364	1.0000
6	0.0000	0.0000	0.0000	0.0000	0.0000	0.0000	1.0000	0.0000	1.0000	0.4000	0.7778	0.6667	0.7273	0.6667
5	0.0000	0.0000	0.0000	0.0000	0.0000	0.0000	1.0000	0.0000	1.0000	0.4000	0.7778	0.6667	0.7273	0.6667
4	0.0000	0.0000	0.0000	0.0000	0.0000	0.0000	1.0000	0.0000	1.0000	0.4000	1.0000	0.6667	0.7273	0.6667
3	0.0000	0.0000	0.0000	0.0000	0.0000	0.0000	1.0000	0.0000	1.0000	0.4000	0.8889	0.6667	0.5455	0.6667
2	0.0000	0.0000	0.0000	0.0000	0.0000	0.0000	1.0000	0.0000	1.0000	0.6000	0.8889	0.6667	0.5455	0.6667
1	0.0000	0.0000	0.0000	0.0000	0.0000	0.0000	1.0000	0.0000	1.0000	0.6000	0.8889	0.6667	0.5455	0.6667
0	0.0000	0.0000	0.0000	0.0000	0.0000	0.0000	1.0000	0.0000	1.0000	0.6000	0.8889	0.6667	0.5455	0.6667
-1	0.0000	0.0000	0.0000	0.0000	0.0000	0.0000	1.0000	0.0000	1.0000	0.6000	0.8889	0.6667	0.5455	0.6667
-2	0.0000	0.0000	0.0000	0.0000	0.0000	0.0000	1.0000	0.0000	1.0000	0.6000	0.8889	0.6667	0.5455	0.6667
-3	0.0000	0.0000	0.0000	0.0000	0.0000	0.0000	1.0000	0.0000	1.0000	0.6000	0.8889	0.7500	0.5455	0.6667
-4	0.0000	0.0000	0.0000	0.0000	0.0000	0.0000	1.0000	0.0000	1.0000	0.6000	0.7778	0.7500	0.5455	0.5556
-5	0.0000	0.0000	0.0000	0.0000	0.0000	0.0000	0.0000	0.0000	1.0000	0.6000	0.7778	0.8333	0.5455	0.5556
-6	0.0000	0.0000	0.0000	0.0000	0.0000	0.0000	0.0000	0.0000	1.0000	0.6000	0.6667	0.8333	0.5455	0.5556
-7	0.0000	0.0000	0.0000	0.0000	0.0000	0.0000	0.0000	0.0000	1.0000	0.6000	0.6667	0.8333	0.5455	0.5556
-8	0.0000	0.0000	0.0000	0.0000	0.0000	0.0000	0.0000	0.0000	1.0000	0.6000	0.6667	0.8333	0.5455	0.5556
-9	0.0000	0.0000	0.0000	0.0000	0.0000	0.0000	0.0000	0.0000	1.0000	0.6000	0.6667	0.7500	0.5455	0.4444
-10	0.0000	0.0000	0.0000	0.0000	0.0000	0.0000	0.0000	0.0000	1.0000	0.6000	0.5556	0.7500	0.5455	0.3333

Main Condition 14 *(Continued)*   **Probabilities**

Secondary Conditions

Tick Variation	1	2	3	4	5	6	7	8	9	10	11	12	13	14
−11	0.0000	0.0000	0.0000	0.0000	0.0000	0.0000	0.0000	0.0000	1.0000	0.6000	0.5556	0.7500	0.5455	0.3333
−12	0.0000	0.0000	0.0000	0.0000	0.0000	0.0000	0.0000	0.0000	1.0000	0.6000	0.5556	0.6667	0.6364	0.3333
−13	0.0000	0.0000	0.0000	0.0000	0.0000	0.0000	0.0000	0.0000	1.0000	0.6000	0.5556	0.6667	0.6364	0.3333
−14	0.0000	0.0000	0.0000	0.0000	0.0000	0.0000	0.0000	0.0000	1.0000	0.6000	0.5556	0.6667	0.6364	0.3333
−15	0.0000	0.0000	0.0000	0.0000	0.0000	0.0000	0.0000	0.0000	1.0000	0.4000	0.5556	0.6667	0.6364	0.3333
−16	0.0000	0.0000	0.0000	0.0000	0.0000	0.0000	0.0000	0.0000	1.0000	0.4000	0.5556	0.6667	0.6364	0.3333
−17	0.0000	0.0000	0.0000	0.0000	0.0000	0.0000	0.0000	0.0000	0.6667	0.4000	0.5556	0.6667	0.5455	0.3333
−18	0.0000	0.0000	0.0000	0.0000	0.0000	0.0000	0.0000	0.0000	0.6667	0.4000	0.4444	0.6667	0.4545	0.3333
−19	0.0000	0.0000	0.0000	0.0000	0.0000	0.0000	0.0000	0.0000	0.6667	0.4000	0.4444	0.5833	0.4545	0.3333
−20	0.0000	0.0000	0.0000	0.0000	0.0000	0.0000	0.0000	0.0000	0.6667	0.4000	0.4444	0.5000	0.4545	0.3333
−21	0.0000	0.0000	0.0000	0.0000	0.0000	0.0000	0.0000	0.0000	0.6667	0.4000	0.3333	0.5000	0.4545	0.3333
−22	0.0000	0.0000	0.0000	0.0000	0.0000	0.0000	0.0000	0.0000	0.3333	0.4000	0.2222	0.5000	0.4545	0.3333
−23	0.0000	0.0000	0.0000	0.0000	0.0000	0.0000	0.0000	0.0000	0.3333	0.4000	0.2222	0.5000	0.4545	0.2222
−24	0.0000	0.0000	0.0000	0.0000	0.0000	0.0000	0.0000	0.0000	0.3333	0.4000	0.2222	0.4167	0.4545	0.2222
−25	0.0000	0.0000	0.0000	0.0000	0.0000	0.0000	0.0000	0.0000	0.3333	0.4000	0.2222	0.4167	0.4545	0.2222
−26	0.0000	0.0000	0.0000	0.0000	0.0000	0.0000	0.0000	0.0000	0.3333	0.6000	0.2222	0.4167	0.4545	0.2222
−27	0.0000	0.0000	0.0000	0.0000	0.0000	0.0000	0.0000	0.0000	0.3333	0.6000	0.2222	0.4167	0.4545	0.2222
−28	0.0000	0.0000	0.0000	0.0000	0.0000	0.0000	0.0000	0.0000	0.3333	0.6000	0.2222	0.4167	0.4545	0.2222
−29	0.0000	0.0000	0.0000	0.0000	0.0000	0.0000	0.0000	0.0000	0.3333	0.6000	0.2222	0.4167	0.3636	0.2222
−30	0.0000	0.0000	0.0000	0.0000	0.0000	0.0000	0.0000	0.0000	0.3333	0.6000	0.2222	0.4167	0.3636	0.2222
−31	0.0000	0.0000	0.0000	0.0000	0.0000	0.0000	0.0000	0.0000	0.3333	0.6000	0.2222	0.4167	0.3636	0.2222
−32	0.0000	0.0000	0.0000	0.0000	0.0000	0.0000	0.0000	0.0000	0.3333	0.6000	0.2222	0.4167	0.3636	0.2222
−33	0.0000	0.0000	0.0000	0.0000	0.0000	0.0000	0.0000	0.0000	0.3333	0.6000	0.2222	0.4167	0.3636	0.2222
−34	0.0000	0.0000	0.0000	0.0000	0.0000	0.0000	0.0000	0.0000	0.3333	0.6000	0.2222	0.4167	0.3636	0.2222
−35	0.0000	0.0000	0.0000	0.0000	0.0000	0.0000	0.0000	0.0000	0.3333	0.6000	0.2222	0.3333	0.3636	0.2222
−36	0.0000	0.0000	0.0000	0.0000	0.0000	0.0000	0.0000	0.0000	0.3333	0.6000	0.1111	0.3333	0.3636	0.2222
−37	0.0000	0.0000	0.0000	0.0000	0.0000	0.0000	0.0000	0.0000	0.3333	0.6000	0.1111	0.3333	0.3636	0.2222
−38	0.0000	0.0000	0.0000	0.0000	0.0000	0.0000	0.0000	0.0000	0.3333	0.4000	0.1111	0.3333	0.3636	0.2222
−39	0.0000	0.0000	0.0000	0.0000	0.0000	0.0000	0.0000	0.0000	0.3333	0.4000	0.1111	0.2500	0.3636	0.2222
−40	0.0000	0.0000	0.0000	0.0000	0.0000	0.0000	0.0000	0.0000	0.3333	0.4000	0.1111	0.2500	0.2727	0.2222
−41	0.0000	0.0000	0.0000	0.0000	0.0000	0.0000	0.0000	0.0000	0.3333	0.4000	0.1111	0.2500	0.1818	0.2222
−42	0.0000	0.0000	0.0000	0.0000	0.0000	0.0000	0.0000	0.0000	0.0000	0.4000	0.1111	0.1667	0.1818	0.2222
−43	0.0000	0.0000	0.0000	0.0000	0.0000	0.0000	0.0000	0.0000	0.0000	0.4000	0.1111	0.0833	0.1818	0.2222
−44	0.0000	0.0000	0.0000	0.0000	0.0000	0.0000	0.0000	0.0000	0.0000	0.4000	0.1111	0.0833	0.1818	0.2222
−45	0.0000	0.0000	0.0000	0.0000	0.0000	0.0000	0.0000	0.0000	0.0000	0.4000	0.1111	0.0833	0.1818	0.2222
−46	0.0000	0.0000	0.0000	0.0000	0.0000	0.0000	0.0000	0.0000	0.0000	0.4000	0.1111	0.0833	0.1818	0.2222
−47	0.0000	0.0000	0.0000	0.0000	0.0000	0.0000	0.0000	0.0000	0.0000	0.4000	0.1111	0.0833	0.1818	0.2222
−48	0.0000	0.0000	0.0000	0.0000	0.0000	0.0000	0.0000	0.0000	0.0000	0.4000	0.1111	0.0833	0.0909	0.2222
−49	0.0000	0.0000	0.0000	0.0000	0.0000	0.0000	0.0000	0.0000	0.0000	0.4000	0.1111	0.0833	0.0909	0.2222
−50	0.0000	0.0000	0.0000	0.0000	0.0000	0.0000	0.0000	0.0000	0.0000	0.4000	0.1111	0.0833	0.0909	0.2222
−51	0.0000	0.0000	0.0000	0.0000	0.0000	0.0000	0.0000	0.0000	0.0000	0.4000	0.1111	0.0833	0.0909	0.1111
−52	0.0000	0.0000	0.0000	0.0000	0.0000	0.0000	0.0000	0.0000	0.0000	0.4000	0.1111	0.0833	0.0909	0.1111
−53	0.0000	0.0000	0.0000	0.0000	0.0000	0.0000	0.0000	0.0000	0.0000	0.4000	0.1111	0.0833	0.0909	0.1111
−54	0.0000	0.0000	0.0000	0.0000	0.0000	0.0000	0.0000	0.0000	0.0000	0.4000	0.1111	0.0833	0.0909	0.1111
−55	0.0000	0.0000	0.0000	0.0000	0.0000	0.0000	0.0000	0.0000	0.0000	0.4000	0.1111	0.0833	0.0909	0.1111
−56	0.0000	0.0000	0.0000	0.0000	0.0000	0.0000	0.0000	0.0000	0.0000	0.4000	0.1111	0.0833	0.0909	0.1111
−57	0.0000	0.0000	0.0000	0.0000	0.0000	0.0000	0.0000	0.0000	0.0000	0.4000	0.1111	0.0833	0.0000	0.1111
−58	0.0000	0.0000	0.0000	0.0000	0.0000	0.0000	0.0000	0.0000	0.0000	0.4000	0.1111	0.0833	0.0000	0.1111
−59	0.0000	0.0000	0.0000	0.0000	0.0000	0.0000	0.0000	0.0000	0.0000	0.4000	0.1111	0.0833	0.0000	0.1111
−60	0.0000	0.0000	0.0000	0.0000	0.0000	0.0000	0.0000	0.0000	0.0000	0.4000	0.1111	0.0833	0.0000	0.1111
−61	0.0000	0.0000	0.0000	0.0000	0.0000	0.0000	0.0000	0.0000	0.0000	0.4000	0.0000	0.0833	0.0000	0.1111
−62	0.0000	0.0000	0.0000	0.0000	0.0000	0.0000	0.0000	0.0000	0.0000	0.4000	0.0000	0.0000	0.0000	0.1111
−63	0.0000	0.0000	0.0000	0.0000	0.0000	0.0000	0.0000	0.0000	0.0000	0.2000	0.0000	0.0000	0.0000	0.1111
−64	0.0000	0.0000	0.0000	0.0000	0.0000	0.0000	0.0000	0.0000	0.0000	0.2000	0.0000	0.0000	0.0000	0.1111

Index

Adversity, probabilities of, *see specific types of adversity*
  determination of, 79–87
  estimation of, 87–99
ALL C, 21–22
ALL D, 21, 23
Assumptions:
  financial market and, 30
  in game theory, 28–29
Axelrod, Robert, 19–24

Bear market trends, 127–132, 134–135
Bell-shaped curve, 79, 113–114, 127, 131
Black-Scholes formula, 79
Blue chip stocks, 31
Bond funds, 31
Broker:
  commission, 49, 118
  risk and, 118
Bullish position, risk/reward variables, 125
Bull market trends, 35, 127–132
Buy orders, in T-bond market, 118–119

Call options, 102
CBOT, 104
Certainty, decision-making under, 7
Closing prices, in bond market, 102–103
Coin toss, probabilities of, 78

Columns, in game table, 15, 17–18
Commissions, brokers', 49, 118
Common stock, 121
Computer programs:
  price movement in bond market, 107, 110
  probability calculations, 98
Computer technology:
  advances in, vii–viii
  digital technology, 3
Connected graph, 8
Consumer Price Index, 100
Cooperate strategies, 19, 21
Crashing market, 35
Crash of '87, 35

Daily price movement, in T-bond market, 119
Day-trading method, T-bond market, 119–120
Defect strategies, 19, 21–22
Digital computers, 3
Don't Play region, *see specific scenarios*
  less risk strategy, 64–66
  more risk strategy, 68
  risk/reward variables and, 123–124
Dow, Charles, vi

Effective targets, 40
Entry price, trading system and, 135
Equilibrium, 15, 18

Equity mutual funds, 1
Eurodollars, 53
Excel, 79
Exit strategy, market-on-close (MOC), 119–120
Expiration dates, 124

Fair strategy, 14–15
Falling market, 127–128
Financial market, generally:
  as iterated game, 23, 78
  as parlor game, 50–54, 101
  price fluctuations in, 34–35
  profit objective, 34–35, 37
  risk acceptance level, 33–35
  speculating *vs.* investing, 31–33, 38
  trends in, 35. *See also* Bear market trends; Bull market trends
  as zero sum game, 24
Floor traders, 31–32
Four-day moving average, 128–129
4-9 oscillator, 128–129, 131–132, 134, 139
401(k) plans, 32
Frequency distribution, *see specific types of distributions*
  adversity probabilities, 82, 84–85, 90–91
  expiring month t-bond future prices, 165–167
  market trend oscillator and, 129
  relative, *see* Relative frequency, prices in bond market
Futures market, *see* Treasury bond futures
  margin costs, 101–102
  risk acceptance levels and, 49
  risk taking in, 31
  time constraints of, 98, 121
  zero sum game and, 24–25

Gambling, 7
Games against nature:
  defined, 25
  Financial Market game as, 52
  Leftover Pie illustration, 26

Oil Prospecting game, 26–28
  state of nature, 26
Game table:
  defined, 12
  Financial Market game, 53–54
  Leftover Pie game, 12–16
  mathematical representation, in game theoretic model, 59–62
  more risk strategy, 66
Game theoretic model:
  application of, 76–78
  construction of:
    completed model, 74–75
    game table, mathematical representation of, 59–62
    less risk strategy, 62–66
    market-strategy notation, 57–58
    more risk strategy, 66–71
    payoff notation, 58–59
    separation of less risk/more risk, 71–74
    speculator strategy notation, 58
  mathematical representation of, 161–164
  order placement and, 118–119
Game theory:
  basic terms and ideas, 4–5
  decision-making problem, 6–8
  defined, 2
  games, characteristics of, 8–12
  games against nature, 25–28
  iterated games, 19–24
  pros and cons of, 28–29
  purpose/application of, 144–145
  simple games, illustrations of:
    Leftover Pie, 12–16
    Prisoner's Dilemma, 17–19
    zero sum game, 24–25
Game tree:
  defined, 8
  for roll a die, flip a coin game, 9–10
  tic-tac-toe, 10–11
Gaps, in bond market, 111
General Motors (GM), stock price distribution illustration, 79–87
Government bonds, 31
Growth funds, 31

Hang Seng stock index, 35–36
Hedging strategy, 32
Histogram:
adversity probabilities, 82, 84–85, 87
market trends, 134
T-bond futures contracts, 104–105
Holding strategy, 98–99, 125
Hunt brothers, 33

Income arbitrage programs, vi
Income funds, 31
Indicators, in trading system, 145
Individual investors, 30
Inferences, price movement in T-bond
market, 110, 113, 122
Inflation:
double-digit, vi
stock prices and, 83
Institutional investors, 30
Insurance companies, 32
Interest rates, 101
International Monetary Market, vi
Investors:
objective of, 38
types of, 31
Iterated games, 19, 78, 119

Leftover Pie:
as game against nature, 26
game table, 12–15
matrix format, 13, 14–15
payoffs, 16
utility and, 13–14
Less risk strategy:
adversity, probabilities of, 87–89
game theoretic model:
Equation Greater Than Zero, 63
probability notations, 58–62
risk/reward variables and, 123–127
T-bond market, 116–117, 119–120
Linear regression, 128
Locus of strategic separation, 72–74
Lognormal price distributions, 79, 98
Long position:
in treasury bond market, 101, 125
zero sum game and, 25
Lotus, 79

Major adversity:
defined, 44, 54
illustrations of, 46–47
less risk strategy, 63–65
more risk strategy, 68
probability of, 71, 90, 96–97
risk/reward variables and, 124
Manhattan Project, 3
Margin costs, 101
Market-on-close (MOC) trades:
illustrations of, 154, 156
overview, 119–120
Market trends, see Bear market trends;
Bull market trends
bond market and, 127–134
impact of, generally, vii, 35
types of, 127–128
Maximin, 14, 16
McMillan, Lawrence G., 79
Microsoft, 40
Minimax, 14, 16
Minor adversity:
classification of, 46
defined, 54
less risk strategy, 63–65
more risk strategy, 66–68
probability of, 71, 93–97
Mixed strategies, defined, 23–24, 55.
See also Game theoretic model
construction
Moderate adversity:
defined, 43
illustrations of, 44–45
Money-losing strategies, risk
acceptance level, 64–66
More risk strategy:
adversity probabilities, 89–90, 95,
98
game theoretic model, 58–62, 66–61
risk/reward variables and, 123–127
T-bond market, 116–117, 119–121
Morgenstern, Oskar, 3–4, 12
Moving averages:
historical perspective, vi
oscillators and, 131–132, 134, 139
types of, 128
Murphy, Joseph E., Jr., 79

Mutual funds:
  hedging techniques, 32
  rate of return, 31–32

Negative payoffs, 4
Neural networks, vii
New York Stock Exchange, 53
Nine-day moving average, 128–129
No adversity, 46
Nominal price, 119
Normal distribution, 79, 113, 125

Oil Prospecting game, 26–28
Optimal strategy, 6
Options, time constraints of, 98, 121
Options as a Strategic Investment
  (McMillan), 79
Order-cancels-order (OCO) trades, 118
Oscillator:
  four-day moving average, 128–129
  4-9, 128–129, 131–132, 134, 139
  3-6, 131–132, 134, 139
Outcome, defined, 2

Payoff(s):
  defined, 4
  notation in game theoretic model,
    58–59
  table, 19
  types of, 4
  utility, 5–6
Pension fund managers, game theory
  application, 30
Perfect information, 10
Play, defined, 8
Positive payoffs, 4
Predictions, in price movements,
  122–123
Premises, financial market and, 30
Price charts:
  illustration of, 35–38
  T-bond futures contract, 103–104
Price fluctuations, *see* Price movement
  influences on, 34–35, 39
  risk acceptance levels and, 39–54
  T-bond futures contracts, 104–114

Price line, 48–49
Price momentum, 128
Price movement:
  classification of, 46, 48
  intraday t-bond, 106–114
  major adversity, 44, 46
  minor adversity, 46
  moderate adversity, 43–45
  no adversity, 46
  zero adversity, 41–44
Price shocks, 101
Prisoner's Dilemma:
  game theory, 17–19
  iterated, 19–24
Probability, generally:
  dispersion, of bond prices,
    127–128
  game theoretic model construction:
    market-strategy notation, 57–58
    speculator strategy notation, 58
Probability triangle:
  adversity, probabilities of, 97
  defined, 61–62
  less risk strategy, 63–65, 122
  more risk strategy, 69–70, 122
  single risk level, 122
Profitability, 25, 39, 88, 99
Profit objective:
  function of, generally, 34–35, 37
  risk acceptance level and, 39–41,
    48–49
  risk/reward variables and, 123–124
  T-bond market and, 119
  in trading system, 135, 138
Pure investments, 32
Pure strategy, 23, 55, 72
Put options, 102

Quick Basic (Microsoft):
  application of, 113–114
  for relative frequencies, 171–174

RANDOM, 21–22
Random variable, 113
Rapoport, Anatol, 21
Rational player, 6, 14

Relative frequency, prices in bond market:
  application of, 117–118
  expiring month, 168–170
  illustration of, 112
  by oscillator conditions, 176–203
Rising market, 127–128
Risk:
  acceptance level, see Risk acceptance level
  decision-making under, 7–8
  and rewards, see Risk/reward values
Risk acceptance level:
  assessment of, 33–35
  less risk, 58–63, 87–89, 116–117, 119–120, 123–127
  more risk, 58–62, 66–74, 89–90, 95, 98, 116–117, 119–121, 123–127
  profit objective and, 39–41, 48–49
  single, 121–122
Risk averse investments, 30
Risk/reward values:
  adversity probabilities and, 86, 99
  testing a trading system, 143
  treasury bond futures, 123–127
Roll a die, flip a coin game, 8–10
Rows, in game table, 15, 17–18

S&P 500, 52
  contract, 102
Saddle point, 15
Sell orders, 118–119, 135
Shelton, Ron, v, vii
Short position, 101, 125
Short sales:
  margin costs, 101
  price movement and, 49
  with zero adversity, 49–50
Short sellers, 25
Sideways market, 127–128
Six-day moving average, 128
Speculating, see Speculator; specific scenarios
  investing vs., 31–32, 38
  mistakes in, 33

Speculator, see specific scenarios
  defined, 31
  objective of, 38
  profit objective and, 49
  risk acceptance level, 49
Spreadsheets, 79, 98
State of nature, 26, 49, 100–101
Statistical analysis, 1, 85, 125
Stochastics, 122, 128
Stock Market Probability (Murphy), 79
Stock purchases, price appreciation and, 31
Stop-loss orders, 118–119
Strategy, defined, 8
Strictly competitive games, 24

Table:
  game, see Game table
  payoff, 19
  price movement in T-bond market, 108–112
Technological advances, impact of, v–vi, 101
10-day moving averages, vi
Theory of Games and Economic Behavior, The, 3–4
Three-day moving average, 128
3-6 oscillators, 131–132, 134, 139
Ticks, bond market trades, 108
Tic-tac-toe, game theory, 8, 10–12
Time frame issues, 98, 121–122, 125
TIT FOR TAT, 20–23
Trading box, 107, 119
Trading system:
  development of, 134–139
  illustrations of:
    downside bias, 147
    MOC close, 154, 156
    money loser, 146, 159
    no trades, 144, 153, 155, 158
    profitable trades, 141, 145, 150–152, 156
    profit objectives and, 142–143, 154
  testing:
    graphic results of, 148–149
    overview, 139–145

Trading volume, T-bond market,
110–112
Transaction costs, 49
Treasury bond futures:
analysis of, generally, 100–106
expiring month prices, 165–167
market trend and, 127–134
practical application, 114–123
price fluctuations, generally, 52. *See
also* Price movement
price movements, intraday, 106–114
risk/reward variables, 123–127
trading system:
development, 134–139
testing, 139–155
Trend analyses, detailed, 130–131
Tucker, Albert, 17

Uncertainty, decision-making under,
7–8
Unfair strategy, 14–15

Upward bias:
bond prices and, 102–103
in stock market, 101
Utility, defined, 5
Utility function, 6
Utility theory, 5

Validity, assumptions and, 29
von Neumann, John, 3, 12

Wall Street Journal, 1, 52
Willing to hold strategy, 49, 124

Zero adversity:
defined, 41–42, 54, 74–75
in game theoretic model, 74–75
illustrations of, 41–43
more risk strategy, 66–68
Zero sum game, 24–25
Z scores, 98, 117